W9-ANN-703

PHYSICAL
SCIENCE
DAYBOOK

In Collaboration with NSTA

TEACHER'S EDITION

GReaT SoURCe
EDUCATION GROUP
A Houghton Mifflin Company

Acknowledgments
Teacher's Edition Reviewer
Charles Harmon
Los Angeles Unified School District
Los Angeles, California

Credits
Writing: Bill Smith Studio
Editorial: Great Source: Sarah Martin, Kathy Kellman, Marianne Knowles, Susan Rogalski; Bill Smith Studio
Design: Great Source: Richard Spencer; Bill Smith Studio
Production Management: Great Source: Evelyn Curley; Bill Smith Studio
Cover Design: Bill Smith Studio

National Science Teachers Association: Tyson Brown, Carol Duval, Juliana Texley, Patricia Warren, Charlene Czerniak

Photos
Page iva: PhotoDisc; **ivb:** Jeff Tinsley, courtesy of the Smithsonian Institution; **1:** Photographic Image Objects; **2a:** PhotoDisc; **2b:** PhotoDisc; **3:** PhotoDisc; **4:** PhotoDisc; **8:** PhotoDisc; **9:** Image State; **11:** Corel; **12–13:** Corel; **14:** Corel; **16–17:** ArtToday; **18a:** Corel; **18b:** PhotoDisc; **20:** PhotoDisc; **21:** Image 100; **22–23:** Corbis Royalty Free; **24–25:** ArtToday; **27:** © Leonard de Selva/CORBIS; **30:** ArtToday; **32–33:** Corel; **34:** Corel; **37a:** ArtToday; **37b:** Corel; **37c:** Corel; **38–39:** Corel; **40:** Phillip Greenspun courtesy of James McLurkin; **41:** Jeff Tinsley, courtesy of the Smithsonian Institution; **42:** Photographic Image Objects; **43:** Corel; **44–45:** Corbis Royalty Free; **46:** Joel Page, Associated Press, AP; **47:** courtesy of Segway LLC; **48:** courtesy of Segway LLC; **48:** Eyewire; **48–49:** ArtToday; **50:** Digital Vision; **51:** Library Of Congress; **52:** ©Tony Anderson/Getty Images; **53:** PhotoDisc; **54:** PhotoDisc; **55:** Photodisc; **56:** © Kelly Overton **57:** © Kelly Overton; **58–59:** PhotoDisc; **60:** © Patrice Ceisel/Visuals Unlimited; **62:** © Bettmannn/CORBIS; **66:** Library of Congress; **68:** ArtToday; **70–71:** PhotoDisc; **72:** © Wayne R. Bilenduke/ Getty Images; **74:** © E. Haucke, G. Ochocki Productions/Photo Researchers; **79:** © Hashimoto Noboru/CORBIS Sygma; **80–81:** PhotoDisc; **83:** Photographic Image Objects; **84:** © Farnsworth Archive; **84–85:** PhotoDisc; **86:** PhotoDisc; **88:** Hulto Archive; **89:** © Bettmann/CORBIS; **90–91:** ArtToday; **92:** Photos.com; **93:** PhotoDisc; **94:** Corel; **94–95:** Corel; **96–97:** PhotoDisc; **99:** NASA; **102–103:** Corel; **104:** PhotoDisc; **106–107:** ArtToday; **107:** © Christie Silver; **108:** Artville; **109:** PhotoDisc; **110–111:** DigitalVision; **112:** PhotoDisc; **114:** ArtToday; **116:** Corbis Royalty Free; **117:** Corel; **120:** Patricia Lanza/California Science Center; **121:** PhotoSpin; **122–123:** PhotoDisc; **124:** © Pool/Reuters/TimePix; **126–127:** Corel; **128:** PhotoDisc; **130:** PhotoDisc; **132–133:** Corel; **133:** PhotoDisc; **134:** Corel; **135:** PhotoDisc; **136:** ArtToday; **136–137:** PhotoDisc; **138:** Corel; **139:** Corel; **141:** Hulton Archive/Getty Images; **142:** PhotoDisc; **144–145:** ArtToday; **146a:** © Nicholas Bergkessel/Photo Researchers, Inc. **146b:** PhotoDisc; **148–149:** PhotoDisc; **150:** © Charles D. Winters/Photo Researchers, Inc. **151:** PhotoDisc; **152–153:** PhotoDisc; **154–155:** Corel; **155a:** Corel; **155b:** Corel; **155c:** Corel; **155d:** Corel; **156:** © Christoph Hellhake/Getty Images; **158:** Jonelle Weaver/FoodPix; **159:** © Swim Ink/CORBIS; **160–161:** PhotoDisc; **162:** Corel; **164–165:** PhotoDisc; **168:** Kenneth Ingham; **171:** © Jim Pisarowicz; **171:** PhotoDisc; **173:** © Bettmann/CORBIS; **174:** ArtToday; **176:** Digital Vision; **177:** Corel; **178:** PhotoDisc; **179:** © Owen Franken/CORBIS; **180–181:** PhotoSpin; **183:** © Ron Leighton; **186:** Getty Images; **188:** PhotoDisc; **189:** PhotoDisc; **190–191:** PhotoDisc; **192:** Corel; **194:** Corel; **194–195:** Corbis; **196:** Corel; **196–197:** Corel; **197:** PhotoDisc; **198:** Biophoto Associates/Photo Researchers Inc. **200:** © AP Photo/Elise Amendola; **204:** Jose Torres; **204–205:** Corel; **206–207:** Photos.com; **208:** Michael Branscom/Lemelson –MIT program; **209:** © Eric Long/ Smithsonian Institution; **212:** © Ron Leighton: **213:** © Ron Leighton; **214–215:** ArtToday; **216:** Artville

Cover: Image Farm

Illustration: All illustrations by Thomas Gagliano, except page 54, Kenneth Batelman and page 82, Jeff Thompson.

Printed in the United States of America.
International Standard Book Number: 0–669-49252-3
1 2 3 4 5 6 7 8 9 10 — DBH — 10 09 08 07 06 05 04 03

Why NSTA Worked On These Books

Scientists write letters, argue incessantly, make mistakes, suffer from jealousy, exhibit both vanity and generosity—all while striving in diverse ways to enlarge human understanding. Among the most important skills they possess is the ability to communicate ideas, defend them against critics, and modify their own positions in the face of contravening evidence. Every literate person—every scientifically literate person—must do this.

The National Science Teachers Association (NSTA) is pleased to participate in the publication of these Science Daybooks because they bring together science, reading, and writing. Most important: The primary sources in the Daybooks—firsthand accounts that scientists and researchers use to communicate their ideas—firmly place science in the context of human endeavor.

What NSTA Did

From the outset, NSTA staff and members collaborated with Great Source editors and developers to ensure that the Daybooks were created from a teacher's perspective and were based on the National Science Education Standards. We helped link important topic areas with primary sources. We suggested activity ideas at the pilot stage and reviewed those submitted by authors during development. We reviewed the teaching plans that accompany student lessons and supported these plans with tips, warnings about misconceptions, and brief activities taken from articles in *Science Scope*—NSTA's middle school peer-reviewed journal. NSTA also provides the *sci*LINKS® extensions that appear throughout the book, directing readers to Web sites that offer further information, additional lessons, and activities.

What Is NSTA

NSTA is the largest organization in the world committed to promoting excellence and innovation in science teaching and learning for all. To address subjects of critical interest to science educators, the NSTA Press publishes projects of significant relevance and value to teachers of science—books on best teaching practices, books that explain and tie in with the National Science Education Standards, books that apply the latest science education research, and classroom activity books. NSTA also considers novel treatments of core science content and is especially eager to publish works that link science to other key curriculum areas such as mathematics and language arts. Hence this project.

Let Us Hear From You

We hope teachers and students benefit from this innovative approach to learning science. Tell us what you think of this joint effort by e-mailing daybooks@nsta.org. For more information about NSTA, please visit our Web site at www.nsta.org.

How to Use This Book

The Great Source *Life Science, Earth Science, and Physical Science Daybooks* are designed to be flexible resources for you to use with your students. Here are a few suggestions for incorporating them into your science curriculum.

Use the *Science Daybooks* as the core of your science program. Throughout the *Science Daybooks*, the lessons reference *ScienceSaurus®*, a middle school science handbook, and *sciLINKS®*, to provide a complete foundation for a middle  school science curriculum. *ScienceSaurus* is a comprehensive reference aligned with the *National Science Education Standards* (grades 5–8), and models scientific investigation and inquiry. The *sciLINKS* Web site provides students with a logical next step to the process of finding out more. With the *Science Daybooks*, we initiate this process by providing students with snippets of readings from "real" science materials. These engage them in the discovery process, and help them apply what they've learned in extended activities. These readings were carefully selected to provide meaningful investigations into every area described by the *National Science Education Standards*. However, unlike a textbook approach that requires students to read about an array of science topics, the *Science Daybooks* allow the students to "get specific" and do the science.

For example, when we study chemical reactions, students gain a basic understanding of how matter interacts by referencing topics 251, 252, and 269 in *ScienceSaurus*. Then, in one of 12 *Physical Science Daybook* lessons from the Interactions of Matter Unit, students focus on the chemical reactions of decomposition by reading an excerpt about mummification written by the Greek historian Herodotus in 450 B.C. They do an activity to compare rates of decomposition. Students go to the *sciLINKS* Web site and enter the keyword "Chemical Reactions" and connect to a vast number of appropriate web sources providing additional research information, and activities. And, they can do additional research and design their own investigations using the models and guidelines found in the *ScienceSaurus* (topics 001–019 and 410–426) and

experience the process of "full inquiry," as outlined in the *National Science Education Standards*.

Supplement your existing science program. The units and topics in the *Science Daybooks* match up with those in most current textbooks. Pick and choose units or chapters as you teach those topics during the year.

Extend science after school or during the summer. It can be difficult to do everything you would like in science class. You may want to extend students' science time to after school. The wealth of extended activities in the *Science Daybooks* allows students (as individuals and/or small groups) to pursue different investigations throughout the year and report their findings to the class. Many of the activities were culled from the best of NSTA's *ScienceScope*, a professional journal for middle school science teachers.

Prepare students for high-stakes assessments with opportunities to write and communicate about science. Most often, state assessments require students to read, comprehend, and write about both fiction and nonfiction passages. The *Science Daybooks* promote critical reading, writing, and thinking about science.

Weave into an integrated science curriculum. Since the *Science Daybooks* are small, inexpensive, and portable, a set of three books can be purchased for the students in the first year of a three-year integrated science curriculum. Determine the units to teach in each of the three years, and pass the books along to the next-level teacher at the end of the year.

There are many ways to make good use of the *Science Daybooks* in your classroom. In whatever way you choose to use them, be assured that these materials provide a foundation for a complete and effective curriculum for the middle school grades.

Scope and Sequence

Correlation with National Science Education Standards, Grades 5–8

	UNIT 1												UNIT 2								
CHAPTER	Ch. 1			Ch. 2			Ch. 3			Ch. 4			Ch. 5			Ch. 6			Ch. 7		
LESSON	1	2	3	4	5	6	7	8	9	10	11	12	13	14	15	16	17	18	19	20	21
Unifying Concepts and Processes																					
Systems, order, and organization	•	•	•	•	•	•	•	•	•	•	•	•				•	•	•	•	•	•
Evidence, models, and explanation		•	•	•		•		•		•			•	•	•	•			•	•	•
Change, constancy, and measurement	•	•	•	•	•						•		•	•					•	•	•
Evolution and equilibrium	•			•	•	•							•								
Form and function							•	•	•	•	•	•			•	•		•			•
Science as Inquiry																					
Abilities necessary to do scientific inquiry		•			•								•								•
Understanding about scientific inquiry							•	•	•	•						•	•			•	
Physical Science																					
Properties and changes of properties in matter													•	•							•
Motion and force	•	•		•	•	•	•	•	•	•	•	•							•	•	•
Transfer of energy		•	•										•	•	•	•		•			
Life Science																					
Structure and function in living systems										•					•					•	
Regulation and behavior																				•	
Diversity and adaptations of organisms										•					•						
Earth and Space Science																					
Structure of the earth system																			•	•	
Earth in the solar system																			•		
Science and Technology																					
Abilities of technological design										•	•	•				•					•
Understanding about science and technology							•	•	•	•	•	•				•	•	•			•
Science in Personal and Social Perspectives																					
Personal health																					
Populations, resources, and environments												•					•				
Natural hazards													•	•							
Risks and benefits												•					•				
Science and technology in society							•	•	•	•	•	•				•	•	•			•
History and Nature of Science																					
Science as a human endeavor							•	•	•	•		•				•	•	•			
Nature of science										•	•	•				•	•				
History of science	•						•	•	•			•				•	•				

	UNIT 3																UNIT 4											UNIT 5									
	Ch. 8			Ch. 9			Ch. 10			Ch. 11			Ch. 12			Ch. 13			Ch. 14			Ch. 15			Ch. 16			Ch. 17			Ch. 18			Ch. 19			Ch. 20		
	22	23	24	25	26	27	28	29	30	31	32	33	34	35	36	37	38	39	40	41	42	43	44	45	46	47	48	49	50	51	52	53	54	55	56	57	58	59	60

Unifying Concepts and Processes

Science as Inquiry

Physical Science

Life Science

Earth and Space Science

Science and Technology

Science in Personal and Social Perspectives

History and Nature of Science

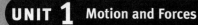

UNIT 1
Motion and Forces

About the Photo

When a roller coaster is poised at the top of a hill, it has tremendous potential energy. As it plunges down the hill, potential energy changes to kinetic energy, the energy of motion.

About the Reading Selections

The reading selections included in the student book include square brackets and points of ellipses—a series of three or four points (periods). Such substitutions were made to simplify or shorten the text. If students are not familiar with these forms of punctuation, offer the following explanations:

► Square brackets show that other words were substituted for words in the original text.
► Points of ellipsis show that words were left out of the original text. Within a sentence, three points are used. At the end of a sentence, four points are used—three points of ellipsis plus the period that ends the sentence.

About the Charts

A major goal of the *Science Daybooks* is to promote reading, writing, and critical thinking skills in the context of science. The charts below describe the types of reading selections included in this unit and identify the skills and strategies used in each lesson.

Balls bounce, apples fall, wheels roll, and birds fly. Forces in nature produce many different types of motion. Sir Isaac Newton was the first person to describe the physical laws that explain how objects around us move. Over the centuries, engineers have used their understanding of motion and forces to build many tools and machines that are useful to us— and some that are just plain fun.

In this unit you'll build a track to determine the relationship between the two forms of energy that keep a roller coaster zipping up and down. Newton's laws of motion will help you explain the movement of a rocket. You'll examine some simple machines, and learn about some modern machines that show off the most recent technology.

8

SELECTION	READING	WRITING	APPLICATION
CHAPTER 1 • UP, DOWN, AND ALL AROUND			
1. "A Law of Motion" (children's science magazine)	• Graphic organizer • Find evidence	• Draw diagrams • Explain your answer	• Write a magazine story
2. "How Does a Roller Coaster Work?" (university science Web site)	• Complete a chart • Read for details	• Make inferences	• Label a diagram
3.	• Read and follow directions	• Record results • Draw conclusions • Make inferences	• Make a hypothesis • Conduct an experiment
CHAPTER 2 • MAY THE FORCE BE WITH YOU			
4. "Forces in the Ollie" (science museum exhibit)	• Use prior knowledge • Read for details	• Make inferences	• Make predictions
5. "Discus Throw" (nonfiction science book)	• Directed reading	• Make calculations • Make comparisons	• Write a limerick
6. "Rocket Boy" (autobiography)	• Directed reading	• Make diagrams	• Hands-on activity

Did You Know?

Engineers in Seattle have developed a robot that washes windows. The toaster-sized robot has been used to clean a giant glass pyramid that sits outside the Louvre museum in Paris, France. Suction cups hold the robot to the pyramid as it moves around. A big squeegee and rotating brush mounted on the robot's hood do the cleaning. The whole thing is controlled by a joystick.

THE CHAPTERS IN THIS UNIT ARE …

9

Answers to *Find Out* Questions

CHAPTER 1
The fastest track is the one with the greatest drop on the first hill. (pp. 16, 19)

CHAPTER 2
Newton's first law of motion explains the unbalanced forces that enable a skateboarder to do "ollies" and other tricks. (pp. 22–23)

CHAPTER 3
Artist Leonardo Da Vinci reasoned that by understanding how each part of a machine worked, he could modify and combine them to create new machines. (p. 31)

CHAPTER 4
Robots are used to automate the milking process. (pp. 43–44)

SCi*L*INKS.
THE WORLD'S A CLICK AWAY

www.scilinks.org
Keyword: Current Research
Code: GSSD04

SELECTION	READING	WRITING	APPLICATION
CHAPTER 3 • DA VINCI'S DESIGNS			
7. "Inventor's Workshop" (science museum exhibit)	• Use prior knowledge • Generate questions	• Label a diagram	• Write a paragraph
8.	• Read and follow instructions • Use a reference book	• Hands-on activity • Draw and label sketches	• Invent a machine
9. "Visions of the Future" (science museum exhibit)	• Interpret diagrams	• Make comparisons • Draw conclusions	• Conduct an interview • Record results
CHAPTER 4 • MODERN MACHINES			
10. "An Idea from Nature" (university newsletter)	• Read for details	• Make comparisons	• Draw conclusions
11. "Robots in the Dairy Barn" (science magazine article)	• Make a list • Read for details	• Decode a diagram • Make calculations	• Hold a debate • Write reflections
12. "Make Way for Segway!" (children's magazine article)	• Describe objects from science fiction • Generate questions	• Make comparisons • Propose solutions	• Conduct an interview • Defend predictions

Up, Down, and All Around

LESSON I
The Wild Ride
Point of Lesson: *Objects tend to resist a change in motion.*

In this lesson, students begin an exploration of the physics of a roller coaster ride. They read an explanation of why, according to Newton's first law of motion, a rider feels glued to the side of a roller coaster car during a turn. Then students diagram the forces on the rider during the turn. They apply their knowledge of unbalanced forces by reporting on a baseball game from a science writer's point of view.

Materials
Enrichment (p. 11), for each student or pair:
► paper or plastic cup
► index card
► coin

LESSON 2
To the Top!
Point of Lesson: *Roller coasters provide an opportunity to study conversions between potential and kinetic energy.*

Students continue their examination of roller coaster physics as they first identify objects with kinetic and potential energy, then read about the potential and kinetic energy transfers during a roller coaster ride. They then label a diagram of a roller coaster to identify where the potential and kinetic energy are greatest during the ride. Students apply their knowledge by diagramming a dive into a pool and describing the energy changes that take place during the dive.

Materials
Science Scope Activity (p. 10B and p. 15), for the teacher:
► foam pipe insulation, 3 m long
for the class:
► index cards with the following labels:
   Maximum GPE
   Maximum KE
   KE > PE
   PE > KE
   acceleration (change in speed)
   friction
   Newton's first law
Connections (p. 16), for the class:
► drawing supplies
► old magazines
► scissors
► clear tape

LESSON 3
The Big Drop
Point of Lesson: *Potential energy is converted to kinetic energy as a ball changes its position on an elevated track.*

In this lesson, students create their own model roller coaster, using a marble as the "car." After testing one suggested design, students raise and lower the starting point of the marble to determine which starting point provides the most potential energy.

Materials
Experiment (p. 18), for each group:
► 1 marble
► pipe insulation sliced lengthwise (2–3 m)
► masking tape
► 2 chairs
► measuring tape
► pencil
► stopwatch

Laboratory Safety
Review the following safety guidelines with students before they do the Experiment in this lesson.

► Promptly pick up any marbles that hit the floor. Do not leave them where people can slip on them.
► If any marble breaks or chips, do not continue to use it. Ask your teacher for a replacement.

Science Scope Activity

Roller Coasters—Thrilling Physics

NSTA has chosen a Science Scope *activity related to the content in this chapter. The activity begins here and continues in Lesson 2, page 15.)*

Time: 30 minutes

Materials: see page 10A

Make one loop in the foam pipe insulation to model a simple single-loop roller coaster. Tack the roller coaster to a bulletin board. (Alternatively, you could simply draw the roller coaster on the board.) The top of the loop should be lower than the starting point, and the ending point should be lower than all other points.

(continued on page 15)

Background Information

Lesson 3

Students who are new to scientific investigation may not understand why it is important to roll the marble from each height three times and average the results, rather than simply rolling the marble once from each height. Explain that if you have only one measurement, you have no means of determining whether that measurement is typical. Repeated trials reduce the possibility of chance errors affecting the results. In fact, the process of scientific investigation includes entire experiments being repeated by different teams of scientists, using the same methods, in order to verify results. This rigorous testing leads to reliable data that can be trusted as true tests of hypotheses.

Point of Lesson

Objects tend to resist a change in motion.

Focus

▶ Motion and forces
▶ History of science
▶ Systems, order, and organization

Skills and Strategies

▶ Making inferences
▶ Recognizing cause and effect
▶ Using space/time relationships
▶ Sequencing

Advance Preparation

Vocabulary

Make sure students understand these terms. Definitions can be found in the glossary at the end of the student book.

▶ force
▶ unbalanced force

Materials

Gather the materials needed for *Enrichment* (p. 11).

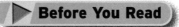

The Wild Ride

How does a roller coaster ride pull you this way and that? Hop on and see.

You bought your ticket. You waited in line. Now it's time for the wild ride. Suddenly—whoosh!—you're falling and turning and mashing into the side of the roller coaster car as it whips around corners!

Roller coaster rides are a thrill. English physicist Sir Isaac Newton (1642–1727) never rode on a roller coaster, but he did describe the forces acting on objects moving up and down and all around.

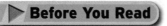 **Before You Read**

THINK ABOUT IT Imagine that you are riding in a car or bus. The table lists ways a car might move. Fill in the table to describe how your body would move (or feel) with each movement of the car.

What the car does	How my body moves or feels
Starts moving	*My body presses into the back of my seat.*
Speeds up	*My body presses harder into the back of my seat.*
Slows down	*I get pulled forward, or toward the front of the car.*
Makes a right turn	*I feel like I'm being pulled to the left side of the car.*
Makes a left turn	*I feel like I'm being pulled to the right side of the car.*
Comes to a stop	*I get pulled forward, or toward the front of the car.*

TEACHING PLAN pp. 10–11

INTRODUCING THE LESSON

This lesson discusses one aspect of Newton's first law of motion—objects tend to resist a change in motion.

Ask students to describe what happens to them when they are riding in a car or bus and it goes around a curve. (They are pulled toward the outside of the curve.) Some students may recall that they feel pulled more on sharper turns. They may also recall that they slide more on hard, slippery seats and less on padded, cloth seats. Ask students to explain why they think they are pulled. Tell them to keep this experience in mind as they work through the lesson.

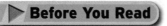 **Before You Read**

THINK ABOUT IT Before students complete the chart, have them visualize themselves riding in a car. Tell them to close their eyes and recall what they experience when a car starts moving, speeds up, slows down, turns right, turns left, and comes to a stop. The point of this exercise is to give students an intuitive understand of how objects in moving vehicles resist any imposed change in their speed or direction.

▶ Read

Here's what happens when a moving car changes direction.

A Law of Motion

*Why do I feel glued to the [out]side [edge]
of the roller coaster car when it whips around a curve?*

Think about what happens if you make a sudden turn when you're driving in a car. If you turn left, you seem to feel a mysterious force pushing you to the right: the kids in the back seat wind up pressed against the passenger-side door. Why is that? Well, before you started your turn, both the car and your body were moving in a straight line. And as Isaac Newton noticed hundreds of years ago, objects move in a straight line unless a force acts to change their motion. (This is part of what we now call Newton's first law of motion.) So when the car begins to turn left, your body keeps going straight for a while—until the car door gets in your way. The same is true on a roller coaster: you keep going straight until the roller coaster car pushes you to the side.

From: Beres, Samantha. "Roller Coaster Science."
Scientific American Explorations.

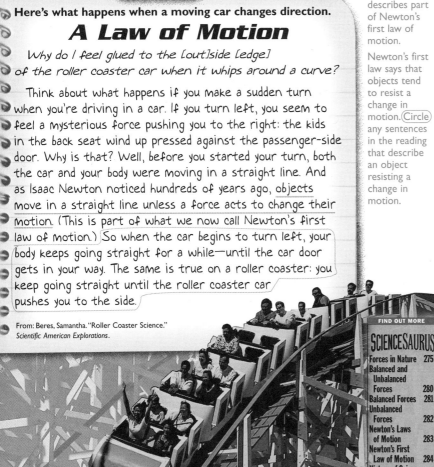

FIND OUT MORE

SCIENCESAURUS

Forces in Nature 275
Balanced and
Unbalanced
Forces 280
Balanced Forces 281
Unbalanced
Forces 282
Newton's Laws
of Motion 283
Newton's First
Law of Motion 284
History of Science
Time Line 442

SCiLINKS
THE WORLD'S A CLICK AWAY

www.scilinks.org
Keyword: Inertia
Code: GSPD01

11

NoteZone (margin notes): Underline the statement that describes part of Newton's first law of motion. Newton's first law says that objects tend to resist a change in motion. Circle any sentences in the reading that describe an object resisting a change in motion.

Enrichment

Time: 15 minutes
Materials: (for each student or pair) paper or plastic cup, index card, coin

The following activity is a surprisingly easy demonstration of Newton's first law. Have students work individually or in pairs, and give them the following instructions:

1. Lay the index card across the top of the cup.
2. Put the coin in the center of the card.
3. With your index finger, flick one edge of the card to push it off the cup. (The coin will drop into the cup.)

Ask students to try to explain their observations. (The card moved sideways because a horizontal force acted on it. The slight horizontal force of friction between the card and the coin was not enough to move the coin. The main force acting on the coin was gravity.) Explain that the tendency of an object at rest to stay at rest is called *inertia*. Inertia also explains what happens when a magician pulls a tablecloth off a fully set table and the objects do not move.

Invite students to try the following variation or make up their own tricks to demonstrate.

▶ Lay a sheet of paper on a table or desk with about 5 cm hanging over the edge. Put one or more coins on the paper. Pull the paper quickly down and away. (The coins will remain on the table or desk.)

▶ Read

As students read, encourage them to mentally review and, if necessary, revise the ideas they had earlier about why they are pushed and pulled in a moving a car.

Encourage students to create a concept map that shows the sequence of events described in the reading in terms of the car's motion and the passenger's motion. (Both the car and the passenger are moving straight forward. The car turns left, but the passenger keeps going straight until he or she hits the door.)

Discuss some other examples of forces that cause a moving object to change speed or direction. Have students generate examples from everyday life. (Examples: A soccer player kicks a rolling ball; a hockey player slaps a puck sliding across the ice; a fence stops a rolling tennis ball; wind blows a leaf falling from a tree.)

CHECK UNDERSTANDING
Skills: Recognizing cause and effect
Ask: *If you were riding in a roller coaster car, in what direction would you slide as the coaster took a right turn?* (to your left) *What unbalanced force would stop you and push you to your right?* (the side of the car)

More Resources

The following resources are also available from Great Source and NSTA.

SCIENCESAURUS

READER'S HANDBOOK

WRITE SOURCE 2000

www.scilinks.org
Keyword: Inertia
Code: GSPD01

PICTURE THIS Sir Isaac Newton discovered that an object at rest tends to stay at rest. Newton also found that an object in motion tends to keep moving at the same speed and in the same direction. So, things tend to keep on doing what they are doing—unless something else happens to them. That something else is called an unbalanced force.

The diagram below shows the top view (looking down from above) of a roller coaster car. Each picture is a snapshot of the car in a different position as it moves along the track. Look at the position of the rider (x) in the first picture. Imagine that the rider can slide across the seat. Draw the position of the rider at the other two points on the track. Add arrows to show the direction the *rider* (not the car) is moving at each point.

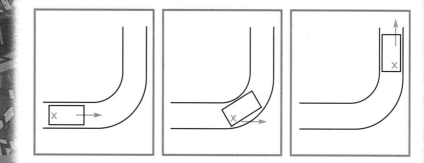

▶ *In what direction is the roller coaster rider moving in the first picture?*
  straight ahead

▶ *What was the unbalanced force that changed the rider's direction of motion?*
  The side of the car pushing on the rider as the car turned made the
  rider's direction of motion change.

▶ *After the turn, in what direction do the rider and car continue to move? Explain your answer in terms of Newton's first law.*
  They begin to move straight ahead again. As long as the track continues
  straight, the rider and the car will continue to move straight because, as
  Newton's first law says, moving objects tend to keep moving at the same
  speed and in the same direction.

12

TEACHING PLAN pp. 12–13

PICTURE THIS Suggest that students turn their book so their bodies are aligned with the initial direction of the roller coaster car. This will help them understand that the track and car turn left. Tell students to visualize being in the car as it takes the sharp left turn. Then have them mark the position of the rider and draw an arrow showing the rider's direction of motion just as the car begins its turn. Have students continue the visualization process to complete the exercise.

Be sure students understand why the rider is at the side of the car in both the second and third frames. Help them see that when the car turns left, the rider slides to the right because there is no force to stop him until he hits the side of the car. Then, when the car is moving straight, the rider stays at the side because there is no force to move him back to the middle. After the turn, the rider continues to move straight again.

You may want to have students work in pairs to complete the diagram, with one student providing instructions while the other draws.

PLAY BALL Imagine that you are a reporter for a science magazine sent to cover a baseball game. You watch as the pitcher throws a ball to the batter, who clobbers the ball with his bat, sending it sailing into the air for a home run.

► *Draw a three-part diagram showing the ball's position and direction of motion at three stages: as the ball is moving toward the batter; as the batter strikes the ball; as the ball sails into the air. Also identify and label the unbalanced force that acted on the ball to change its direction of motion.*

► *Below your diagrams, describe the pitch and the hit for your magazine story. Try to make the story exciting while still explaining the science of what happens to the ball.*

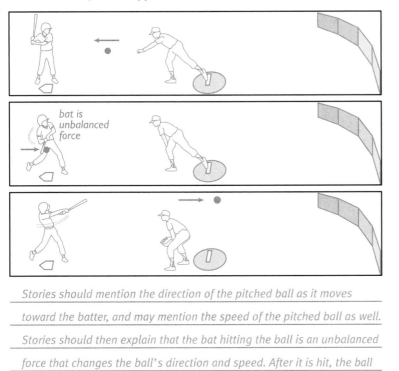

bat is
unbalanced
force

Stories should mention the direction of the pitched ball as it moves

toward the batter, and may mention the speed of the pitched ball as well.

Stories should then explain that the bat hitting the ball is an unbalanced

force that changes the ball's direction and speed. After it is hit, the ball

moves in almost the opposite direction, away from the batter, toward the

outfield, and at a different speed.

13

Assessment
Skill: Recognizing cause and effect

Use the following task to assess each student's progress:

Have students use Newton's first law to explain how car safety belts can save lives. (When a car brakes suddenly or hits another object, the passenger's body continues to move forward as the car stops. The seat belt acts as an unbalanced force to stop the body from moving forward. If the passenger were not wearing a seatbelt, he or she would continue to move forward until stopped by an unbalanced force such as the dashboard or windshield. This collision would result in injury.)

► **Take Action**

PLAY BALL Suggest to students that they think of the three boxes on this page as frames in a slow-motion video replay. If they need help getting started, ask: *What is the direction of the ball just after the pitcher throws it?* (straight ahead, toward the batter) *What force causes the motion?* (the movement of the pitcher's arm) *What is the direction of that force?* (straight ahead, toward the batter) Then direct students to record this information graphically in the top frame.

Help students organize their descriptions of the play by suggesting that they use each diagram as the basis for a short paragraph. Remind them that they should explain both the story of the batter's home run and the science of what happens to the ball.

Before they begin writing, students may find it helpful to make two lists of words to include in their articles: one of baseball terms (such as *pitch, hit, base, run, outfield, home run*) and the other of science-related words and phrases that apply to this situation (such as *force, unbalanced force, direction, motion, speed*).

Point of Lesson

Roller coasters provide an opportunity to study conversions between potential and kinetic energy.

Focus

► Motion and forces
► Transfer of energy
► Systems, order, and organization

Skills and Strategies

► Sequencing
► Making inferences
► Interpreting scientific illustrations
► Using space/time relationships

Advance Preparation

Vocabulary

Make sure students understand these terms. Definitions can be found in the glossary at the end of the student book.

► gravity
► mass

Materials

Gather the materials needed for *Science Scope Activity* (p. 10B and p. 15) and *Connections* (p. 16).

To the Top!

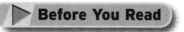

You've got potential—energy, that is.

The chains creak as the roller coaster you are riding is dragged up the first hill. You reach the top. *This isn't so bad*, you think to yourself. The car hesitates for a second. Then it plunges downhill, picking up speed. The thrill you feel has a lot to do with energy changing forms. It's exciting, and it's physics!

▶ **Before You Read**

COMPARING ENERGY FORMS Imagine climbing the ladder of a high dive. When you get to the platform, you walk to the far edge and pause. At that moment, standing high above the water, you have potential energy. *Potential energy* is the energy an object has because of its position or its height. The higher the diving platform, the more potential energy you have. Now imagine diving off the platform. As you dive, your potential energy is converted to *kinetic energy*—the energy of motion.

Think of other examples of when people or objects have potential energy that changes to kinetic energy. Fill in the chart with your ideas. Some examples are already filled in to get you started.

Object or Person	Position with Potential Energy	Motion Showing Kinetic Energy
Rubber band	Stretched out	Snapping back
Ball	In the air after it was tossed	Falling back
Book	On the shelf	Falling off the shelf
Acorn	Hanging on the tree	Falling to the ground
Child on a swing	When the swing is all the way back or all the way forward	Moving forward or backward
Arrow	In the bow with the bowstring pulled back	After it's released and is flying through the air

14

TEACHING PLAN pp. 14–15

INTRODUCING THE LESSON

This lesson introduces the concepts of potential and kinetic energy. Briefly review the meaning of each term with students: Potential energy is the energy an object has because of its position or height—for example, a book resting on a shelf. Kinetic energy is the energy an object has due to its motion—for example, a bowling ball rolling along a lane toward the pins.

Explain that an object's potential energy can change to kinetic energy, and vice versa. Help students recall situations in which the potential energy of an object begins to change to kinetic

energy. (Examples: a leaf falling from a tree, snow sliding off a roof) Then have students give examples of an object whose kinetic energy is converted to potential energy. (Example: a tossed ball as it rises up into the air)

▶ **Before You Read**

COMPARING ENERGY FORMS Expand on the examples that students cited in the chart. Ask: *How could you give one ball more potential energy than another ball?* (Toss one ball higher in the air than the other one.) *How might you*

give one rubber band more potential energy than another one? (Stretch one rubber band more than the other one.) Then ask: *How could the kinetic energy of one book falling from a shelf be more than the kinetic energy of another book falling from a shelf?* (One book could fall from a higher shelf.)

▶ **Read**

Here's how Dr. Louis Bloomfield, a physics professor, explains potential and kinetic energy on a roller coaster.

HOW DOES A ROLLER COASTER WORK?

A roller coaster is [basically] a gravity-powered train. When the chain pulls the train up the first hill, it transfers an enormous amount of energy to that train. This energy initially takes the form of gravitational potential energy—energy stored in the gravitational force between the train and the earth. But once the train begins to descend the first hill, that gravitational potential energy becomes kinetic energy—the energy of motion. The roller coaster reaches maximum speed at the bottom of the first hill, when all of its gravitational potential energy has been converted to kinetic energy. It then rushes up the second hill, slowing down and converting some of its kinetic energy back into gravitational potential energy. This conversion of energy back and forth between the two forms continues. [B]ut energy is gradually lost to friction and air resistance, so that the ride becomes less and less intense until finally it comes to a stop.

transfer: to move from one place to another
initially: at first
descend: move downward
maximum: most, greatest
converted: changed
conversion: change

friction: the force that resists motion, causing objects to slow down and stop
air resistance: friction caused as an object moves through air
intense: strong

From: Bloomfield, Louis A. "How Does a Roller Coaster Work?"
(www.howthingswork.virginia.edu)

Underline the first time potential energy is changed to kinetic energy.

Circle the first time kinetic energy is changed to potential energy (not including when the chain pulls the train up the hill to begin the ride).

FIND OUT MORE

SCIENCESAURUS
Forms of Energy 300

SCLINKS
THE WORLD'S A CLICK AWAY
www.scilinks.org
Keyword: Kinetic/
Potential Energy
Code: GSPD02

15

Science Scope Activity
(continued from page 10B)

Procedure:

1. Tell students to visualize a car traveling along the roller coaster's track. Encourage them to think about where the car would have the greatest potential energy, where it would have greatest kinetic energy, and so on.

2. Invite groups of students to take turns placing each label at an appropriate point on the track.

3. After one group finishes labeling the roller coaster, ask the other groups to critique that group's work. Have students note which cards were placed correctly and which incorrectly and to explain why they think so. Encourage students to identify an alternate point, if any, where each card could be placed correctly. If necessary, guide students to recognize that many of the cards can be correctly placed in more than one location.

▶ **Read**

Encourage students to form a mental picture of what is happening on the roller coaster as they read. Help them with their imaging by explaining that the roller coaster car's energy does not change from potential to kinetic all at once. Instead, the change happens gradually and continuously as the roller coaster car moves down a hill. The change from kinetic energy back to potential energy is also a gradual, continuous process that occurs as the car climbs the next hill.

Students will probably notice that the excerpt uses the term *gravitational potential energy* rather than simply *potential energy.* Point out that gravitational potential energy refers specifically to the energy an object has because of its height above Earth. Review the definition of *gravity* with the class. (The force of attraction between any two objects; on Earth, the force of gravity causes unsupported objects to fall to the ground.) Explain that the force of gravity pulling a falling object toward Earth is what gives a falling object its energy.

CHECK UNDERSTANDING
Skill: Generating ideas
Describe to students a "Sky Drop" type of amusement park ride, in which a car carrying riders is hoisted to the top of a tall tower and, after hanging there for a moment, is released and allowed to fall. Ask: *During which part of the ride is the car's potential energy changing to kinetic energy?* (PE is converted to KE continuously as the car falls.) *When is the car's potential energy the greatest?* (PE is greatest as the car hangs at the top of the tower.)

More Resources

The following resources are also available from Great Source and NSTA.

ScienceSaurus

Forms of Energy   300

Reader's Handbook

Visualizing and Thinking Aloud   664

www.scilinks.org
Keyword: Kinetic/Potential Energy
Code: GSPD02

Connections

Time: 20–30 minutes
Materials: thesaurus, drawing supplies, old magazines, scissors, clear tape

WRITING Invite students to write and illustrate short poems about an object's energy changing from kinetic to potential or vice versa. Encourage them to use a thesaurus to help find vivid verbs and adverbs. Allow students to choose any form of poetry that they feel suits their subject. Illustrations may be hand-drawn, collages of pictures cut from magazines, or clip art obtained on the Internet.

TEACHING PLAN pp. 16–17

▶ Explore

SEQUENCE THE ENERGY CHANGES Professor Bloomfield explains that an object has gravitational potential energy because of its height above the ground. Gravity is the force of attraction that exists between all pairs of objects. The greater the mass of the objects, the greater the force of attraction is. Since Earth is so massive compared to other objects nearby, we are usually only aware of the gravitational force due to Earth's mass. As the chain pulls the roller coaster car up the hill, farther and farther away from Earth, the car gains more and more gravitational potential energy.

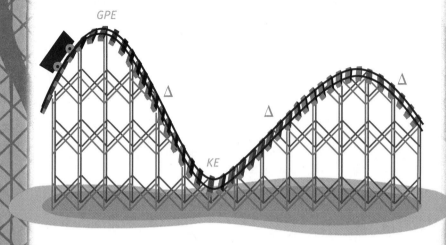

▶ *At which point on the track will the car's gravitational potential energy be the greatest? Label this point "GPE."*
▶ *At which point on the track will the car's kinetic energy be the greatest? Label this point "KE."*
▶ *Use a small triangle (Δ) to label three places where an energy conversion is taking place.*

MAKE AN INFERENCE Consider where on a hill a roller coaster car moves the slowest, and where on a hill it moves the fastest. How does the car's kinetic energy seem to be related to its speed?

The greater the kinetic energy, the greater the speed. As kinetic energy increases, so does speed.

16

▶ Explore

SEQUENCE THE ENERGY CHANGES
Point out to students that they have an intuitive understanding of gravitational potential energy. Ask students to remember how scary heights can be. Allow a few students to give examples. Summarize their examples by saying that heights are scary because you know that a fall will hurt badly. Then ask a volunteer to use the term *potential energy* to explain why falling from a greater height is worse than falling from a lower height. (You start with more potential energy, so you build up more kinetic energy as you fall and are moving faster when you hit the ground.)

If needed, help students label the diagram. If students are having difficulty labeling the point where the car's GPE is the greatest, point out that although there are two hills, one is higher than the other; the higher one would provide the greater gravitational potential energy. On the other hand, the car's KE will be greatest at the bottom of the bigger hill, when all the car's GPE has been converted to KE. At any place where the car is moving up or down, an energy conversion is taking place.

MAKE AN INFERENCE If students are having difficulty determining where on a hill a roller coaster moves the fastest, have them reread the excerpt. (The roller coaster picks up speed on its way down the hill and goes the fastest as it nears the bottom.) If students have difficulty visualizing the roller coaster example, ask them to imagine themselves bicycling or skateboarding down a hill.

▶ Propose Explanations

APPLY THE CONCEPT Imagine once again that you are on the platform of a high dive. On the diagram below, draw and label your position in the following three places:

    1. gravitational potential energy greatest, kinetic energy least
    2. gravitational potential energy and kinetic energy about equal
    3. gravitational potential energy least, kinetic energy greatest

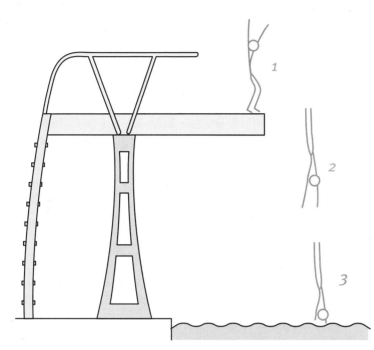

▶ **Describe the energy change that takes place as you dive off the platform.**

The gravitational potential energy that I built up and stored as I climbed

the ladder began to change to kinetic energy when I jumped off the edge

to make the dive. I had the most kinetic energy just as I hit the surface

of the water.

17

Assessment

Skill: Drawing conclusions

Use the following task to assess each student's progress:

Tell students to imagine the following situation: Two divers of equal mass are about to dive into a pool from separate diving boards. Diver A has greater potential energy than Diver B. Ask: *What can you infer about Diver A's position compared with Diver B's position? Explain your reasoning.* (Diver A must be on a higher board than Diver B. The higher the diving board, the more potential energy the person will have.) *Which diver will be going faster when he or she hits the water? How do you know?* (Diver A will be going faster because he or she has more potential energy to be changed into kinetic energy. The greater the kinetic energy, the greater the speed.)

▶ Propose Explanations

APPLY THE CONCEPT As necessary, guide students to use what they have learned about energy conversions to determine how to label their drawings. Students may have particular difficulty with label 2, *gravitational potential energy* and *kinetic energy about equal*. Remind students that an object's potential energy is not converted to kinetic energy all at once. Rather, the diver's potential energy is steadily and continuously converted to kinetic energy throughout the entire fall. Help students use this information to determine

when the diver's potential and kinetic energy would be about equal. (about halfway between the platform and the water)

For an extra challenge, ask students to describe what happens to the diver's kinetic energy when he or she hits the water. (The kinetic energy must be converted to something else because the diver's speed decreases greatly.) Ask: *If the diver's speed decreases, where does the energy go?* As a hint, remind students that any kind of motion is evidence of kinetic energy. Help students see that some of the energy is transmitted to the water, forming waves and a splash.

Point of Lesson

Potential energy is converted to kinetic energy as a ball changes its position on an elevated track.

Focus

▶ **Transfer of energy**
▶ **Evidence, models, and explanation**
▶ **Change, constancy, and measurement**

Skills and Strategies

▶ **Designing an experiment to test a hypothesis**
▶ **Measuring**
▶ **Collecting and recording data**
▶ **Interpreting data**
▶ **Drawing conclusions**

Advance Preparation

Vocabulary

Make sure students understand this term. The definition can be found in the glossary at the end of the student book.

▶ **hypothesis**

Materials

Gather the materials needed for *Experiment* (below).

Up, Down, and All Around

The Big Drop

Have you got what it takes to go the distance?

Higher, faster, farther! The higher a roller coaster car, the more potential (stored) energy it has. The more potential energy it has, the more kinetic (motion) energy it will have when it reaches the bottom of the hill. But will the car have enough kinetic energy to roll up that next hill?

▶ Experiment

GOING THE DISTANCE

Test your own ideas about roller coaster track design.

What You Need:
- one marble
- pipe insulation sliced lengthwise (2-3 meters)
- masking tape
- two chairs
- measuring tape
- pencil
- stopwatch

What to Do:
1. Set up the track in a semicircular shape as shown.
2. Hold the marble at the top of one side of the track. Measure its height from the floor and record it in the table. This is starting point A.
3. Let the marble go. Measure how many seconds the marble rolls before it comes to a complete stop. Record the time in the table.
4. Repeat two more times and find the average roll time. Record the average in the table.
5. Now mark any lower spot on the track to start the marble from. This is starting point B. Measure the height from the floor and record it in the table. Repeat steps 3 and 4.
6. Study your results for starting points A and B. How do you think the starting height affects the total time the marble rolls? Choose a third starting point to test your hypothesis. Write a prediction about the results using an "if/then" statement: IF something happens, THEN something else will happen.
   Predictions will vary.

7. Measure the starting height and record it. Repeat steps 3 and 4, starting the marble at the new position.

18

TEACHING PLAN pp. 18–19

INTRODUCING THE LESSON

This lesson gives students an opportunity to do hands-on experiments with potential and kinetic energy. Ask students what they can tell you about potential and kinetic energy. Help students review what they learned in the previous lesson.

▶ Experiment

Time: 45 minutes
Materials: 1 marble, pipe insulation sliced lengthwise (2–3 m), masking tape, two chairs, measuring tape, pencil, stopwatch

▶ Have students work in groups of four.
▶ Tell students to make sure the sides of the track are sloped, not vertical.
▶ To keep the track from swaying, students can let the center touch the floor.
▶ Help students measure time accurately. Remind them to start the timer at the same moment they release the marble and stop it the moment the marble stops rolling.
▶ Point out that to find an average in step 4, they must add the three times and then divide by 3.

Students may wonder why the marble does not continue to convert potential energy to kinetic energy and keep rolling forever. Explain that the marble's energy is gradually lost to friction as it rolls back and forth on the track. Friction is a force that opposes motion between two touching surfaces, and energy is needed to overcome it. If there were no friction, the marble would continue rolling back and forth to the same height forever.

The average roll time for each starting point should correspond to its height. The higher the starting point is, the longer the total roll time will be.

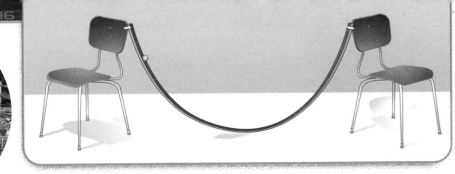

What Do You See?

Starting Point	Height (cm)	Roll Time #1 (sec)	Roll Time #2 (sec)	Roll Time #3 (sec)	Average Roll Time (sec)
A (top of track)					
B (lower spot)					
C (your choice)					

Propose Explanations

DRAW CONCLUSIONS

▶ Look at your prediction from step 6. How does your data support or not support your hypothesis?

Answers will vary. Example: I thought it would stop sooner if it started

lower, and it did, so I was right.

MAKE INFERENCES Kinetic energy is the energy an object has because of its motion.

▶ Which starting point height gave the marble the most kinetic energy? What evidence do you have to support your answer?

Starting point A gave the marble the most kinetic energy. The evidence

is that it kept moving longer.

Potential energy is the energy an object has because of its position. The marble's potential energy is converted to kinetic energy as it rolls down the track.

▶ What can you infer about which starting position provided the greatest amount of potential energy?

Starting point A, because the marble had the most kinetic energy

when it started there.

FIND OUT MORE

SCIENCESAURUS
Testing
  Hypotheses   007
Gathering Data 009
Recording Data 010
Drawing
  Conclusions   013
Forms of Energy 300

SCILINKS.
THE WORLD'S A CLICK AWAY
www.scilinks.org
Keyword: Kinetic/
Potential Energy
Code: GSPD02

19

More Resources
The following resources are also available from Great Source and NSTA.

SCILINKS.
THE WORLD'S A CLICK AWAY

www.scilinks.org
Keyword: Kinetic/Potential Energy
Code: GSPD02

Assessment
Skill: Making inferences

Use the following task to assess each student's progress:

Tell students to imagine they are in a bicycle race and will ride up three hills that are identical in height and slope. They will approach the first hill from a long, flat road. They will start up the second hill after biking down a short hill. They will hit the third hill after coming down a very high, steep hill. Ask: *Which of the three identical hills will be easiest to ride up?* (the third hill) *Why?* (The rider would have the greatest amount of kinetic energy after coming down the high, steep hill, and this would help him or her up the third hill.)

▶ Propose Explanations

DRAW CONCLUSIONS Whether their data support their hypotheses or not, all students should recognize that the higher the starting point, the longer the roll time.

MAKE INFERENCES If necessary, clarify for students that the marble with the most potential energy also had the most kinetic energy, which allowed it to roll back and forth the longest.

To help students describe the energy conversions that took place as the marble rolled back and forth on the track,

ask: *At what points had all the marble's kinetic energy become potential energy?* (when it reached then end of a roll in one direction and paused momentarily) *At what point had all its potential energy become kinetic energy?* (at the bottom where the track touches the floor) Have students label these points on the diagram.

CHECK UNDERSTANDING
Skill: Drawing conclusions
Ask: *Imagine yourself on a roller coaster. At which moment do you have the greatest gravitational potential energy? Explain.* (Once the car has been pulled up the track to the starting point; this is the highest point on the track and so has the greatest GPE. I know it is the highest point on the track because the car does not rise higher than its initial starting point.)

May the Force Be With You

LESSON 4

On Board With Forces

Point of Lesson: *Newton's first law explains how a skateboarder can create an unbalanced force on his board to pop it up into the air.*

The skateboard maneuver known as the *ollie* provides a springboard for exploring the effects of unbalanced forces on an object's motion. Students read a description of the forces in an ollie, then identify those forces in a diagram. They relate the skateboard's movements to Newton's first law of motion and consider how changing the size of any one force would change the motion of the skateboard. Finally, students think of other examples of forces causing objects to change direction.

Materials
Read (p. 21), for the class:
► videotape of skateboarders (optional)
Enrichment (p. 21), for each group:
► 2 marbles
► wooden board
► 2–3 wooden blocks
Propose Explanations (p. 23), for each student or pair:
► rubber ball, table tennis ball, or rubber eraser

Laboratory Safety
Review the following safety guideline with students before they do the *Enrichment* activity in this lesson.

► Handle the marbles carefully. Do not throw them. Promptly pick up any marble that falls on the floor.

LESSON 5

Mass Action

Point of Lesson: *Newton's second law explains why a modern discus can be thrown farther than the discus used by ancient Greek Olympic competitors.*

Newton's second law of motion is explored through the discus throw event at the Olympics in Ancient Greece. Students determine how the acceleration of a discus of a certain mass changes as the force on it is increased. They explore the relationship between the discus's acceleration, its speed, and the distance it travels and compare the properties of ancient and modern discuses. The lesson ends with students composing limericks about Newton's second law.

Materials
Enrichment (p. 25), for each group:
► skateboard
► 2 bricks
► stopwatch
Take Action (p. 27), for the class:
► book of limericks

Laboratory Safety
Review the following safety guidelines with students before they do the *Enrichment* Activity in this lesson.

► Do not ride the skateboard during this activity.
► Do not stack the bricks on the skateboard. Place them side by side.
► Handle the bricks carefully. Do not drop them or toss them.
► Stay off the track while classmates are rolling skateboards.

LESSON 6

Rocket Reaction

Point of Lesson: *Rocket action demonstrates the action and reaction forces described by Newton's third law.*

A passage from the book *Rocket Boys* introduces students to Newton's third law of motion. Students then observe the motions of a balloon that is inflated and released. Finally, they identify the forces acting on the balloon and explain its motion in terms of Newton's third law.

Materials
Activity (p. 29), for each student:
► 1 small balloon

Laboratory Safety
Review the following safety guidelines with students before they do the Activity in this lesson.

► If you are allergic to latex, do not do this activity.
► Only one student should blow up each balloon. Do not share balloons.
► Hold the balloon firmly with your hand while you are inflating it so you do not accidentally inhale it.

Background Information

Lesson 4

Vectors in a diagram are a means of showing the size and direction of forces acting on an object. Vectors typically are introduced in physics courses at the high school level. However, the diagram on page 22 of the student book includes an example of informal vectors, if you want to expose students to this concept. The upward arrow indicates the larger force of the ground pushing up on the skateboard, and the downward arrow shows the smaller force of gravity pulling down on the skateboard. The two arrows indicate that there is a net unbalanced force on the skateboard, in an upward direction. (In a true vector diagram, the arrows would be labeled with the size of each force in Newtons, and the length of each arrow would be strictly in proportion to the magnitude of that force.)

ground pushing up

gravity pulling down

Lesson 6

A common misconception in the early days of rocketry was that the gases expelled from a rocket (the action) push against the gases in the atmosphere, which in turn propel the rocket forward (the reaction). This misconception still pops up today, and it may be worth discussing with your students. If rockets required an atmosphere to push against, then of course no rockets would be able to accelerate after leaving Earth's atmosphere. Since rockets do change speed and direction in space, acceleration clearly is possible. The correct explanation is that expanding gases from a rocket push against the inner walls of the chamber in which the fuel is burned, not necessarily against any atmosphere. You can relate this to the balloon activity in the lesson by having students draw arrows showing forces pushing against the inside wall of the balloon.

Point of Lesson

Newton's first law explains how a skateboarder can create an unbalanced force on his board to pop it up into the air.

Focus

► Evidence, models, and explanation
► Change, constancy, and measurement
► Motion and forces

Skills and Strategies

► Recognizing cause and effect
► Making inferences
► Predicting
► Sequencing
► Communicating
► Interpreting scientific illustrations

Advance Preparation

Vocabulary

Make sure students understand these terms. Definitions can be found in the glossary at the end of the student book.

► force
► gravity
► physics

Materials

Gather the materials needed for *Read* (p.21), *Enrichment* (p. 21), and *Propose Explanations* (p. 23).

TEACHING PLAN pp. 20–21

On Board With Forces

Can understanding physics improve your skateboard tricks?

Skateboarders love to perform, but like all performers they need lots of practice with basics. A stunt called the *ollie*, jumping up in the air with the board under their feet, is one of those basics. The physics is basic, too. A skateboarder just creates an unbalanced force on the board to make it pop up and follow his feet into the air.

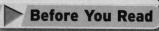
Before You Read

HOW DO THOSE TRICKS WORK? Skateboard stunts can seem like magic until you understand the science that makes them possible. Think of a trick you do, perhaps on skates, on a trampoline, in a pool, or another place. Describe in detail the actions needed to make the trick work. Use words like *push, crouch, twist, crunch, slam,* or *lean.*

> *Answers will vary. Example: To do a "180" on in-line skates,*
> *you have to jump up and also twist your body at the same*
> *time. Part of the trick is to begin twisting before you leave*
> *the ground, and then twisting your legs and feet while you*
> *are in the air. You have to bend your legs when you land.*

UNIT 1: MOTION AND FORCES

20

INTRODUCING THE LESSON

This lesson introduces students to part of Newton's first law of motion—an object will stay in motion at the same speed and in the same direction unless acted on by an unbalanced force.

Ask students to think for a moment about what causes motion, or movement. Ask them to describe what makes an object move from one place to another. Students may suggest that pushing, pulling, throwing, and dropping objects cause them to move. Explain to students that in each of these cases, a force acting on the object causes it to move.

Ask students to identify those cases in which the force of gravity was acting on the object. Students might think that gravity was acting only on the dropped object. Explain that gravity was acting on the object in every example but was most noticeable when the object was dropped.

Before You Read

HOW DO THOSE TRICKS WORK? After students answer the question, ask a volunteer to define the word *force*. (A force is any push or pull.) Then have students work in groups of three or four to choose a sport and discuss the different ways that force is used in the sport. Have the groups make a list of as many different uses of force in their chosen sports as they can. Students may want to create diagrams that illustrate the uses of force in the sports.

▶ Read

In skateboarding lingo, an *ollie* is a jump. The jump is usually done while rolling forward, but the physics is the same whether the skateboard is moving fast, slow, or not at all. The jump begins when the skater bends his knees and jumps. Here's what happens next.

FORCES IN THE OLLIE

[As the skater jumps upward,] his rear foot exerts a much greater force on the tail of the board than his front foot does on the nose, causing the [tail to drop.] As the tail strikes the ground, the ground exerts a large upward force on the tail. The result of this upward force is that the board bounces up....

With the board now completely in the air, the skater slides his front foot forward [and] ...begins to push his front foot down, ...leveling out the board. Meanwhile, he lifts his rear leg to get it out of the way of the rising tail of the board. If he times this motion perfectly, his rear foot and the rear of the board rise in perfect unison, seemingly "stuck" together.

exerts: pushes
leveling out: making flat
unison: together

From: "Frontside Forces and Fakie Flight: The Physics of Skateboarding Tricks." *Exploratorium.* (www.exploratorium.edu/skateboarding/trick02.html)

Underline the three different objects that exert a force on the board when a skater performs an ollie.

FIND OUT MORE

SCIENCESAURUS

Balanced Forces	281
Unbalanced Forces	282
Newton's First Law of Motion	284

SCiLINKS
THE WORLD'S A CLICK AWAY

www.scilinks.org
Keyword: Force
Code: GSPD03

21

Enrichment

Time: 15–20 minutes
Materials: (for each group) 2 marbles, 2–3 wooden blocks, wooden board

Tell students that several forces often act on one object at the same time. Have students keep a lookout for all the forces that cause motion or a change in motion in the following exercises.

First, have students use the blocks and board to build a ramp they can roll marbles down. Then have them place two marbles at the top of the ramp and release them at the same time. Ask them to compare the relative speeds of the two marbles. (The speeds should be about the same.) Have students identify the force that caused the marbles to roll down the ramp. (the force of gravity) Emphasize that without the force of gravity, the marbles would not have rolled.

Next, have students place both marbles at the top of the ramp again. This time, tell them to release one marble and at the same time push the other with their finger. Ask them to compare the relative speeds of the two marbles. (The one that was pushed should roll faster.) Ask students to use the term *force* to explain why one marble rolled faster than the other. (The push was an added force. Since there was more force, there was a greater motion.)

▶ Read

Time: will vary
Materials: videotape of skateboarders (optional)

Encourage students to make a sequence of diagrams that illustrates "in slow motion" the series of actions described in the reading.

After students have finished reading the passage, you may want to show the class a videotape of skateboarders in action. Play the tape in slow motion so students can see each movement of the skater and the board. Ask students to relate what they are seeing to the steps described in the reading and the steps illustrated in their diagrams. If any of your students are skateboarders, have them describe the sport to the class and explain how they perform different tricks.

CHECK UNDERSTANDING
Skill: Sequencing
Ask: *What are the first two things that happen when a skateboarder performs an ollie?* (As she jumps upward, her rear foot pushes down on the tail of the board, causing it to strike the ground, and then the board bounces back up.) *What causes the board to change its direction of motion?* (striking the ground)

More Resources

The following resources are also available from Great Source and NSTA.

SCIENCESAURUS

READER'S HANDBOOK

SCI
LINKS.
THE WORLD'S A CLICK AWAY

www.scilinks.org
Keyword: Force
Code: GSPD03

▶ **Explore**

IDENTIFY THE FORCES

Study the diagram at right. The arrows show the direction and relative size of the different forces acting on the skateboard at the beginning of the ollie maneuver.

▶ *Describe the forces acting on the board at this moment. In which direction are the forces acting? Which force is greater?*

  Gravity is pulling down on the board and the ground is pushing up on the board. The upward force is greater.

ground pushing up   gravity pushing down

Newton's first law of motion says that objects at rest tend to stay at rest unless acted upon by an unbalanced force. It also says that objects in motion tend to stay in motion with the same speed and direction, unless acted upon by an unbalanced force.

▶ *What does Newton's first law say will happen when the force of the ground pushing up on the board is suddenly much greater than the force of gravity pulling down on the board?*

  Since there is an unbalanced force, the direction or speed of the board will change.

Newton's first law says that once the board lifts off the ground, it will continue moving upward unless it is acted upon by an unbalanced force.

▶ *What is the unbalanced force acting on the board that causes it to stop rising, change direction, and begin falling?*

  gravity and the skater dropping (or the weight of the skater)

22

TEACHING PLAN pp. 22–23

▶ **Explore**

IDENTIFY THE FORCES As students examine the diagram, explain that the force of the ground pushing up is a result of the force of the skater slamming the board down onto the ground. Point out that the diagram shows the precise moment when the skater has lifted his weight off his rear foot in preparation for launching into the air. At that moment, gravity is the only force pulling the board downward.

Now ask students to imagine they are holding a ball in their hand. Have them identify as many forces as they can that

are acting on the ball. (Gravity is pulling down, and their hand is pushing upward on the ball with an equal force.) Ask students to imagine what would happen if they pushed upward on the ball with a force that is stronger than gravity. (If they pushed up hard and released the ball at the same time, it would move upward into the air.) Lead students to see that pushing up hard on the ball and releasing it is analogous to the ground pushing up on the skateboard at the same moment that the skater lifts his weight off his rear foot.

MAKE INFERENCES Think about what you have learned about the forces necessary to make a skateboard bounce into the air.

▶ *What do you think the skater could do to make the board go higher?*

If he pushed down harder and jumped higher, then the board would go

higher.

▶ *What would produce just a "baby" ollie?*

If the skater didn't push hard, then the board wouldn't go as high.

THINK ABOUT IT The ground pushes up on the tail of the skateboard only after the skater slams the tail down to hit the ground.

▶ *Think of another situation where slamming an object down to the ground causes the object to pop up into the air.*

Answers may vary, but many students will think of bouncing a ball.

Think about bouncing a basketball. To get the best bounce, you need plenty of air in the ball. You also need a good surface. A surface that will push back on the ball will provide the unbalanced force to send the ball back into the air.

▶ *Describe what makes a good surface for bouncing a basketball.*

A good surface would be hard and smooth and flat, like a wood floor or

blacktop. A bad surface would be squishy and bumpy, like grass or

gravel.

▶ *Why do you suppose it would be much more difficult for a skater to do an ollie on soft ground instead of on pavement?*

When the tail slams into the ground it would just sink instead of

bouncing back. The ground wouldn't push back hard enough to create

an unbalanced force on the skateboard.

23

Connections

LANGUAGE ARTS The word *force* has many meanings outside of science, but each meaning is related to the idea of causing something to happen. (being forced to do something, being a force for change in the community, forcing your hand) Have students brainstorm different ways they have used the word *force* other than in science. Then have them add to their lists by consulting a dictionary. Encourage students to think of instances when different "forces" acted on something or someone and what the result was. Could they describe the forces in terms of being "balanced" or "unbalanced"? For example, being forced to clean up one's room could be seen as an unbalanced force acting on a student.

Assessment

Skill: Recognizing cause and effect

Use the following question to assess each student's progress:

How does a skateboarder use unbalanced forces to perform an ollie? (He presses down on the rear of the board, slamming it into the ground and creating an unbalanced force that launches him into the air.)

MAKE INFERENCES As needed, point out that the harder the board strikes the ground, the harder the ground pushes back. This is an example of Newton's third law, which states that any time one object pushes on another, the second pushes back on the first with an equal force.

Ask students to identify some situations in which they may have experienced Newton's third law. (Students may say that the harder they hit a wall, the more it hurts, or the harder they pull on a rubber band, the harder the rubber band pulls back.)

Time: 15–20 minutes
Materials: (for each student or pair) rubber ball, table tennis ball, or rubber eraser

THINK ABOUT IT If students are having difficulty answering the questions, encourage them to do some tests with rubber balls, table tennis balls, or rubber erasers. Have them try to bounce the object on a carpeted floor, a wooden floor, cement, and grass. Ask them to write a description of how well the object bounced on each surface. Then discuss how each surface affected the way the object bounced.

Point of Lesson
Newton's second law explains why a modern discus can be thrown farther than the discus used by ancient Greek Olympic competitors.

Focus
▶ Change, constancy, and measurement
▶ Motion and forces

Skills and Strategies
▶ Recognizing cause and effect
▶ Using numbers
▶ Comparing and contrasting
▶ Drawing conclusions

Advance Preparation

Vocabulary
Make sure students understand these terms. Definitions can be found in the glossary at the end of the student book.

▶ acceleration
▶ mass

Materials
Gather the materials needed for *Enrichment* (p. 25) and *Take Action* (p. 27).

Mass Action

Discus throwing is both art and science.

Imagine tossing around a gallon jug of water. That's about the mass of the discus thrown by the ancient Greeks in Olympic competition, so don't confuse a discus with a Frisbee! The discus used by the ancient Greeks was a large, round, flat disc made of marble, bronze, or lead. They weren't all the same, but a typical discus may have had a mass anywhere between two and six kilograms. The discus throw was the first of five events in the Olympic pentathlon competition.

▶ **Read**

In the year 708 B.C., Lampis, a young athlete and discus thrower from the city-state of Sparta, came to test his strength and skill in the 18th Olympiad.

DISCUS THROW

Lampis waited patiently near the balbis. He carried a bronze discus on his shoulder. He rubbed the discus with fine sand so that he could get a firm grip. One of the contestants was about to complete his first discus throw. His body strained to bring the utmost force behind the throw. Lampis wondered whether the simple style of his rival, requiring only one step, might be more effective than his own, which needed three. Each contestant in the discus throw had five chances. A judge marked the best of the throws with a peg.

When his turn came, Lampis took his place on the balbis. His right foot was forward, bearing his weight. Holding the discus in his left hand, he let it swing forward and took it in his right. Then as the discus

FIND OUT MORE

SCIENCESAURUS

Newton's Second
Law of Motion 285
Physical Science
Equations 298

SCILINKS.
THE WORLD'S A CLICK AWAY

www.scilinks.org
Keyword: Force
Code: GSPD03

TEACHING PLAN pp. 24–25

INTRODUCING THE LESSON
This lesson introduces students to Newton's second law of motion—the acceleration of an object by a force is inversely proportional to the mass of the object and directly proportional to the force.

Ask students if they know what determines how much force is needed to move an object. Students should realize that the amount of force needed to move an object depends on how much mass the object has, which is related to how heavy it is.

Some students may misunderstand the term *acceleration*, thinking it applies only to objects speeding up. Emphasize that acceleration is not the speed of an object but the *change* in an object's speed or direction. A car pulling away from a stoplight is accelerating, but so is a car slowing down for a stoplight. Make sure students understand that anything that is increasing or decreasing in speed or changing direction of motion is accelerating.

▶ **Read**

As students read, ask them to pantomime the motions the discus thrower is going through before and during his throw. Ask them to underline any passages that tell them how the discus thrower is preparing to generate the maximum amount of force. ("...as the discus arced vigorously down and back, he bent his body to the right....")

arced vigorously down and back, he bent his body to the right, turning his head so that he could see the right side of his body. Then, putting the whole force of his body into the movement, Lampis threw the discus. His throw was timed to the rhythm of flute music. The young Spartan saw the pegs set down by the judge and knew that he had done better than any of his competitors.

balbis: the sloped platform the discus was thrown from
bronze: a metal made of a mixture of copper and tin
utmost: greatest

rival: opponent
effective: powerful
arced: swung in a circular path
vigorously: quickly

From: Glubock, Shirley and Alfred Tamarin. *Olympic Games in Ancient Greece.* HarperCollins.

Explore

FLYING FARTHER Newton's first law explains that an object that is not moving will not start moving until an unbalanced force acts on it.

▶ **What unbalanced force acted on Lampis's discus to make it start moving?**

Lampis's hand throwing it

Newton's second law explains the relationship between the unbalanced forces acting on an object, the mass of the object, and the acceleration of the object that results. (Acceleration is a measure of how quickly the speed or direction of an object is changing.) Newton came up with the equation $F = m \times a$ to explain how these three factors are related.

Use Newton's equation to calculate the acceleration of a discus in each of the following cases:

A *force* of	will give a *mass* of	an *acceleration* of
16 Newtons	4 kg	4 m/s²
12 Newtons	4 kg	3 m/s²
8 Newtons	4 kg	2 m/s²
4 Newtons	4 kg	1 m/s²

25

NoteZone

What changes would a left-handed discus thrower make?

He would start with his left foot forward. He would start with the discus in his right hand. Then he would switch it to his left hand and bend to his left side.

Enrichment

Time: 30 minutes
Materials: (for each group) skateboard, 2 bricks, stopwatch

Students can develop a qualitative understanding of Newton's second law by accelerating two objects of different masses. You may choose to do this activity outdoors or indoors.

Choose a smooth straight surface to work on. Have teams of students mark off a 5-meter track. One team member should stand at the finish line with a stopwatch. Another student should place the skateboard at the starting point and then push it as hard as he or she can toward the finish line. The student with the stopwatch should time how long it takes the board to travel 5 meters. Then have each team repeat the activity, this time with two bricks placed securely on the board. (Encourage students to use the same amount of force in both trials.) Have them compare the times it took the board to complete the 5-meter track in both trials. Students should relate travel time to the acceleration of the board. (The greater the acceleration, the faster the course was completed.) Guide them to conclude that in $F = m \times a$, as *m* increases, *a* decreases for the same force.

Explore

FLYING FARTHER Point out that in the equation $F = m \times a$, *F* stands for force, *m* stands for mass, and *a* stands for acceleration. If students are having difficulty filling in the chart, tell them to write an equals sign and a multiplication sign in each row. The first row, for example, would show the following:

16 Newtons = 4 kg × __ m/s²

Acceleration is measured in m/s². To help students understand that acceleration tells how fast the speed is changing, read m/s² as *meters per second,*

per second. Explain that an object with an acceleration of 4 m/s² will move 4 m/s faster during each second than it did during the previous second.

CHECK UNDERSTANDING
Skill: Communicating
Organize students into groups of three or four. Tell the groups to imagine that they are a team of sports commentators at the 18th Olympiad. Have each group write a brief script describing the action taking place in the discus throw using the terms *force, mass,* and *acceleration.* Encourage students to make the broadcast as humorous as possible.

More Resources

The following resources are also available from Great Source and NSTA.

www.scilinks.org
Keyword: Force
Code: GSPD03

Connections

PHYSICAL EDUCATION Average acceleration can be calculated using the following formula:

Acceleration =
$$\frac{\text{ending velocity} - \text{starting velocity}}{\text{time it takes to change velocity}}$$

(continued on page 27)

> How would using more force change the acceleration of the discus? (Use the data in the chart on page 25 to find the answer.)

More force would make the discus accelerate more.

The greater the acceleration of the discus, the greater its speed will be when it leaves the thrower's hand.

> How would using more force change the speed of the discus as it is thrown?

More force would make the speed of the discus greater.

Finally, the greater the speed of a discus when it leaves the hand of the thrower, the farther it will travel.

> How would using more force change the distance the discus flies?

More force would make the discus go farther.

MAKE COMPARISONS The discus used by the ancient Greeks varied from one competition to another. The mass might be 1.5 kg or 4.5 kg. But for any one contest, all athletes used the same discus.

> Use Newton's second law to explain why this would be important for a fair competition.

If they used different discuses, the one that was lighter would go farther

because it would get more acceleration from the same force. Or someone

who wasn't as strong could throw a discus with less mass just as far as

a stronger person who had to throw a discus with more mass.

Today, a typical discus is made of wood instead of marble or bronze, and has metal only around the rim. The mass of today's standard Olympic discus is 2 kg.

> If Lampis competed in the discus throw today, what do you think his reaction might be when he first picked up a modern wood discus?

He would be excited because the new discus would probably be lighter

than the one he used, and so it would be easier to throw far.

26

TEACHING PLAN pp. 26–27

> **Explore** *(continued)*

Help students see that in the discus throw, increased force on the discus means increased acceleration of the discus, which means increased speed of the discus, which means increased throw distance. The more force the athlete applies to the discus, the farther it will travel.

MAKE COMPARISONS Ask students to imagine the force needed to roll (accelerate) a bowling ball compared with the force needed to roll a volleyball. (Rolling the bowling ball would require more force.) Then encourage students

to remember examples from their own experience that illustrate the difficulty of throwing or rolling (accelerating) something heavy compared with something light. Remind them that even pushing or sliding an object that started off at rest involved accelerating it.

Point out that manufacturers of certain sports equipment used in competition must guarantee that their products meet standards for mass. While some sports allow equipment variations (tennis rackets, baseball bats), oftentimes equipment is strictly regulated (golf balls and golf clubs, for example). Ask students to think of examples when a

difference in equipment mass would give a competitor an advantage. (Examples: running shoes and bicycles with less mass, bowling balls with greater mass) Encourage students to share their own experiences.

WRITE A LIMERICK

A limerick is a five-line poem. The first, second, and fifth lines rhyme with each other and have about nine syllables per line. The third and fourth lines rhyme with each other and have five or six syllables each. The following limerick was written about Newton's second law.

> Said Sir Isaac: "I've got a great notion
> That force is a changer of motion.
> Let's put it this way:
> F equals *ma*
> The rest is just sweat and devotion."
> – A. P. French

Use this limerick as a model to write your own limerick about Lampis throwing the discus.

► *Start by listing terms that relate to the second law, then think of words that rhyme with those terms.*

Encourage students to use the words

force, mass, *and/or* acceleration *in*

their limericks.

_____

_____

_____

► *Next, write a limerick.*

Example: If you're wishing to move a large horse

You'll need to apply a great force —

You can tempt it with grass,

But to move that large mass

You have to push on it hard of course.

_____

▲ **Sir Isaac Newton**

27

(continued from page 26)
Have students use the equation on page 26 to solve the following problems:

After the first 2 seconds of a 100-meter race, a sprinter's speed was 8 m/s. What was her average acceleration in that time period?
(8 m/s − 0 m/s = 8 m/s; then 8 m/s ÷ 2 s = 4 m/s²)

In the next two seconds her speed increased to 9 m/s. What was her average acceleration in that time period?
(9 m/s − 8 m/s = 1 m/s; then 1 m/s ÷ 2 s = 0.5 m/s²) She ran at a steady rate for the rest of the race.

Discuss at what point during the race the sprinter's acceleration was greatest. (at the beginning) Ask students how this compares with their own experience in races. (You have to push hard to get going, but after a while your speed stays about the same.)

Assessment

Skill: Recognizing cause and effect

Use the following task to assess each student's progress:

Use Newton's second law to explain why it is harder to handle a full shopping cart than an empty one. (It takes more force to change the speed or direction of a full cart because the full cart has more mass.)

Time: will vary
Materials: book of limericks

WRITE A LIMERICK Some students may in general be reluctant to write poetry. Encourage them by pointing out that since limericks are almost always a little silly, writing them is not as difficult as writing some other forms of poetry. To make the rhyming easier, the final word may even repeat the last word of the first or second line.

To help students get started, bring a book of limericks to class (such as *Lear's Book of Nonsense*), and let them pass the book around and read some of the limericks aloud.

Point of Lesson

Rocket action demonstrates the action and reaction forces described by Newton's third law.

Focus

► Evidence, models, and explanation
► Abilities necessary to do scientific inquiry
► Motion and forces

Skills and Strategies

► Interpreting data
► Observing
► Making and using models
► Recognizing cause and effect
► Comparing and contrasting
► Communicating

Advance Preparation

Vocabulary

Make sure students understand these terms. Definitions can be found in the glossary at the end of the student book.

► gas
► pressure

Materials

Gather the materials needed for *Activity* (p. 29).

CHAPTER 2 / LESSON 6

May the Force Be With You

Rocket Reaction

What does it take to make a rocket soar?

What could a balloon possibly have in common with a rocket? Plenty! Both would flop without Newton's third law of motion.

NOTEZONE

Underline the words that describe the motion of the gases as they move through the nozzle.

FIND OUT MORE

SCIENCESAURUS
Newton's Third Law of Motion 286

SCiLINKS
THE WORLD'S A CLICK AWAY
www.scilinks.org
Keyword: Force
Code: GSPD03

▶ **Read**

Homer Hickam is 14 years old. His teacher, Miss Riley, has brought Homer and his model rocket to see the school principal.

Rocket Boy

"The McDowell County Science Fair is in March. Miss Riley believes you should be allowed to represent the school.... Are you prepared to answer tough questions?"

"Yes, sir."

"All right then.... What makes a rocket fly?"

"Newton's third law. For every action, there is an equal and opposite reaction."

He stabbed the drawing of the nozzle. "And this peculiar shape? What's it for?"

"That is a DeLaval nozzle. It's designed to convert slow-moving, high-pressure gases into a stream of low-pressure, high-velocity gases. If the gases reach a sonic velocity at the throat, they will go supersonic in the diverging part of the nozzle, producing maximum thrust."

"You taught him all this, Miss Riley?"

"No, he taught it to himself."

nozzle: narrow opening
convert: change
velocity: speed
sonic: traveling at the speed of sound

supersonic: traveling faster than the speed of sound
diverging: widening
thrust: push

From: Hickham, Homer H. *Rocket Boys.* Delacorte Press.

TEACHING PLAN pp. 28–29

INTRODUCING THE LESSON

This lesson introduces students to Newton's third law of motion—for every action there is an equal but opposite reaction.

Draw out misconceptions by asking students to explain what happens when you apply a force to a wall. Most students will say nothing happens because the wall does not move. Explain that while the wall does not move, it does in fact push back with an equal force. If it did not, when you leaned on the wall you would go through it.

▶ **Read**

After students finish the reading, draw the following diagram on the board.

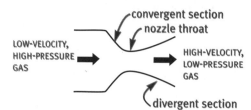

LOW-VELOCITY, HIGH-PRESSURE GAS → convergent section / nozzle throat → HIGH-VELOCITY, LOW-PRESSURE GAS / divergent section

Explain that the nozzle is located at the bottom of the rocket, where the gases move out. The DeLaval nozzle was invented by Swedish engineer Gustav DeLaval. While working on steam engines, he discovered that a nozzle that alternately converged and diverged produced the maximum thrust. This nozzle is part of every rocket engine in use today.

The movie "October Sky" is based on the novel from which this excerpt was taken. After students read the passage, they may be interested in seeing the movie. If you choose to show the movie, pause it occasionally to discuss how Homer Hickam applied his knowledge of Newton's laws of motion to the design of his rockets. Preview the movie first to make sure it is appropriate for your students.

▶ Activity

WATCH IT FLY

Build your own balloon rocket.

What You Need: one small balloon

What to Do:
1. Blow up the balloon and pinch the neck closed.
2. In an open area, hold the balloon horizontally and then release it.
3. Observe what happens to the balloon.

WHAT DO YOU SEE?

▶ *What happened to the balloon when you let go of the neck? Draw the balloon as it looked right before and right after you let go of the neck. Use an arrow to show what direction the balloon moved.*

▶ *What two things are moving in the second part of your drawing? (Hint: What comes out of the balloon?)*

air (out of the neck) and the balloon

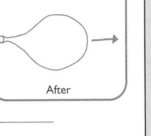

Before

After

▶ Propose Explanations

IDENTIFY FORCES Newton's third law says that for every action there is an equal and opposite reaction. That means that every time one object exerts a force on another object, the second object exerts an equal force back on the first object.

▶ *Can you identify the two opposite forces in your balloon diagram?*

One force is air pushing against the balloon. The other force is the balloon pushing against the air.

▶ *Identify the two opposite actions in your balloon diagram.*

the air rushing out of the neck of the balloon; the balloon moving in the opposite direction

▶ *How is your balloon like Homer's rocket?*

The air rushing out of the neck of the balloon is like the gases rushing out of the nozzle of the rocket. Both of these actions have opposite reactions: the movement of the balloon or rocket.

29

More Resources

The following resources are also available from Great Source and NSTA.

SCIENCESAURUS
Newton's Third Law of Motion   286

www.scilinks.org
Keyword: Force
Code: GSPD03

Enrichment

Have students use information they have researched on the Internet to make a time line of the development and uses of rockets.

Assessment

Skill: Recognizing cause and effect

Use the following task to assess each student's progress:

Tell students to imagine they are wearing roller skates and holding a huge inflated balloon with the neck facing away from them. Ask, *What would happen if you opened the neck of the balloon?* (I would be pushed in the direction opposite the direction in which the air is escaping from the neck of the balloon.) *What would happen if you were not wearing roller skates?* (If I have skates on I might roll, but if I'm not wearing skates I might just feel the push without going anywhere.)

▶ Activity

Time: 10–15 minutes
Materials: 1 small balloon

▶ Have students work individually.
▶ Before students move on to the Propose Explanations questions, check their drawings to make sure they show the neck of the balloon pointing one way and movement occurring in the opposite direction.

▶ Propose Explanations

IDENTIFY FORCES After students have completed the questions, ask them if they have ever seen the space shuttle launched into orbit. If so, have them describe what the launch looked like. (Students may describe the gases streaming out of the bottom of the shuttle's rockets.) Ask: *What two equal but opposite forces are involved in launching a rocket?* (Students should realize that liftoff depends on the fact that the gases push the rocket upward with the same force that the rocket pushes the gases downward.)

CHECK UNDERSTANDING
Skill: Recognizing cause and effect
Have students draw a simple diagram to show the forces involved when a swimmer pushes off the wall as he or she turns while swimming laps. (Student diagrams should show an arrow near the swimmer's feet pointing toward the wall and another arrow pointing from the wall toward the swimmer.) Ask: *How does Newton's third law help the swimmer start the next lap quickly?* (Pushing off the wall propels the swimmer into the next lap.)

Da Vinci's Designs

LESSON 7
Curious Minds
Point of Lesson: *Leonardo da Vinci used his understanding of how simple machines work to invent new machines.*

Students are encouraged to think of machines in a new way. They first read an explanation of how Leonardo da Vinci's way of observing the world influenced his understanding of how things work. Students then analyze a diagram of a machine and identify the simple machines that make it up. They consider how da Vinci's broad interests and ability to combine ideas from several sources contributed to his inventions.

Materials
Science Scope Activity (p. 30B and Part 1, p. 31), for each pair:
► wooden block (approximately 15 cm × 20 cm) with two holes drilled in one end about 10 cm apart
► rubber band
► plastic spoon
► wooden ruler
► tape
► 2 screws
► screwdriver

Laboratory Safety
Review the following safety guidelines with students before they do the Science Scope Activity, Part 1, in this lesson.
► Handle rubber bands responsibly to avoid injury by a rubber band or by any part of the catapult that attaches to the rubber band.
► Do not test your catapult during this part of the activity. Everyone in the room must be wearing safety goggles before testing can occur.

LESSON 8
Gadget Gawking
Point of Lesson: *Simple machines make up gadgets we use every day.*

In this lesson, students analyze a common compound machine and identify the simple machines that make it up. They then review each type of simple machine, and invent their own compound machine to help perform an everyday task.

Materials
Activity (p. 34), for each student or pair:
► drawing paper
► a compound machine (such as a rotary eggbeater, handheld can opener, rotary drill, hand wrench, mechanical pencil sharpener, or bicycle)

Propose Explanations (p. 35), for the teacher:
► picture of a gear or an actual gear

Laboratory Safety
Review the following safety guideline with students before they do the Activity in this lesson.
► Use care when handling the simple machines, especially those with sharp edges or meshed gears.

LESSON 9
Leo's Machines Today
Point of Lesson: *Machines similar to those designed 500 years ago by Leonardo da Vinci are actually in use today.*

Students view da Vinci's sketches for a flying machine and a diving suit and compare them with photographs of a modern helicopter and SCUBA tank. They compare and contrast da Vinci's designs (which were never built) with the modern designs and speculate about what people may have thought of his ideas at the time. The lesson ends with students researching an older machine, comparing it with a newer one that has the same function, and identifying advantages and disadvantages of each machine.

Materials
Science Scope Activity (Part 2, p. 37), for each pair:
► catapult from Lesson 7
► miniature marshmallows
► meter stick
► safety goggles

Laboratory Safety
Review the following safety guidelines with students before they do the Science Scope Activity, Part 2, in this lesson.
► Wear safety goggles whenever anyone in the room is using a catapult, whether they are testing or in competition.
► Do not use catapults to fling anything other than marshmallows.

Science Scope Activity

Classroom Catapults

NSTA has chosen a Science Scope *activity related to the content in this chapter. The activity begins here and continues in Lesson 7, page 31, and Lesson 9, page 37.*

Time: 30 minutes for each Part

Materials: see page 30A

Tell students they will be building a catapult, which is a lever used for flinging things. The lever increases the speed of the object being flung and/or the distance the object moves. In da Vinci's time, large catapults were used for warfare. They are commonly used today by acrobats.

(continued on page 31 and page 37)

Background Information

Leonardo da Vinci

Leonardo da Vinci (1452–1519) embodied the concept of the "Renaissance Man," a person who excels in many fields of endeavor. He was recognized in his own time as an extraordinarily intelligent and innovative artist and engineer. Although he was well known to other artists and thinkers, he was not able to read many of the published works of his time. Although he grew up in an intellectual family environment, he did not receive the formal classical education usually given to a "man of letters" and therefore did not read Latin, the language in which European scholars published. His lack of formal education is cited by some historians as a reason for his very original ways of thinking. Rather than read what others had written about a subject, da Vinci examined objects and phenomena directly, relying on his own observations and reasoning in order to understand how they worked. Such direct observation is, of course, the foundation of scientific inquiry as it is understood and practiced today.

Point of Lesson

Leonardo da Vinci used his understanding of how simple machines work to invent new machines.

Focus

► Motion and forces
► History of science
► Science as a human endeavor
► Systems, order, and organization
► Science and technology in society

Skills and Strategies

► Making inferences
► Generating ideas
► Interpreting scientific illustrations

Advance Preparation

Vocabulary

Make sure students understand these terms. Definitions can be found in the glossary at the end of the student book.

► force
► simple machine
► work

Materials

Gather the materials needed for *Science Scope Activity*, (p. 30B and *Part 1* p. 31).

Da Vinci's Designs

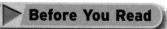

CURIOUS MINDS

Five hundred years ago, an Italian artist sketched designs for dozens of fantastic machines.

Leonardo da Vinci was born in Florence, Italy, in 1452. Leonardo worked as a painter, draftsman, sculptor, architect, and engineer. He is remembered mainly as an artist, but Leonardo's notebooks show that he worked constantly to gain new knowledge as a scientist. He wrote notes and drew sketches of things in his world that interested him (almost everything!). He also drew pictures of his ideas for inventions of new machines.

▲ Leonardo da Vinci

▶ Before You Read

RECOGNIZING SIMPLE MACHINES A machine is a tool you use to make work easier. Machines can be very complex, but there are a few machines that are called *simple machines*. Simple machines make work easier by changing the size or direction of a force. These machines were used for many centuries, even before Leonardo's time.

► *Have you ever seen any of these simple machines in use, either by themselves or as part of another machine? Write down any examples you can think of. Describe what the machine does.*

Possible answers: Pulley—in window blinds to move the blinds up and down. Wedge—in a knife to cut. Lever—in a can opener to open a can. Wheel and axle—in a door knob.

Inclined plane—in a wheelchair ramp to make it easier to move a wheelchair to a higher level. Screw—in a clamp to push two things together.

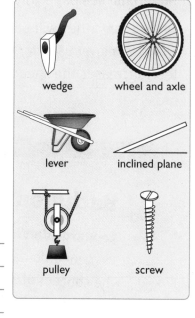

wedge — wheel and axle
lever — inclined plane
pulley — screw

UNIT 1: MOTION AND FORCES

30

TEACHING PLAN pp. 30–31

INTRODUCING THE LESSON

This lesson discusses simple machines and Leonardo da Vinci's technique for designing compound machines.

Solicit a definition of *machine* from students. Some may think that machines include only large construction vehicles such as bulldozers or household appliances such as dishwashers. Remind students that a machine is any device that makes a task easier. Machines can include such simple things as scissors and a stapler. Explain that using a machine to help with a task usually allows people to use less strength than they would

otherwise need. That is, the machine increases the force a person is able to apply to an object.

Ask students to look around the room and list any machines they see. (Examples: pencil sharpener, scissors, stapler)

▶ Before You Read

RECOGNIZING SIMPLE MACHINES Give students a brief review of the six different simple machines shown. Explain that a gear can be considered another type of simple machine, but it can also be considered a type of wheel and axle.

Be sure students can think of at least one instance of having used each of these simple machines in their own lives.

Go back to the list of classroom machines. Challenge students to identify some of the simple machines that make up those classroom machines. (For example, a stapler has a lever; a pencil sharpener has wheels and axles [gears], and its blades are wedges.)

▶ Read

As an apprentice, Leonardo spent lots of time taking apart machines in order to understand them better.

INVENTOR'S WORKSHOP

Leonardo's fascination with machines probably began during his boyhood. Some of his earliest sketches clearly show how various machine parts worked. As an apprentice [to a famous artist], Leonardo observed and used a variety of machines. By studying them he gained practical knowledge about their design and structure.

Many ancient machines were in common use in Leonardo's time. For example, water wheels turned millstones to grind grain and Archimedes' screws lifted water from streams providing a ready supply for drinking and washing.

Artists and craftsmen in Leonardo's time knew how to build and repair the familiar kinds of machines. The idea of inventing new kinds of machines, however, would not have occurred to [many of] them.

Leonardo developed a unique new attitude about machines. He reasoned that by understanding how each separate machine part worked, he could modify them and combine them in different ways to improve existing machines or create inventions no one had ever seen before.

Leonardo set out to write the first systematic explanations of how machines work and how the elements of machines can be combined.

---

fascination: great interest
apprentice: a person who works for an expert to learn a trade or skill
millstones: circular stones

Archimedes' screw: machine used to lift water
unique: one of a kind
systematic: orderly

From: "Inventor's Workshop." *The Museum of Science.*
(www.mos.org/sln/Leonardo/InventorsWorkshop.html)

© GREAT SOURCE. COPYING IS PROHIBITED.

NOTEZONE

What else would you like to know about Leonardo's work after reading this excerpt?

FIND OUT MORE

SCIENCESAURUS

Simple Machines	288
Inclined Plane	289
Wedge	290
Screw	291
Lever	292
Wheel and Axle	293
Pulley	294

SCiLINKS
THE WORLD'S A CLICK AWAY

www.scilinks.com
Keyword: Simple Machines
Code: GSPD04

31

Science Scope Activity

(continued from page 30B)

Procedure

Part 1: Building the Catapult
Have students work in pairs, and give them the following instructions.

1. Tape the plastic spoon to the ruler, with the bowl of the spoon near one end of the ruler and facing up.
2. Use a screwdriver to fix the two screws into the end of the wooden block. Leave about 0.5 cm of each screw protruding from the wood.
3. Stretch the rubber band over the two screws. Use the band to hold the ruler upright. The band may need to be twisted or tied to hold the ruler tightly.

Have each pair present their catapult. Then ask the class to answer the following questions:

▶ *How does your catapult compare with other students' catapults?* (Students may note differences such as the position of the spoon on the ruler or the direction the spoon is facing.)

▶ *How do you think the design of your catapult might affect the distance it can fling an object? Why?* (Answers will vary.) Allow differences of opinion at this point, but encourage discussion. Tell students they may not test their catapults at this point but may alter the design if they want.

(continued on page 37)

▶ Read

Ask students if they have seen a machine disassembled or even opened up. Some may have seen the inside of a watch when a battery was replaced, for example, or some may have helped repair a lawnmower or watched a piano being tuned. Discuss how seeing the hidden components helped them gain some understanding of how the machine works.

Some small machines are now made with a transparent plastic case that allows you to see all the insides without taking the machine apart. Invite students to bring in any such machine they may have at home to share with the class.

CHECK UNDERSTANDING
Skill: Making Inferences
Ask: *What science skills did Leonardo da Vinci make use of when coming up with ideas for new machines?* (Students' answers should indicate that they understand da Vinci used many science skills, including observing, classifying, diagramming, measuring, and inferring.)

More Resources

The following resources are also available from Great Source and NSTA.

SCIENCESAURUS

READER'S HANDBOOK

www.scilinks.com
Keyword: Simple Machines
Code: GSPD04

PICTURE THIS! Leonardo took apart plants, animals, and machines in order to be able to draw them realistically. He also drew the things he saw in order to be able to understand them. Here is a sketch of a machine that probably was used in Leonardo's time to haul water up out of a well.

▶ *Review simple machines in your textbook or your ScienceSaurus handbook. Use your book to help you find the simple machines that make up this one. Use arrows to label each simple machine you find.*

Parts that might be identified include the wheel and axle, the lever,

possibly wedges as teeth on the gear, and the inclined plane.

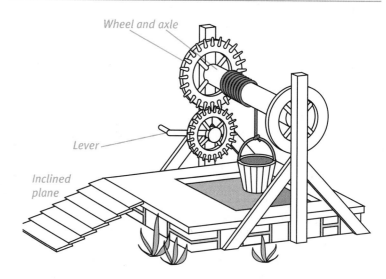

▶ *Write what you think the role of each labeled part is. Use information from your reference book to help you.*

wheel and axle—When the wheel turns, the axle turns, lifting the pail.

lever—The lever is used to turn the bottom wheel, which turns the top wheel and the axle.

inclined plane—People can mount the platform more easily.

32

TEACHING PLAN pp. 32–33

▶ **Explore**

PICTURE THIS! Help students picture how a well winder would have been used. Tell them to imagine a person pushing down on the handle. Ask: *What would happen?* (The bottom wheel would turn, counterclockwise.) *What would happen next?* (The top wheel would turn, clockwise.) Continue leading students through the axle turning, the rope unwinding, and the bucket dropping. Lead students to see that after the bucket had hit the water and filled, the person would wind in the

opposite direction to bring the bucket back up.

As students answer the Explore questions, encourage them to approach the problem in the same way that da Vinci would have. That is, they should consider each piece of the machine separately in order to be able to understand what its role is.

WRITE A PARAGRAPH Leonardo was a painter who learned to build his own canvases and mix his own paints. He was a sculptor who learned to build the molds needed to cast bronze statues. By taking apart and studying the parts of living and nonliving things, Leonardo was able to understand how things work. Accurate drawings helped him record what he had learned so that he could review the information later.

People who make major new discoveries are often people who put *ideas* together in new ways, not just things. How do you think being interested in many different subjects made it possible for Leonardo to come up with ideas for building three of his most famous inventions: a flying machine, a parachute, and an underwater breathing machine? What ideas or observations might have led him to these inventions?

Since he knew things about different subjects, he could take ideas from

different subjects and put them together. He could take the idea of a bird

and the idea of a machine and come up with a flying machine. He could

take the idea of a fish and the idea of a machine and come up with a

machine for underwater swimming. He could see a leaf falling and think

of a parachute for people. Since he could draw well, he could show his

ideas on paper.

People often have new ideas that they don't pay attention to because they think the ideas might be silly. Try to remember any interesting ideas you might have had for a new machine, but ignored. Describe one of your ideas below.

This is a brainstorming exercise. Ideas might not be practical.

Possible answer: I would make a remote control collar for my dog so I

wouldn't have to go out to walk him in the rain or in the dark. The collar

would be more like a harness. It would work like reins on a horse and

tell him which way to go. The collar could send back signals to my

remote control so I could see where he was. Then I would push a joystick

to send signals to the collar.

33

Connections

PHYSICAL EDUCATION Remind students that a lever is a rod that pivots at a fixed point. In the case of a seesaw, the fixed point is the center stand. In the case of a hammer, the fixed point is the handle end you are holding. Our skeletal system also includes levers. Some joints are pivots for bones acting as levers. Have students do a simple exercise such as an arm curl, and ask them to identify which bones are working together as a lever and which joint is acting as a pivot. (forearm bones and elbow)

Assessment

Skill: Solving problems

Use the following task to assess each student's progress:

Organize students into small groups. Tell them to imagine that they are engineers in ancient Egypt and the pharaoh has ordered them to build a huge pyramid using blocks of stone that each weigh more than a ton. Remind students that they will not have any modern machines with engines to help them with their task. Ask students to tell how they might build the pyramid and describe how they might use simple machines to do the job. (Students might suggest using wheels and axles, levers, and inclined planes to transport the heavy blocks and lift them into position.)

► **Take Action**

WRITE A PARAGRAPH Dean Kamen is a 21st century inventor who uses his understanding of current technology to create new machines. After Kamen observed some of the challenges facing people in wheelchairs, he applied his knowledge of science and engineering to create the Ibot. This wheelchair can raise the seated person to eye level with people who are standing and can transport a person up and down stairs without help from another person.

To give students an idea of the process involved in linking ideas to create something new, you might share these two examples of inventions by young people. In 1873, a 13-year-old boy invented earmuffs so he could skate outside for a longer time in cold weather. In 1987, a 6-year-old girl invented an edible pet food spoon. It could be used to get food out of a can and then be fed to her cat so she did not have to wash the spoon.

Encourage students to remember a situation that makes them wish "someone" would invent a machine that made a certain task easier or more pleasant. To help students brainstorm ideas, suggest that they think about some of the daily chores they have to do. Have them jot down difficulties or annoyances that come up in these everyday activities.

Point of Lesson
Simple machines make up gadgets we use every day.

Focus
► Motion and forces
► Form and function
► Systems, order, and organization

Skills and Strategies
► Observing
► Using space/time relationships
► Making and using models

Advance Preparation

Vocabulary
Make sure students understand this term. The definition can be found in the glossary at the end of the student book.

► simple machine

Materials
Gather the materials needed for *Activity* (below) and *Propose Explanations* (p. 35).

Gadget Gawking

You can try out Leonardo's methods for understanding how machines work.

Leonardo da Vinci wanted to understand how compound machines work, so he took them apart. He studied the pieces and sketched what he saw. The most basic parts of a compound machine are simple machines. By finding out how the simple machines worked, Leonardo was able to put them together in new ways to make new machines.

SKETCH A GADGET

What You Need: drawing paper, pencils, erasers, a compound machine (such as a rotary eggbeater, a handheld can opener, a rotary drill, a hand wrench, a mechanical pencil sharpener, or a bicycle)

What to Do:
1. Choose a compound machine and study it carefully. Watch how each part moves and try to identify any simple machines.
2. Sketch the machine while it is not moving. Also make separate sketches to show the details of any small parts.
3. Draw other pictures of your machine from different views to show all the working parts.
4. Add arrows to your sketches to show the direction in which each part moves.

Drawings will vary.

Refer to your textbook or your *ScienceSaurus* handbook to help you label the simple machines you found in this compound machine.

FIND OUT MORE

SCIENCESAURUS

Simple Machines	288
Inclined Plane	289
Wedge	290
Screw	291
Lever	292
Wheel and Axle	293
Pulley	294

SCLINKS
THE WORLD'S A CLICK AWAY

www.scilinks.org
Keyword: Simple Machines
Code: GSPD04

UNIT 1: MOTION AND FORCES

34

TEACHING PLAN pp. 34–35

INTRODUCING THE LESSON
This lesson focuses on the simple machines found in some common household gadgets. Although many compound machines can be powered by electricity, hand tools tend to be easier to analyze. Ask students to list hand-powered tools they might have at home that would be called compound machines. If students have difficulty, suggest that they think about gadgets with moving parts used in the kitchen or in the garage. It might also help them to think about gadgets owned by their grandparents. (Possible gadgets include pruning shears, post-hole dig-gers, jar openers, cheese graters, and salad spinners.) For each compound machine mentioned, have students identify the simple machines that make it up.

Activity

Time: 50 minutes
Materials: drawing paper, pencils, erasers, a compound machine (such as a rotary eggbeater, a handheld can opener, a rotary drill, a hand wrench, a mechanical pencil sharpener, or a bicycle)

Remind students that scale is important when sketching a working machine. To draw each part of the machine in proportion to the other parts, students might want to measure all the parts of the machine, decide how much larger or smaller they want to draw the machine, and then multiply or divide the measurements by that number.

To minimize frustration, allow ample time for drawing. Invite students to use extra paper so they have space to show details. If possible, provide high quality erasers and correction fluid.

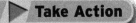

▶ Propose Explanations

PUTTING IT TOGETHER What is the function of the compound-machine gadget you examined?

Answers will depend on the machine.

Refer to the drawings in Lesson 7 on page 30 to help you recognize the simple machines in this compound machine.

▶ **What is the role of each simple machine in this gadget?**

Answers will depend on the machine.

▶ **How do the various parts work together to accomplish the task of the compound machine?**

Answers will depend on the machine. Answers should include a

description of how one part causes another part to move.

▶ Take Action

BE AN INVENTOR Be an inventor for a day. Imagine a new compound-machine gadget that would make your life easier. For example, can you invent a machine to make your bed? Before you begin, review the ways that each simple machine can be used to make work easier. How could you combine two or more simple machines to increase their usefulness?

Sketch your invention in the box. Identify the simple machines that you combined. Then explain what your machine does and how it works.

Drawings will vary.

Possible idea: A machine that opens

the refrigerator door from a distance

and takes out food. The machine is made of a pair of pliers (two levers)

with handles attached to a pulley system. The pliers open the door,

grab the food, and place it in a basket. The pulley system is used to

bring the basket across the room.

35

More Resources

The following resources are also available from Great Source and NSTA.

SCIENCESAURUS

Simple Machines	288
Inclined Plane	289
Wedge	290
Screw	291
Lever	292
Wheel and Axle	293
Pulley	294

www.scilinks.org
Keyword: Simple Machines
Code: GSPD04

Assessment
Skill: Classifying

Use the following questions to assess each student's progress:

What compound machines have you used today? Name one. What simple machines make up that compound machine? (Sample answer: I used a pair of scissors, which is made up of two levers and two wedges.)

Time: 5 minutes
Materials: picture of a gear or an actual gear

PUTTING IT TOGETHER The compound machine that students draw may contain gears. A gear is considered a simple machine by some and a compound machine by others. Find a picture of a gear or an actual gear to show the class. Ask students to try to identify the two simple machines that make up a gear. If necessary, point out that a gear is a combination of a wheel and axle and many wedges. Students can label the gears either as gears or as wheels and axles plus wedges.

▶ Take Action

BE AN INVENTOR Tell students to consider the materials from which they would make their simple machine. Explain that different materials have different properties, such as hardness, heat resistance, and flexibility. Choosing the right kind of material can make a machine much more effective. For example, if the machine becomes hot or works in a hot environment, it should not be made of a material that might melt or catch fire.

CHECK UNDERSTANDING
Skill: Making inferences
Tell students to think about a kitchen knife. Ask: *What two simple machines does it include?* (a wedge and a lever) *What is the role of each machine?* (The wedge cuts, and the lever increases the force applied.)

Point of Lesson

Machines similar to those designed 500 years ago by Leonardo da Vinci are actually in use today.

Focus

► Motion and forces
► History of science
► Science and technology in society
► Abilities of technological design
► Form and function

Skills and Strategies

► Comparing and contrasting
► Making inferences
► Collecting and recording data

Advance Preparation

Materials

Gather the materials needed for *Science Scope Activity, Part 2* (p. 37; see materials list p. 30A).

LEO'S MACHINES TODAY

Leonardo's inventions were hundreds of years ahead of their time.

The first time someone jumped from a high place using a parachute was in France in 1783. Armies used tanks for the first time during World War I in 1917. The first airplane with landing gear that folded up came out in 1933. Yet, all these ideas were sketched in detail by Leonardo da Vinci in the late 1400s and early 1500s.

▶ **Read**

See how Leonardo's sketches compare to similar modern machines.

Visions of the Future

Leonardo described and sketched ideas for many inventions hundreds of years ahead of their time. But it seems [that] very few of these were ever built and tested during his life. Though his notes suggest that he wished to organize and publish his ideas, he died before he could accomplish this important goal. After his death, his notebooks were hidden away, scattered, or lost, and his wonderful ideas were forgotten.

Centuries passed before other inventors came up with similar ideas and brought them to practical use.

[Here are two] modern inventions [that] Leonardo envisioned...in his notebooks over 500 years ago.

UNIT 1: MOTION AND FORCES

36

TEACHING PLAN pp. 36–37

INTRODUCING THE LESSON

This lesson discusses how many of the machines Leonardo da Vinci imagined in the 1400s are similar to modern machines used today.

Ask students to guess when the following machines were invented: zipper (1893), telephone (1876), airplane (1903), helicopter (1939), CD player (1979). Students are unlikely to know exact dates, but they may be able to infer the general time period when many machines were first used.

Some students may be surprised to find out that civilizations existing

thousands of years ago were quite technologically advanced. Ask: *What civilization do you think first pumped water to irrigate fields?* (the Babylonians, around 1700 B.C.) *What was the largest building in the world until the Empire State Building was constructed?* (the Great Pyramid of Cheops, built in Egypt around 2900 B.C.) Use these two questions to make the point that technology developed in ancient civilizations was often the basis for inventions that followed.

▶ **Read**

Ask: *What do you think it means to be "ahead of your time"?* (You have ideas that most other people don't accept while you are alive, but in the future your ideas will be valued.) Have students review the diagram of the wooden well winder on page 32 to help them imagine the daily life of people living in the 1400s. Remind students that there was no gasoline-powered transportation or electricity and very little leisure time. Ask: *Who in the 1400s might have been interested in Leonardo's sketches of flying machines or diving equipment?*

Leonardo sketched several different designs for flying machines including this one [at the right] with a rotating [propeller]. He intended to power it with a wound-up spring.

[The picture on the left] is a U.S. Navy helicopter capable of carrying heavy loads. The first helicopter that could carry a person was designed and flown [with a gasoline-powered engine] by Paul Cornu in 1907....

Leonardo sketched designs for several different diving suits. Most required a diver to breathe air from the surface through long hoses. In this design, he imagined a crush proof air chamber attached to the diver's chest to allow the diver to swim freely without connection to the surface.

Modern SCUBA divers can swim freely underwater while breathing compressed air from tanks on their backs. Jacques-Yves Cousteau and Emile Gagnon invented [the] self-contained breathing apparatus [shown at left,] in 1943.

---

envisioned: pictured
capable: able
SCUBA: Self-Contained Underwater Breathing Apparatus

compressed: squeezed together
apparatus: equipment

From: "Visions of the Future." *The Museum of Science.* (www.mos.org/sln/Leonardo/InventorsWorkshop.html)

NOTEZONE

For each pair of pictures, draw lines to connect parts of Leonardo's invention to similar parts of the modern machine.

propeller—
propeller

air chamber—
air tank

FIND OUT MORE

SCIENCESAURUS
Simple Machines 288
History of Science
Time Line 440

SCILINKS
THE WORLD'S A CLICK AWAY
www.scilinks.org
Keyword: Simple Machines
Code: GSPD04

Science Scope Activity
(continued from p. 31)

Part 2: Using the Catapult

Tell students that they must wear safety goggles at all times and that they may not use anything other than marshmallows as missiles. Also explain that they will compete to see whose catapult flings a marshmallow the greatest distance. Then give students the following instructions.

4. Prepare for the competition by testing the catapult you built in Lesson 7. Aim away from other people. Hold one marshmallow in the bowl of the spoon, pull back on the spoon, and then release both the spoon and marshmallow.
5. If you wish, make adjustments to your catapult to make it shoot the greatest possible distance.
6. When you are ready to compete, each group will get three chances to fling a marshmallow. The group that flings a marshmallow farthest wins.
7. Measure and record the distance each marshmallow travels.

After the competition, have students answer the following questions:

Which catapult flung best? (Answers will vary.) *What made some catapults fling better?* (Possibilites: a tighter rubber band, a greater "wind-up," a longer lever arm)

Encourage students to offer a variety of ideas.

As students look at the pictures of da Vinci's flying machine, tell them more about its design. It is also known as an "aerial screw." Can students see why? Point out that the rotating propeller is one piece of linen cloth wrapped around the center post like the threads of a screw. Thus, the propeller is really a giant screw. As a hypothetical team of men on the platform turned the shaft, or as a spring unwound, the rotating propeller would move through the air. Remind students that this machine was never built but existed only in the mind and notebook of da Vinci. Have students compare the screw design of da Vinci's machine with modern day propellers on the helicopter. Point out that helicopter propellers also act as screws.

CHECK UNDERSTANDING

Skill: Predicting

Have students think of a machine they use today. Tell them to imagine how it might be different 50 years from now. Ask: *What new technology might it make use of?* (Answers will vary. Students will probably predict the use of electronics to automate many of the mechanical tasks performed by machines.)

More Resources
The following resources are also available from Great Source and NSTA.

www.scilinks.org
Keyword: Simple Machines
Code: GSPD04

Enrichment
To help students learn more about the invention process, invite them to visit one of the Web sites listed below and report their findings to the class.

▶ Invent America! is a national competition for students in grades K–8. This annual event was created to help children develop creative thinking and problem solving skills through inventing. Read about winning inventions and get information about how to enter the competition. (www.inventamerica.com)

(continued on page 39)

Teaching Plan pp. 33–34

▶ **Explore**

MAKE COMPARISONS As students compare Leonardo's inventions with modern machines, help them recognize components of modern machines that were not available in Leonardo's time. For example, students should note that the fossil fuel-powered engine used in modern helicopters was invented only a little more than 100 years ago. Leonardo's helicopter was designed to be powered only by a spring (or a team of men). With compressed air tanks, SCUBA divers today can carry much larger amounts of air than would have been possible in Leonardo's time because of the technology involved in controlling gases under high pressure.

THINK ABOUT IT Explain to students that many of today's inventions are funded with money from investors. The investors expect that the invention will be purchased by enough people to make a profit for them in the future. Have half of the class pretend they are investors and the other half pretend they are inventors. Each inventor should come up with an idea for a new machine and suggest what its uses could be. They should then present their ideas to the investors. The group of investors should then choose which invention they want to fund. Afterwards, tally which inventions got the most funding and discuss why.

▶ **Explore**

MAKE COMPARISONS
▶ *How is Leonardo da Vinci's design for a helicopter similar to a modern-day helicopter? How is it different?*

Possible answer: They both involve moving parts that spin. They both have a propeller. A wound-up spring powers Leonardo's and a gas engine powers the modern one. Their shape is different. The shape of the propellers is different.

▶ *How is Leonardo's design for an underwater breathing machine similar to the one invented in 1943? How is it different?*

Possible answer: They both allow breathing underwater and involve carrying air along with the diver underwater. The modern version uses compressed air the diver carries on the back, while Leonardo's used regular air the diver carried on the chest.

THINK ABOUT IT Leonardo drew sketches of many inventions that weren't actually built until centuries later. One of those is the parachute, which he drew sketches of in the late 1400s.

▶ *Why do you suppose people of his time might not have recognized this as a useful invention? (Hint: Think about how parachutes are used today.)*

Possible answer: They didn't have airplanes or even hot air balloons so there wouldn't have been much need for a parachute.

When the Wright brothers were working on building the first airplane in the 1890s and early 1900s, most people thought they were just foolish. Even after the first successful flight, few people were impressed.

▶ *How do you suppose people in the 1400s probably reacted to Leonardo's idea for a helicopter?*

Possible answer: People might have thought he was crazy. People might have thought that trying to fly like a bird went against the laws of nature. Some people were probably also excited about the possibility.

38

MACHINES THEN AND NOW Many machines that we use today had previous versions that were different. Some older machines, such as rotary eggbeaters, look much as they did many years ago. Others, such as bicycles, look different.

Interview an adult to learn about some old machines. Find out what has changed from the old machine to the new machine. How is the new machine better? Can it do more? What are its advantages over the older version? How does the new machine make life easier? Are there any disadvantages with the new version? Record the results of your interview below.

Machine

Answers will vary. Possible answer: pencil sharpener

How the Machine Has Changed

Answers will vary. Students should give details about materials, weight, power source, size, cost, durability, availability. Possible answer: It used to be turned by hand. Usually it would be screwed onto a wall or tabletop. On most of them, there was a size selector. You could turn the size selector so the right-sized hole was lined up with the blades. Then you put the pencil in and turned the crank. That would make the blades turn that cut away the wood and made a point on the pencil. Now the power comes from electricity. They aren't screwed onto a wall, they just go anywhere.

How the New Machine Makes Life Easier

Answers will vary. Students should give details about the amount of energy required, the energy source, the time saved, safety improvements, ease of use. Also consider disadvantages that might be related to durability, cost, or compatibility with other machines. Possible answer: It's easier because you don't have to turn the crank. They also sharpen faster, so you can sharpen a lot of pencils pretty fast. You only need one hand to hold the pencil. I don't know if they're more expensive or not. One problem is that you can't take apart the new ones very well.

39

(continued from page 38)

▶ The National Inventors Hall of Fame in Akron, Ohio, was founded in 1973 by the National Council of Patent Law Associations, now the National Council of Intellectual Property Law Associations, and the Patent and Trademark Office of the U.S. Department of Commerce. Read about many inventions and discoveries and their inventors. (www.infoplease.com/ipa/A0004638.html)

▶ FIRST (For Inspiration and Recognition of Science and Technology) is an organization founded by inventor Dean Kamen and committed to motivating students to learn about science and technology. FIRST sponsors national competitions in robotics for high school students and for 9–14 year-old students. (www.usfirst.org)

Assessment

Skill: Using space/time relationships

Use the following questions to assess each student's progress:

Which do you think was invented first, the motorcycle or the bicycle? Why? (The design of the motorcycle is similar to the design of the bicycle, but it uses more advanced technologies, so the bicycle must have been invented first.)

▶ **Take Action**

MACHINES THEN AND NOW Tell students that an interview involves a series of questions. In most cases, one person (the interviewer) poses the questions and another (the person being interviewed) answers them. The purpose of an interview is to draw out and share with an audience what a certain person knows about a certain subject.

Tell students that the interview will go more smoothly if they prepare questions beforehand. Students also might want to do some research before they conduct the interview so they know what machines were common during the person's lifetime and can prompt the person as needed. Tell students to try to elicit technical information from the person as well as an account of his or her experiences with the machine.

Modern Machines

Robot Ants

Point of Lesson: *Engineers often get ideas for new machines from nature.*

A student engineer studied ant colonies as a model for his robots. In this lesson, students read about the engineer's work, then compare the structure and behavior of the robot ants to the structure and behavior of real ants.

Materials

Milking Machines

Point of Lesson: *Machines can be used to do jobs that used to be done by people.*

Students examine the differences between traditional milking machines and new robotic ones, which do not require human assistance to operate. They calculate the time saved by farmers who invest in the newer, more expensive machines and stage a debate about the advantages and disadvantages of machine labor compared with human labor.

Materials
Science Scope Activity (p. 40B and p. 43), for each group:
▶ list of pre-1950 devices (see page 40B)

Activity (p. 45), for each group:
▶ index cards

Connections (p. 45), for the class:
▶ research sources about historical debates

Transporting Humans

Point of Lesson: *Any new technology has its limitations.*

An article about the recently invented Segway human transporter leads to a consideration of the relative safety and usefulness of various single-person vehicles. Students read a news article about the Segway, then compare its working parts with those of a bicycle. They are then asked to consider the limitations of the Segway and to suggest ways in which those limitations could be addressed. Finally, students research sidewalk vehicle regulations in their own community and predict whether the Segway would be permitted where they live.

Materials
Enrichment (p. 47), for the class:
▶ research sources about methods of transportation throughout history
▶ index cards

Propose Explanations (p. 49), for the class:
▶ local newspapers containing editorial cartoons

Connections (p. 49), for the class:
▶ recordings of songs that mention modes of transportation

Science Scope Activity

Scavenger Hunt Science

NSTA has chosen a Science Scope activity related to the content in this chapter. The activity begins here and continues in Lesson 11, page 43.

Time: will vary

Materials: list of pre-1950 devices

Tell students that in this activity, they will research one mechanical device that was invented before 1950 and is still in use today. Divide the class into small groups. Give each group a copy of the following list of devices.

- large ice tongs
- ice cream scoop
- slide rule
- clothes iron
- eggbeater
- letter opener
- bread-making machine
- icebox
- knife
- paperweight
- clock
- toothbrush
- bicycle
- lemon squeezer
- insecticide sprayer

(continued on page 43)

Background Information

Lessons 10 and 11

Although the term *robot* conjures up images of metallic humanoids working in space, the vast majority of robots are used in factories, especially in the auto industry. The term *robot* comes from a Czech word meaning "drudgery," and indeed, most of the tasks that robots perform are repetitive and boring, such as assembly-line work. All robots have moving parts. Unlike the robot ants described in the lesson, however, most stay in one place as they do their jobs or move by following a predetermined track. It is surprisingly difficult to get a robot to sense a changing environment and respond to it, and engineers typically try to make a robot only as complex as it needs to be to complete its task. The Tech Museum of Innovation (San Jose, California) hosts an excellent Web site on robotics: www.thetech.org/robotics

Point of Lesson

Engineers often get ideas for new machines from nature.

Focus

▶ Motion and forces
▶ Form and function
▶ Science and technology in society
▶ Nature of science

Skills and Strategies

▶ Comparing and contrasting
▶ Making inferences

Advance Preparation

Vocabulary

Make sure students understand this term. The definition can be found in the glossary at the end of the student book.

▶ light

Enrichment

In the future, robots that work together might be used for dangerous jobs that require cooperation. For example, they might be used to inspect pipes in nuclear power plants or to find and pick up unexploded bombs. Have students write about how they think robotic ants might be used in the

(continued on page 41)

TEACHING PLAN pp. 40–41

INTRODUCING THE LESSON

This lesson focuses on how scientists sometimes look to nature for ideas when designing new technology.

Find out what students already know about robots by asking them to explain what a robot is. Students may think that robots are built only to resemble humans and do humanlike tasks. If necessary, clarify that the term *robot* refers to any machine that works automatically or by remote control. Explain that robots come in all shapes and sizes.

Ask students to list some places where robots might be used. (factories,

Robot Ants

Some robots are not much bigger than your thumb.

Ants live together in large groups called colonies. Ants in colonies work together to get big jobs done quickly. Perhaps you've seen a group of ants marching in a line between a food source and their nest. When engineer James McLurkin was a college student at the Massachusetts Institute of Technology, he studied how ant colonies cooperate. Then he used this knowledge about nature to develop new machines that cooperate.

▲ James McLurkin

▶ Read

NOTEZONE

Underline the parts of the robot that sense things in its environment.

(Circle) the parts of the robot that send and receive messages.

FIND OUT MORE

SCIENCESAURUS
Steps in Technology
Design   357
Military and Space
Technology   366

SCILINKS.
THE WORLD'S A CLICK AWAY

www.scilinks.org
Keyword: Robots
Code: GSPD05

40

James McLurkin created a colony of tiny robot ants.

An Idea from Nature

They can go around obstacles, look for food and even play tag. They're programmed to behave like ants in a colony, but they're not insects—they're matchbook-sized robots....

Each [robot ant] has a pair of tiny treads powered by a battery and two motors.... The robots are guided away from objects they hit and toward [light] sources by antennae and light sensors. [T]hey also have mandibles powered by a third motor to pick up bits of "food"—quarter-inch balls [0.5 cm] of crumpled brass.

Mr. McLurkin's goal is to have the robots behave cooperatively like an ant colony, [looking for] food and communicating with each other about where to find it. They do this with the aid of (infrared transmitters and receivers) (similar to those used by television remote controls) and software. If one robot finds food, it sends out the message "I found food." [O]thers in the [area] that receive [the signal] respond by heading toward the sender and signaling "I found a robot that found food." [In this way, they] eventually spread...the word to the entire group....

mines, laboratories, and so on) Robots have been designed to build cars, go inside active volcanoes, and even explore the surface of Mars.

▶ Read

After students have finished the reading, ask: *Do robot ants communicate as effectively as real ants?* (No; robot ants get confused if they receive signals from more than four other robots at once.)

Show students how difficult it is to receive multiple communications at the

same time. Organize the class into groups. Have each group form a circle with one student standing in the center. The students in the circle should, one by one, start to give simple instructions (such as, "Pat your head") to the student in the center. The student should try to follow all of the instructions. At first, following the instructions will be easy, but as more students join in, the task will become more difficult.

So goes the theory. In practice, Mr. McLurkin has found that the robots...get confused if they receive signals from more than four other robots at once....

obstacles: objects in the way
treads: heavy rubber belts that act as tires
antennae: feelers used to sense the environment
light sensors: instruments that respond to light
mandibles: jaws

infrared transmitters: instruments that send out signals
receivers: instruments that take in signals
software: part of a computer that processes information
theory: idea

From: Waugh, Alice. "MIT Senior's Robot Begets 'Ant' Farm." *MIT News.* (web.mit.edu/newsoffice/nr/1995/40009.html)

▶ **Explore**

COMPARING ANTS Using the excerpt and the ant diagram, find and label the following parts of the robotic ant: mandibles, treads, and antennae.

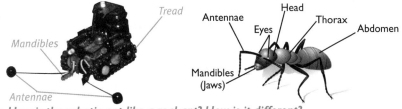

▶ **How is the robotic ant like a real ant? How is it different?**

Like: It has mandibles for picking things up and antennae to sense

things in the environment. Different: It has treads instead of legs,

infrared receivers instead of eyes, and it is not alive.

▶ **How are the robotic ants like an ant colony? How are they different?**

The robotic ants are like an ant colony because they communicate with

one other and work together. They are different because they get

confused if they get information from too many other robots.

▶ **How might being able to communicate with one another make the robotic ants more useful as robots?**

Since they can communicate, they can work together to do a job that a

single robot might not be able to do.

41

(continued from page 40)
future. Tell them to include a description of how the robots work together and how they get the job done, including the parts of the robots that are involved.

More Resources
The following resources are also available from Great Source and NSTA.

ScienceSaurus
Steps in Technology Design   357
Military and Space Technology   366

SCILINKS.
THE WORLD'S A CLICK AWAY

www.scilinks.org
Keyword: Robots
Code: GSPD05

Assessment
Skill: Making inferences

Use the following task to assess each student's progress:

Have students list five machines that might have been inspired by things in nature. Be sure they identify the natural element that might have inspired each machine. (Sample answers: Airplanes could have been inspired by birds, man-made dams by beaver dams, Jacuzzis by natural whirlpools, solar cells by plant leaves, and tongs by crab pincers.)

▶ **Explore**

COMPARING ANTS Ask: *Why do you suppose James McLurkin didn't design the robots to look exactly like real ants, with a thorax and abdomen and six legs?* (The robots were designed to perform the same tasks as ants, but there was no need to include all the features of a real ant. The features of the robot ant could accomplish the same tasks, and they were simpler to build.)

Have students compare the robot's treads to the ant's six legs. Ask: *Where have you seen treads before?* (on other machines, such as tractors and tanks)

Which do you think is better, legs or treads? Why? (Students should recognize that although treads allow the robot to move across a variety of surfaces, having six legs would probably provide more flexibility.)

CHECK UNDERSTANDING
Skill: Organizing information
Remind students that communication involves a number of separate tasks and is not as simple as it may seem. Have students list all of the communication tasks the robots can complete and what sort of equipment is needed to perform each of these tasks. (send out signals—infrared transmitter; receive signals—receivers; understand signals—software; know where signal is coming from—antennae and light sensors)

Point of Lesson

Machines can be used to do jobs that used to be done by people.

Focus

▶ **Systems, order, and organization**
▶ **Motion and forces**
▶ **Science and technology in society**
▶ **Nature of science**

Skills and Strategies

▶ **Communicating**
▶ **Interpreting scientific illustrations**
▶ **Using numbers**
▶ **Making inferences**
▶ **Generating ideas**

Advance Preparation

Materials

Gather the materials needed for *Science Scope Activity,* (p. 40B and p. 43), *Activity* (p. 45), and *Connections* (p. 45).

Milking Machines

A machine can get the milk out of a cow, and the farmer doesn't even have to be there.

Do you have milk with your cereal? Do you butter your toast? Do you eat ice cream? Have you ever had a grilled cheese sandwich? If your answer to any of these questions is yes, you can thank the people who milk dairy cows twice a day, seven days a week, 365 days a year. The cows produce milk all the time, and so they have to be milked on time, all the time. Milking machines have existed for years, but getting them on and off the cows is tedious and time-consuming work.

Recently, engineers have invented a new kind of milking machine. It is still very expensive, but before long it might make the lives of many dairy farmers a whole lot easier.

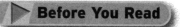
▶ Before You Read

THE OLD-FASHIONED WAY Many machines you use every day do jobs that were once done by people. For example, bread-making machines automatically knead and bake bread. An automatic car wash can clean the outside of the car while you relax inside.

▶ *What other machines do jobs that people once did? If you're not sure, ask an older person. List the machines below, along with the job they do and a brief explanation of how the job used to be done.*

Answers will vary. Examples: A washing machine does the job of

washing clothes. People used to wash them by hand. A food processor

chops food that people used to chop by hand. A checkout scanner at

the store records the price of an item, which a person used to have to

enter into a cash register by hand.

42

TEACHING PLAN pp. 42–43

INTRODUCING THE LESSON
This lesson introduces the idea that robots can be used to perform some tasks normally done by humans, such as milking a cow.

Some students may have heard people complain about new technology that takes jobs away from people. Students may have the idea that new technology always causes people to lose their jobs. Explain that the opposite often occurs. When a new machine is invented, people are given jobs making the machine, repairing the machine, adver-

tising the machine, and so on. Also, a new technology can allow people who are doing unpleasant jobs to do jobs that they find more interesting.

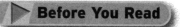
▶ Before You Read

THE OLD-FASHIONED WAY Have students identify some of the machines they listed in their answers. Write the names of the machines on the board. Ask students to write a description of what their life would be like without one of the machines on the list. Then ask students to go one step further and imagine what life would be like without *any* of the machines on the list.

▶ Read

Can dairy cows be trained to milk themselves?

Robots in the Dairy Barn

The dairy farms of Europe are as [charming] as ever, but for the past 10 years they've had something American farms lack: robotic milking technology. Labor costs are higher [in Europe], so as many as half the European dairies have the machines, which can milk cows 24 hours a day with no human [contact].... Lately, American farmers have begun to wonder if the machines...are worth a try....

With the right equipment, cows can be trained to milk themselves. They are [led in]to the machine with food, but soon learn to go there whenever their udders are full. When a cow enters the milking station, a computer scans an [identification] tag on her collar (1). A robotic arm swings under her udder (2) and washes it. A laser locates the exact position of her teats, attaches four [milking] cups (3), and starts milking. Milk from each teat is measured by a computer that releases the cups when milk flow stops. The robotic arm disinfects the udder, swings back (4), and the cow exits (5).

robotic: automatic
technology: equipment
udders: the sacs on cows that hold milk
laser: narrow beam of light
teats: parts of the udder that milk comes out of
disinfects: cleans off germs that might cause disease

From: Lanigan, Diane. "With the Right Equipment, Cows Can Be Trained to Milk Themselves." *Popular Science Newsfiles.* (www.popsci.com/popsci/science/article/0,12543,265562,00.html)

An earlier milking machine ▶

NOTEZONE

<u>Underline</u> four parts of the robotic milking machine.

FIND OUT MORE

SCIENCESAURUS

Steps in Technology Design	357
Limits on Technology Design	358
Natural Limits on Technology	359
Economic Limits on Technology	360
Society and Research	364
Society's Values	365
Tradeoffs	369
Reasonable People Disagree	373

SCiLINKS.
THE WORLD'S A CLICK AWAY

www.scilinks.org
Keyword: Robots
Code: GSPD05

Science Scope Activity
(continued from page 40B)

Procedure
Give students the following instructions.

1. Choose one item on the list, and write a report that answers the following questions about the device:
   ▶ *What job was your device designed to do?*
   ▶ *When was your device first manufactured?*
   ▶ *What was the cost of the device when it was first offered for sale?*
   ▶ *What is the cost of the device today?*
   ▶ *Why do you think your device has stood the test of time?*
2. Present your report to the class. Use graphics such as illustrations, graphs, and charts in your presentation.
3. When everyone has reported, create a class time line that shows when each device was first used.

▶ Read

After students finish the reading, ask a volunteer to read aloud the statement that describes the function of the laser in the milking machine. Then elaborate on the definition by explaining that a laser is an extremely bright beam of a single wavelength (color) of light. As the beam hits the teats, the light is scattered in different directions and picked up by light sensors. The computer uses the information from these light sensors to determine the exact location of the teats. The suction cups can then be moved into the correct position to hook onto the teats.

The word *laser* is actually an acronym, a word that is formed from the first letters of a name or phrase. "Laser" is derived from the phrase *light amplification by stimulated emission of radiation*. Have students look up the meaning of any words they do not understand.

Theodore Maiman invented the first working laser in 1960. Many people called it "the invention without a use." Today, however, lasers have thousands of uses, from reading CDs and DVDs to making extremely precise cuts during eye surgery.

CHECK UNDERSTANDING
Skill: Making inferences
Ask: *What might go wrong with a robotic milking machine? What might the result be?* (Answers will vary. Examples: If a cow's tag fell off, the computer might not know what to do next, and the cow would not get milked. Or the cow might move her leg and get in the way of the robotic arm; the arm might get stuck, and the cow would not get milked.)

More Resources

The following resources are also available from Great Source and NSTA.

SCILINKS.
THE WORLD'S A CLICK AWAY

www.scilinks.org
Keyword: Robots
Code: GSPD05

DECODE A DIAGRAM The diagram shows the steps in milking a cow with a robotic milking machine. Compare the diagram to the description in the reading.

▶ **What human action is replaced by each of the numbered steps in the diagram?**

1 *leading the cow into the milking station*

2 *cleaning the cow's udder*

3 *attaching the vacuum cups and starting them*

4 *disinfecting the udder*

5 *letting the cow out*

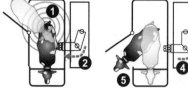

A FARMER'S LIFE Dairy farmers have a hard time taking a day off. Dairy cows must be milked twice a day on a regular basis. If they are not, they will stop producing milk. The work is hard and one person can't do it alone. Recently, many people who own small dairy farms have decided that it is just not possible to make a living as a farmer. Too much hard work and not enough profit make them want to give up. But some people think that robotic milking machines might make it possible for more families to keep their small dairy farms.

▶ **Old milking machines were operated by people. It used to take about five minutes to milk one cow. If a farmer had 50 cows, how long did it take to milk them all?**

50 x 5 = 250 minutes, or 4 hours 10 minutes

▶ **How much time did he spend milking each day if he milked the whole herd twice a day?**

4 hours 10 minutes x 2 = 8 hours 20 minutes

▶ **How might a robotic milking machine make a dairy farmer's life easier?**

The farmer doesn't have to herd the cows into the barn. He doesn't have to milk the cows himself twice a day, every day of the year. He can be away from home for more than a few hours.

44

TEACHING PLAN pp. 44–45

▶ **Explore**

DECODE A DIAGRAM Some students may have difficulty understanding the diagram because the illustrations are not in sequential order. Suggest that students form groups to illustrate the robot's work through a series of five consecutive panels. Tell students to use the reading on page 43 to create their illustrations, not the diagram on this page. Display the illustrations in the classroom, and have each group describe what is occurring in each panel.

A FARMER'S LIFE To help students understand the human side of the math equations they complete in this section, have them create a daily schedule of activities for the dairy farmer described. Include key activities such as waking up and going to sleep; eating breakfast, lunch, and dinner; and working. Then have students create a daily schedule for their own life. Afterwards, have students discuss the similarities and differences between their lives and the life of a dairy farmer with a herd of approximately 50 cows.

DEBATE THE ISSUE Within every group of people, you will find differences of opinion. One way that people share different ideas is through a debate. A debate is not an argument. Each side is allowed to present its position without being disturbed. Then questions are asked and answered in order to explore the issue further.

Hold a debate about the advantages and disadvantages of having machines do jobs that people used to do.

What You Need:
• index cards

What to Do:
1. Form a team with classmates.
2. Begin by reviewing the list of machines you made on page 42.
3. Write the name of each machine on an index card. For each machine, decide what its advantages (or disadvantages) are and write them on the card. For example, an advantage might be "The machine gives people more free time." A disadvantage might be "The machine causes pollution."
4. With your teammates, develop a list of points to make to present your position on each machine. If necessary, do additional research to find new points.
5. Hold a debate with the other side by taking turns making your case about each machine.
6. As the other team makes its case, write down any additional questions you want to ask them.
7. Ask the other team your side's questions. They will do the same with your team.

Write Reflections
What did you learn from the debate? Did the arguments you heard make you change your mind about anything? If so, what?

Answers will vary.

45

Connections
Time: will vary
Materials: research sources about historical debates

SOCIAL STUDIES Tell students that many debates, including those held in the United States Congress, are organized according to standard procedures. Have students use books, articles, and the Internet to research famous historical debates in this country. Direct students to pay particular attention to the formal procedures that were used to regulate the debates. You may want to have students create a flowchart describing the steps in the procedure (for example, presentation, cross-examination, and rebuttal).

Assessment
Skill: Generating questions

Use the following question to assess each student's progress:

What questions might a farmer consider when trying to decide whether to invest in milking machine technology? (Answers will vary. Examples: How many hours per day do I spend milking the cows? Do I have enough time to do everything that needs to get done in the day? How might I use extra time to make my business more profitable? How might having extra time improve my life?)

Time: 1 class period
Materials: index cards

▶ Before students start the debate, explain that they do not necessarily have to debate the side of the issue that they agree with.
▶ After the students form teams, tell each team that they should not only develop arguments for their side of the issue but also prepare a list of possible responses to make to the other team's statements. Teams may also want to practice making their arguments and refuting the other team's possible arguments before the actual debate.
▶ You may want to give students time limits for each portion of the debate. For example, you could give each team eight minutes to make opening statements, four minutes to cross examine, eight minutes to make rebuttal speeches, and four minutes to make closing remarks. Also allow time for the teams to prepare their rebuttal speeches and closing remarks.

Point of Lesson
Any new technology has its limitations.

Focus
► Systems, order, and organization
► Motion and forces
► Science as a human endeavor
► Science and technology in society

Skills and Strategies
► Communicating
► Comparing and contrasting
► Making inferences
► Generating ideas

Advance Preparation

Vocabulary
Make sure students understand these terms. Definitions can be found in the glossary at the end of the student book.

► speed
► technology

Materials
Gather the materials needed for *Enrichment* (p. 47), *Propose Explanations* (p. 49), and *Connections* (p. 49).

Transporting Humans

Imagine moving down the sidewalk without an ounce of effort!

Throughout history, inventors have taken existing machines and ideas, added their own ideas, and created new machines. One idea inventors are always trying to improve upon is how to more easily transport objects and people from one place to another. The wheel was invented thousands of years ago. But inventors are still working on new ways to use it today!

One of those inventors is Dean Kamen. He has created the Segway—a machine designed to carry one person along the sidewalk.

▲ Dean Kamen

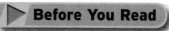
► Before You Read

BEAM ME UP Movies, television shows, comics, and books often show us what the future might look like, especially in terms of technology. Science-fiction writers have come up with fascinating ideas for how to transport individual people easily from one place to another.

What unusual or original method have you seen for transporting humans? How did it work? Where could it take people? If you can't think of any you have seen, what would you like to invent? Write about an imaginary human transportation system in the space below.

Answers will vary. Example: In the television series Star Trek, *people could be transported from another location to the space ship. They seemed to dissolve and be reassembled in a matter of seconds. It would be great not to have to get on a plane to go across the continent.*

UNIT 1: MOTION AND FORCES

TEACHING PLAN pp. 46–47

INTRODUCING THE LESSON
This lesson introduces a new transportation technology—the Segway, or human transporter.

Find out what students know about transportation by first asking what the term means. (the process of moving something from one place to another) Then ask students to identify some methods of transportation that people use.

Students may not realize how important transportation is in their lives. To help students understand the importance of modern transportation tech-

nology, ask them to raise their hands if they ride in a car or bus in school. Then ask students to raise their hands if they have to use a car or bus to get to the grocery store. Then ask: *Where does the food in the grocery store come from?* (It comes from all over the world.) *If there were no airplanes, trucks, trains, or boats, what food would be available to you?* (only local foods)

► Before You Read

BEAM ME UP After students list some of the imaginary forms of transportation for the future, ask them to tell how likely it is for that form of transportation to become a reality. Then ask: *Fifty years from now, how do you think people and products might be moved from one place to another?* (Accept all reasonable answers.)

NOTEZONE

What else do you want to know about Segway after reading this?

▶ Read

Inventor Dean Kamen wants to improve the way we get around with a new machine.

Make Way for Segway!

Segway looks like a cross between a scooter and a lawnmower. The battery-powered scooter travels as fast as 17 miles per hour and has internal gyroscopes that make it difficult to fall from or knock over. A gyroscope is a wheel-like device that maintains its steady position no matter how it is moved.

Segway's coolest feature may be that its speed and direction are controlled by the rider's shifting weight. Riders navigate with a bicycle-like handlebar. By simply standing up straight, the scooter takes you wherever you want to go. It doesn't have brakes, but is smart enough to sense when the rider wants to stop....

Kamen is already famous for a variety of inventions including a wheelchair that climbs stairs. The New Hampshire-based inventor hopes Segway will one day be used on city sidewalks, where riders won't need a license. He also hopes his latest invention will replace cars in big cities and help the environment by cutting down on car use and pollution.

device: piece of equipment
navigate: steer

From: El Nabli, Dina. "Make Way for Segway!" *Time for Kids.*
(www.timeforkids.com/TFK/news/printout/0,9187,187023,00.html)

The Segway ▶

FIND OUT MORE

SCIENCESAURUS

Steps in Technology Design	357
Limits on Technology Design	358
Natural Limits on Technology	359
Economic Limits on Technology	360
Society and Research	364
Tradeoffs	369
Community Decision-Making	370
Reasonable People Disagree	373

47

Enrichment

Time: will vary
Materials: research sources about methods of transportation throughout history, index cards

Tell students that they are going to design and develop a transportation museum for the class. Give students the following instructions:

1. As a class, brainstorm a list of different vehicles and methods of transportation.
2. Divide the list of transportation items among the class members. Each student will then be responsible for finding or creating a picture or model of the transportation item that he or she was assigned and for researching information about the item, including when it was invented, who invented it, and what its use is.
3. Write the name of your item and the information you learned on an index card.

Assemble all the models, pictures, and information cards on a large table. Allow students time to arrange the items in museumlike display (most likely, in chronological order).

▶ Read

After students read the passage, encourage them to try to think of any benefits of the Segway that are not mentioned in the reading. Also ask them to name some potential problems. (Examples: The batteries could run out when you are far from home. Your legs might get tired from standing still on the platform instead of walking, riding a bike, or sitting in a vehicle.)

Finally, ask students to name some of the benefits they thought of, besides cutting down on car use and pollution. (Examples: People will save time by traveling more quickly than they could by walking and by not having to wait for buses and subways. The Segway would help people who have trouble walking but don't need a wheelchair, giving them more mobility and independence.)

CHECK UNDERSTANDING
Skill: Recognizing cause and effect
Ask: *How might the Segway make people use cars less?* (People would hop on a Segway for short trips to the store, to travel around their town or city, or to go to work if their commute was only a few miles from home.) *How would using cars less help the environment?* (When cars burn gasoline, pollutants are released into the air, so using cars less would reduce air pollution.)

More Resources

The following resources are also available from Great Source.

ScienceSaurus

Reader's Handbook

Write Source 2000

COMPARE BICYCLES AND SEGWAYS The bicycle is a familiar machine for moving people. You can probably name all the bicycle's main parts: frame, seat, handlebars, pedals, chain, gears, brakes.

The important parts of the Segway are a bit harder to see. The Segway has two electric motors powered by batteries. The motors are connected to large plastic wheels with rubber tires. Each wheel can spin by itself. The two wheels can turn in different directions at the same time. Because of this the machine can turn in a complete circle without moving forward or backward. Special sensors keep track of the rider's position. The rider's position tells the motors how the rider wants to move. A twist grip on the handlebars allows the rider to steer. A red button allows the rider to stop the machine.

▶ *How is a Segway similar to a bicycle?*

Answers will vary. Examples: It carries one

person. It can be steered and stopped.

It is not enclosed. It has two wheels.

▶ *How is a Segway different from a bicycle?*

Answers will vary. Examples: It is powered by electricity, not a human.

It keeps the rider balanced, while the rider has to balance a bicycle.

Its wheels are side-by-side, rather than one behind the other. It has no

seat. It can turn without moving forward.

▶ *What might make the Segway safer to use in places where a bicycle is not safe to use?*

It is easy to turn and responds to the slightest input. It also is designed

so that people won't get hurt if they bump into each other.

▶ *When would a bicycle be better to use than a Segway? When would a Segway be better to use than a bicycle?*

Answers will vary. Example: A bicycle is better for exercise. Bikes are good

on dirt trails and when you want to go fast. A Segway would be better

for a person who wants to move without using a lot of energy or cannot

exercise because of health problems. It would be good on city sidewalks.

48

TEACHING PLAN pp. 48–49

Explore

COMPARE BICYCLES AND SEGWAYS If students are having difficulty answering the Explore questions, help them by creating a graphic organizer on the board or overhead projector. Start by writing *Bicycles* on one side of the board and *Segways* on the other side. Have students call out features of each form of transportation. Then have volunteers draw lines connecting the features that are the same in bicycles and Segways.

Next, create another graphic organizer that focuses on the uses, settings, or populations for which each is suited. Again write *Bicycles* on one side of the board and *Segways* on the other side. Have students name groups of people who might use each device, places they might go with each device, and the purposes of the trips. Write students' responses on the board. Then ask volunteers to circle the people, places, or purposes that appear in only one list.

▶ Propose Explanations

NOTHING'S PERFECT When you see a transporter in a science-fiction movie, it seems like a perfect machine. It does a great job and doesn't cause any problems. Real life inventions are not so perfect. They have limitations—characteristics that make them less useful than their inventors hoped.

▶ **What limitations does the Segway have? List at least three. Look back at the picture on page 48 for ideas.**

Answers will vary. Example: There is no place to carry bags. The rider is

exposed to the weather. There is no room for another passenger.

▶ **What might be a solution to one of these limitations?**

Answers will vary. Example: It could have hooks to hang shopping

bags, and some kind of awning over it to protect from rain and snow.

▶ Take Action

FIND OUT MORE Dean Kamen sees his invention being ridden on sidewalks in cities. Not everyone agrees that this is a good idea. List all the vehicles you have seen on sidewalks. Include those with motors and without motors—for example, scooters and motorized scooters. Contact the police department in your town or a nearby city. Find out which of these vehicles are allowed on sidewalks today. Based on what you learn, write whether you think the Segway would be allowed. Explain your prediction.

Possible vehicles: bicycles, tricycles, baby strollers, roller skates,

skateboards, scooters, motorized scooters. Sample opinion: In our town,

downtown, you can't ride anything on the sidewalks. So if the police were

fair they would not allow Segways either. But maybe they will say Segways

are safer because people won't get hurt when they hit each other.

49

Connections

Time: will vary
Materials: recordings of songs that mention modes of transportation

MUSIC Tell students that many songs include modes of transportation in their themes. Bring some examples to class for students to listen to. (Examples include John Denver's *Leavin' on a Jet Plane,* Harry Dacre's *A Bicycle Built for Two*, the Hollies' *Bus Stop*, and the Beach Boy's *Little GTO*.) After students listen to the examples you brought in, have small groups write their own songs about the Segway. Encourage students to have fun with the lyrics.

Assessment

Skill: Concept mapping

Use the following task to assess each student's progress:

Have students create a concept map that shows the pros and cons of using Segways on sidewalks. (Pros: Segways would allow people to move more quickly and would help some people with disabilities get around more easily. Cons: Segways might cause injury to pedestrians or increased congestion on sidewalks.)

▶ Propose Explanations

Time: will vary
Materials: local newspapers containing editorial cartoons

NOTHING'S PERFECT Tell students to imagine they are news reporters doing an editorial on the Segway. Explain that an editorial is an opinion piece in a newspaper. An editorial contains facts, but it also presents the writer's feelings and opinions on the subject. Have students use the information that they have learned in this lesson to write the editorial. As an alternative, you could let students draw cartoons about the

Segway in the style of modern editorial cartoons. You may want to bring in copies of local newspapers to show students examples of editorial cartoons.

▶ Take Action

FIND OUT MORE Tell students to imagine that they are on the Board of Public Safety for their community. The topic of the day is whether to allow Segways on the community's sidewalks, streets, and in public parks. Tell students to list questions they would consider before deciding whether and where to allow Segways

to be used. Also encourage them to suggest tests that could be done to answer the questions. (For example: Could a pedestrian be hurt if a Segway hit him or her? To find out, the Board could require tests using a mannequin to represent the pedestrian.)

UNIT 2 Electricity and Magnetism

About the Photo

As a boy, Thomas Edison had a small lab in the basement of his house. Later he established this laboratory complex in New Jersey, just 12 miles west of New York City. The site has been maintained to inspire visitors, complete with the industrious and industrial smells of grease and chemicals. Among more than 1,000 other inventions, Edison used the lab to find a way to use electricity to produce light, replacing messy and dangerous oil lamps the world over.

Is it nature or technology?

Electricity is a form of energy, and magnetism is a force. Both are found in nature. And both have been harnessed by people for their own uses. Remember that the energy that powers your TV, telephone, and computer is the very same kind of energy that creates enormous bolts of lightning across the sky. Magnetic materials can be found in the rocks that make up Earth, but they can also be used to produce electricity and to make train travel more efficient.

In this unit you will learn about how magnetism is related to electricity. You'll explore the causes of static electricity and the origin of the electric light bulb. You'll learn the role of Earth's magnetic field in two mysterious happenings in nature. And you'll discover how everyday devices like computers depend on the precise control of electricity.

50

About the Charts

A major goal of the *Science Daybooks* is to promote reading, writing, and critical thinking skills in the context of science. The charts below describe the types of reading selections included in this unit and identify the skills and strategies used in each lesson.

SELECTION	READING	WRITING	APPLICATION
CHAPTER 5 • HOW SHOCKING!			
13. "The Zapper Slide" (science journal article)	• Use prior knowledge • Read for details	• Label a diagram • Explain your answer	• Hands-on activity • Record observations • Suggest solutions
14. "Dog OK after Lightning Hits" (news service article)	• Use prior knowledge • Main idea	• Explain your answer • Make inferences	• Create a graphic organizer
15. "An Amazon Adventure" (Web site posting)	• Read for details • Main idea	• Make inferences	
CHAPTER 6 • EDISON AT WORK			
16. "Edison Sets a Goal" (PBS program transcript)	• Brainstorming • Make a list • Directed reading	• Explain your answer • Draw conclusions	• Interpret a quote • Describe a personal experience
17. "A Flitting Butterfly" (PBS program transcript)	• Directed reading	• Explain your reasoning • Critical thinking	• Comparing spoken and written words
18. "Edison vs. Westinghouse" (PBS program transcript)	• Use prior knowledge • Read for details	• Persuasive writing	• Make a poster

? Did You Know?
A lightning bolt can produce hundreds of millions of volts of electricity. The average wall outlet produces about 120 volts.

© GREAT SOURCE. COPYING IS PROHIBITED.

▲ Edison's laboratory

51

Answers to *Find Out* Questions

CHAPTER 5
Static electricity can build up on a plastic slide and transfer to a child, causing a painful shock. (p. 53)

CHAPTER 6
Thinner wires have greater resistance, and this greater resistance produces more light. (p. 64)

CHAPTER 7
They have a built-in navigation system that uses Earth's magnetic field to tell them where they are and in which direction they are going. (pp. 74–77)

CHAPTER 8
The uniform rows in a plowed field gave the inventor of television the idea of using a magnetic field to keep the electrons used to form a television image in neat rows. (p. 83)

SCI LINKS
THE WORLD'S A CLICK AWAY

www.scilinks.org
Keyword: Science Fair
Code: GSSD03

SELECTION	READING	WRITING	APPLICATION
CHAPTER 7 • IT'S MAGNETIC			
19. "Aurora in the Sky" (children's science book)	• Identify action verbs • Critical thinking	• Interpret a diagram • Make comparisons	
20. "Magnetic Personalities" (newspaper science Q & A column)	• Use prior knowledge • Describe a situation	• Interpret a map • Cite supporting evidence	• Write a research report
21. "Fast Track" (science news magazine)	• Sketch observations • Directed reading	• Explain your understanding • Make comparisons	• Hands-on activity • Make observations
CHAPTER 8 • ELECTRONICS			
22. "Imagine That!" (children's nonfiction book)	• Describe personal experiences • Read for details	• Problem solving • Critical thinking	• Create an image
23. "Under a Telephone Pole" (poem)	• Critical reading • Interpret a poem	• Record observations	• Create a graphic organizer
24. "Analytical Engine" (teacher resource book)	• Decipher a code • Generate questions	• Fill in a chart • Calculate binary and decimal numbers	• Write a coded message

CHAPTER 5

Overview

How Shocking!

LESSON 13

Zap Attack!

Point of Lesson: *Static electricity can produce a shock when discharged to a person's body.*

Students explore the phenomenon of static electricity by reading an article about static charges on plastic playground slides. They then label a diagram to show where charges build up and discharge as a person travels down a slide. In a hands-on activity, students test whether it is possible to pretreat a surface with a dryer sheet in order to prevent static buildup and discharge.

Materials

Before You Read (p. 52), for teacher demonstration (optional):
► plastic comb
► hair dryer

Enrichment (p. 53), for each group:
► clear jar or drinking glass
► two strips of aluminum foil (1 cm × 4 cm)
► index card
► paper clip
► tape

Activity (p. 55), for each pair or group:
► very small pieces of paper
► 2 or more blown-up balloons
► small piece of wool
► dryer sheet

Connections (p. 55), for the class:
► dictionary with information on word origins
for teacher demonstration (optional):
► piece of amber
► piece of fur or wool

LESSON 14

Hot Dog

Point of Lesson: *Lightning is a form of static discharge.*

The strange but true tale of Sport, a dog who survived being hit by lightning, introduces students to this powerful electrical phenomenon. After reading a newspaper report of Sport's misadventure, students analyze and label a diagram to show the path that charges are most likely to take during a lightning strike. Students then identify the energy transfers that occur during a lightning strike.

Materials

Before You Read (p. 56), for the class:
► photographs of lightning

Enrichment (p. 57), for the class:
► research sources about lightning safety procedures
► posterboard
► art supplies

LESSON 15

Electric Eel

Point of Lesson: *Some animals use electrical discharge to catch their prey.*

Students discover a fish that can generate electricity in its body. They read one man's description of his encounter with an electric eel in the Amazon rain forest. Students analyze a diagram to explain why the man was reluctant to touch the electric eel, even though his guide was telling everyone it was safe to do so. They then infer how the time an eel takes to recharge might affect its behavior when attacking its prey.

Materials

Introducing the Lesson (p. 60), for teacher:
► photographs of electric eels (optional)

Background Information

Lesson 14

Lightning rods are often installed to protect buildings from the kind of damage described in the newspaper article from which this lesson's reading was taken. To be effective, a lightning rod must be connected electrically to the ground by a conductor, such as a wire. "Grounding," as this is called, seems to accomplish two things. If the rod is hit, grounding provides lightning with a safe path to a source of neutralizing charges (the ground). A lightning rod also provides a path for charges from the ground to disperse into the air above the rod, where they neutralize the charge in the air and help prevent strikes in the first place.

Lesson 15

Electric eels (*Electrophorus electricus*) are not true eels (order Anguilliformes) but are actually another type of fish. The term "eel" in this case simply refers to the eel-like shape. One major difference between electric eels and true eels is that all true eels have teeth, but electric eels do not.

The electric eel has thick skin that acts as an insulator and protects the fish from shocking itself. If the electric eel is injured and its skin is punctured, it runs the risk of electrocuting itself.

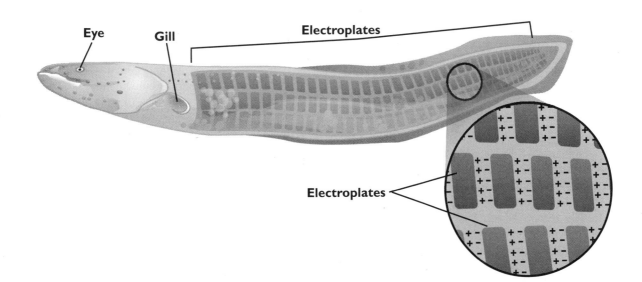

Eye   Gill   Electroplates

Electroplates

Point of Lesson
Static electricity can produce a shock when discharged to a person's body.

Focus
▶ Transfer of energy
▶ Change, constancy, and measurement
▶ Evolution and equilibrium
▶ Evidence, models, and explanation

Skills and Strategies
▶ Observing
▶ Collecting and recording data
▶ Recognizing cause and effect
▶ Making inferences

Advance Preparation

Vocabulary
Make sure students understand these terms. Definitions can be found in the glossary at the end of the student book.

▶ charge
▶ electricity
▶ energy
▶ humidity
▶ negative charge
▶ positive charge

Materials
Gather the materials needed for *Before You Read* (below), *Enrichment* (p. 53), *Activity* (p. 55), and *Connections* (p. 55).

ZAP ATTACK!

Static electricity is everywhere. Are you shocked?

Have you ever felt a shock when you touched a metal doorknob after walking across a carpet? That same energy can also make your hair hard to comb in the winter. And it can make your clothes cling to each other and to you when they come out of the dryer.

This annoying energy comes from something called electric charge. Everything in the world is chock full of particles with charge, either positive or negative. The particles with negative charge are called electrons, and the ones with positive charge are called protons. Any two opposite charges pull toward each other, but any two like charges try to push apart. When a huge number of like charges are all forced onto one object with no escape route, the result is called static charge, or static electricity.

▲ Static cling makes laundry stick together.

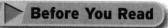 **Before You Read**

OUCH! Even when you know it's coming, a shock from static electricity feels like a surprise, and it is always a little unpleasant. Sometimes the jolt catches you completely off guard, and sometimes it really hurts.

▶ *Think of a time when you got an electric shock. Describe the situation. Can you remember what the weather was like?*

Answers will vary. Students may describe cold weather, dry air conditions, and movement such as walking on a carpet.

▶ *Have you ever shocked another person? Described what happened.*

Answers will vary. Students may describe a situation such as walking across a carpeted floor to get a pencil from a sibling. When their hands touched, they both got a shock.

UNIT 2: ELECTRICITY AND MAGNETISM

TEACHING PLAN pp. 52–53

INTRODUCING THE LESSON
This lesson explains the phenomenon of static electricity.

Students may think that static electricity is caused by new charges being created on an object. Explain that static electricity is actually caused by a separation of charges that normally exist in pairs (one positive, one negative). For example, when two materials are rubbed together, some of the electrons are pulled off one material and "stick" to the other material. In this way, the charges are separated. When two objects with opposite charges built up on them come into contact, a shock is produced.

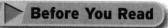 **Before You Read**

Time: 10 minutes
Materials: plastic comb, hair dryer (optional)

OUCH! Explain that static electricity is more common in dry conditions than in humid conditions. The reason is, when air contains enough water vapor, water molecules can collect on the surfaces of objects. A layer of water molecules keeps the objects' surfaces from actually touching, so the charges cannot be transferred.

Students who live in very humid climates may be unfamiliar with static electricity or may need prompting to remember their experiences with it.

You may also want to perform a simple demonstration, such as running a comb through your hair after using a hair dryer. Negative charges will collect on the comb, leaving each strand of hair with an overall positive charge. Because like charges repel, the strands will move away from each other, creating a "flyaway" effect.

Read about how children might get a "charge" out of playing on a plastic slide.

The Zapper Slide

Can [enough] static charge build [up on] plastic playground equipment to harm someone?

Static electricity can build up when materials such as plastic are rubbed. The friction involved in the rubbing can either remove electrons from the plastic leaving the plastic positively charged or add extra electrons onto the plastic leaving it negatively charged....

Let's take a slide as an example of the [plastic] playground equipment.... As [a] child slides down the slide, [his or her] clothes will rub on the plastic and a [static] charge could...build up on both the child and the slide.

Is this charge enough to hurt someone? Ask Peter Ledlie, a father playing on a plastic slide with his daughter:

...It was during a warm day here in Phoenix, (85 deg[rees F]) [29.4 degrees C] with humidity around 15 [percent]. I went on a plastic slide, and could feel and hear the charges building up as I went down. I put my hands out at the end to stop, and brushed by one of the [metal] bolts, getting a painful zap!

friction: force created by rubbing
electrons: negatively charged particles

From: "Can a Static Charge [on] Plastic Playground Equipment ... Harm Someone?" *ScienceNet Quick Links.* (www.sciencenet.org.uk/database/Biology/0107/b00982d.html)

Fowler, Steve. "Are Children's Slides at Fast Food Restaurants a Static Hazard?" *ESD Journal.* (www.esdjournal.com/static/believeit/slides/slides.htm)

FIND OUT MORE

SCIENCESAURUS
Atomic Structure 256
The Law of
  Electric Charges 315
Static Electricity 316

SCiLINKS.
THE WORLD'S A CLICK AWAY
www.scilinks.org
Keyword: Static Electricity
Code: GSPD06

53

Enrichment

Time: 30 minutes
Materials: clear jar or drinking glass, two strips of aluminum foil (1 cm × 4 cm), index card, paper clip, tape

Have students work in small groups to construct a simple electroscope—a device that detects the presence of static electricity. Give students the following instructions.

1. Bend the paper clip to form a hook on one end and a straight wire on the other end (like a letter J).
2. Push the straight end of the paper clip up through the center of the index card so the hook hangs down. Tape the paper clip to the card to hold it in place.
3. Stack the two foil strips and hang them vertically on the hook.
4. Put the index card on top of the glass or jar so the strips hang down inside it.
5. Charge various objects by rubbing them. Hold each object near the top of the paper clip. Observe what happens to the foil strips. (They separate.) Remove the object and observe again. (The strips come back together.)

Explain that when the charged object is brought near the paper clip, it induces the opposite charge in both strips. Because both strips have the same charge (positive-positive or negative-negative) and like charges repel, the strips move away from each other.

► **Read**

To help students understand how the selection is organized, have them identify the role of each paragraph. (first paragraph—asks a question; second paragraph—explains the phenomenon in scientific terms; third paragraph—gives a real-world example of the phenomenon; fourth paragraph —answers the first question by giving a specific example of an event) Point out that the selection answers the first question by moving from the most general information to the most specific.

Explain that neither friction nor rubbing is necessary to create static electricity. Any time two different materials come in contact with each other and then are separated, one tends to give up electrons and the other tends to accept them. Rubbing increases the number of contact-separation events, and friction is simply a by-product of rubbing.

CHECK UNDERSTANDING
Skill: Recognizing cause and effect
Ask: *What causes static electricity?* (Sample answer: When one object rubs against another object, positive or negative charges may build up on the surfaces of the objects.)

More Resources

The following resources are also available from Great Source and NSTA.

ScienceSaurus

Reader's Handbook

SCILINKS.
THE WORLD'S A CLICK AWAY

www.scilinks.org
Keyword: Static Electricity
Code: GSPD06

Explore

HOW DID PETER LEDLIE GET ZAPPED? As Peter Ledlie came down the slide, charges built up on him and on the slide.

▶ *What made this happen?*

His clothes rubbed against the plastic and the rubbing caused static

electricity to build up on him and on the slide.

Below is a diagram of Peter Ledlie on the slide. Add plus (+) and minus (−) signs to show positive and negative charges built up on Peter and on the slide. (Hint: There may be more than one correct way to do this.)

Students could show negative charges on the man and positive charges on the slide, or positive charges on the man and negative charges on the slide. In any case, man and slide must be oppositely charged. Students should circle the bolt the man is touching.

A shock is felt when static discharge occurs. Static discharge occurs when a charged object touches another object and the built-up charges move quickly off the charged object. The charges move most quickly when the object touched is a conductor—a material that charges move through easily. Metal is a good conductor.

▶ *On the diagram, circle the spot where the discharge took place.*

▶ *If there hadn't been a metal bolt on the side of the slide, do you think Peter Ledlie would have gotten shocked? Explain your answer.*

No, because there would have been no discharge of the charges built up

on him.

54

TEACHING PLAN pp. 54–55

Explore

HOW DID PETER LEDLIE GET ZAPPED?
Students may be concerned because they do not know which object develops a positive charge and which develops a negative charge. Encourage students to share their completed diagrams, and point out that the important factor is having two oppositely charged objects, not determining which object is positively charged and which is negatively charged.

As a class, discuss students' answers to the last question. Explain that static electric charges build up most often on

materials that are insulators and do not conduct electricity well, such as plastic or fabrics. In contrast, electrons move easily thorough materials that are conductors, such as metal. As a result, static discharge often occurs when insulators with built-up charges touch conductors.

Point out that static discharge can sometimes be dangerous, such as when it occurs near a highly flammable substance such as gasoline. Explain that the trucks that deliver gas to the underground tanks at filling stations use a grounding device that leads charge away from the gasoline; this

prevents static discharge. People who are preparing to put gas into their cars or other containers should touch something metal before they approach the tank, and all containers should be placed on the ground while they are being filled.

ZAPPING STATIC

Can dryer sheets help you avoid "the shock"?

What You Need:
- very small pieces of paper
- blown-up balloons
- small piece of wool
- dryer sheets

What to Do:
1. Make a pile of very small bits of paper on your desk.
2. Rub one side of a balloon with a piece of wool for about 30 seconds.
3. Pass that part of the balloon over the pieces of paper. Write your observations in the chart.
4. Now rub one side of the wool with the dryer sheet for about 30 seconds. Then use that side of the wool to rub another balloon in the same way as the first balloon.
5. Pass that part of the balloon over the pieces of paper again. Write your observations in the chart.

What Do You See?

	Observations
Balloon rubbed with wool	*The pieces of paper should be attracted to the balloon.*
Balloon rubbed with dryer-sheet-treated wool	*The pieces should not be attracted to the balloon.*

What Happened?

▶ *Describe what happened in steps two and three in terms of "built-up charges."*

Students should describe how charges built up on the balloon

when they rubbed it. These charges attracted pieces of paper.

▶ *What can you infer about how the dryer sheet affected the build-up of charges on the wool and the balloon?*

It seemed to keep charges from building up.

▶ *How might you be able to stop the "zap attack" of a plastic slide?*

Students might suggest rubbing the parts of children's clothes

that will touch the slide with dryer sheets.

55

Connections

Time: 20 minutes
Materials: dictionary with information on word origins; piece of amber and piece of fur or wool (optional)

LANGUAGE ARTS Have students use a dictionary to find the origin of the word *electricity*. (from the Greek *elektron*, which means "amber") Explain that the ancient Greeks studied static electricity. They discovered that when amber (fossilized resin) was rubbed with fur, the amber would attract objects such as feathers. If possible, use amber and fur or wool to demonstrate this phenomenon. Point out that word origins often reveal information about the meaning of the word.

Assessment
Skill: Communicating

Use the following task to assess each student's progress:

Have each student make a warning sign that tells people how to avoid being "zapped" by static electricity on a playground slide. (Examples: Use a dryer sheet to rub your clothing before going down the slide; use the slide only on days with high humidity; be careful not to touch the metal bolts.)

▶ **Activity**

Time: 20 minutes
Materials: very small pieces of paper, blown-up balloons, small piece of wool, dryer sheets

This activity works best on a cool, dry day. Have students work in pairs or small groups. Students could use confetti or small pieces of notebook paper, copier paper, or newspaper. If you are conducting this activity on a humid day, running the wool through a clothes dryer or blowing it with a hair dryer immediately before the activity may help.

The paper will eventually fall off the balloon. If students observe this, coach them to the conclusion that the opposite charges attract the paper to the balloon, but the charges eventually balance out while the balloon and paper are in contact.

Explain to students how dryer sheets work to prevent the buildup of charges. Point out that the wool and the latex balloon need to be in direct contact for the balloon to pull electrons away from the wool. Dryer sheets contain a chemical that sticks to and coats the fibers of the wool. This very thin chemical layer prevents contact between the wool and the balloon, so no charges are transferred. Have students relate this information to what they learned about humidity and water molecules in the Before You Read discussion described on page 52 of this Teacher's Edition.

Point of Lesson

Lightning is a form of static discharge.

Focus

▶ Properties and changes of properties in matter
▶ Transfer of energy
▶ Evidence, models, and explanation
▶ Change, constancy, and measurement
▶ Natural hazards

Skills and Strategies

▶ Interpreting scientific illustrations
▶ Making inferences
▶ Recognizing cause and effect

Advance Preparation

Vocabulary

Make sure students understand these terms. Definitions can be found in the glossary at the end of the student book.

▶ charge
▶ electrical energy
▶ energy
▶ negative charge
▶ positive charge
▶ static electricity

Materials

Gather the materials needed for *Before You Read* (below) and *Enrichment* (p. 57).

TEACHING PLAN pp. 56–57

INTRODUCING THE LESSON

This lesson discusses lightning as a form of electrical energy and describes the effects of lightning strikes.

Lead a class discussion to find out what students know about lightning. Students may think that lightning cannot strike twice in the same place. Explain that although this is a common saying, it is not true. In fact, many places are struck by lightning several times a year. Some tall buildings have been struck by lightning several times within just a few minutes.

Point out that many people and animals that have been struck by lightning have survived, despite the very high voltages involved. Explain that damage done to a living thing by electricity depends on voltage (strength), current (rate of delivery), and total exposure time.

▶ Before You Read

Time: 15 minutes
Materials: photographs of lightning

LIGHTNING STRIKES To help students answer the second question, provide photographs of lightning for them to examine. Use the questions in the text as the basis for a class discussion.

Students may have interesting or exciting stories to share about structures or people they know that were struck by lightning. Be aware that some students may be afraid of lightning or may have had frightening experiences. Reassure students that there is only a 1-in-600,000 chance that a person in the United States will be struck by lightning in his or her lifetime. Also explain that they can decrease their chances further by practicing lightning safety.

UNIT 2: ELECTRICITY AND MAGNETISM

How Shocking!

HOT DOG

Scientists think lightning may strike somewhere on Earth a hundred times each second.

Lightning is a form of static electricity. Like the shock you sometimes get after walking across a carpeted room, lightning is caused by the sudden release of positive or negative charges that have built up on an object. As you might have guessed, however, a lightning bolt is a lot more powerful than a carpet shock.

◀ Sport survived, but the house was damaged as shown above and below this doorway

▶ Before You Read

LIGHTNING STRIKES Lightning can be frightening, and it is dangerous. Fortunately, it's not too hard to predict when lightning is likely to happen. People can stay safe by staying indoors at those times.

▶ *When have you seen lightning? Did the lightning strike anything? What was the effect?*

Lightning usually occurs during a thunderstorm. Students may have heard a loud noise when lightning strikes. They may have seen trees split, electrical appliances damaged, and even fires started.

▶ *What did the lightning look like? Where did it seem to begin and where did it appear to go?*

Usually lightning looks like a jagged bolt, but it can also look like a ball and it can fill the sky like a sheet. It looks like it starts in the sky and goes toward the ground or just across the sky.

56

© GREAT SOURCE. COPYING IS PROHIBITED.

▶ **Read**

NOTEZONE

Underline the effect that lightning had on objects on the ground.

One day lightning struck the house of Sally Andis. Afterwards, she discovered something so strange that she told the local newspaper about it.

Dog OK after Lightning Hits

WASHINGTON, Ind. — A dog hit by lightning that struck a tree and traveled through the chain that had been holding him escaped with singed fur and a wounded paw, but no serious injuries.

After Sally Andis saw the bolt hit a tree near her rural southwestern Indiana home on Wednesday night, the dog was nowhere to be seen. The lightning broke the chain, and the heat burned a ring around the tree where the chain had been fastened. Four black paw prints were left on concrete outside the home's back door, where the dog, a beagle named Sport, had been standing.

▲ **Sport left blackened paw prints on the concrete where he was standing when lightning struck.**

When Ms. Andis found the dog, his fur was singed and his body felt hot. He was panting and bleeding from one paw. A trip to the veterinarian assured the family that Sport will be OK, but Ms. Andis told the Washington Times-Herald that the dog no longer wants to leave her side.

The family's house, about eight miles south of Washington, didn't fare so well. The lightning blew bricks 30 to 40 feet [9 to 12 meters] out of the home's foundation and damaged a door frame. Every appliance in the house had its cord blown out of the outlets, and the bolt left smoke outside and inside the house.

singed: slightly burned
rural: in the country
fastened: attached
assured: told

fare: do
foundation: the solid base on which a house is built

From: "Dog OK After Lightning Hits." *The Associated Press.*

FIND OUT MORE

SCIENCESAURUS
The Law of
Electric Charges 315
Static Electricity 316

SCI LINKS.
THE WORLD'S A CLICK AWAY
www.scilinks.org
Keyword: Static
Electricity
Code: GSPD06

57

Enrichment

Time: will vary
Materials: research sources about lightning safety procedures, poster-board, art supplies

Have students work in pairs or small groups to research lightning safety and create posters for display in the school hallways. Provide materials such as pamphlets, printouts, or videos from the American Red Cross. The following Web sites are also good sources of information:

www.weather.com/safeside/lightning/
www.lightningsafety.noaa.gov/
www.redcross.org/services/disaster/keepsafe/readythunder.html

Students may also be interested in the following site written for young-sters by a young lightning strike survivor:

www.azstarnet.com/~anubis/zaphome.htm

Provide class time for students to share their posters and discuss what they learned about lightning safety. If possible, invite a volunteer from a local safety organization to visit the class and answer students' questions. Alternatively, have your class give a safety presentation to another class in your school.

▶ **Read**

Point out that the reading came from a newspaper article, and explain that newspaper reporters use the "5 Ws" to guide them as they ask questions and write their stories. Have students create a 5 Ws graphic organizer similar to the one shown below. Encourage them to fill in the organizer as they read. When students have finished their organizers, have volunteers share their answers to the five questions. Provide time for students to discuss problems they had using the organizer and to ask any questions they have about the reading.

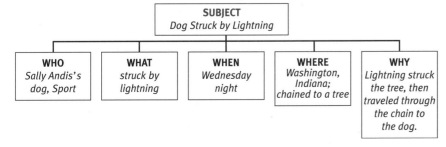

SUBJECT				
Dog Struck by Lightning				
WHO	**WHAT**	**WHEN**	**WHERE**	**WHY**
Sally Andis's dog, Sport	struck by lightning	Wednesday night	Washington, Indiana; chained to a tree	Lightning struck the tree, then traveled through the chain to the dog

CHECK UNDERSTANDING
Skill: Comparing and contrasting
Have students compare a lightning strike and the shock you get when you walk across a carpet and touch a doorknob. *What do they have in common?* (Both are caused by the build-up and discharge of static electricity.) *How do they differ?* (A lightning bolt is much more powerful than the shock from the doorknob.)

More Resources

The following resources are also available from Great Source and NSTA.

SCILINKS.
THE WORLD'S A CLICK AWAY

www.scilinks.org
Keyword: Static Electricity
Code: GSPD06

WHAT MAKES LIGHTNING STRIKE? Normally, clouds contain an even mix of negative and positive charges. During a rainstorm, however, positive charges move up to the tops of tall clouds. As a result, an overall negative charge is produced at the bottom of the clouds.

Remember that like charges repel each other. Positive charges push other positive charges away. Negative charges push other negative charges away. In this way, charges in the bottom of clouds can affect the charges that build up on objects beneath them—including the ground.

The following diagram shows storm clouds forming above a house and tree. Using the information you just learned, label the diagram to show what charges, positive (+) or negative (−), are building up in the tops and bottoms of the clouds. Then infer what charges would be building up on the tree and on the ground beneath the clouds.

Students should show negative charges on the bottom of the clouds and positive charges on the top of the clouds. They should also show positive charges on the tree and the ground surface.

Opposite charges in the clouds and on the ground want to move toward each other. But the charges do not move easily through air. So the charges try to follow the shortest, easiest path through the air.

▶ *What object in Sally Andis's yard did the lightning hit? Use what you just learned to explain why this might have happened.*

The tree. The charges took the shortest path between the base of the

clouds and the ground, so they struck the tallest object on the ground.

If you are unexpectedly caught outside in a lightning storm, experts advise that you get into a "lightning position."

▶ *Describe what you think the "lightning position" might be. How would it keep you as safe as possible?*

It would be very low to the ground as lightning takes the shortest path

between the clouds and the ground, so being lower would create a

longer path.

58

Teaching Plan pp. 58–59

WHAT MAKES LIGHTNING STRIKE? To help students complete their diagrams, have them first reread the first paragraph on this page and label the clouds. Then ask: *What kind of charges are on the bottom of the cloud?* (negative) *What effect do negative charges have on other charges?* (They push negative charges away and pull positive charges closer.) *What do you think happens to the negative charges in the ground below the storm clouds?* (They are pushed away from the clouds.) Help

students see that this would leave positive charges near the surface.

Students may wonder about charges built up on the house. Explain that positive charges would build up on the house, too. Ask: *If there were no tree next to the house, where do you think the lightning would strike, and why?* (It might strike the house because the path between the clouds and the house is shorter than the path between the clouds and the ground.)

Explain that the "lightning position" involves squatting or crouching, not lying flat on the ground. This is impor-

tant because after lightning hits the ground it may spread out along the surface. A position that minimizes your contact with the ground is therefore much safer. Also make sure students understand that lightning follows the shortest and easiest path, but it does not always strike the tallest object. It may strike the most conductive object, so it is also important to move away from metal or water.

ENERGY CHANGES All lightning starts out as electrical energy. But it is soon converted to other forms of energy.

▶ *Based on your experience and the reading, try to come up with four other forms of energy that electrical energy is converted to during a lightning strike. Draw a graphic organizer to show your ideas. Give evidence for all four of your answers.*

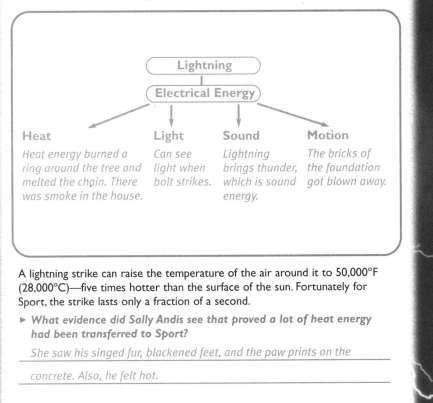

A lightning strike can raise the temperature of the air around it to 50,000°F (28,000°C)—five times hotter than the surface of the sun. Fortunately for Sport, the strike lasts only a fraction of a second.

▶ *What evidence did Sally Andis see that proved a lot of heat energy had been transferred to Sport?*

  She saw his singed fur, blackened feet, and the paw prints on the

  concrete. Also, he felt hot.

Lightning causes about 10,000 forest fires in the United States each year.

▶ *How do you think lightning might start forest fires?*

  If the air around the trees is five times hotter than the sun, that would

  be hot enough to burn the trees just like a match does.

59

Connections

MATH Tell students that an average lightning strike contains about 1 billion joules of electrical energy. Also tell them that it takes 100 joules to light a 100-watt light bulb for one second. Ask: *For how many hours could an average lightning strike light one bulb?* (about 2,778 hours) *For how many days?* (about 116) *Months?* (4)

Assessment
Skill: Sequencing

Use the following task to assess each student's progress:

Have students describe the buildup and movement of electric charges that result in a lightning strike. (Positive charges move to the tops of clouds, and negative charges move to the bottom. As a result, positive charges move to the surface of the ground below the clouds. Opposite charges from the clouds and the ground discharge, following the shortest, easiest path between them.)

▶ **Propose Explanations**

ENERGY CHANGES Review how energy changes from one form to another, using the following examples:

▶ When you turn on a light switch, electrical energy is converted to light energy.

▶ Space heaters convert electrical energy to heat, or thermal energy.

▶ Turning on a blender converts electrical energy to mechanical energy.

▶ Radios convert electrical energy to sound energy.

Students may want to refer to *ScienceSaurus* item 300 or another science reference book to review the different forms of energy.

Encourage students to review the reading when they construct the graphic organizer, paying particular attention to evidence described in the reading.

You may want to discuss the history of fire management in this country and its consequences. For many decades, forest fires, even small ones, were actively put out. The unintended result of this diligence, however, was the accumulation of flammable materials on the

forest floor. When these areas eventually caught fire, they burned hotter and longer than they naturally would, causing greater devastation. Today, the U.S. Forest Service includes controlled burns in its forest management plans.

Point of Lesson

Some animals use electrical discharge to catch their prey.

Focus

► Transfer of energy
► Structure and function in living systems
► Form and function

Skills and Strategies

► Interpreting scientific illustrations
► Recognizing cause and effect
► Making Inferences

Advance Preparation

Vocabulary

Make sure students understand these terms. Definitions can be found in the glossary at the end of the student book.

► cell
► electric charge
► electricity

► energy
► voltage
► volts

Materials

Gather the materials needed for *Introducing the Lesson* (below).

How Shocking!

Electric Eel

▲ An electric eel

The electric eel makes its own electricity in order to survive.

Electric eels are actually fresh-water fish that live in rivers in the Amazon rain forest. They can reach 3 meters (about 9 feet) in length and weigh more than 20 kilograms (about 44 pounds).

NOTEZONE

Underline what the electric eel uses to produce electricity.

FIND OUT MORE

SCIENCE SAURUS

The Law of
Electric Charges 315
Current Electricity 317
Electric Circuits 318

SCiLINKS
THE WORLD'S A CLICK AWAY
www.scilinks.org
Keyword: Static Electricity
Code: GSPD06

UNIT 2: ELECTRICITY AND MAGNETISM

60

▶ **Read**

One group of adventurers got a first-hand look at this very strange fish.

An Amazon Adventure

I heard the cry "Grab your camera and come see this!" One of the older fishermen of the area knew that we were interested in strange animals and had brought an electric eel that he had caught to the lodge....

The guides were encouraging people to touch the eel so they could feel the electric charge. When it was caught, it had discharged most of its energy and the guides were claiming that all you could feel was a slight tingling since it took some time for the animal to recharge. At full power, an electric eel has the ability to produce a charge...[strong] enough to stun or knock out a human or other large animal. Usually, the eels stun their prey and eat them when they can't move.

The charge is produced in [special] cells [called electroplates] found all along the tail of the animal. There are about 200 to 250 of these cells per centimeter of length. Larger eels...produce more energy [than smaller eels]. I declined the offer to touch it. ...I am not going to touch a big electric eel any more than I am going to stick my finger in a wall socket.

prey: an animal hunted by another

From: Frostick, Robert. *An Amazon Adventure—Electric Eel.*
(jajhs.kana.k12.wv.us/amazon/eel.htm)

TEACHING PLAN pp. 60–61

INTRODUCING THE LESSON
Time: 10 minutes
Materials: photographs of electric eels (optional)

This lesson describes the electric eel and explains how it uses electrical energy to catch its prey. Ask students who have seen electric eels in aquariums to describe the fish, or show the class photographs of electric eels.

▶ **Read**

In the reading, the writer describes his decision not to touch the electric eel. Ask students whether they think they would have touched the eel under the same circumstances. Encourage students to suggest methods they could use to determine whether it was safe to touch the eel. (Examples: watching other people touch the eel; using instruments to measure the charge) Ask: *Even if someone else had touched the eel without getting hurt, would you know that it was still safe to touch? Why or why not?* (No; the eel recharges over

time, so it could be fully charged by the time another person touched it.)

Students might be interested to know that the electric eel can produce a charge of 600–1,000 volts at a current of 1 ampere. Typical household electric outlets provide 120 volts and a current of about 100 amperes.

▶ Propose Explanations

WHAT'S THAT SHOCK? Each electroplate cell in the eel's body makes about 0.15 volts of electrical energy (about $\frac{1}{1000}$ the voltage from a wall outlet). These cells are lined up in long rows, like beads on a string. When the electroplates are all activated at once, the eel can discharge up to 600 volts of electrical energy. That's about 5 times the volts from an electrical wall outlet!

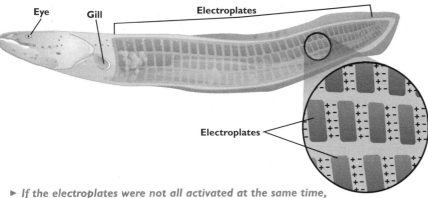

Eye   Gill   Electroplates

Electroplates

▶ *If the electroplates were not all activated at the same time, how would this affect the electric eel's ability to catch prey?*

The shock might not be great enough to stun the eel's prey, making it

hart for the eel to capture food.

In the reading, the guides said that it was not dangerous to touch the eel.

▶ *What made it safe for a few moments?*

The eel needed time to recharge.

▶ *What can you infer from this information about how an eel would need to time its attacks on prey?*

The eel would have to wait a few minutes between each attack. If the

first strike didn't work, it would have to wait before trying again.

61

More Resources

The following resources are also available from Great Source and NSTA.

SCIENCESAURUS

The Law of Electric Charges	315
Current Electricity	317
Electric Circuits	318

READER'S HANDBOOK

Reading Actively	43

SC*I*LINKS.
THE WORLD'S A CLICK AWAY

www.scilinks.org
Keyword: Static Electricity
Code: GSPD06

Assessment

Skill: Organizing information

Use the following question to assess each student's progress:

How do electric eels produce an electric shock? (They separate positive and negative charges in special cells called electroplates, then activate the cells to produce electricity.)

▶ Propose Explanations

WHAT'S THAT SHOCK? Have students look at the enlarged view of a section of electroplates, and draw their attention to the positive and negative charges that have built up. Ask: *What have you learned in this chapter about the separation and buildup of unlike charges? What do they have the potential to do?* (Students should recall from the slide and lightning examples that when opposite charges move toward each other, or discharge, an electric shock is produced.) Explain that activation of the electroplates is triggered by signals from nerve cells. The signals cause the opposite charges to move toward each other, producing a small voltage. Since the electroplates are all lined up in a long series, just as batteries are in a flashlight, together they provide enough voltage to stun anything in the water nearby, even a horse!

After students have answered the questions, discuss their answers. Ask: *Do you think the electric eel has many predators? Why or why not?* (No, because other animals would get shocked if they tried to eat the eels.)

CHECK UNDERSTANDING
Skill: Generating ideas
Point out that electric eels do not have teeth. Ask: *Why is it important for the electric eel to be able to stun its prey before eating it?* (Without teeth, the eel would probably not be able to hold onto struggling prey. Stunning the prey keeps it motionless so the eel can eat it.)

Edison at Work

LESSON 16

Try, Try Again

Point of Lesson: *Edison knew that genius was more perspiration than inspiration.*

Students are introduced to Thomas Edison through an account of the invention of the light bulb. The process of technological design is illustrated through the repeated failures Edison's team experienced while seeking a workable filament. Students explore the electrical reasons for the shape and size of light bulb filaments. They then consider how Edison's methods of dealing with the public and with failed experiments reveal the underlying values that drove him to be such a prolific inventor.

Materials

Enrichment (p. 63), for each group:
► prices and packages for 3–5 different types of light bulbs (fluorescent; regular, clear, and frosted incandescent; halogen; mercury vapor; or sodium vapor)
► sample electric bill showing price per kWh
► Light Bulb Efficiency and Cost Worksheet (copymaster page 226)

Explore (p. 64), for teacher demonstration:
► small glass jar with cork stopper
► nail
► two 50-cm lengths of insulated copper wire with ends stripped to expose wire
► 6-V dry cell battery
► several strands of thin iron wire (such as single strands of picture wire)

LESSON 17

Organized Chaos

Point of Lesson: *Edison depended both on the input of colleagues and on his own ideas.*

Students read a passage describing the main work space in Edison's Menlo Park laboratory, which was set up to encourage collaboration among all the workers. Students identify the advantages of such an arrangement and consider the importance of keeping careful records of laboratory work. They then identify words and phrases in the reading selection that indicate it is a transcript of interviews and narration.

Materials

Explore (p. 67), for the class:
► videotape and transcript of PBS program *Edison's Miracle of Light* (transcript available at www.pbs.org/wgbh/amex/edison/filmmore/transcript)

LESSON 18

Fighting Change

Point of Lesson: *Fear of the competition affected Edison's scientific decisions and behavior.*

Students discover a moment in history by reading an account of the competition between Edison's direct-current power plants and the alternating-current power plants championed by Westinghouse. Students compare the two kinds of current and how they are generated. They then consider factors that may have led Edison to work against alternating current, even though he ultimately lost this battle. Finally, students have the opportunity to research sources of energy that are used to generate electricity in their area and design a persuasive poster about one energy source.

Materials

Explore (p. 70), for teacher demonstration:
► simple hand-cranked generator with wire leads (available from most laboratory supply companies)
► flashlight bulb in socket

Take Action (p. 71), for the class:
► research sources about power plants

for each student:
► poster board
► art supplies

Background Information

Lesson 16

Edison's incandescent bulb was revolutionary, but it wasn't the first electric light source. Arc lamps were introduced at the Philadelphia Centennial Exhibition in 1876—three years before Edison produced his incandescent bulb. These lamps made use of the arc of light produced when electric current passes through an ionized gas. Most of today's homes are lighted by incandescent bulbs. However, modern versions of arc lamps—including fluorescent lamps, neon signs, mercury vapor lamps, and sodium lamps—are used to light businesses, public buildings, streets, parks, and stadiums.

In addition to meticulously detailing his investigations, Edison kept notes on other ideas, observations, and even poetry that came to him as he worked. Most of these writings have been collecting dust since Edison's death in 1931. The Thomas A. Edison Papers Project was started in 1978 to collect and publish Edison's writings so scientists and historians could study Edison's work. The Project, which is centered at Rutgers University in New Jersey, discovered more than 4 million pages of Edison's notebooks. To date, only about one-third of a million of these pages have been published in some format. For more information, visit the Project's Web site at edison.rutgers.edu/about.htm.

Point of Lesson

Edison knew that genius was more perspiration than inspiration.

Focus

► Evidence, models, and explanation
► Science as a human endeavor
► History of science
► Science and technology in society
► Transfer of energy

Skills and Strategies

► Making inferences
► Recognizing cause and effect
► Drawing conclusions

Advance Preparation

Vocabulary

Make sure students understand these terms. Definitions can be found in the glossary at the end of the student book.

► electric current
► electricity
► electron
► experiment
► patent

Materials

Gather the materials needed for *Enrichment* (p. 63) and *Explore* (p. 64).

Try, Try Again

How does someone become a great inventor? Does it take brains, hard work, or both?

Thomas Edison was one of the most famous men of his time. This creative genius patented more than 1,000 inventions. Edison is best known for his work on the incandescent light bulb and the phonograph, or record player. He even had a small studio for making silent films at his laboratory. Later, he figured out how to match sound with pictures, making it possible to create "talkies," movies with sound. Edison was often called the "Wizard of Menlo Park," named after his laboratories in Menlo Park, New Jersey.

The readings in this chapter come from the transcript of a television program (*Edison's Miracle of Light*) about Thomas Edison and the invention of the light bulb. A transcript is a written record of what people said. In this transcript, you will read what was said by the narrator of the TV program and by experts on Edison.

► **Before You Read**

▲ Edison's electric lamp

ELECTRICITY AT WORK Edison held 389 separate patents for inventions related to electric light and power. That's a lot of inventions!

► *Look around you and think about all the things you use that are powered by electricity. Make a list of ten electrical appliances in your home or school. What do these things have in common?*

Lists will vary, but will likely include television, computer and

accessories, microwave oven and other kitchen appliances, CD player,

lamp, hair dryer, various electric tools, vacuum cleaner, and so on.

Students should note that they all plug into a source of electrical

power—usually the wall socket. Some students may know that these

devices change electrical energy into another form of energy.

62

TEACHING PLAN pp. 62–63

INTRODUCING THE LESSON

This lesson introduces students to the work of Thomas Edison and describes how Edison and his team invented the first practical incandescent light bulb.

Students may not realize how recently Edison lived and worked. Explain that Edison invented the light bulb in 1879 and that the first central power station to provide electric power to homes and businesses was opened in New York in 1882. However, it was not until the 1930s that most farms and rural areas had access to electric power.

Have students calculate how long ago people started using electric power at home. Then ask: *How do you think the invention of the electric light bulb changed people's lives?* (Examples: People could work later in the evening; electric light may have been less of a fire concern than lanterns or firelight.)

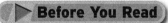
► **Before You Read**

ELECTRICITY AT WORK After students have answered the question in this section, discuss the appliances that they

listed. Encourage students to share their lists and work together to brainstorm as long a list as possible. Then choose an item from the list and ask: *How long do you think people have been using this appliance? Why do you think it was invented? How do you think this appliance has changed people's lives?* (Answers will vary based on the appliance chosen. Most electrical appliances have been in use for 100 years or less.)

▶ Read

The program narrator talks with historian Paul Israel about Edison's most important invention—the light bulb.

Edison Sets a Goal

Narrator: On this historic day—September 15th [1878]— Thomas Edison surprises reporters by announcing his biggest project yet. He says he has solved a problem that has confounded the greatest scientific minds of the nineteenth century—a practical electric lightbulb. As if that were not enough, he says he will also invent a new industry to provide electric power—mysterious invisible energy to run machines and trains. He will harness Niagara Falls to light up America and change the world. [I]ncredibly, he tells the reporters he will have it done in only six weeks....

Edison went to work. He set his Menlo Park team of engineers, mathematicians, glassblowers and draftsmen to the task of creating a practical incandescent lamp.... [They] quickly assembled a number of prototype light bulbs. Not one of them worked.

[Historian] Paul Israel: One of his assistants approached him about all these failed experiments that they had had. He said, "No, they're not failures. They taught [me] something that I didn't know. They taught me what direction to move in...."

Narrator: ...For over a year, [Edison] and his team narrowed down their search for the perfect filament. The breakthrough came in the fourteenth month. The material—a piece of lampblack scraped from the chimney of a common lantern.

confounded: confused or puzzled
harness: make use of
draftsman: person who draws diagrams and plans for an invention
incandescent: producing light by making something hot enough to glow

prototype: an early model
filament: the threadlike wire in a light bulb that electricity flows through, making it glow
lampblack: finely powdered carbon

From: "The American Experience: Edison's Miracle of Light." *PBS Online.* (www.pbs.org/wgbh/amex/edison/filmmore/transcript/index.html)

NOTEZONE

Underline the object Edison said he could invent.

Circle what Edison said he would create to make that invention usable.

FIND OUT MORE

SCIENCESAURUS

Current Electricity	317
Electric Circuits	318
Steps in Technology Design	357

SCILINKS
THE WORLD'S A CLICK AWAY

www.scilinks.org
Keyword: Light Bulbs
Code: GSPD07

63

Enrichment

Time: 30 minutes
Materials: (for each group) prices and packages for 3–5 different types of light bulbs (fluorescent; regular, clear, and frosted incandescent; halogen; mercury vapor; or sodium vapor), sample electric bill showing price per kWh, Light Bulb Efficiency and Cost Worksheet (copymaster page 226)

Have students use the packages to compare how efficiently different light bulbs convert electrical energy to light energy. Explain that the watt (W) is the unit for measuring the rate at which energy is used. The watt rating given on the package tells how much electrical energy the bulb uses when it is lit.

Also tell students that the amount of light given off by a bulb is measured in lumens and is also listed on the package. The efficiency of a bulb can be described by the ratio of lumens to watts.

Have students record the information for 3–5 different kinds of light bulbs in the chart provided on the copymaster. Then have them calculate the efficiency of each type of bulb by dividing lumens by watts.

Next, have students follow the steps on the copymaster to find the total cost of purchasing and using two different types of bulbs for their predicted lifetimes.

▶ Read

Point out that the incandescent light bulb Edison set out to create is basically the same as the standard light bulbs commonly used in homes today. Other examples of incandescent bulbs include flashlights and most car headlights. Explain that halogen bulbs are also a type of incandescent bulb.

Tell students that Edison's incandescent bulb was not the first electric light, but it was the first that was practical for indoor use.

When students have completed the reading, ask: *How did Thomas Edison use the methods of scientific inquiry in the process of inventing the light bulb?* (Examples: He made hypotheses about which materials would work in his bulb; he gathered data on both things that worked and things that did not work; he made inferences about what direction to follow.)

CHECK UNDERSTANDING
Skill: Solving problems
Ask students to write a set of instructions describing how to invent a new product, based on the steps Thomas Edison followed in inventing the incandescent bulb. (Students' instructions should include some of the following steps: decide what you want to invent, get skilled workers to help you develop and test several prototypes, keep working until you succeed.)

More Resources

The following resources are also available from Great Source and NSTA.

www.scilinks.org
Keyword: Light Bulbs
Code: GSPD07

THE FILAMENT SEARCH Some electrical appliances have wires that heat up when the appliance is switched on. A toaster oven and an electric stove are two examples.

▶ *Describe any changes you see in a toaster oven when it is turned on. What other kind of energy besides heat energy is being produced?*

It gets red. Light energy is produced.

Where there is heat, there is light, at least in wires. Edison knew that if he ran an electric current through a wire, the wire would get hot and glow, giving off light.

What makes a wire with current running through it produce heat and light? Resistance. Resistance is a measure of how much a wire resists the movement of electrons through it. The greater the resistance, the greater the amount of heat and light produced.

The amount of resistance in a wire depends on two things: how thick the wire is and how long it is. Thicker wires have less resistance than thinner wires. And shorter wires have less resistance than longer wires.

▶ *Since Edison wanted to produce light, what sort of wire do you think he chose for his light bulb, a thick or thin wire? Explain.*

He would have chosen a thin wire, as thin wires have greater resistance and therefore give off more light.

The light bulb that Edison and his team came up with had a lampblack filament. The lampblack was long and thin and wrapped into a coil shape.

▶ *Why do you suppose Edison's team wrapped the filament into a coil?*

They could fit a longer length of filament into the bulb if it was coiled. And greater length equals more resistance equals more light.

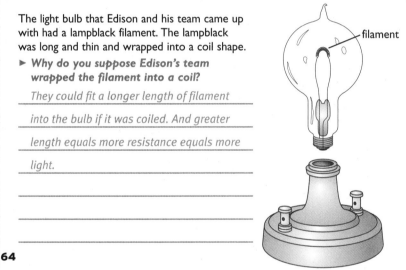

filament

64

Teaching Plan pp. 64–65

▶ Explore

Time: 30 minutes
Materials: small glass jar with cork stopper, nail, two 50-cm lengths of insulated copper wire with ends stripped to expose wire, 6-V dry cell battery, several strands of thin iron wire (such as single strands of picture wire)

Note: To save time, you may want to construct the device beforehand and simply show students how it works. However, watching you assemble the components would be a valuable learning experience for students.

THE FILAMENT SEARCH To help students visualize a filament and understand how it is used in a light bulb, perform the following demonstration. Carefully use a nail to drill two small holes in the cork stopper. Push the two copper wires through the holes so the ends hang about 5 cm below the cork. Bend the end of each copper wire into a hook so that the iron wire can be wrapped around the hooks to create a filament. Wrap several strands of iron wire together and stretch them across the space between the two copper hooks. Wrap the iron wire securely around the copper hooks. Place the

cork stopper in the jar with the filament inside the jar. Carefully connect the other ends of the copper wires to the battery terminals so the filament glows. When the filament burns out, disconnect the wires and wait for the filament to cool before opening the jar.

Ask: *How could we produce a brighter light?* (Example: Use a wire with greater resistance—a thinner wire or a longer wire.) Make a coiled filament and repeat the demonstration.

THE MIND OF AN INVENTOR Most inventions are announced to the public after they have been developed and tested. Often the press and other scientists are invited to watch a demonstration of the new product in action.

▶ *How was Edison's announcement about the light bulb different than the usual?*

Edison just talked about his idea and didn't have anything to show.

▶ *What does this tell you about Edison as a person?*

Answers will vary. Example: Edison believed that something could be done and he and his team could make it happen. Some will say he was confident and bold. Some may say he was overconfident.

Edison is famous for saying, "Genius is one percent inspiration and 99 percent perspiration."

▶ *How does the reading give clues to what Edison meant?*

The reading says it took Edison's team 14 months of failed experiments to come up with the solution to the problem of what material could be the filament in a light bulb. Edison meant that being very successful comes from a little bit of talent but mostly from sticking with a problem until it is solved.

Edison said that the unsuccessful light bulbs were not "failures." He learned what would not work and tried something different.

▶ *Describe an experience where you learned from something that might have seemed like a failure.*

Answer will vary. Look for examples where students recognize the value of not immediately getting the result they were looking for.

65

Connections

WRITING Explain that inventors usually keep detailed records of their work. In fact, Thomas Edison wrote down every detail of his investigations. Ask: *Why do you think it is important for inventors to keep detailed records of their investigations?* (Example: to keep track of what they have tried and what worked and what did not so they can apply that information to a new investigation) Encourage students to brainstorm a description of what should be included in an inventor's notebook. Then challenge students to write a notebook entry for the invention of the incandescent bulb based on what they have learned in this lesson.

Assessment
Skill: Concept mapping

Use the following task to assess each student's progress:

Have each student create a concept map to show the relationships between the following terms: *electric current, resistance, heat, light, length, thickness, wire* (Students' maps should show that electric current moving through a wire creates heat because the wire resists the movement of electrons through it. This heat produces light. Thinner, longer wires have more resistance and therefore produce a brighter light.)

▶ **Propose Explanations**

THE MIND OF AN INVENTOR You might want to introduce the concepts of public relations and advertising at this point or later in the chapter. Point out that Edison's laboratory was almost always open to the press and that Edison often tried to keep his work in the public eye. Ask: *How do you think this helped Edison in his work?* (Example: It helped him create public interest in his products.) *Do you think it helped the public, too? If so, how?* (Example: It helped people learn about new inventions that they could use in their daily lives.) Encourage students to discuss any possible disadvantages to Edison's use of public relations. (Some of his ideas might have been picked up by other inventors and used to make rival products.)

Have students go back to the reading and compare how long Edison said it would take him and his team to invent the incandescent light bulb and how long it actually took. (predicted: 6 weeks; actual: 14 months) Ask: *Why did it take so much longer than Edison expected?* (Edison's team could not find just the right filament.)

After students have answered the questions in this section, ask: *What do you think other inventors could learn from Thomas Edison?* (Examples: Don't give up until you find a solution; don't rule out any possibilities until you have tested them.)

Point of Lesson

Edison depended both on the input of colleagues and on his own ideas.

Focus

▶ Systems, order, and organization
▶ Understanding about scientific inquiry
▶ Understanding about science and technology
▶ Science as a human endeavor
▶ Nature of science

Skills and Strategies

▶ Understanding that scientists share their results to form a common core of knowledge
▶ Drawing conclusions
▶ Evaluating source material

Advance Preparation

Vocabulary

Make sure students understand these terms. Definitions can be found in the glossary at the end of the student book.

▶ data
▶ experiment
▶ laboratory

Materials

Gather the materials needed for *Explore* (p. 67).

TEACHING PLAN pp. 66–67

Organized Chaos

Edison's research was a group science project that lasted for years.

People often imagine that inventors work all alone in a laboratory. But Edison's approach to inventing was very different.

▲ Edison's laboratory

NOTEZONE

Underline the sentences that describe how Edison worked together with his team.

(Circle) the sentences that describe how Edison separated himself from his team.

▶ **Read**

Later in the transcript, Edison biographer Neil Baldwin talks about Edison's approach to inventing.

A Flitting Butterfly

[Biographer] Neil Baldwin: The second floor of [his research laboratory] was an unobstructed space, like a loft space, you might say. Several people could be working together on one thing, and there were all these notebooks that were next to each project, that were open, that you would write in. You know, whatever you were doing, you would make an entry on that. And Edison was constantly circulating throughout the hall, stopping here and stopping there and working with all the different people all the time, sort of like a butterfly almost, flitting from one flower to another. And then he had his own desk off in the corner by the window, facing the wall. If he sat there, then you weren't supposed to bother him.

I think his hearing loss definitely was one of the reasons why he was able to screen out a lot of buzz from the outside world…. People would say to him, "Why don't you invent a hearing aid? Isn't that an obvious thing for you to want to discover?" He would say, "I want to have this condition, because it helps me be a better creator and a better inventor."

unobstructed: not closed up, open
loft: large open space at the top of a building

circulating: moving around
flitting: moving quickly from place to place

From: "The American Experience: Edison's Miracle of Light." *PBS Online.*
(www.pbs.org/wgbh/amex/edison/filmmore/transcript/index.html)

FIND OUT MORE

SCIENCE**SAURUS**
Current Electricity 317
Electric Circuits 318
Asking Scientific
Questions 003
Doing Research 005

UNIT 2: ELECTRICITY AND MAGNETISM

66

INTRODUCING THE LESSON

This lesson describes Thomas Edison's cooperative laboratory, where teams of people worked on many different projects at once.

Have students describe what they think of when they hear the word *inventor*. Students may think of inventors as solitary figures, working alone and in secret. Explain that Edison developed a new way for inventors to work by building a research laboratory and a production factory in the same place. Products that were invented at Edison's "invention factory" could be produced in the factory and sold to the public, often at

low prices. Many modern companies follow this model.

▶ **Read**

After students read the excerpt, discuss the work environment in Edison's laboratory. Ask: *How was Edison's laboratory like a classroom?* (Example: People worked together on projects, and Edison's desk—like a teacher's desk—was in the same room.) *Do you think you would have enjoyed working there? Why or why not?* (Some students may think the environment would have been creative and fun, while others may

think the noise and collaboration would have been distracting.)

Point out that there could be many different projects going on at once. Ask: *Why do you think having different projects underway was better than having everyone work on the same project?* (Examples: It made people more creative because there were more ideas being generated; people working on different projects might come up with ideas that could help one another.)

AN INVENTOR'S WORKSHOP To an outsider, Edison's laboratory might have looked disorganized. It also might have surprised some people to see the boss moving among his workers, rather than working in a separate office.

▶ *What do you think might be some advantages to Edison's open-space laboratory and his way of supervising his workers?*

Answers will vary. Example: People could see everyone else, so it was

easy to ask for help or an opinion from another worker. Edison could see

his workers if he wanted to, or turn his back on them if he needed to

concentrate. His way of wandering around the lab was casual, so it

wouldn't make workers nervous to see the boss checking on their work.

Although Edison's laboratory may have looked disorganized, its research methods were not. In science, it is very important to keep careful records of observations and data from experiments. Next to each experiment in Edison's laboratory sat a notebook.

▶ *Why do you think keeping notebooks by each experiment was better than having each worker carry around his or her own notebook?*

The notebook made it possible for workers to read the observations and

data of others and see what had been done before. They could then use

this information when considering their own questions or planning their

own experiments.

COMPARING SPOKEN AND WRITTEN WORDS The excerpts you have read are from a transcript of the television program, *Edison's Miracle of Light*. A transcript is a written record of everything that was said in a discussion.

▶ *Read the transcript paragraphs in this lesson carefully. What clues tell you that biographer Neil Baldwin was talking, not reading from a written script? Explain your reasoning.*

He uses very informal language, such as "you know" and "sort of." You

wouldn't expect words like that in the book he wrote about Edison.

67

More Resources

The following resources are also available from Great Source.

SCIENCESAURUS

Asking Scientific Questions	003
Doing Research	005
Current Electricity	317
Electric Circuits	318

WRITE SOURCE 2000

Watching Documentaries	358

Assessment
Skill: Generating questions

Use the following task to assess each student's progress:

Imagine you are a researcher trying to discover whether Edison's laboratory is more productive than a more traditional laboratory. What questions would you ask in your research? (Example: How many successful new products are developed in Edison's laboratory in one year compared with the number developed by the same number of people working in a traditional laboratory?)

AN INVENTOR'S WORKSHOP Have students describe what they see in the laboratory pictured on page 66. Tell them that Edison and his colleagues experimented with many different materials and kept the laboratory well-stocked. Ask: *Why do you think people might have thought the laboratory looked disorganized?* (Example: With so many people working on different projects and testing many different materials, the laboratory was probably crowded and cluttered.)

Time: 1 hour (You may need to divide the viewing into two sessions.)
Materials: videotape and transcript of PBS program *Edison's Miracle of Light* (transcript available at www.pbs.org/wgbh/amex/edison/filmmore/transcript/)

COMPARING SPOKEN AND WRITTEN WORDS Show the videotape to the class, and allow students to follow the written transcript as they watch.
Caution: The program contains a graphic description of the first execution conducted by electric chair, which may be disturbing to some students.

CHECK UNDERSTANDING
Skill: Making inferences
Ask: *How do you think Edison's partial hearing loss might have made him a better inventor?* (Example: It allowed him to focus on whatever he was thinking about and not be distracted by what was going on around him.)

Point of Lesson

Fear of the competition affected Edison's scientific decisions and behavior.

Focus

▶ Systems, order, and organization
▶ Risks and benefits
▶ Science and technology in society
▶ Science as a human endeavor
▶ History of science

Skills and Strategies

▶ Making inferences
▶ Comparing and contrasting
▶ Interpreting scientific illustrations
▶ Drawing conclusions

Advance Preparation

Vocabulary

Make sure students understand these terms. Definitions can be found in the glossary at the end of the student book.

▶ electron   ▶ power
▶ energy   ▶ technology
▶ magnet   ▶ voltage

Materials

Gather the materials needed for *Explore* (p. 70) and *Take Action* (p. 71).

68

Fighting Change

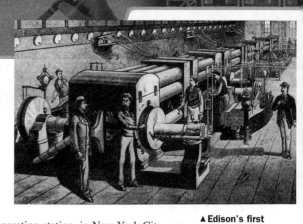
▲ Edison's first electric lighting station

Edison was not just an inventor. He was also a very successful businessman—for a while.

Edison's first electric power generating station, in New York City, was opened in 1882. By the year 1887, there were one hundred and twenty-one Edison central power stations generating electricity in the United States. Each power station was surrounded by the homes and businesses that used the electricity. All the lamps and equipment used in homes and businesses had been made in factories owned by Edison. So it seemed that it would be only a matter of time before Edison would become very wealthy. But when a competitor came along, Edison seemed to lose his confidence.

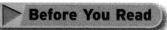
▶ Before You Read

THINK ABOUT IT Sometimes competition is fun, but sometimes it's scary. People react differently to a challenge. For instance, you might eagerly accept an invitation to play in a tennis match against a well-known older player. Or you might be afraid of looking bad and turn down the invitation, saying that you're too busy to play.

▶ *Think of a time when you, or someone you know, was offered a challenge. Describe that person's reaction. Was the challenge taken as a threat or as an opportunity for friendly competition? Was the challenge accepted or did the person find a reason to avoid the situation? Why do you suppose the person reacted as they did?*

Answers will vary. Example: I knew someone who was really good at

math and loved doing hard math problems. Everyone said she should

be on the math team, but she kept saying she didn't think it would be

fun. I think she might have just been scared of making a mistake and

looking foolish.

68

TEACHING PLAN pp. 68–69

INTRODUCING THE LESSON
This lesson describes the development of alternating current and explains how Edison reacted to the threat of competition.

Encourage students to discuss how they think competition works in the business world. Ask: *What happens when a company makes a successful new product? How do other companies react?* (Example: Other companies try to make similar products; some companies may go out of business if their product is replaced by the new product.)

Students may think that science is essentially an intellectual activity and is not affected by financial concerns or human emotions. Point out that science takes place in the real world, and real-world considerations apply, including personalities. Scientists are real people and are often driven by the same fears and concerns that affect other people.

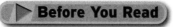
▶ Before You Read

THINK ABOUT IT Encourage students to talk about the different reactions people might have to being challenged.

Ask: *Why might someone be excited about a challenge? Why might someone be afraid?* (Example: People might be excited by the chance to test their skill and learn something new; people might be afraid of looking bad or losing something important to them.) Ask students to describe what they think are some positive responses to losing a competition and what they think are negative responses. (Students may say that congratulating the winner or making improvements in your work or play are positive responses, while giving up and making negative statements about the winner are negative responses.)

▶ Read

Here's what was said in the television show *Edison's Miracle of Light* about Edison and how he reacted when new competition came on the scene.

Edison vs. Westinghouse

Narrator: ...Edison had shown the world how profitable electric power could be, but now other inventors and other businessmen wanted part of the action. Competitors began rushing into the field with rival products and technological refinements. One of the most threatening of these new competitors was George Westinghouse. Westinghouse challenged Edison with a brand-new system based on high-voltage alternating current. Edison's direct-current power plants could only send electricity a mile or so—any farther away and lightbulbs grew dim—but Westinghouse's newly-developed technology could reach for hundreds of miles with little loss of power. The advantages of alternating current were obvious to most people, but Edison could not or would not see them....

[Biographer] Neil Baldwin: The reason Edison was so against alternating current was not only because it was proposed by a compet[itor], but because, on some level, he saw it as the wave of the future and he saw that ultimately it would win and triumph, and he could see the seeds of his destruction there.

Rather than adapt to the new technology, the inventor who had once been so visionary now decided to fight against change. He launched a new propaganda campaign denouncing alternating current as too dangerous.

profitable: making money
competitors: challengers
rival: similar
refinements: improvements
alternating current: electric current that reverses direction back and forth
direct current: electric current that does not reverse direction

ultimately: in the end, eventually
seeds of his destruction: events that would later lead to failure
visionary: full of new ideas
propaganda: one-sided information
campaign: long-term effort to convince
denouncing: criticizing strongly

From: "The American Experience: Edison's Miracle of Light." *PBS Online.* (www.pbs.org/wgbh/amex/edison/filmmore/transcript/index.html)

NOTEZONE

Underline ways in which Westinghouse's system differed from Edison's.

FIND OUT MORE

SCIENCESAURUS

Current Electricity	317
Electric Circuits	318
Research Bias	368
Tradeoffs	369

69

Enrichment

Tell students that the alternating current proposed by Westinghouse eventually won out over Edison's direct current and is the type provided by electric companies today. Challenge students to imagine what the world would be like today if Edison had succeeded in convincing people not to use alternating current. (Example: Under Edison's system, there would have to be a power supply station every mile or so, and anyone farther than one mile from a power station would not have a source of electricity.) Have students write a brief newspaper or magazine article describing what the United States would be like today if Edison's system were still in use. Encourage students to be creative as they imagine the consequences of using direct current to provide electricity. Ask students to consider the following questions: *Would every house and business have electricity? How would the system affect the distribution of people?* Provide class time for students to share their ideas.

▶ Read

Students may be interested to know that Westinghouse did not invent the system of high-voltage alternating current. The system was developed by Nikola Tesla, a scientist who briefly worked for Thomas Edison. Westinghouse hired Tesla and bought the rights to use his invention. The rivalry between Tesla and Edison has been the subject of several books, feature films, and even an opera.

After students have completed the NoteZone activity, ask volunteers to read the text they underlined. Point out that the narrator claims that the advantages of alternating current were obvious to most people. Ask: *Why do you think Edison was so resistant to alternating current?* (Example: He wanted his system to be used so he could profit from it.) *How do you think Edison could have used the new technology to his advantage?* (Students may say that Edison could have developed a better way of using alternating current, or he could have tried to work with Westinghouse so they could both profit.)

CHECK UNDERSTANDING
Skill: Comparing and contrasting
Ask: *How was Westinghouse's system for delivering electricity an improvement over Edison's?* (Westinghouse's system allowed electricity to travel for hundreds of miles with little loss of power. Edison's system could send electricity only a mile or so.)

More Resources

The following resources are also available from Great Source.

Connections

MUSIC Explain that Thomas Edison made a major contribution to music by inventing the phonograph, the first device that could record and play back sound. The first recordings were made on tin foil wrapped around cylinders and could be played only a few times. Later cylinders were made of hard wax. Eventually, other companies began producing disk-shaped records, which became very popular.

(continued on page 71)

▶ Explore

COMPARING AC AND DC Electricity is the movement of electrons. Wires are made of metal, and metals have lots of loose electrons. So how do you produce electricity in a wire? You get those electrons to start moving. And how do you do this? With a magnet. All you have to do to produce electricity in a closed loop of wire is to move the wire past a magnet.

If the wire is moved past the magnet in one direction, the electrons will move through the wire in one direction. But if the wire is moved back and forth past the magnet, the electrons will move through the wire in alternating directions.

▶ *Look at the diagrams below. One shows direct current (DC). The other shows alternating current (AC). Based on what you just learned, label each diagram "DC" or "AC." Also indicate which system was used by Edison and which was used by Westinghouse.*

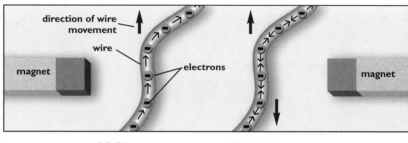

direction of wire movement

wire

magnet

electrons

magnet

<u>DC, Edison</u>　　　　<u>AC, Westinghouse</u>

When you send either kind of electricity over very long distances, you always lose some power. Westinghouse and Edison were in agreement on that fact. Both men knew they would have to start out with extremely high voltage electricity at the power plant in order for the electricity to make it out to distant homes and businesses. Voltage is "oomph." With enough voltage, electricity can move long distances over wires. But high voltage is also extremely dangerous. If you sent it into people's houses you could kill them!

What Westinghouse knew that Edison didn't was how to build a little device called a transformer. A transformer can raise or lower the voltage of AC electricity.

▶ *How could Westinghouse use a transformer to keep people safe in their homes but still send out high-voltage electricity from the power plant?*

He could send out high-voltage electricity to get it to a wide area, but

then use the transformer to reduce the voltage just before it went into

people's houses.

70

▶ Explore

Time: 15 minutes
Materials: (for teacher demonstration) simple hand-cranked generator with wire leads (available from most laboratory supply companies), flashlight bulb in socket

COMPARING AC AND DC Help students understand that an electric current is created in a wire either when the wire is moving past a magnet or when a magnet is moving past the wire. The idea behind producing either AC or DC electricity is that the mechanical energy of a wire and magnet moving past

each other can be converted to electrical energy if the wire is part of a closed circuit. Demonstrate by using a hand generator to light a light bulb. (Attach each lead from the generator to one of the socket clips and rotate the crank.)

Invite students to describe other places they may have noticed or even participated in the conversion of mechanical energy to electrical energy. Some may have seen hand-cranked radios or bicycle lights that use the energy of a spinning wheel. Explain that generators convert mechanical energy into electrical energy, and electric motors convert electrical energy into mechanical energy.

Remind students that in Lesson 16, they read about Edison's intention to "harness Niagara Falls to light up America." Ask: *What role might Niagara Falls have played in Edison's plan to provide electricity to his customers?* (He could have used the mechanical energy of the falling water to move a magnet or a wire to produce electricity.)

TEACHING PLAN pp. 70–71

UNDERSTANDING EDISON Edison was an inventor. But he was also a business owner. Banks had given him money to build his electrical power companies. It took a long time for him to make his companies profitable.

▶ *Why do you think Edison the business person was against AC electricity?*

Because he knew AC was better than DC and didn't want any competition

to threaten his investment. He might have realized that if he didn't stop

it at the beginning, his company would not be able to compete.

Actually, Edison didn't completely understand AC electricity. He had taught himself most of what he knew about science. He didn't have all the necessary math skills to understand AC electricity.

▶ *How might Edison's education have affected his response to AC electricity?*

Since he didn't understand the science and math of AC electricity, he

might have been afraid to work with it. He might have felt angry about it,

or scared that he would be left out.

> ## ▶ Take Action

WHERE DOES YOUR POWER COME FROM? To create electricity, either a wire is moved past a magnet, or a magnet is moved past a wire. That movement takes energy. So, in order to generate electricity, power plants first need some other source of energy. Some burn a fuel such as oil for energy. Others get their energy from nuclear reactions, and some get energy from the power of waterfalls.

People disagree about what the best source of energy for generating electricity is. Do research to find out what sources of energy are used in power plants in your area. Then find out the pros and cons of using that type of energy. Decide whether you think this is the best possible source of energy for your area, or whether you think another source would be better.

▶ *Make a poster to show your position. Make your poster persuasive by showing important facts and using interesting graphics.*

71

(continued from page 70)

If possible, have students listen to the early Edison recordings, available at www.pbs.org/wgbh/amex/edison/sfeature/songs.html.

Assessment
Skill: Drawing conclusions

Use the following task to assess each student's progress:

Ask students to use the information in the reading to compare the way a scientist might react to a new idea with the way a businessperson might react. Then have them determine whether Thomas Edison was acting as a scientist or a businessperson when he opposed the introduction of alternating current. (Example: A scientist would compare the new idea with the old idea and maybe try to further improve on it. A businessperson would consider whether the new idea could be used to make money or whether it would hurt the business. Thomas Edison was acting as a businessperson when he opposed alternating current.)

> ## ▶ Propose Explanations

UNDERSTANDING EDISON Encourage students to put themselves in Edison's place and imagine how they would feel if they saw that their success was threatened. Ask: *How would you feel if you thought all your hard work was going to waste? What if you couldn't understand the new technology well enough to use it yourself?* These questions may help students answer the questions in this section.

> ## ▶ Take Action

Time: will vary
Materials: research sources about power plants, posterboard, art supplies

WHERE DOES YOUR POWER COME FROM? Provide research materials, or help students locate appropriate materials. Online resources can be found by searching the Department of Energy Web site at www.energy.com. In addition, your local utility company may be able to provide information in print or online resources.

Encourage students to identify the sources of mechanical energy that are currently being used to generate electricity in your area, and to research alternative energy sources. Point out that some alternative energy resources are more practical in some parts of the country than in others. For example, solar power may not be practical in a rainy Northwestern climate, and hydroelectric power is not feasible in a desert region.

It's Magnetic

LESSON 19

Tongues of Flame

Point of Lesson: *Earth is surrounded by a magnetic field that bends inward near the poles.*

An arctic explorer's description of the aurora borealis introduces students to the topic of Earth's magnetic field. Students interpret a diagram of Earth's magnetic field and use it to explain why auroras are more often visible in areas near the poles than in areas near the equator.

Materials

Introducing the Lesson (p. 72), for the class:

▶ globe or world map

LESSON 20

Coming Home

Point of Lesson: *Some animals seem to be sensitive to Earth's magnetic field and use it to navigate.*

Students begin the lesson by thinking about ways they navigate on land. They then read a newspaper article describing some evidence that sea turtles may use Earth's magnetic field to navigate in the ocean. On a map showing the migratory route of loggerhead turtles, students identify places where sensing the magnetic field would help keep turtles on track. Next, students explain how the results of an experiment support the hypothesis that turtles can sense magnetic fields. Finally, students do research to find out what other animals may be able to sense Earth's magnetic field.

Materials

Before You Read (p. 74), for teacher demonstration:

▶ directional compass

Enrichment (p. 75), for each group:

▶ directional compass
▶ 50 m of string with marks at 5-m intervals
▶ 5 index cards
▶ marker or pencil
▶ Migratory Routes (copymaster page 227)

Explore (p. 76), for the class:

▶ world map or globe

Propose Explanations (p. 76), for teacher demonstration:

▶ 1 spool insulated wire
▶ scissors or wire stripper
▶ 6-V battery
▶ directional compass
▶ ring stand with support rod
▶ knife switch and connecting wire

LESSON 21

On the Fast Track

Point of Lesson: *The attractive and repulsive forces of magnetism can be used to improve train travel.*

Students explore a practical application of electromagnets—maglev trains. After reading a newspaper article about magnetically levitated trains, students interpret diagrams that show the way electromagnets are used to both raise and propel these trains. The lesson ends with an activity in which students first build a model electromagnetic train, then compare their model with a real maglev train.

Materials

Before You Read (p. 78), the class:

▶ 2 bar magnets

Enrichment (p. 79), for the class:

▶ atlas or other resource that gives distances between U.S. cities

Explore (p. 80), for each student or pair:

▶ 2 bar magnets

Activity (p. 81), for each pair or group:

▶ 6-volt dry cell
▶ scissors or wire stripper
▶ long steel nail
▶ paper clips
▶ plastic-covered copper wire (1 m)
▶ 4 drinking glasses
▶ square piece of cardboard
▶ tape

Laboratory Safety

Review the following safety guidelines with students before they do the Activity in this lesson.

▶ Use care when handling the scissors, nail, and other sharp objects.
▶ If you are not sure how to strip wire using scissors, ask your teacher for help.
▶ Leave the electromagnet connected to the battery only as long as needed to complete the activity, and make sure to disconnect it when you are finished.

Background Information

Lesson 19

The term *solar flare* refers to the periodic, sudden eruptions of the sun's surface that send charged particles (electrons and protons) streaming outward. These flares create a solar wind of charged particles that travels toward Earth at nearly the speed of light. When the incoming charged particles collide with gas molecules in Earth's atmosphere, they excite the molecules, causing them to emit different colors of light. We see this light show as an aurora.

Lesson 20

Biologists have studied the migration of sea turtles for decades, but it is only relatively recently that individual turtles could be tracked with some degree of reliability. Early work on sea turtle migration involved tagging turtles when they were on a beach, then watching for the tagged turtles in other areas along their suspected migration route. In the late twentieth century, new technology enabled scientists to start tracking turtles by satellite. A satellite transmitter is attached to the back of an adult or nearly adult turtle. When the turtle surfaces, its unique transmitter signal is picked up by one or more satellites. For a number of reasons, the system is not foolproof. It does, however, provide far more data than the old method. Information about "adopting" a specific sea turtle and tracking its progress is available at the Caribbean Conservation Corporation's Sea Turtle Survival League Web site: www.cccturtle.org.

Point of Lesson

Earth is surrounded by a magnetic field that bends inward near the poles.

Focus

► Structure of the earth system
► Motion and forces
► Evidence, models, and explanation

Skills and Strategies

► Interpreting scientific illustrations
► Recognizing cause and effect
► Making inferences

Advance Preparation

Vocabulary

Make sure students understand these terms. Definitions can be found in the glossary at the end of the student book.

► atmosphere   ► magnet
► aurora   ► magnetic field
► force   ► pole

Materials

Gather the materials needed for *Introducing the Lesson* (below).

TONGUES OF FLAME

What's that up in the sky?

Nineteenth-century polar explorers had to be hardy and courageous. They saw their adventure as a test of their character. They also hoped to become rich and famous. But when they saw the northern lights—also called the aurora borealis—they became poets. The aurora is a spectacular light show that occurs in the skies mainly near Earth's north and south poles. In 1893, the crew of the Norwegian ship *Fram* was treated to one such light show as they were trapped in the arctic ice around the north pole.

▲ Aurora borealis

UNIT 2: ELECTRICITY AND MAGNETISM

NOTEZONE

Underline the action verbs that describe the aurora.

FIND OUT MORE

SCIENCESAURUS
Electricity and
Magnetism   314
Magnetism   320

SCILINKS.
THE WORLD'S A CLICK AWAY

www.scilinks.org
Keyword: Earth's
Magnetic Field
Code: GSPD08

72

Fram sailor Fridtjof Nansen was so moved by seeing the northern lights that he wrote about it in his journal.

Aurora in the Sky

Presently the aurora borealis shakes over the vault of heaven its veil of glittering silver—changing now to green, now to red. It spreads, it contracts again, in restless change, next it breaks into waving, many-folded bands of shining silver, over which shoots billows of glittering rays; and then the glory vanishes. Presently it shimmers in tongues of flame over the very zenith; and then again it shoots a bright ray right up from the horizon, until the whole melts away in the moonlight, and it is as though one heard the sigh of a departing spirit. Here and there are left a few waving streamers of light, vague as a foreboding—they are the dust from the aurora's glittering cloak.

vault: arch that forms a ceiling
billows: big waves
zenith: the highest point
horizon: where the sky seems to meet earth or sea

vague: dim or unclear
foreboding: a feeling that something bad will happen
cloak: long, loose coat

From Savage, Candace. *Aurora: The Mysterious Northern Lights.* Sierra Club Books.

TEACHING PLAN pp. 72–73

INTRODUCING THE LESSON

Time: 10 minutes
Materials: globe or world map

This lesson explains how Earth's magnetic field and charged particles from the sun interact to produce the magnificent displays of light known as *auroras*.

Explain that auroras occur at both the north and south poles of Earth. Point out these areas on a globe or world map. Tell students that the light show that occurs at the north pole is called the *aurora borealis*, and the show that occurs at the south pole is called the *aurora australis*.

► Read

After students have completed the NoteZone activity, ask volunteers to identify the verbs they underlined. Then ask students to explain what makes the writing in the excerpt so poetic. Ask: *Is it only the verbs, or are there other poetic words in the reading?* Have students locate other poetic words. (nouns such as *vault, veil, glory,* and *spirit* and adjectives such as *glittering* and *restless*)

Next, challenge students to rewrite the excerpt, substituting more scientific language for the poetic phrases. For example, instead of "vault of heaven," students might use the word "sky." Discuss whether the different descriptions have different effects on the reader. Ask: *Which description do you think is more factual? Which one makes you want to see the aurora?* (Some students may prefer the poetic version because it is more descriptive, while others may think the scientific description is easier to understand.)

46

▶ Explore

WHAT CAUSES AN AURORA? What do you think of when you hear the word *magnet*? You might picture a horseshoe magnet or the bar magnet on a toy. You probably don't, however, think about Earth. But Earth too acts as a sort of giant magnet.

Like any magnet, Earth has a north and south pole. It also has a magnetic field that surrounds it. This magnetic field acts like a shield, protecting Earth from charged particles that come towards it from the sun.

Look at the diagram below. It shows the magnetic lines of force that describe the shape of the magnetic field around Earth.

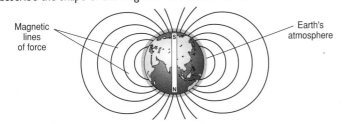

Magnetic lines of force

Earth's atmosphere

▶ **What do you notice about the lines of force near the poles? How are they different from the lines of force near other parts of Earth?**

The lines come down into the poles. They don't form a shield here as they do around other parts of the planet.

▶ **Imagine charged particles coming in from the sun toward Earth. Where do you think the particles would be most likely to enter Earth's atmosphere?**

at the poles, where the lines do not form a shield

Auroras form where charged particles from the sun enter Earth's atmosphere.

▶ **Look at a map of Earth. Why do you think auroras are more likely to be seen in Alaska and New Zealand than in Mexico and Texas?**

Alaska and New Zealand are near Earth's magnetic poles, where the lines of force do not form a shield to protect the atmosphere from charged particles. So here the particles enter the atmosphere and create the auroras. Mexico and Texas are near the equator, where the lines of force protect Earth from the incoming charged particles.

73

More Resources

The following resources are also available from Great Source and NSTA.

SCIENCE SAURUS
Electricity and Magnetism   314
Magnetism   320

READER'S HANDBOOK
Reading Know-how:
   Kinds of Paragraphs   55
Focus on Language: Examining
   Figurative Language   426

WRITE SOURCE 2000
Sample Science Observation
   Report   212

SCILINKS
THE WORLD'S A CLICK AWAY

www.scilinks.org
Keyword: Earth's Magnetic Field
Code: GSPD08

Assessment
Skill: Using space/time relationships

Use the following task to assess each student's progress:

Ask students to explain the role of magnetism in creating auroras. (Earth's magnetic field surrounds it, forming a shield. At the poles, however, the field bends inward, allowing charged particles from the sun to enter the atmosphere and create auroras.)

▶ Explore

WHAT CAUSES AN AURORA? Clarify for students that the bar magnet shown inside Earth in the diagram does not really exist. It is included only to show that the magnetic field around Earth is the same as what you would expect if there were a magnet inside.

Also explain that the magnetic south pole of Earth is located near the geographic north pole (and vice versa). A compass needle points to geographic north because the north pole of the magnetized needle is attracted to Earth's magnetic south pole.

Students may think they need to know where the sun is in the diagram to predict where the particles enter the atmosphere. Tell students to imagine that the particles are coming from all directions. Ask: *What would happen to particles entering from the east?* (They would strike the magnetic lines of force.) *From the north?* (They would not be blocked by the lines of force but could enter the atmosphere.) *South?* (same as north) *West?* (same as east)

CHECK UNDERSTANDING
Skill: Comparing and contrasting
Ask: *What happens when charged particles from the sun approach Earth's atmosphere near the equator?* (They are stopped by Earth's magnetic field.) *What happens when charged particles approach the atmosphere near the poles?* (They enter the atmosphere and cause the aurora.)

Point of Lesson

Some animals seem to be sensitive to Earth's magnetic field and use it to navigate.

Focus

► Evidence, models, and explanation
► Structure and function in living systems
► Motion and forces

Skills and Strategies

► Interpreting scientific illustrations
► Making inferences
► Recognizing cause and effect
► Communicating

Advance Preparation

Vocabulary

Make sure students understand this term. The definition can be found in the glossary at the end of the student book.

► magnetic field

Materials

Gather the materials needed for *Before You Read* (below), *Enrichment* (p. 75), *Explore* (p. 76), and *Propose Explanations* (p. 76).

Coming Home

How would you find your way home if you were in the middle of the ocean?

The migration route of a loggerhead turtle is more than 12,000 kilometers long and takes anywhere from 5–10 years to complete. Turtles can't read maps, so how do they find their way along this amazing journey? Scientists have found that these turtles have their own built-in navigation system based on magnetism. This system lets them know at any time exactly where they are on Earth, and what direction they are heading!

▲ A loggerhead turtle

 **Before You Read**

FINDING YOUR WAY People use different tools and clues to help them find their way when they travel. Maps show us where we are, and the streets or paths we need to take to get somewhere else. Or maybe we already know where we are going, but we use certain objects as clues to know when and where to make the correct turns to get us there.

► *Think about the route you take to school each morning. Maybe you walk, or maybe you are driven. What clues from the environment (objects) do you use that tell you the correct route to take?*

Answers will vary. Example: I follow directions from road signs. I also use objects such as mail boxes, stoplights, and buildings as clues for where to turn to stay on course. For example, I know that I go straight until I get to the traffic light and then I go left at the gas station.

A compass is a tool that uses Earth's magnetic field to tell you which direction you should go in order to head north, south, east, or west.

► *Describe a situation where having a compass might be helpful to you.*

A compass would be helpful if I were in the woods and there were no signs to follow. Or if I were out at sea and couldn't tell which direction I was heading.

74

TEACHING PLAN pp. 74–75

INTRODUCING THE LESSON
This lesson explains why scientists think sea turtles use Earth's magnetic field to navigate.

Ask students what they know about animal migration. Students may give examples of geese or other migratory birds, caribou, or monarch butterflies. Ask: *How do you think these animals find their way along their journeys?* Students may think that the animals are taught by their parents or that they follow an older animal. Explain that sea turtles typically travel alone and that they begin their migratory journey as soon as they hatch. Tell students that

these amazing facts made scientists wonder how sea turtles found their way.

▶ **Before You Read**

Time: 5 minutes
Materials: directional compass

FINDING YOUR WAY In addition to describing routes they travel every day, encourage students to talk about trips they have made less frequently, such as visiting a museum or a relative's house. Ask: *How many times do you have to go somewhere before you know the way? If you have gone some-*

where only once before, what clues let you know you are going the right way? (Example: I know the way after three trips. On my second trip, I recognize landmarks.)

Show students how to use a compass to find north, south, east, and west. Also familiarize them with the heading degrees—0° through 360°. Explain that Earth's magnetic field is not strong enough to influence most magnetic objects, but it is strong enough to influence the small magnetized needle in a compass.

▶ Read

Kathy Wollard, who writes for the newspaper *Newsday*, answers science questions from young readers. Here she answers a question about the wandering ways of sea turtles.

Magnetic Personalities

"How can sea turtles find their way back to the place where they were born after many years to lay eggs?" asks Ving Kim of Flushing, [New York].

Scientists think sea turtles navigate the oceans by sensing Earth's magnetic fields and following them like a map.

Arcing out from the north and south ends of our planet is an invisible magnetic force field... Overall, Earth's magnetic field is only approximately 1/20,000th as strong as that of a refrigerator magnet, so it can't attract paper clips. But it can influence a swinging compass needle—or a traveling sea turtle.

In experiments with newborn sea turtles, when scientists changed the direction of a magnetic field in a saltwater tank, swimming turtles would change direction, too. Baby sea turtles apparently sense both the direction and intensity of the Earth's field. Regional magnetic fields are like navigational buoys to turtles in the open sea, helping them to stay on course and swim in the warmest, food-rich currents.

navigate: steer a course
arcing: following a curved line
intensity: strength
regional: in a small area

buoys: floating objects that mark a spot
currents: moving rivers of ocean water

From: Wollard, Kathy. "Sea Turtles' Magnetic Personalities." *Newsday.*

NOTEZONE

Underline how Earth's magnetic field influences a traveling sea turtle.

FIND OUT MORE

SCIENCESAURUS

Electricity and
Magnetism   314
Magnetism   320
Electromagnetism   321

SCILINKS
THE WORLD'S A CLICK AWAY

www.scilinks.org
Keyword: Earth's
Magnetic Field
Code: GSPD08

75

Enrichment

Time: 40–45 minutes
Materials: (for each group) directional compass, 50 m of string with marks at 5-m intervals, 5 index cards, marker or pencil, Migratory Routes (copymaster page 227)

Have students work in groups of three. Choose a large, open area outdoors free of obstructions. Give each group a compass and a copy of the Migratory Routes.

Tell students that they will use a compass to model the migratory navigation of the loggerhead turtle. Briefly review how to use the compass.

Assign each group one of the routes on the sheet—A, B, C, or D. Tell students to use the compass and the marked string to follow the route. Have each group select a different starting point and mark it with an index card labeled with their initials and the word *Start*. At each turning point along the route, have them place another initialed card to mark their place.

When all groups have finished, challenge them to trade routes and retrace the other's path from its starting point. If both groups have followed the directions correctly, the second group should be able to pick up all the cards left by the first group.

▶ Read

Ask students what they think "scientists changed the direction of the magnetic field in a saltwater tank" means. Help them see that if one end of the tank were the "south pole" and the other end the "north pole," reversing the poles would change the direction of the magnetic field. Tell students that later they will learn how the scientists switched the tank's north and south poles.

Explain that Earth's magnetic field is stronger at the poles and weaker at the equator. Then ask students what they think the term "regional magnetic fields" in the reading's last paragraph means. Lead students to understand that since Earth's magnetic field varies in strength and direction from one region to another, we can describe different regions—or areas—of Earth in terms of their magnetic influence.

When students have completed the NoteZone activity, ask volunteers to read the text they underlined. Then ask: *According to the reading, what two different aspects of Earth's magnetic field can sea turtles detect?* (the direction and the intensity)

CHECK UNDERSTANDING
Skill: Drawing conclusions
Ask students to explain what experimental evidence made scientists think that sea turtles can sense Earth's magnetic field. (When scientists changed the direction of the magnetic field in the tank, the sea turtles changed direction.) Then ask: *What steps do you think these scientists took to be sure of their findings?* (They must have repeated the experiment many times with many different turtles.)

More Resources

The following resources are also available from Great Source and NSTA.

SCIENCESAURUS

MATH ON CALL

www.scilinks.org
Keyword: Earth's Magnetic Field
Code: GSPD08

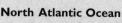

FOLLOW THAT TURTLE The path on the map below shows the approximate migration route of loggerhead turtles in the North Atlantic Ocean. Ocean currents are shown as black arrows.

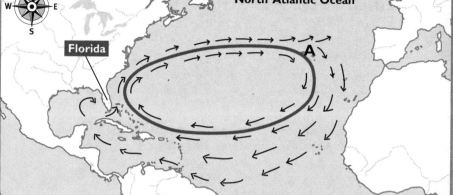

The turtles hatch on the beaches of eastern Florida. Soon they head east and enter the ocean currents that will take them around the Atlantic. The turtles use the ocean currents to help carry them on their journey, but scientists think they use Earth's magnetic field to help them stay on the correct course.

Earth acts like a giant, weak magnet. Like any magnet, Earth has a north pole and a south pole. The magnetic field is strongest at these places. It gets weaker as you move towards the equator. At the equator, the field is the weakest.

Researchers hypothesize that loggerhead turtles can detect Earth's magnetic field—both the direction (north or south) and the strength (strong or weak).

▶ **Look at point "A" on the map. What is happening to the ocean currents at this place?**

They are splitting into two different directions.

▶ **How might a loggerhead turtle use the strength of Earth's magnetic field to know if it went the wrong way at point "A"?**

If it felt a very strong magnetic field, it would know that it had gone too

far north. It needed to follow the current that split off to the south.

76

TEACHING PLAN pp. 76–77

Time: 10 minutes
Materials: world map or globe

FOLLOW THAT TURTLE To orient students to the map shown on this page, have them find the same area on a large world map or globe. Have them use the globe or world map to label all the continents on the map on this page. Also have them note the location of the equator. (It runs through Ecuador, well south of the turtles' migration route.)

Help students compare the strength of the magnetic field near Europe to the strength near Africa. (It would be stronger near Europe.)

Then tell students that scientists have tagged sea turtles in Florida as part of a program to learn about the turtles' migratory pattern. Some of the turtles tagged in Florida have been found living in the Azores and Madeira. Have students locate these places on the map. Ask: *What path do you think the turtles took from Florida to the Azores or Madeira?* (Students should describe a path that follows the migration route.)

▶ Propose Explanations

Time: 15 minutes
Materials: (for teacher demonstration) 1 spool insulated wire, scissors or wire stripper, 6-V battery, directional compass, ring stand with support rod, knife switch and connecting wire

WHICH WAY IS UP? Use the following demonstration to show the magnetic field around a current-carrying wire. Loop the insulated wire into a coil with a diameter of about 15 cm. The more loops you have, the stronger the magnetic field will be. Use the ring stand to hang the coil parallel to a wall. Use

Propose Explanations

WHICH WAY IS UP? The group of researchers wanted to test their hypothesis that loggerhead turtles are able to use Earth's magnetic field to determine direction (north or south). So they set up an experiment.

The researchers put a number of baby turtles in a big pool in the laboratory. They then created a magnetic field around the pool by wrapping large coils of wire around it and running electricity through the wire. (Electricity running through a wire creates a magnetic field around the wire.) This magnetic field was meant to imitate Earth's magnetic field. By changing the direction the electricity traveled through the wire, they could change the direction of the magnetic field around the pool.

The researchers found that when they changed the direction the electricity flowed through the wire, the turtles in the pool started swimming in the opposite direction.

▶ *How does this result support the researchers' hypothesis?*

The turtles reacted to a change in the magnetic field around them by

changing the direction they were swimming in. This suggests that the

turtles used cues from the magnetic field to decide which direction

(north or south) they were supposed to swim to stay on course.

▶ Take Action

RESEARCH OTHER MAGNETIC PERSONALITIES Sea turtles are not the only animals that use magnetism to navigate. Honeybees, monarch butterflies, green sea turtles, a bird called the bobolink, a salamander called the eastern red-spotted newt, frogs, homing pigeons, trout, sharks, and whales do, too. How do they do it?

Choose an animal with a magnetic personality. Go to the library or use the Internet to find out how the animal uses magnetism and how scientists think it works. Be sure to include how far the animal migrates and where it lives during different times of the year.

Answers will vary.

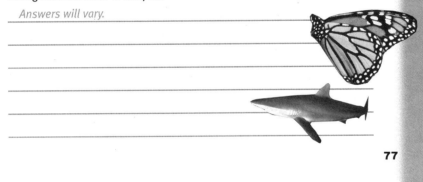

77

Connections

MATH Tell students that newborn loggerhead turtles have an average length of about 4.5 cm and an average mass of 20 g. Loggerhead turtles take about 15 years to grow to their adult size, when their average length is 91 cm and their average mass is 113.5 kg. Ask students to calculate the average (mean) annual rate of growth in cm and kg. (cm: about 5.8 cm/year; kg: about 7.6 kg/year) Ask: *Does this tell you how much a loggerhead turtle will grow in any given year? Why or why not?* (No, because it is only an average; loggerhead turtles may have years with large growth spurts and other years with very little change in size.)

Assessment

Skill: Interpreting scientific illustrations

Use the following questions to assess each student's progress:

How does the strength of Earth's magnetic field change as the turtles travel down the right side of the migration path shown on page 76? (It gets weaker.) *How does Earth's magnetic field change as the turtles travel up the left side of the path?* (It gets stronger.)

---

scissors or a wire stripper to strip the ends of the wire. Connect the ends to the battery to produce a current in the wire. Hold the compass in the center of the loop, and open and close the circuit. (A knife switch in the circuit makes this easier.) The compass needle will move as current flows. Ask: *How does this demonstration show that there is a magnetic field around the wire?* (The needle moves when there is a current in the wire, and we know compass needles respond to magnetic fields.) Reverse the wires on the battery to reverse the direction of the current, and demonstrate the effect on the compass

needle. (The needle will move in the opposite direction.) Point out that this demonstration models the experiment described in the text.

▶ Take Action

RESEARCH OTHER MAGNETIC PERSONALITIES Information about magnetic navigation can be found at the following Web sites:

www.abc.net.au/science/k2/trek/4wd/ Over57.htm

www.sciencenews.org/sn_arc99/ 11_27_99/fob7.htm

www.nwf.org/nationalwildlife/1999/ compass.html

www.exploratorium.edu/theworld/ sonar/navigation.html

When students have completed their research, provide class time for them to share their findings.

Point of Lesson

The attractive and repulsive forces of magnetism can be used to improve train travel.

Focus

► Change, constancy, and measurement
► Science and technology in society
► Motion and forces

Skills and Strategies

► Observing
► Comparing and contrasting
► Making inferences
► Interpreting scientific illustrations

Advance Preparation

Vocabulary

Make sure students understand these terms. Definitions can be found in the glossary at the end of the student book.

► electricity   ► power
► magnet   ► speed
► pole

Materials

Gather the materials needed for *Before You Read* (below), *Enrichment* (p. 79), *Explore* (p. 80), and *Activity* (p. 81)

On the Fast Track

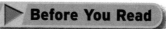

How would you like to ride a train that would move you to your destination almost as fast as a plane?

Imagine getting in a bullet-shaped train and gliding to your destination at almost 500 kilometers (about 300 miles) per hour. Magnetism could make it possible. In the early 1960s, two American scientists patented a new kind of train called a *maglev* train. The name stands for "magnetically levitated train," because the train floats just above the track. Maglev trains are very expensive to build, but several different groups are experimenting with new designs that could slash the costs greatly. If these designs prove practical, we could someday see maglev trains zooming between American cities.

► Before You Read

ZOOM! Maglev trains use magnets to float a fraction of an inch above the tracks. To get an idea how this works, experiment with two bar magnets.

Look at the magnets. One end should be marked "S" (south) and one end marked "N" (north). Place both north poles together, then both south poles together, and finally, one north pole and one south pole together.

► *In the space below, draw pictures to show what you did and what you observed.*

> *The north poles will repel each other and the south poles will repel each other. The north and south poles will attract each other.*

► *What conclusion can you draw about how magnets behave? Use the following terms:* like poles, opposite poles, attract, *and* repel *(push away).*

like poles repel, opposite poles attract

TEACHING PLAN pp. 78–79

INTRODUCING THE LESSON

This lesson introduces students to maglev trains and describes how the trains rely on magnetism to achieve high speeds.

Ask students: *What are the fastest ways to travel from one place to another?* (Students may mention planes, cars, or high-speed trains.) Ask: *What factors do you think might limit the speed of cars and trains?* (Examples: safety issues, fuel consumption, comfort) Students may think that high-speed trains, such as the TGV in France, already regularly travel at speeds over 500 kilometers per hour (about 300

mph). Explain that although some high-speed trains currently in use are capable of reaching speeds over 500 kph, they usually travel at speeds closer to 250 kph (150 mph).

► Before You Read

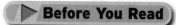

Time: 15 minutes
Materials: 2 bar magnets

ZOOM! Have students work individually or in pairs. If students work in pairs, make sure each student has the opportunity to experiment with the magnets. As students work with the magnets, ask questions to guide their

exploration. For example, ask: *How close can you get the two magnets before you feel the magnetic force between them?* (Answers will vary depending on the strength of the magnets.) Before moving on with the lesson, make sure students understand that like poles repel and opposite poles attract. Write the combinations *N-N*, *S-S*, *N-S*, and *S-N* on the board, and have volunteers label each combination *attract* or *repel*.

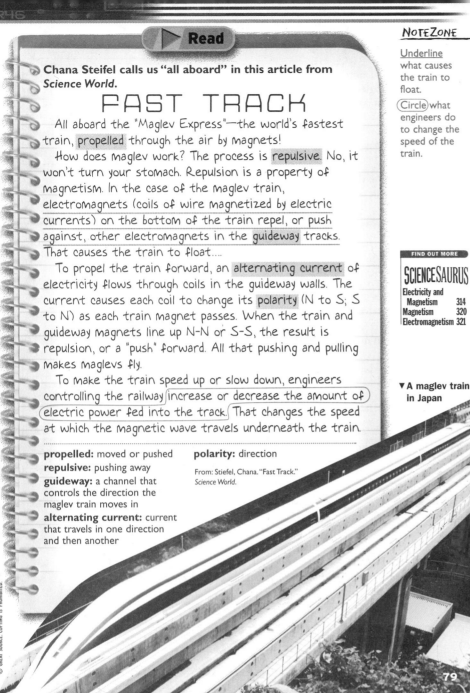

Read

Chana Steifel calls us "all aboard" in this article from *Science World*.

FAST TRACK

All aboard the "Maglev Express"—the world's fastest train, propelled through the air by magnets!

How does maglev work? The process is repulsive. No, it won't turn your stomach. Repulsion is a property of magnetism. In the case of the maglev train, electromagnets (coils of wire magnetized by electric currents) on the bottom of the train repel, or push against, other electromagnets in the guideway tracks. That causes the train to float....

To propel the train forward, an alternating current of electricity flows through coils in the guideway walls. The current causes each coil to change its polarity (N to S; S to N) as each train magnet passes. When the train and guideway magnets line up N-N or S-S, the result is repulsion, or a "push" forward. All that pushing and pulling makes maglevs fly.

To make the train speed up or slow down, engineers controlling the railway increase or decrease the amount of electric power fed into the track. That changes the speed at which the magnetic wave travels underneath the train.

propelled: moved or pushed
repulsive: pushing away
guideway: a channel that controls the direction the maglev train moves in
alternating current: current that travels in one direction and then another

polarity: direction

From: Stiefel, Chana. "Fast Track."
Science World.

FIND OUT MORE

SCIENCESAURUS

Electricity and Magnetism	314
Magnetism	320
Electromagnetism	321

▼ A maglev train in Japan

Enrichment

Time: 20 minutes
Materials: atlas or other resource that gives distances between U.S. cities

Tell students that maglev trains have a top speed of over 300 miles per hour (about 500 kph), which will make them twice as fast as the fastest commuter trains in the United States today and about five times as fast as automobiles. Explain that commercial airplanes typically reach speeds of about 450 miles per hour (about 750 kph). Have students choose two U.S. cities and use the distance between them to calculate how long it would take to travel from one city to another by car, by conventional train, by maglev train, and by airplane. Then ask: *Which vehicle would you prefer to take, and why?* Encourage students to speculate about how the introduction of maglev trains might affect travelers in the United States.

Read

Remind students of your demonstration in Lesson 20 that electric current moving through a wire produces a magnetic field. Also remind them that they saw how the polarity of the magnetic field can be reversed by reversing the direction of the electric current. Encourage them to keep the demonstration in mind while they read the excerpt.

Point out that the two diagrams on page 80 explain the two processes described in the reading: making the train float and making it move forward.

Encourage students to refer to the diagrams as they read.

After students have finished the reading, help them compare traditional trains and maglev trains. Ask: *How are conventional trains moved along the track?* (The engine pulls the cars.) *How are maglev trains moved?* (They are powered by magnetic repulsion.)

Ask volunteers to share their answers to the NoteZone activity.

CHECK UNDERSTANDING
Skill: Concept mapping
Have each student create a concept map to explain how electric current powers and controls a maglev train. (Concept maps should include the following: Electric currents create electromagnets on the bottom of the train and in the tracks. An alternating current switches the polarity of the electromagnets in the guideway walls so the train moves forward. Increasing or decreasing the electric power in the track makes the train speed up or slow down.)

More Resources

The following resources are also available from Great Source.

SCIENCESAURUS

READER'S HANDBOOK

Connections

SOCIAL STUDIES Tell students that China, Japan, Germany, and the United States all have programs to develop and test maglev train routes. Point out that these countries have different population densities. In 1996, the population density of the United States was 28.7 people per square kilometer; of Japan, 371.3 people per square kilometer; and of Germany, 234.1 people. In 1995, 94 percent of China's population lived on only about 36 percent of the land; the population density of the most densely populated areas of China was 320.6 people per square kilometer.

(continued on page 81)

▶ **Explore**

PUSH ME, PULL ME

The diagram to the right shows a maglev train and the electromagnets that lift it off the track. The "N" and "S" show the north or south polarity of each electromagnet.

▲ Side view of maglev train floating above track

▶ *Study the diagram.*
What allows the train to float above the track?

The N poles of the train's electromagnets are lined up with the N poles on the track's electromagnets. Since like poles repel each other, the train is repelled from the track and "floats" above it.

Electromagnets below a maglev train lift it off the track. A completely different set of electromagnets beside the train make it move forward. The diagram below shows how electromagnets on the sides of the train and on the guideways might be arranged.

▶ *Draw an arrow to show which direction you think this train is moving.*

▶ *Why do you think the train is moving that direction?*

The "S" electromagnets on the back of the train will be repelled by the "S" electromagnets on the guideways near the back of the train. The repulsion will push the train to the left.

▲ Top view of maglev train moving between guideways

As soon as the train has moved forward one "notch," the electromagnets on the guideways will flip to the opposite polarity.

▶ *Explain how you think that could keep the train moving forward.*

Switching the poles would keep the same poles (N-N or S-S) aligned at the back of the train. This would keep the train moving forward by repulsion.

80

TEACHING PLAN pp. 80–81

 **Explore**

Time: 10 minutes
Materials: 2 bar magnets

PUSH ME, PULL ME Have students compare the diagrams on this page with the sketch they made in Before You Read on page 78 to confirm their answers. Some students may want to work with the magnets again at this point. Encourage them to predict what will happen when they position the magnets as shown in the diagrams. Then let them use the magnets to test their predictions.

To help students interpret the second diagram, have them reread the third paragraph of the reading selection. Ask: *Why does the train move forward?* (When like poles of the magnets are lined up, they repel each other; this causes the train to move forward.) Point out that the south pole of the electromagnet on the right/rear end of the train in the diagram would be repelled by the south pole of the electromagnet on the guideway. As a result, the train would move toward the left.

Then ask: *Why is it important for the alternating current to cause each electromagnet in the guideway to change its polarity as each train magnet passes?* (Each magnet on the train must always be near a like-pole guideway magnet that will repel it, pushing the train forward.)

YOUR OWN MAGNET TRAIN

Build an electromagnet to power a train of paper clips.

What You Need:
- 6-volt dry cell
- scissors or wire stripper
- long steel nail
- paper clips
- plastic-covered copper wire (1 m)
- 4 drinking glasses
- square piece of cardboard
- tape

What to Do:

1. First, make an electromagnet. Strip the insulation off about 5 cm at the ends of the wire.
2. Wrap the wire at least 12 times around the nail. (The more you wrap it, the more powerful your electromagnet will be.)
3. Connect the ends of the wires to the posts of the dry cell.
4. Pass the nail over a pile of paper clips. The nail should attract the clips. Disconnect one wire and the clips will fall.
5. Now set up your train. Draw your train track on the cardboard. Tape each corner of the cardboard to a drinking glass.
6. Hook the paper clips into a train and put them on the track.
7. Move the electromagnet below the cardboard to pull your train around the track.

nail

What Do You See?

▶ *What force moved your train along the track?*

magnetic force of attraction

▶ *How is your model train similar to a maglev train? How is it different?*

Both the model and the maglev train use electromagnets. The model train was not levitated. The model train moved forward because of forces of attraction, instead of repulsion. Also, my train had no electromagnet. The maglev train has electromagnets on both the train and the track.

81

(continued from page 80)

Ask students how the population density of a country might affect whether it decides to invest in maglev train technology, which is quite expensive. (Students may suggest that maglev trains would make financial sense only in areas with high enough population density to justify their cost.)

Assessment

Skill: Drawing conclusions

Use the following question to assess each student's progress:

What role does electric current play in the function of a maglev train? (Electric current creates the electromagnets that levitate the train and move it forward along the track by repulsion.)

▶ **Activity**

Time: 40–45 minutes
Materials: 6-volt dry cell, scissors or wire stripper, long steel nail, paper clips, plastic-covered copper wire (1 m), 4 drinking glasses, square piece of cardboard, tape

▶ Have students work in pairs or small groups.
▶ You may want to set up a sample apparatus to show students how to tape the cardboard to the drinking glasses to create a secure work surface.

▶ Encourage students to test the electromagnet with the wire wrapped fewer than 10 times around the nail and with the wire wrapped more than 12 times. Ask: *Which electromagnet is more powerful? How can you tell?* (The one with the wire wrapped around the most times can pick up the most paper clips.)
▶ After students have completed step 4, ask: *How is an electromagnet different from a regular magnet?* (A regular magnet is always magnetized, but an electromagnet works only when an electric current is flowing.)

▶ Challenge students to design a model of the maglev train. How could they levitate the train using magnets? How could they use magnets to propel the train? Have them sketch and describe their ideas. If time permits, have them try some of their ideas using bar magnets or electromagnets.

Electronics

LESSON 22
Plowboy Inventor
Point of Lesson: *Television images are sent through wires as a series of electrical signals.*

An account of how a beet field inspired Philo T. Farnsworth to invent modern television introduces this chapter on electronics. After reading the account, students work with an analogy and with a page from the inventor's sketchbook to understand the system of image transfer that he devised. They then learn how electrons are controlled in a television set and practice creating an image using a grid of small boxes, as a television does.

Materials
Enrichment (p. 83), for each student:
► newspaper photographs (both color and black-and-white)
► magnifier
Explore (p. 85), for each student:
► 2 sheets of graph paper

LESSON 23
A Copper Wire
Point of Lesson: *Telephones convert voice vibrations into an electric current that moves through copper wires.*

Students read a poem celebrating the telephone wire and the connections between people that it makes possible. They then identify the energy transfers that take place as a spoken message is transmitted from one telephone and received by another.

Materials
Explore (p. 87), for each student:
► physical science textbook or other source such as *ScienceSaurus*, section 300

LESSON 24
Zeroes and Ones
Point of Lesson: *Computers use binary code to control the flow of electricity and perform operations.*

In this lesson, students meet Ada Byron Lovelace, the woman who suggested using binary code to program an early computer. After reading an account of Lovelace's work with Charles Babbage (whose "analytical engine" was a precursor to the computer), students explore the basis of binary code. They first practice simply changing base 10 numbers to binary numbers, then learn how to convert letters and words into ASCII code, then into binary, and finally into bytes.

Materials
Enrichment (p. 89), for each pair:
► stopwatch
► calculator
► two sets of arithmetic problems involving adding, subtracting, multiplying, or dividing—one set of 5 multidigit problems and one set of 20 single-digit problems
► answer key for problems
Connections (p. 90), for the class:
► International Morse Code (copymaster page 228)

Background Information

Lesson 23

In 1916, when Carl Sandburg wrote the poem featured in this lesson, telephone calls were completed through a series of separate connections. Each connection was made by hand by a switchboard operator in a central office. In general, the longer the distance between the two phones, the greater the number of switchboard operators who were needed and the longer it took to complete the connections. Also, the number of lines that were available for long-distance calls was limited, and only one call could be carried at a time on each line. These facts made long-distance calling relatively expensive, and most people placed long-distance calls only to convey news that was both urgent and important, such as a death in the family.

Today, copper wires still connect your home telephone to the local network, but long-distance calling is handled by computers that instantly route and connect your call to the phone you are trying to reach. Thousands of calls can be carried simultaneously over fiber-optic lines or via satellite. In addition to correctly routing calls, computers also identify which long-distance carrier you have chosen and track the cost of the call, according to the calling plan you have with that carrier. All this automation means that the relative cost of a long-distance call today is a fraction of what it was in Carl Sandburg's time.

Point of Lesson
Television images are sent through wires as a series of electrical signals.

Focus
▶ Systems, order, and organization
▶ Understanding about science and technology
▶ Science as a human endeavor
▶ Transfer of energy

Skills and Strategies
▶ Solving problems
▶ Interpreting scientific illustrations
▶ Making inferences
▶ Recognizing cause and effect

Advance Preparation

Vocabulary
Make sure students understand these terms. Definitions can be found in the glossary at the end of the student book.

▶ electric current
▶ electron
▶ lens
▶ magnetic field
▶ technology

Materials
Gather the materials needed for *Enrichment* (p. 83) and *Explore* (p. 85).

TEACHING PLAN pp. 82–83

Plowboy Inventor

How did a field of sugar beets inspire a 14-year-old boy to help invent something that would change the world?

Inventors get their ideas by looking at the world around them. Does the shape of an airplane remind you of anything? Maybe a bird? Early flight engineers looked at birds when coming up with ideas about how to build a machine that could fly. Even the neatly plowed rows of a sugar-beet field could be inspiring to a young electronics engineer.

Electronics is a type of technology that deals with electrons in motion. You use electronics every time you watch TV, talk on the phone, or use the computer.

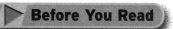 **Before You Read**

USING ELECTRONICS
▶ *How do you personally use electronics in your daily life? Describe what you use and how it helps you.*

Examples: microwave oven: lets me heat food quickly; CD player: plays

music and lets me pick what music I want; alarm clock: makes noise at

the right time to wake me up; TV: shows TV programs; phone: lets me

talk to my friend and get messages.

_____

_____

_____

_____

_____

82

UNIT 2: ELECTRICITY AND MAGNETISM

INTRODUCING THE LESSON
This lesson discusses the invention of television and describes how television images are transmitted by electrical signals.

Explain that all television sets receive signals that tell them how to display the images being transmitted. Ask students: *What are some of the devices that send signals to a television set?* (Students may mention a broadcast tower, cable, a satellite, a VCR, or a DVD player.) Students may not realize that the signals sent to the television from these different devices contain basically the same type of information.

For example, the signal from a VCR or DVD player contains the same type of information as the signal from a TV antenna that picks up transmissions from a broadcast tower.

▶ **Before You Read**

USING ELECTRONICS Students may have difficulty distinguishing between electronic devices and simpler electrical devices. Explain that in general, electrical devices are those that simply use electricity as a source of energy. In contrast, electronic devices have small parts made from materials called semi-

conductors (such as transistors and diodes) that control the flow of electrons to produce specific effects. (In the earliest days of electronics, vacuum tubes were used instead of semiconductor devices, but they served the same purpose.) Point out that in the past, devices such as irons, toasters, and curling irons were simple electrical devices; they would heat up when they were plugged in and turned on. Today, these types of appliances are often electronic. For example, many irons have an automatic shut-off function that uses an electronic timer.

▶ Read

Philo T. Farnsworth spent his boyhood days working on the family farm in Rigby, Idaho. Plowing the sugar-beet fields one day in 1921, he was suddenly hit by an idea that led him to invent television.

Imagine That!

Philo was an <u>avid</u> reader of popular-science magazines. Inspired by articles in their pages, he had been trying for more than a year to figure out how to create television. As his future wife later wrote, "Bit by bit he collected information that eventually led him to discover for himself that mysterious, <u>vitally</u> important particle called the electron, the study of which would define his life.... Philo tried to imagine a way to use electrons to <u>eliminate</u> the <u>mechanical</u> method of <u>transmitting</u> pictures." The solution first came to him when he looked back over his shoulder in the sugar-beet field. He saw <u>the neat rows his harrow had just made in the earth.</u> The pattern gave him an idea for using electrons in similar rows to make the television picture.

avid: very eager
vitally: extremely
eliminate: get rid of
mechanical: using a machine with moving parts
transmitting: sending
harrow: plow

From: Tucker, Tom. *Brainstorm! The Stories of Twenty American Kid Inventors.* Farrar, Straus and Giroux.

An early television set ▶

NOTEZONE

Underline the image in nature that inspired Philo's invention.

FIND OUT MORE

SCIENCESAURUS

Atomic Structure	256
Current Electricity	317
Electric Circuits	318
Magnetism	320
Electromagnetism	321

83

Enrichment

Time: 20 minutes
Materials: (for each student) newspaper photographs (both color and black-and-white), magnifier

Have students use a magnifier to examine dark, light, and grayish areas of a black-and-white newspaper photo. Ask them to describe what they see. (tiny black dots, close together in dark areas and farther apart in lighter areas)

Then have students look at a color photo. Ask: *What colors are the dots?* (Students might see individual dots of blue, red, yellow, and black or combinations of these colors where dots overprint.) *Are these the same colors you see when you look at the picture without the magnifier?* (No, I see all different colors.) Explain that blue (cyan), red (magenta), and yellow are the primary colors of pigment. Tell students that color newspaper pictures are created by combining just these three primary colors and black.

Finally, relate this exercise to the tiny dots, called *pixels,* on a television screen. Explain that just as our brain perceives the individual dots in a newspaper picture as one complete image, it also perceives the separate pixels on a television screen as one picture. The pixels on a television screen give off light in three colors that our brain combines to produce all the colors we see. These three colors are red, green, and blue—the primary colors of light.

▶ Read

Explain that people had been working on the idea of television for many years before Philo came up with his idea. What made Philo's idea unique was that it used electronic means to dissect and reconstruct the transmitted images. Previous inventors had relied on mechanical means to dissect the image and turn it into an electrical signal. Typically this was done by focusing light from the scene onto a spinning disk with holes. As the light passed through the holes, it was broken down into small bits that were translated into electrical signals and sent out through wires. Philo realized that this mechanical method was too slow and imprecise, so he searched for an electronic way to break down images into electrical signals. The result was his Image Dissector, diagrammed on page 84.

CHECK UNDERSTANDING
Skill: Classifying
Have students identify the two different methods of transmitting images described in the reading. (mechanical and electronic) Ask: *Which method was pioneered by Philo?* (electronic)

More Resources

The following resources are also available from Great Source.

SCIENCESAURUS

WRITE SOURCE 2000

Connections

WRITING Tell students that in October 1938, the writer E.B. White, author of *Charlotte's Web* and *Stuart Little*, wrote a magazine essay about the role he thought television would play in modern society. He said that television could become "either a new and unbearable disturbance of the general peace or a saving radiance in the sky." Have students write a short persuasive essay of their own explaining which of the two possibilities they think best describes television's role in society today. Students will probably believe that both are true. Encourage them to describe ways in which television is helpful and ways in which it is harmful.

TEACHING PLAN pp. 84–85

▶ Explore

SENDING AN IMAGE Help students understand why an image must be "dissected" before it can be converted to signals carried by electric current. Ask students if they are familiar with the idea of pixels, the individual dots on a television screen. If they are not, you could use the Enrichment activity on page 83 to introduce and illustrate the concept. Explain that a television picture is created by electron beams that zig-zag across the screen, lighting up each tiny pixel 30 times per second.

Our brain combines the individual pixels into a complete picture. The signal that hits each pixel carries information from the corresponding spot of the objects in front of the TV camera.

Students may be aware that television signals are sent through cable wires. Signals can also be sent by satellites and broadcasting towers. Explain that in these cases, the electrical signals are converted to radio waves, sent through the air, and then changed back into electrical signals by the receiver on the television set.

As students examine the Image Dissector diagram, point out that the photoelectric plate was housed in a vacuum tube, represented in the diagram by the rectangular-shaped outline. Also point out that the coil of wire Philo drew above the vacuum tube represented a wire that in the actual model wrapped around the entire device.

▶ Explore

SENDING AN IMAGE A television camera's job is to take an image from one place and send it to another place—your television. The question is, how can the image be sent?

Think about a 1000-piece jigsaw puzzle. The image it shows is made up of 1000 smaller pieces of the image. Let's say you had a completed jigsaw puzzle. And let's say you wanted to pass the puzzle to a friend in the next room, but there was a wall between you with only a small hole in it.

▶ *How might you transfer the puzzle to your friend?*

I could take apart the puzzle and pass it through the hole piece by piece.

▶ *How could you make it very easy for your friend to reassemble the puzzle? Record your ideas.*

I could pass one row of pieces at a time, starting from the top and moving toward the bottom. He could just put the pieces back together in the order he received them, and the image would be correct.

Now think about a television camera. It takes an image, breaks it down into many tiny parts, and sends the parts to your television. Your television then puts the parts back together to re-form the image. Each "part" is an electric signal (electrons) sent through a wire.

This drawing of a television camera is one that Philo made while he was still in high school. The picture shows the lens of the camera on the left. The lens focuses the optical (light) image onto a photoelectric plate. This plate changes the light into electrical signals that form an electron image. The signals then travel through wires to your television. Strong light produces strong signals, while low light produces weaker signals. In this way, the signals can carry information about light and dark areas of the image.

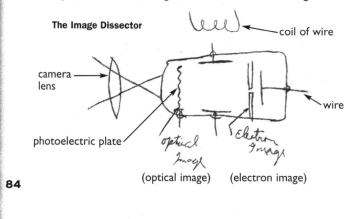

The Image Dissector

coil of wire

camera lens

wire

photoelectric plate

(optical image)   (electron image)

84

Philo called his camera the Image Dissector. To *dissect* something means to take it apart.

► *Why do you think Philo called his camera the Image Dissector?*

It broke the image down into many smaller parts that could be sent

to the television.

Philo came up with the idea of using a magnetic field to hold the electrons in straight rows as they came off of the photoelectric plate and moved toward the wires. Philo knew that electric current moving through a wire creates a magnetic field. So he wrapped the Dissector with a coil of wire carrying an electric current. This produced a magnetic field around the Dissector that guided the electrons in rows as orderly as those he saw in his beet field.

► *Why do you think it was important that the electrons traveled in an orderly way? (Hint: Think about passing the jigsaw puzzle pieces to your friend in the next room.)*

so that they could be reassembled in an orderly way to re-form the image

correctly

SIGNALS CREATE AN IMAGE Look at the following series of "electric signals." Imagine that they are coming through the wire to your black-and-white television. An "off" signal produces a tiny black square on the screen. An "on" signal produces a tiny white square. When you stand back, all the tiny squares work together to form a larger image.

off–off–off–off–off–off–on–on–on–off–off–on–off–on–off–off–on–on–
on–off–off–on–off–off–off–on–off–off–off–on–off–off–off

► *Fill in the "screen" below to see the image formed by the electric signals received. Begin at the top left. If the signal is "on," leave the box blank. If the signal is "off," blacken the box with your pencil.*

1	2	3	4	5
6	7	8	9	10
11	12	13	14	15
16	17	18	19	20
21	22	23	24	25
26	27	28	29	30
31	32	33	34	35

► *What do you see on your "screen"?*

the letter "P"

Assessment
Skill: Organizing information

Use the following question to assess each student's progress:

How did Philo use electricity and magnetism to create a clear television image? (He used a photoelectric plate to convert light images to electrical signals [electrons] that traveled through wires to recreate the images on a television screen. He used a magnetic field [produced by a current-carrying coil of wire] to direct the electrons coming off the photoelectric plate and keep them in parallel lines so they would recreate the images correctly.)

Have students look back at the diagram on page 84 as they read the second paragraph on this page. After students answer the second question, explain that inventors working in Philo's time already knew that a photoelectric plate could be used to change light into electrical signals of varying intensities. The problem was that the electrons did not come off the plate in straight, parallel lines. Philo had read a research article that explained how a magnetic field could be used to guide a beam of electrons. He put this knowledge to use by wrapping his Image Dissector in a coil of current-carrying wire, thus creating a magnetic field that kept the electrons coming off the photoelectric plate moving in straight, parallel lines.

Time: 15 minutes
Materials: 2 sheets of graph paper

SIGNALS CREATE AN IMAGE As an extension of this activity, have students use graph paper to create an image they want to "transmit." Tell students to create the image by darkening some squares on the graph paper and leaving others blank. Then have students write a series of "on/off" signals that represent their image pixel by pixel. Finally, have students work in pairs to decode each other's images on another sheet of graph paper using only the series of signals. When students have decoded the signals, have them compare the "received" image with the "transmitted" image.

Point of Lesson

Telephones convert voice vibrations into an electric current that moves through copper wires.

Focus

► Systems, order, and organization
► Transfer of energy
► Understanding about science and technology
► Science and technology in society

Skills and Strategies

► Observing
► Interpreting scientific illustrations
► Concept mapping

Advance Preparation

Vocabulary

Make sure students understand these terms. Definitions can be found in the glossary at the end of the student book.

► conductor   ► metals
► electric current   ► sound
► electricity   ► vibration
► energy

Materials

Gather the materials needed for *Explore* (p. 87).

UNIT 2: ELECTRICITY AND MAGNETISM

Electronics

A Copper Wire

▼ Telephone wires

Copper wires have made it possible for us to talk with people around the world whenever we want.

Have you ever wondered how your voice is carried from your home telephone to the telephone of a friend many miles away? Here's a hint: Look at the wires that connect your phone to the wall, and the wires that run from one telephone pole to another. Your words travel as electric signals through these wires, connecting you to people all over the country.

► **Read**

NOTEZONE

In line 4, Sandburg lists examples of something he calls "it." What is the "it"?

speech, words

FIND OUT MORE

SCIENCE**SAURUS**

Current Electricity   317
Electric Circuits   318

SC**I**INKS.
THE WORLD'S A CLICK AWAY

www.scilinks.org
Keyword: Alexander
Graham Bell
Code: GSPD09

86

Carl Sandburg (1878–1967) was one of America's greatest poets. In 1916 he wrote a poem praising the thin copper wires that connected Americans.

Under a Telephone Pole

I AM a copper wire slung in the air,

Slim against the sun I make not even a clear line of shadow.

Night and day I keep singing—humming and thrumming:

It is love and war and money; it is the fighting and the tears, the work and want,

Death and laughter of men and women passing through me, carrier of your speech,

In the rain and the wet dripping, in the dawn and the shine drying,

A copper wire.

From: Sandburg, Carl. *Chicago Poems.*

© GREAT SOURCE. COPYING IS PROHIBITED.

TEACHING PLAN pp. 86–87

INTRODUCING THE LESSON

This lesson uses a poem by Carl Sandburg to introduce students to the role of copper wires in carrying telephone messages as electrical signals.

Ask students: *What kinds of telephones have you used?* Students may mention conventional phones, cordless phones, cell phones, and even Internet phones. Students may also mention picture phones, wrist phones, and phones with no number pad in which you simply speak the number. Have students speculate about how their voice is transmitted from one phone to the other.

► **Read**

Students may be surprised to find a poem in a science book, since many poems tend to reflect on personal issues such as love, loss, and beauty. Ask: *Why might someone write a poem about science and technology?* (Example: to describe how they feel about the technology and its effect on society) Encourage students to look for clues about the poet's feelings toward the technology he is describing. Ask: *How do you think Carl Sandburg felt about telephone wires?* (Example: He was amazed that a wire too thin to cast

a shadow could carry messages about such important issues as death, love, and war.)

▶ Explore

HOW A TELEPHONE WORKS Put your fingers on your throat and say the alphabet out loud.

▶ *What do you feel?* vibrations

When you speak, vibrations in your voice box create sound waves that travel through the air to the ear of someone nearby. But sound waves can't travel through telephone wires.

Look at the following diagram of a telephone. When you talk into the mouthpiece (the transmitter), your voice vibrates a metal disk. These vibrations are then converted to an electric current that varies just as your voice varies as you speak. This varying current moves through telephone wires to the phone of your friend. There, in the earpiece (receiver), the electric current is converted back to sound waves and your friend hears your voice.

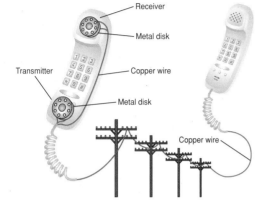

▶ *In the space below, draw a graphic organizer that shows the energy conversions involved in a telephone call.*

sound energy   →   electrical energy   →   sound energy
(voice)   (varying current)   (voice)

▶ *What form of energy is the copper wire described in the poem carrying?*

electrical energy

87

More Resources

The following resources are also available from Great Source and NSTA.

SCIENCESAURUS

READER'S HANDBOOK

SCILINKS
THE WORLD'S A CLICK AWAY

www.scilinks.org
Keyword: Alexander Graham Bell
Code: GSPD09

Assessment

Skill: Drawing conclusions

Use the following question to assess each student's progress:

How does electric current enable your friend to hear you speak when you are far away? Explain what happens at both the transmitter and at the receiver. (The transmitter in my phone converts my voice vibrations into a varying electric current. The electric current moves from the transmitter in my phone to the receiver in my friend's phone. At my friend's receiver, the current is converted back into sound energy, and the friend hears my voice.)

▶ Explore

Time: 10–15 minutes
Materials: physical science textbook or other source such as *ScienceSaurus*, section 300

HOW A TELEPHONE WORKS To help students identify the energy conversions involved in a telephone call, first ask them to identify all the events that occur. Then have them identify the type of energy involved in each event. For example, ask: *What is the first thing that happens during a phone call?* (Example: The person receiving the call says "Hello.") Then ask: *What kind of*

energy does that involve? Students may not realize that speech is sound energy. Point out that speech begins with the vibrations of the vocal cords in the voice box, a form of sound energy. If necessary, have students review the forms of energy explained in a science textbook or other source such as *ScienceSaurus*, section 300.

CHECK UNDERSTANDING
Skill: Interpreting scientific illustrations
Have students identify where in the diagram on this page the energy conversions are taking place. (at the metal disks)

Point of Lesson
Computers use binary code to control the flow of electricity and perform operations.

Focus
► Science and technology in society
► History of science
► Systems, order, and organization

Skills and Strategies
► Using numbers
► Sequencing
► Creating and using tables

Advance Preparation

Vocabulary
Make sure students understand these terms. Definitions can be found in the glossary at the end of the student book.

► data
► electric current
► technology

Materials
Gather the materials needed for *Enrichment* (p. 89) and *Connections* (p. 90).

Zeroes and Ones

In the 1800s, a woman created the code of computer technology.

Ada Byron Lovelace lived during a time when women did not study mathematics. Back in the 1800s, few girls even went to school. But Ada's father was a famous poet. Her mother was a mathematician and a member of the royal family in England. This meant she had opportunities other women did not, including a private tutor. Ada's tutor introduced her to other mathematicians. These meetings led Ada to make a suggestion that would change the world.

Her suggestion had to do with the binary number system, which uses only the digits 0 and 1 instead of all the digits from 0 to 9. Today, all computers use the binary number system to store and transmit information.

▲ Ada Byron Lovelace

 ▶ **Before You Read**

BREAKING THE CODE Codes are invented for many purposes. Sometimes a code is used to send secret messages. The person who receives the coded message has a "key" to unlock the code. See if you can translate this coded message using the key provided.

Nbui dbo cf gvo. Math can be fun.
(key: a ⟶ b)

► *What was the secret to this code?*

Each letter in the real message is represented in the coded message

by the next letter in the alphabet.

UNIT 2: ELECTRICITY AND MAGNETISM

88

TEACHING PLAN pp. 88–89

INTRODUCING THE LESSON
This lesson introduces students to codes and describes how binary code is used in computers.

Students may think that codes are used only to deliver secret messages. Explain that a code is any system of communication in which symbols from one set are replaced by symbols from another set according to a specific rule. For example, written words are a code for spoken words. Sign language is a code of gestures for spoken words. Point out that bar codes—which contain product information that has been coded into a series of vertical lines—appear on almost every product and that anyone can get the key for creating and reading them.

▶ **Before You Read**

BREAKING THE CODE Ask students: *What is your experience with codes? When have you seen codes used? Have you ever made up a code? What was it based on? How did you use it?* (Students may recall having seen codes used in war movies, may have learned about Morse code in scouting, or may describe codes they have invented themselves to send secret messages to a friend.)

Explain that every code has a key that explains how the code works. Help students see that the key **a ⟶ b** means that every *a* in the original message has been replaced by the letter *b* in the code. Ask: *How do you think the letter* b *is represented in this code?* (Every *b* is represented by the letter *c*.) Then ask: *What is the general rule for writing a message using this code?* (Represent each letter in the original message with the one that follows it in the alphabet.) *What is the general rule for decoding the message?* (Replace each letter in the code with the letter that comes before it in the alphabet.)

▶ Read

Ada's private tutor introduced her to mathematician and inventor Charles Babbage. At the time, Babbage was working on a calculating machine he called the *difference engine*.

ANALYTICAL ENGINE

Soon after that, Ada and her mother were invited to Babbage's workshop, where he described his project. He was building a machine that would be capable of calculating tables of numbers by computing their differences. At that time, all [complex calculations were done] by hand, which was extremely time consuming, and filled with errors. When Ada saw the machine, she immediately recognized its tremendous potential. She began to work with Babbage....

After many years of working on the difference engine, [Babbage] abandoned it for a better plan—the analytical engine. This machine would be able to do much more than generate tables. It would perform a variety of functions by receiving commands from a series of punched cards. Babbage got this idea from a weaving loom designed by J. M. Jacquard. If the cards could tell the loom which threads to pick up, Babbage reasoned they could direct the machine as to which gears to operate.

▼ Babbage's analytical engine

computing: calculating
analytical: something that breaks down and examines data in order to understand it
generate: make
functions: tasks

weaving loom: a machine that weaves threads together to create cloth
gears: toothed wheels that make up the mechanical part of the analytical engine
operate: make work

From: Reimer, Luetta and Wilbert Reimer. *Mathematicians Are People, Too. Stories from the Lives of Great Mathematicians Vol 2.* Pearson Education, Inc., publishing as Dale Seymour Publications.

NoteZone

What more do you want to know after reading this?

FIND OUT MORE

SCIENCESAURUS
Science, Technology and Society 354
Decimals 378

SCILINKS
THE WORLD'S A CLICK AWAY
www.scilinks.org
Keyword: Computer Technology
Code: GSPD10

89

Enrichment

Time: 30 minutes
Materials: (for each pair) stopwatch; calculator; two sets of arithmetic problems involving adding, subtracting, multiplying, or dividing—one set of multidigit problems and one set of 20 single-digit problems; answer key for problems

Have students work in pairs to compare the time it takes to perform calculations by hand with the time it takes to perform the same calculations using a calculator, a type of digital computer. Provide each pair with the list of multidigit problems. One student should keep time as the other works out the problems, first by hand and then using the calculator. Then have students switch roles.

Ask: *What was the time difference between the two methods?* (Using the calculator will probably be much faster for most students.) Give students the answer key so they can check their results. Then ask: *Which method was more accurate?* (most likely, using the calculator)

Have students repeat the activity with the single-digit problems. (Students will probably find that the brain is quicker than the calculator in this case.) Ask: *When are calculators most helpful?* (for solving math problems with large numbers)

▶ Read

After students have read the excerpt, walk them through the following comparison of Babbage's analytical engine and a modern computer: The analytical engine was mechanical—it was operated by a series of cards with holes punched in them. Today's computers are electronic—they are operated by a series of electrical signals. Both devices follow commands to perform complex tasks, but today's computers can do many more things than Babbage's analytical engine, and they are much faster.

To help students visualize how the punched cards could have given commands to the analytical engine, ask them to recall the answer sheets for a multiple-choice standardized test on which they darken one oval per row. Tell them to imagine that each darkened oval was a punched hole. By "reading" the pattern of punched holes in each row on a card passing through the machine, the analytical engine could receive a series of commands. By responding to all the individual commands, the machine would complete a computation.

CHECK UNDERSTANDING
Skill: Communicating
Ask: *How did Babbage's analytical engine receive commands?* (from a series of punched cards)

More Resources

The following resources are also available from Great Source and NSTA.

SCIENCESAURUS

MATH ON CALL

SCILINKS.
THE WORLD'S A CLICK AWAY

www.scilinks.org
Keyword: Computer Technology
Code: GSPD10

Connections

Time: 30 minutes
Materials: International Morse Code
(copymaster page 228)

LANGUAGE ARTS Tell students that one of the most widely used codes in the world is International Morse Code, which was developed in 1851 as a refinement of the original code developed by Samuel Morse in 1838. Morse code consists of a series of dots, dashes, and spaces; it can be

(continued on page 91)

► **Explore**

BINARY NUMBERS The decimal number system we use everyday is a "base 10" system that uses ten digits—0, 1, 2, 3, 4, 5, 6, 7, 8, and 9. Computers, on the other hand, can only read two digits—0 and 1. That's because computers are electronic devices and can only read whether a switch is ON or OFF. To a machine, the digit 1 means ON, and 0 means OFF. The two-digit number system computers use is called the "base 2" system, or binary number system.

Use the table below to help you translate the decimal numbers 12, 13, and 20 into binary numbers. First, finish filling in the binary place values in the second row of the chart. (The first three have been done for you.) The small number above the "2" tells you how many times to multiply the "2" by itself. So, for example, 2^2 becomes 2×2 or 4. Similarly, 2^3 becomes $2 \times 2 \times 2$.

BINARY PLACE VALUES							
2^7	2^6	2^5	2^4	2^3	2^2	2^1	2^0
128	64	32	16	8	4	2	1
12 0	0	0	0	1	1	0	0
13 0	0	0	0	1	1	0	1
20 0	0	0	1	0	1	0	0

Now, follow these steps to convert the number 12, in the third row, to binary:
1. Find the greatest place value that is less than or equal to 12. This is 8, so write a "1" in the eights place to show that you have one group of 8.
2. Then, since you need 4 more to make 12, write a "1" in the fours place.
3. Fill in the empty boxes to the right of the 1s with 0s as placeholders.
► *What is the sequence of 1s and 0s in base 2 that has the same value as 12 in base 10?*

1100

Now try converting 13.
1. Begin by writing a "1" in the eights place to show that 13 has one group of 8.
2. You need 5 more to make 13. Put "1"s in the two places that add up to 5.
3. Fill in the empty boxes between the 1s with 0s as placeholders.
► *What is the sequence of 1s and 0s in base 2 that has the same value as 13 in base 10?*

1101

Go to the last row of the chart and fill in the boxes to show the binary form of the number 20.
► *What is the sequence of 1s and 0s that has the value of 20 in base 10?*

10100

90

TEACHING PLAN pp. 90–91

► **Explore**

BINARY NUMBERS To help familiarize students with the base 2 number system, first demonstrate how to analyze numbers using the base 10 system. On the board, draw the table of base 10 place values shown here. Then ask

students to help you fill in the table to show the values of numbers such as 410, 1852, 27, and 9, as shown. Point out that the base 2 system works exactly the same way, but only the digits 0 and 1 can be used. (The base 10 system uses the digits 0, 1, 2, 3, 4, 5, 6, 7, 8, and 9.)

You may want to lead the class through the answer to the first question on this page and then have them complete the next two questions on their own or working in pairs. For additional challenge, have students convert the base 10 numbers 62, 7, 300, and 175 to binary numbers. (62 = 111110; 7 = 111; 300 = 100101100; 175 = 10101111)

	10^4 10,000	10^3 1,000	10^2 100	10^1 10	10^0 1
410			4	1	0
1,852		1	8	5	2
27				2	7
9					9

Propose Explanations

HOW IS BINARY CODE USED IN COMPUTERS? What does the computer do with this binary code? A "1" turns a switch controlling electric current ON. A "0" turns a switch controlling electric current OFF. As the flow of electric current is started and stopped, operations like calculating and writing letters are performed.

For example, when you send e-mail to a friend, you use words and letters. But the computer "codes" each letter into a number. Almost all computers use a standard code called ASCII. In ASCII code, all letters are coded as base 10 numbers. Then the computer changes these numbers into binary code. But that is not all it has to do.

The computer must read numbers as bytes. A byte is a group of eight binary digits made of 1s and 0s. It changes each binary number into an eight-digit number by adding 0s onto the beginning. For example, the number 1 would be 00000001. To write numbers the way a computer reads them, use exactly eight digits (0 or 1) each time you write a number.

▶ *Go back to the chart on page 90. Fill in the chart with 0s as needed to make each number a byte.*

▶ *What byte represents the base 10 number "12" in binary code?*

00001100

Take Action

WRITE A MESSAGE IN COMPUTER CODE The table below shows the base 10 ASCII code for all lower case letters. Write the word "hi" in ASCII code. Then convert each ASCII code number in the word into an eight-digit binary number (byte). Use the chart on page 90 to help you with the conversion.

ASCII code for lower case letters							
a	97	h	104	o	111	v	118
b	98	i	105	p	112	w	119
c	99	j	106	q	113	x	120
d	100	k	107	r	114	y	121
e	101	l	108	s	115	z	122
f	102	m	109	t	116		
g	103	n	110	u	117		

ASCII   *104 105*

Binary   *01101000 01101001*

91

(continued from page 90)

transmitted using long and short electrical, mechanical, or visual signals. Provide each student with a copy of the code, and have students write a message in code. Then have them exchange and decode the messages. For an additional challenge, encourage students to deliver the messages by tapping a pencil on a desk.

Assessment
Skill: Sequencing

Use the following task to assess each student's progress:

Remind students that when they write an E-mail message to a friend, their typed words become electronic signals that the computer can read, store, and send to their friend's computer. Have students describe the conversions their typed words go through to become electronic signals. Then have them describe the conversions that must happen at their friend's computer to turn the electronic signals back into words they can read. (At my computer, each letter is coded into an ASCII number, and then each ASCII number is coded into an eight-digit binary number—a byte. The bytes make an electric current switch ON and OFF. At my friend's computer, the ON and OFF signals become binary code, which becomes ASCII code, which becomes letters.)

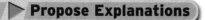

Propose Explanations

HOW IS BINARY CODE USED IN COMPUTERS? Remind students that all computer information is delivered in bytes, groups of eight binary digits. Explain that bytes flow through computers without spaces between them. That is, computers read one long, uninterrupted string of binary numbers. To illustrate this point, draw any four consecutive bytes on the board without spaces between them. Ask: *How do bytes allow computers to decide where a coded letter begins or ends?* (Because each coded letter is exactly eight digits

long, a new letter begins every eight digits.) To illustrate this point, draw a vertical line after each group of eight binary digits on the board.

Take Action

WRITE A MESSAGE IN COMPUTER CODE If students have trouble converting "hi" into binary code, make sure they understand that the ASCII code for the letters "h" and "i" is given in the chart. Remind students that they can then use the binary place values chart on page 90 to convert their base 10 numbers into binary code. Remind

them to use zeros as placeholders so their numbers are eight digits long.

If students want an extra challenge, encourage them to try to write their first and last names in ASCII and then binary. For an even greater challenge, place the binary-coded names in a box, then have students draw out "names" and try to translate them back to letters to identify the people who created them.

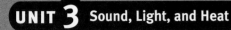

UNIT 3 Sound, Light, and Heat

About the Photo

From low-energy radio waves to high-energy gamma rays, all forms of electromagnetic radiation move easily through space. Earth's atmosphere acts to block many of the sun's high-energy waves that would be harmful to living things. But out in space, a person would be fully exposed to these damaging waves. Special suits help protect astronauts in space from being harmed by electromagnetic radiation from the sun.

About the Charts

A major goal of the *Science Daybooks* is to promote reading, writing, and critical thinking skills in the context of science. The charts below describe the types of reading selections included in this unit and identify the skills and strategies used in each lesson.

Switch on the radio, flip on the light, and sit by the fire.

Sound, light, and heat may seem very different, but all have something in common. They are all forms of energy. Sound we can hear, light we can see, and heat we can feel. These forms of energy can also cause objects around them to change. We don't think of sound as breaking objects very often. But like all forms of energy, sound is capable of changing matter.

I n this lesson you will look at different forms of energy—how they travel and what effect they have on objects around them. You'll find out how astronauts protect themselves from getting sunburned in space and how doctors can use sound to help heal patients. You'll see how mirrors can be used to create optical illusions and why certain fabrics keep you warmer than others.

92

© GREAT SOURCE. COPYING IS PROHIBITED.

SELECTION	READING	WRITING	APPLICATION
CHAPTER 9 • THE ENERGY OF WAVES			
25. "The Voyage of the Frog" (children's novel)	• Describe prior experience • Critical thinking • Directed reading	• Make inferences • Cite supporting evidence	• Conduct research • Complete a table
26. "What Does Outer Space Feel Like?" (astronomy Web site)	• Describe prior experience • Read for details	• Interpret a diagram • Critical thinking	• Conduct an interview
27. "What's up with 'zapped' foods?" (children's health magazine)	• Read for details	• Explain your answer	• Think about safety
CHAPTER 10 • SOUNDING OFF			
28. "A Shattering Sound" (technology newsletter)	• Use prior knowledge • Directed reading	• Make inferences	• Hands-on activity • Create a model
29. "The Physics of Music" (children's science magazine)	• Make a concept map • Read for details	• Analyze data from a table • Make inferences • Compare and contrast	• Write a paragraph
30. "Stop the Bleeding" (science news Web site)	• Critical thinking	• Make inferences	• Write a journal entry

? Did You Know?

Astronauts in space have to touch their helmets together in order to hear each other talk. That's because sound waves need to travel through a medium, and there is no air in space. But the sound waves can travel through the solid materials that make up the helmet.

Answers to *Find Out* Questions

CHAPTER 9
Yes; without the ozone layer between you and the sunlight, you could get a nasty sunburn in just a few seconds. (p. 99)

CHAPTER 10
Patterns in frequencies make some sounds pleasant, or musical. More random sounds are just noise. (p. 110)

CHAPTER 11
Optics, the science of light, makes it possible to create the illusion of a living head without a body. (p. 121)

CHAPTER 12
Your tongue is more likely to be burned by pie filling because it contains more heat energy than pie crust at the same temperature. (p. 128)

SCI LINKS.
THE WORLD'S A CLICK AWAY

www.scilinks.org
Keyword: Developing Classroom Activities
Code: GSSD05

93

SELECTION	READING	WRITING	APPLICATION
CHAPTER 11 • LIGHT IT UP!			
31. "Ben Franklin's Spectacles" (original letter)	• Reading for details	• Logical thinking	• Interpret an adage
32. "Color It In" (Australian TV series)	• Use your imagination • Generate questions	• Explain your answer • Make comparisons	• Hands-on activity • Visual perception • Propose explanations
33. "Magic: The Science of Illusion" (science museum exhibit)	• Use prior knowledge • Read for details	• Label a diagram • Use a protractor	• Propose explanations
CHAPTER 12 • HEATING THINGS UP			
34. "Steady as She Goes" (children's science magazine)	• Recall prior experiences • Read for details	• Interpret a technical diagram	• Write a scientific description
35. "Hot Stuff" (physics Web site)	• Directed reading	• Logical thinking	• Explain your reasoning
36. "It's Fuzzy Wuzzy Time " (backpacking magazine)	• Make a list • Critical reading	• Make comparisons	• Hands-on activity • Record data • Cite evidence to support answer

The Energy of Waves

LESSON 25

Battering Waves

Point of Lesson: *Mechanical waves, such as water waves, carry energy from one place to another.*

An excerpt from an adventure novel introduces mechanical waves. Students read a description of a small sailboat riding waves during a storm, then infer the conditions that would cause such large waves to form. Students interpret a diagram showing the parts of a wave and recognize the relationship between a wave's amplitude and how much energy it carries. Finally, they identify the forces that cause waves in some everyday objects and materials.

Materials

Introducing the Lesson (p. 94), for the class:
► rope (at least 3 m long)

Read (p. 95), for each group:
► materials to represent waves (optional)

Enrichment (p. 95), for each pair or group:
► aluminum baking pan
► water
► cork
► wooden stirring stick

Connections (p. 97), for the class:
► video or photographs of person surfing

LESSON 26

Do Astronauts Get Sunburned?

Point of Lesson: *Ultraviolet waves carry energy that can damage human skin cells.*

A scientist's answer to a seemingly simple question introduces students to energy in the form of electromagnetic waves. After reading a description of what would happen if an astronaut removed a glove in space, students interpret a diagram of the electromagnetic spectrum and relate a wave's frequency to its energy. They then compare electromagnetic waves that are used in everyday life and those that should be used only by trained professionals. Finally, students relate the energy of ultraviolet waves to sunburned skin and explore ways to prevent sunburn.

Materials

Enrichment (p. 99), for each pair or group:
► metal washers
► colored construction paper

LESSON 27

Zapped Foods

Point of Lesson: *Gamma rays contain energy that can be used to make food safe.*

In this lesson, students explore the use of gamma rays to sterilize food. An imaginary diary entry by a teen whose father works in the food industry introduces this use of gamma rays. Students identify disease-causing contaminants that are killed by gamma rays, then use their knowledge of electromagnetic waves to explain why workers must be shielded from gamma rays during the food irradiation process.

Materials

Enrichment (p. 103), for each student:
► drawing compass
► protractor

Background Information

Waves

Waves are classified as either mechanical or electromagnetic. Mechanical waves, such as sound waves, can only be propagated through matter. The wave causes a disturbance that presses molecules of matter together and then pulls them apart as it passes through. Without the particles of matter to compress and pull apart, mechanical waves do not exist.

Electromagnetic waves, which include all wavelengths of electromagnetic radiation, do not require a medium to propagate and can therefore travel through empty space. Electromagnetic waves are produced by all stars, including our sun. As the sun's rays move toward Earth's surface, most of the high-frequency, high-energy waves are filtered out by the ozone layer of the atmosphere. The energy of these waves can be harmful to living things, but their energy also makes them useful in combating disease.

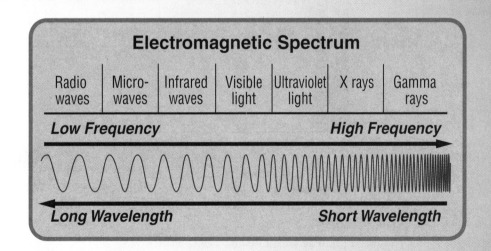

Electromagnetic Spectrum						
Radio waves	Micro- waves	Infrared waves	Visible light	Ultraviolet light	X rays	Gamma rays

Low Frequency → *High Frequency*

Long Wavelength ← *Short Wavelength*

Point of Lesson

Mechanical waves, such as water waves, carry energy from one place to another.

Focus

► Evidence, models, and explanation
► Transfer of energy
► Motion and forces

Skills and Strategies

► Communicating
► Recognizing cause and effect
► Making inferences
► Creating and using tables

Advance Preparation

Vocabulary

Make sure students understand these terms. Definitions can be found in the glossary at the end of the student book.

► energy
► wave

Materials

Gather the materials needed for *Introducing the Lesson* (below), *Read* (p. 95), *Enrichment* (p. 95), and *Connections* (p. 97).

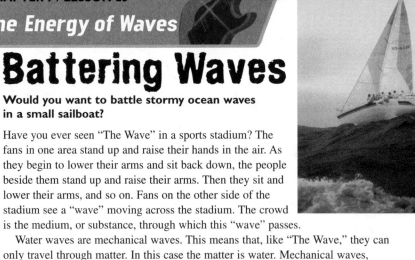

Battering Waves

Would you want to battle stormy ocean waves in a small sailboat?

Have you ever seen "The Wave" in a sports stadium? The fans in one area stand up and raise their hands in the air. As they begin to lower their arms and sit back down, the people beside them stand up and raise their arms. Then they sit and lower their arms, and so on. Fans on the other side of the stadium see a "wave" moving across the stadium. The crowd is the medium, or substance, through which this "wave" passes.

Water waves are mechanical waves. This means that, like "The Wave," they can only travel through matter. In this case the matter is water. Mechanical waves, including water waves, carry energy from one place to another.

▶ Before You Read

WATER WAVES Think about times when you have seen waves. You might have seen them in an ocean, lake, pond, or pool. Perhaps you've seen a movie or television show where a boat was being knocked about by the waves. Or, maybe you've even had such an experience of your own.

► *What experiences have you had with waves? Describe one experience.*

Answers will vary. Example: I was once in a rowboat that got rocked back

and forth by big waves coming from a fast motorboat that passed by.

_____

_____

_____

_____

_____

_____

_____

94

TEACHING PLAN pp. 94–95

INTRODUCING THE LESSON

Time: 5–10 minutes
Materials: rope (at least 3 m long)

This lesson describes mechanical waves and how they transfer energy. Find out what students already know about waves by asking them what they think of when they hear the word *wave*. Explain that there are many different kinds of waves. Tell students that in this lesson, they will be looking at mechanical waves—waves that travel through matter.

Explain that all waves carry energy from one place to another. Mechanical waves transfer energy by causing particles to vibrate, which vibrate nearby particles, and so on. If there are no particles to vibrate, a mechanical wave cannot move.

To demonstrate how mechanical waves move through matter, have two students each hold one end of a long rope. Then have one student shake his or her end of the rope gently up and down. Point out that the wave travels across the room but the rope does not. Ask students to identify the medium through which the wave is traveling. (the rope)

▶ Before You Read

WATER WAVES After students think about their experiences with water waves, have them list all other types of mechanical waves they can think of. (Examples: sound waves, earthquakes, waves on the surface of water, and waves in a Slinky, a rope, a flag, or flapping sheets on a clothesline)

▶ Read

In the novel *The Voyage of the Frog*, a 14-year-old boy named David sails alone into the Pacific Ocean aboard the *Frog*, a small sailboat. During a storm, the waves threaten his boat and his life.

The Voyage of the Frog

The wind had increased in strength. He climbed onto the cabin and reefed the main [sail] down to half size but left the jib full. Then he went back to the helm, brought her around, and the sails filled and the *Frog* started taking the swells.

There were waves coming in now as well, on top of the swells, growing in chop and intensity each moment. The *Frog* was slamming, making noise, but he held her angled up into the wind and took it. Spray came over the bow and covered him, soaking him, but he…would not…let the sea have her….

The wind became worse. <u>The waves grew until they were larger than the swells they rode on,</u> towering over him, burying the bow. <u>More than once he was knocked off his feet by a wall of water</u> coming back over the side of the cabin but he never let go of the helm, rose and took it again and again, held her through wave after wave when they rose over him, walls of water, mountains of water moving down on him, down on the *Frog*.

---

reefed: reduced the size of the sail by rolling it and tying it down
jib: a triangular sail in front of the main sail
helm: the steering wheel of a boat

swells: long waves that move continuously without breaking
chop: short, slapping motion
intensity: strength
bow: front section of a boat

From: Paulsen, Gary. *The Voyage of the Frog.* Orchard Books.

NOTEZONE

What do you think was the source of energy carried by the waves?

the wind

<u>Underline</u> three clues to the amount of energy in the waves.

FIND OUT MORE

SCIENCESAURUS
Characteristics of a Wave — 306
Kinds of Waves — 307

SCiLINKS
THE WORLD'S A CLICK AWAY
www.scilinks.org
Keyword: Ocean Waves
Code: GSPD11

95

Enrichment

Time: 15 minutes
Materials: aluminum baking pan, water, cork, wooden stirring stick

Have students work in pairs or small groups. Give them the following instructions.

1. Fill an aluminum baking pan half full with water.
2. When the water is still, use the stirring stick to tap the surface of the water. Watch how the water moves.
3. Place a cork in the water. Again, tap the surface of the water with the stirring stick. Watch how the cork moves. Then try to move the cork to the side of the dish by tapping the water with the stick.

Ask: *How did the water move when you tapped it?* (The water moved up and down in waves. The waves moved out in all directions.) *How did the cork move when you tapped the water?* (The cork moved up and down.) *Were you able to move the cork to the side of the dish? How can you explain your observations?* (No, the cork stayed in the same place. Students will probably offer different explanations for this. Some may realize that the waves were passing through the water, but the water itself only moved up and down, not sideways. As a result, the cork bobbed up and down but was not carried sideways.)

▶ Read

Time: 40–45 minutes for performing skits
Materials: materials to represent waves (optional)

Students may enjoy acting out the reading, since it is so full of action. Divide the class into groups. Tell the groups to create a skit that re-enacts this scene in the voyage of the *Frog*. Tell students to concentrate on the movement of the waves in the story. They may want to create props to represent the waves. Students could build their props with old sheets, cardboard, ropes, or other materials.

Let each group perform its skit for the rest of the class. Afterwards, lead students in a discussion about how the waves were moving. Ask: *How would you describe the motion of the waves?* (repetitive, choppy, up-and-down, and so on)

CHECK UNDERSTANDING
Skill: Communicating
Ask students to describe a mechanical wave in their own words. (Sample answer: A mechanical wave carries energy from one place to another. It can only move through matter.)

More Resources

The following resources are also available from Great Source and NSTA.

SCIENCESAURUS

READER'S HANDBOOK

www.scilinks.org
Keyword: Ocean Waves
Code: GSPD11

WIND AND WAVES Sailors—like David in *The Voyage of the Frog*—depend on energy from the wind to power their boats. Moving air particles push against the sails and move the boat forward.

Winds blowing over the ocean also transfer their energy to the water, creating ocean waves. The size of the waves created by wind and the amount of energy they contain is determined by several factors. Three of these factors are shown in the chart. Each one affects the amount of energy that is transferred from the wind to the water. The greater the amount of energy that is transferred, the larger the waves are.

Factors Affecting the Size of Water Waves		
Wind Velocity	**Wind Duration**	**Fetch**
the speed at which the wind blows in a certain direction	the length of time the wind blows	the area the wind blows over

▶ **What can you infer about the velocity of the wind in the reading from The Voyage of the Frog? What clues help you make this inference?**

The wind is fast. The reading tells first that the wind had increased in

strength and then it became worse.

▶ **What can you infer about the duration of the wind in the reading? What clues help you make this inference?**

The wind duration is long. The text says that the wind "had" increased in

strength, indicating that the wind has already been blowing for a time.

Also, it says "again and again," indicating a passage of time.

▶ **What can you infer about the fetch of the wind? What clues help you make this inference?**

The reading does not say anything about the area covered by the wind,

but it gives a sense that this is a large storm, which would mean that

the fetch is large.

▶ **What do the clues about wind velocity, wind duration, and fetch tell you about the amount of energy in the waves that struck the Frog?**

Together they created very large waves with a lot of energy in them.

96

TEACHING PLAN pp. 96–97

▶ Explore

WIND AND WAVES Before students complete the questions in this section, ask: *How would you describe the size of the waves that would be created by a gentle breeze that does not last long?* (Small waves would be created.) *How much energy would these waves carry?* (The wind would not transfer much energy to the water, so the waves would not carry much energy.)

Then ask: *How would you describe the size of the waves that would be created by a strong, steady wind that blows over a large area?* (Large waves would

form.) *How much energy would be transferred from the wind to the water?* (a lot of energy) *How much energy would these waves contain?* (a lot of energy)

After students complete the section, have them create a graphic organizer illustrating the relationship between the amount of energy a wave contains and the size of the wave. (Students' graphic organizers should show a direct relationship between the size of a wave and the amount of energy carried by the wave.)

HOW STRONG ARE THE WAVES? All water waves have the same basic shape. The dashed line in the diagram represents the water surface at rest. A wave moving along the water surface has a crest and a trough. The crest is the highest point of the wave and the trough is the lowest. Amplitude is the distance from the resting point to the crest of the wave. The greater the amplitude, the greater the amount of energy the wave carries.

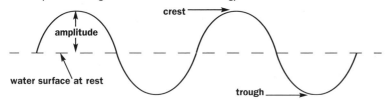

▶ *What can you infer about the amplitude of the waves that struck the Frog? What evidence do you have?*

The amplitude is large. The waves were like walls or mountains of

water. The waves towered over David and buried the bow of the boat.

▶ *What does this tell you about the amount of energy in the waves in the story?*

The amount of energy in the waves was very great.

▶ *The wind transferred some of its energy to the water, making waves. What did the waves transfer some of their energy to? What evidence do you have?*

The waves transferred energy to the boat and David. They slammed into

the Frog *and knocked David over.*

▶ Take Action

THAT'S DISTURBING! In *The Voyage of the Frog*, the wind's motion is the "disturbing force" that creates the ocean waves. Every mechanical wave has a disturbing force that creates it. For each kind of wave below, write what might be the disturbing force. If necessary, do some research to get ideas.

Mechanical Wave	Disturbing Force
A flag waving at the top of a flagpole	*wind*
Ripples in a pond	*Answers will vary. Example: a fish jumping*
Vibrations of a guitar string	*someone plucking the string*

97

Connections

Time: will vary
Materials: video or photographs of person surfing

PHYSICAL EDUCATION Show students a video or photographs of someone surfing. Ask students to describe how the surfer interacts with the large waves. (Students should note that the surfer attempts to ride the front of the wave into shore, staying between the crest of the wave and the level water surface.)

Assessment

Skill: Making inferences

Use the following task to assess each student's progress:

Tell students that all sounds we hear are created by sound waves. Like other mechanical waves, sound waves have a certain amplitude. Ask: *What can you infer about the amplitude of sound waves that produce loud music compared with the amplitude of sound waves that produce soft music?* (Example: Loud music seems to carry more energy than soft music. I know this because loud music can hurt my ears. Therefore, loud music must be produced by sound waves of a larger amplitude than the sound waves that produce soft music.)

▶ Propose Explanations

HOW STRONG ARE THE WAVES? Tell students that amplitude is not the only variable involved in how much energy a wave has. Ask students to examine the wave diagram on this page and try to think of another way a wave's energy can vary. Students may notice the distance between two wave crests (wavelength) or how close together the waves are (related to frequency). Students will probably not know the terms for these concepts, but they might be able to describe them.

Ask students to make an inference about how frequency is related to energy level. Lead students to understand that the frequency of a wave is directly related to its energy level. That is, the greater the number of waves that strike per second, the more energy is transferred.

▶ Take Action

THAT'S DISTURBING! To help students identify the disturbing forces, ask them what they would do to get a flag to wave, to get ripples to form in a pond, or to get guitar strings to vibrate.

Students might be interested to know that there is another disturbing force besides wind that can create large waves in the ocean. An earthquake that occurs in Earth's crust below the ocean can cause huge waves. These waves are called tsunamis. Often when tsunamis hit land, they cause mass destruction.

Point of Lesson
Ultraviolet waves carry energy that can damage human skin cells.

Focus
▶ Evidence, models, and explanation
▶ Transfer of energy
▶ Personal health

Skills and Strategies
▶ Communicating
▶ Interpreting scientific illustrations
▶ Making inferences
▶ Collecting and recording data

Advance Preparation

Vocabulary
Make sure students understand these terms. Definitions can be found in the glossary at the end of the student book.

▶ electromagnetic wave
▶ heat
▶ temperature

Materials
Gather the materials needed for *Enrichment* (p. 99).

Do Astronauts Get 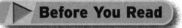 SUNBURNED?

With no protection, an astronaut in space would be sunburned in just seconds.

Imagine standing on a beach watching the waves come in to shore. Step into the water and you can feel each wave hit your legs. While you stand there, other waves are hitting you, too. They are waves that come from the sun and they are called electromagnetic waves. Like all waves, electromagnetic waves carry energy. While water waves can only travel through matter, electromagnetic waves can also travel through a vacuum, or a place without matter. Much of space is a vacuum.

When astronauts go into space, they must wear space suits, complete with gloves and helmets, to survive in the vacuum. Inside their space suits they have oxygen to breathe. Space suits also protect them from the energy of the sun's electromagnetic waves.

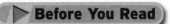 **Before You Read**

FEEL THE BURN Have you ever been sunburned? Where were you? Do you remember what the weather was like? What time of year was it? What time of day? Do you remember what you were wearing? Write about your experience.

Answers will vary. Example: Last winter when we went to Arizona I got
sunburned. It was sunny, but it didn't seem very hot so I didn't think I
needed sunscreen. I spent a whole day outside only wearing shorts
and a T-shirt and I got burned everywhere.

UNIT 3: SOUND, LIGHT, AND HEAT

98

TEACHING PLAN pp. 98–99

INTRODUCING THE LESSON
This lesson looks at electromagnetic waves and how they can affect human health.

Point out to students that you can tell water waves carry energy because you can feel their power as they hit your legs when you are at the beach. Ask students how they can tell that the waves from the sun also carry energy. If necessary, remind them that heat and light are both forms of energy. (You can feel the heat of the sun warming your skin, and the bright light makes you squint.)

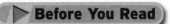 **Before You Read**

FEEL THE BURN As students write about their experiences with sunburn, they will be thinking about how sunlight affects their skin. Ask students how sunlight affects other materials. (Students may note that sunlight will fade the color in fabrics, heat rocks and metals, melt snow, and so on.)

This would be a good opportunity to point out that while some rays from the sun are harmful, life on Earth depends on energy from the sun.

Remind students that plants use light energy from the sun to convert carbon dioxide and water into sugars and starches. These substances provide food for both the plants themselves and the animals that eat them.

> ▶ **Read** 🔲🔳

What would happen if an astronaut took off a glove during a space walk? Here's how physics professor Philip Plait answered that question.

WHAT DOES OUTER SPACE FEEL LIKE?

Space doesn't feel like anything, because there is nothing to feel! Space is a vacuum (or near enough). It's a common question to ask how hot space is (or how cold), but space itself has no temperature. However, the Sun is hot, and [it gives off that energy in the form of electromagnetic waves]. You [or any other object] absorb [some of] that [energy] and feel heat. Near the Earth, a person floating in space would...not receive enough [heat energy] to keep from freezing! You yourself would radiate away your heat, and that's why spacesuits have heaters in them....

Surprisingly, the worst thing that might happen [if you took off your glove] is that you'd get a bad sunburn. Without the Earth's protective ozone layer between you and the raw sunlight, the ultraviolet light from the Sun could give you a nasty sunburn in just a few seconds! If you're an astronaut doing a tricky maneuver, better pack the sunblock!

ozone layer: a layer of the atmosphere
ultraviolet light: high-energy electromagnetic waves
maneuver: a procedure requiring skill

From: Guess, Malcolm. "What Does Outer Space Feel Like?" *Bad Astronomy.* (www.badastronomy.com/mad/1999/space_feel.html)

◀ Astronaut Winston Scott in a spacesuit, on Columbia mission STS-87

99

NOTEZONE

Underline the type of electromagnetic waves that can give you a sunburn.

Circle what protects you from electromagnetic waves when you are on Earth.

FIND OUT MORE

SCIENCESAURUS

Characteristics of a Wave	306
Kinds of Waves	307
Electromagnetic Spectrum	309

Enrichment

Time: 2 or 3 days (partial class time)
Materials: metal washers, colored construction paper

Encourage interested students to do the following activity to explore the effect of ultraviolet light on common materials.

Have students work in pairs or small groups. Give students the following instructions:

1. Place small pieces of colored construction paper outside in direct sunlight. Use a variety of colors.
2. Place washers on the paper.
3. Leave the setup outside for two or three days.
4. Remove the washers and examine the paper.

Ask: *What happened to the construction paper?* (Except for the areas covered by washers, the color faded.) *What evidence do you have that ultraviolet light from the sun broke down the different paper dyes at different rates?* (Some colors faded more than others did.) *What evidence do you have that ultraviolet light did not travel through the washers?* (The spots under the washers did not fade at all.)

> ▶ **Read**

Have students read the passage to themselves silently. Then have a volunteer reread the second paragraph aloud. Draw students' attention to the term "raw sunlight" in the second sentence. Ask: *What do you think that means?* (Answers will vary.) Students should note that the word *raw* was used to show that in space, sunlight is not changed or filtered in any way. The term emphasizes the difference between sunlight in space and sunlight on Earth. Sunlight that strikes Earth's surface has been filtered by the atmosphere, in particular the atmosphere's ozone layer.

CHECK UNDERSTANDING
Skill: Making inferences
Tell students that scientists have found that the ozone layer is thinner than it used to be. Ask: *Why would it concern scientists to find out that the ozone layer in the atmosphere is getting very thin in some places?* (If the layer became too thin, it wouldn't protect us from harmful ultraviolet light from the sun.)

More Resources

The following resources are also available from Great Source.

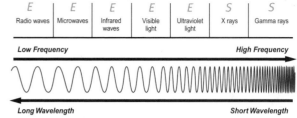

> Explore

INTERPRET A DIAGRAM The diagram shows all the types of electromagnetic waves given off by the sun. The waves are in the order of their frequencies, starting with the lower frequencies at the left. Remember, frequency is the measure of how many waves pass by a point each second.

E	E	E	E	E	S	S
Radio waves	Microwaves	Infrared waves	Visible light	Ultraviolet light	X rays	Gamma rays

Low Frequency ——————→ High Frequency

Long Wavelength ←—————— Short Wavelength

The higher the frequency of the waves, the more energy they carry. The more energy a wave carries, the more dangerous it is to living things. Luckily, the atmosphere protects Earth from most high-energy waves. You read that a layer of ozone in the atmosphere protects us from most of the ultraviolet light from the sun. But some ultraviolet light still gets through.

▶ *Why might ultraviolet light waves cause sunburn when visible light waves do not?*

Ultraviolet light waves carry more energy.

WHICH WAVES ARE SAFE? All the electromagnetic waves shown in the diagram above are given off by sources other than the sun as well. Radios and microwave ovens are common household objects. Infrared heat lamps are used in restaurants to keep food warm. Every room at home has at least one light bulb that gives off visible light. Ultraviolet lamps are sometimes used at amusement parks to give a Day-Glo effect. Other types of electromagnetic waves are used only by trained professionals. X rays are used by doctors to create pictures of the body. Gamma rays are used in hospitals to sterilize medical equipment.

▶ *Mark each type of electromagnetic wave shown on the diagram above. Use an "E" to label the types that can be used by everyone. Use an "S" to label the types that require special training.*

▶ *How are the frequencies of the waves related to who can use them? Why do you think this is?*

The ones with lower frequencies can be used by all because they

have less energy. The highest frequencies are only used by professionals.

They have so much energy they are dangerous.

100

Teaching Plan pp. 100–101

> Explore

INTERPRET A DIAGRAM Draw students' attention to the diagram of the types of electromagnetic waves given off by the sun. Explain that wavelength (labeled in the bottom portion of the diagram) is the distance between the crest of one wave and the crest of the next. Ask students to study the diagram and describe how wavelength and frequency seem to be related. (The longer the wavelength, the lower the frequency.)

Before students answer the question, have them label the "high energy" and "low energy" sides of the diagram. (The left side is low energy and the right side is high energy.) Help students answer the question by having them compare the positions of visible light and ultraviolet light on the diagram to determine which carries more energy. (ultraviolet light)

WHICH WAVES ARE SAFE? Ask: *What are the two highest-energy waves given off by the sun?* (X rays and gamma rays) Explain that X rays and gamma rays are stopped by the oxygen and nitrogen in the atmosphere before they reach Earth's surface. Ask: *Why do you think it is especially important that these particular rays from the sun are stopped by the atmosphere?* (They would injure living things more than ultraviolet light does because they have more energy.) Tell students that they will learn more about gamma rays in the next lesson.

Propose Explanations

ULTRAVIOLET WAVES AND SKIN Scientists have discovered a direct connection between exposure to ultraviolet light and certain kinds of skin damage. Scientists don't know exactly how ultraviolet light damages skin. What they do know is that the energy of these waves causes chemical reactions inside skin cells. These reactions probably release substances that damage the cell. The result of too much ultraviolet light is sunburn, deep wrinkles, thickened skin, brown spots, and possibly skin cancer. In addition to damaging skin, ultraviolet light can cause damage to the eyes.

One way to protect yourself from sunburn is to use sunblock or sunscreen. These contain substances that either absorb or reflect ultraviolet wavelengths. Either action prevents most (but not all) of the damaging waves from reaching your skin.

▶ *Professor Plait suggests that an astronaut's skin could be protected from sunburn by a sunblock. Why might sunblock not be enough to prevent sunburn out in space?*

In space, the astronaut does not have the protection of the ozone layer.

The amount of ultraviolet light reaching her skin will be much greater.

Sunblock might not be able to block out all the energy.

▶ *What jobs here on Earth might expose people to more skin and eye damage than usual? (Hint: Damage is not only caused by lack of protection, but by spending long periods of time in bright sunlight.)*

Answers will vary. Examples: lifeguards, letter carriers, farmers, ski

instructors, fishers, park rangers

Take Action

CONDUCT AN INTERVIEW Sunburn greatly increases the risk of certain skin and eye cancers. For people who need to be outside all day every day, sunny weather can be a serious danger. Interview a lifeguard or someone else who works all day in the sun to find out what they do to protect their skin and eyes. Record what you find out below.

wear a hat, sunglasses, and tightly woven clothing that covers the skin;

wear SPF 15 or higher sunscreen

101

Connections

MATH Students may be interested to know that all electromagnetic waves (including visible light) travel through space at a speed faster than anything else known—about 300,000,000 m/s. The distance from the sun to Earth is about 150,000,000,000 m. Have students calculate the time it takes for light to travel from the sun to Earth. If necessary, give them the following hint: speed = distance ÷ time. (time = distance ÷ speed; time = 150,000,000,000 m ÷ 300,000,000 m/s = 500 seconds, or about 8 minutes). Then have students calculate the time it takes the sun's reflected light to travel from the moon to Earth. The distance to the moon is about 384,000,000 m. (384,000,000 m ÷ 300,000,000 = 1.28 seconds)

Assessment
Skill: Communicating

Use the following questions to assess each student's progress:

What kind of electromagnetic waves cause skin damage? (ultraviolet waves) *Do they have long or short wavelengths?* (short) *Is their frequency high or low?* (high) *How is frequency related to the energy of the wave?* (The higher the frequency, the more energy it carries.)

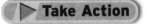

Propose Explanations

ULTRAVIOLET WAVES AND SKIN Invite a health care professional to visit the class and give a presentation about skin cancer. Ask the presenter to concentrate on the most common causes of skin cancer and how people can protect their skin from the sun. Encourage students to prepare a list of questions for the presenter before he or she arrives. Also suggest that they take notes as the presenter speaks. After the presenter leaves, have students write a summary of the major points the presenter made. You may want to

have students use the information provided by the presenter to make a skin care pamphlet that can be placed in the school's library.

Take Action

CONDUCT AN INTERVIEW Before students conduct their interviews, ask them what they already know about sunscreens and sunblocks. (Students will probably mention that they protect the skin from ultraviolet waves and that their SPF numbers describe their strength.) Ask: *What does SPF stand for?* (sun protective factor) *What does*

the SPF number represent? (how many times longer a person can stay in the sun without getting a sunburn) Explain that an SPF of 15, for example, means if you can stay in the sun for 10 minutes without getting sunburned, with the lotion you can stay 15 times longer— in this case, 150 minutes. Emphasize, though, that the extended time applies only if the lotion is not rubbed off accidentally or washed off when the user swims. It is always a good idea to reapply lotion before the SPF time limit runs out.

Point of Lesson

Gamma rays contain energy that can be used to make food safe.

Focus

► **Evidence, models, and explanation**
► **Transfer of energy**
► **Science and technology in society**
► **Risks and benefits**
► **Personal health**

Skills and Strategies

► **Interpreting scientific illustrations**
► **Communicating**
► **Making inferences**

Advance Preparation

Materials

Gather the materials needed for *Enrichment* (p. 103).

More Resources

The following resources are also available from Great Source.

SCIENCESAURUS

READER'S HANDBOOK

TEACHING PLAN pp. 102–103

Zapped Foods

Electromagnetic waves have uses as well as dangers.

If you buy fast-food burgers or chicken, you might have eaten food zapped with electromagnetic waves. Sound dangerous? It's actually been done to protect you. Over a century ago, scientists discovered that electromagnetic waves can be used to kill bacteria in food. Today, this process is becoming more and more common.

NOTEZONE

Underline the type of electromagnetic waves that can be used to kill bacteria.

FIND OUT MORE

SCIENCESAURUS

102

▶ **Read**

What would you write in your diary if your dad was going to work in a place that "zapped" meat? Here's one writer's idea.

What's up with "zapped" foods?

Dear Diary,

Bad news! We have to move. My dad got a job...at [a] meat lab.... [H]e will be working with meat that is irradiated (ear-RAY-dee-ay-ted).... [H]e'll be using gamma rays to zap and kill bacteria in the meat. It's the bacteria that make people sick....

I asked my science teacher about irradiation.... He told me to look it up...and give a report to the class.... I did some research, and here's what I've written so far:

"Irradiation makes foods safe to eat by killing the bacteria in meat and poultry. It also kills trichina (trih-KY-nuh) worms in pork and insects in wheat, potatoes, flour, spices, tea, fruits, and vegetables...."

Foods aren't changed when they are irradiated. A raw apple stays crisp and juicy, and meat isn't cooked.... Of course the big question is—is it really safe?

© GREAT SOURCE. COPYING IS PROHIBITED.

INTRODUCING THE LESSON

This lesson focuses on the use of the energy in electromagnetic waves to kill dangerous bacteria in food.

Ask students to describe what happens to food on the shelf or in the refrigerator if it is not eaten in a reasonable amount of time. (It goes bad, gets moldy, or loses its taste.) Describe the process of pasteurization to students. Explain that pasteurization uses heat to kill microscopic organisms in food. Tell students that milk and fruit juices are two kinds of foods that are commonly pasteurized. Ask: *Why is pasteurization*

not a good choice for meat? (The heat would cook the meat.)

▶ **Read**

Tell students that not everyone approves of irradiating food. Some scientists believe that irradiating food destroys nutrients as well as bacteria. For example, they have evidence that fruits and vegetables lose some of their vitamin A and vitamin C. Other scientists worry that irradiating food may cause harmful, cancer-causing molecules to form in food. Still others worry about trans-

porting and handling the radioactive material (usually cobalt 60) that produces the gamma rays. Accidents could expose large numbers of people to dangerous levels of radiation. Ask: *What questions would you want answered before you made a decision about whether or not to buy irradiated foods?* (Examples: Can I get sick from eating irradiated foods? Is the danger from the irradiation greater or less than the danger from bacteria?)

Here's what I found out:

"The process can't be used on all foods, but it is used on many. It not only kills bacteria that will make you sick, but it also keeps foods fresh.... That means some foods don't need to be refrigerated after going through the irradiation process."

Amanda

irradiated: treated with electromagnetic radiation

bacteria: microscopic organisms, some of which cause diseases

trichina worms: tiny worms found in pork that can cause serious disease

From: Murphy, Dee. "What's Up with 'Zapped' Foods?" *Current Health*.

 **Explore**

HOW DOES IT WORK? Gamma rays are one type of electromagnetic wave. Circle their position on the diagram on page 100.

Electromagnetic waves with higher frequencies carry more energy than those with lower frequencies.

▶ *Compared to other electromagnetic waves, are gamma rays high-energy or low-energy? Explain how you know.*

high-energy because they have higher frequencies than all the other

waves

▶ *How is the energy in gamma waves used to make food safe?*

It is used to kill the bacteria, trichina worms, and insects in food that can

make people sick. The high-energy waves kill these organisms.

In food irradiation plants, packaged food is placed on a moving belt that carries the food into a sealed room. There the food is exposed to gamma rays. Then the moving belt carries the food out of the room. All workers are carefully protected from getting anywhere near the gamma rays.

▶ *Why do you think the "zapping" is done by machines while people are far away?*

The gamma rays are high energy and could harm a person's cells.

103

Enrichment

Time: will vary
Materials: drawing compass, protractor

According to one survey, almost half of people questioned were willing to buy irradiated meat or poultry products, about 31 percent would not buy them, and the rest were not sure. Have students survey people they know to find out if they would buy irradiated meat or poultry. (Students may need to explain what irradiation is.) Tell students to ask the people to explain their positions. Have students show their results in a circle graph. (To create a circle graph, determine what percentage of the total number of participants each group makes up, then multiply that number by 360. For example, a group that was 25 percent of the total would be represented by a 90° sector: $0.25 \times 360° = 90°$).

Assessment

Skill: Designing an experiment

Use the following task to assess each student's progress:

Have students design an experiment to test the effectiveness of gamma rays in keeping food fresh. Ask: *How would the experiment be set up? What variables would you need to keep in mind?* (Experiment designs should include controlling all variables except the one being tested: exposure to gamma rays.)

▶ **Explore**

HOW DOES IT WORK? Have students refer back to the diagram on page 100. Ask them to identify the highest-energy electromagnetic waves (gamma rays) and the lowest-energy waves. (radio waves)

Explain that although gamma rays are harmful to living things, they can also be used to treat people with cancer. Doctors focus a narrow beam of gamma rays on cancerous tumors inside a person's body. The high-energy rays kill the growing tumor without damaging the rest of the person's body.

Invite students to conduct a debate about whether their community should allow irradiated foods to be sold in grocery stores. If students decide to allow it, ask what restrictions or safety checks the community might require. If students decide not to allow irradiated foods, ask them to identify factors that might influence them to change their minds.

CHECK UNDERSTANDING
Skill: Making inferences
Remind students that gamma waves are at the high-frequency end of the electromagnetic spectrum. Ask: *How do the wavelength, frequency, and energy of gamma waves compare with the wavelength, frequency, and energy of other electromagnetic waves?* (Gamma waves have the shortest wavelength, the highest frequency, and carry the most energy.)

Sounding Off

LESSON 28

Bad Vibrations

Point of Lesson: *Sound waves can move or change matter.*

Sound can shatter a glass! An article describing a professor's demonstration of this phenomenon leads students to consider the evidence showing that sound is a form of energy. Students then perform an activity modeling how the pressure created by sound waves shattered the glass.

Materials

Before You Read (p. 104), for each student:
- ▶ rubber band

Read (p. 105), for the class:
- ▶ water glasses or wine glasses of different shapes and sizes (optional)

Enrichment (p. 105), for each group:
- ▶ tuning fork
- ▶ plastic cup
- ▶ water

Activity (p. 107), for each student:
- ▶ 2 plastic foam coffee cups

LESSON 29

Good Vibrations

Point of Lesson: *Music is a pattern of sounds that are mathematically related.*

Students explore what makes a sound musical or nonmusical. By reading about Caribbean steel drums, students discover the traits of musical tone—pitch, volume, and timbre—and relate these traits to the frequency and wavelength of sound waves. Students then analyze data to determine which of two sets of tones was produced by a musical instrument. Finally, they compare and contrast music and noise and describe the sound of their favorite musical instruments.

Materials

Science Scope Activity (p. 104B and p. 109), for students working in small groups or individually; assorted craft supplies such as:
- ▶ cardboard
- ▶ plastic wrap
- ▶ glue
- ▶ paper cups
- ▶ rubber bands
- ▶ string
- ▶ tape
- ▶ shoe boxes
- ▶ straws

Explore (p. 110)
for each pair:
- ▶ 3-m length of rope
for the class:
- ▶ recording of sounds at different pitches (optional)

Take Action (p. 111), for the class:
- ▶ recordings of musical instruments (optional)

Laboratory Safety

Review the following safety guidelines with students before they do the *Science Scope* Activity in this lesson.
- ▶ Handle the rubber bands responsibly to avoid injuring yourself and others.
- ▶ Do not share any wind instruments you invent. Only one person's mouth should be used on any one wind instrument.

LESSON 30

Healing Vibrations

Point of Lesson: *Ultrasound is a form of sound energy used in medicine.*

Ultrasound has uses in medicine beyond imaging. Students read an article describing two ways that ultrasound is used to heal wounds: one method is in use, the other is experimental. They then compare the frequencies of ultrasound to the frequencies of sound that humans can hear to explain why everyday sounds do not cause the changes that ultrasound does. The lesson ends with students proposing an engineering problem that could be addressed using sound energy.

Materials

Science Scope Activity

Lend Me Your Ears

NSTA has chosen a Science Scope *activity related to the content in this chapter. The activity begins here and continues in Lesson 29, page 109.*

Time: 30 minutes
Materials: see page 104A

Lead the class in a discussion about different types of musical instruments that people have invented. Have students brainstorm a list of as many instruments as they can, and write the list on the board. Ask students to explain how each instrument is similar to and different from the others. Also ask them to suggest different ways that musical instruments can be classified. For example, instruments are usually classified as woodwind, brass, percussion, string, keyboard, and (in modern times) electronic.

(continued on page 109)

Background Information

Sound Waves

Sound waves are mechanical waves. That is, they only move through matter. A plucked string on a guitar will vibrate, causing a disturbance that presses molecules of air together and then pulls them apart as it travels through them. When the disturbance reaches our eardrums, it causes them to vibrate, too. With a little help from the brain, we hear a sound.

The total amount of energy carried by a wave is determined by both its amplitude and its frequency. The larger the wave (amplitude) and the more times it strikes an object in a given amount of time (frequency), the more energy it will transfer. Loud sounds transfer more energy than soft sounds, and high-frequency waves transfer more energy than low-frequency waves. Due to their ability to change matter, high-frequency waves have medical applications, as students will see in Lesson 30.

Point of Lesson
Sound waves can move or change matter.

Focus
► **Properties and changes of properties in matter**
► **Motion and forces**
► **Transfer of energy**
► **Evidence, models, and explanation**
► **Change, constancy, and measurement**

Skills and Strategies
► **Observing**
► **Making inferences**
► **Recognizing cause and effect**
► **Making and using models**

Advance Preparation

Vocabulary
Make sure students understand these terms. Definitions can be found in the glossary at the end of the student book.
► **vibration**
► **wave**

Materials
Gather the materials needed for **Before You Read** (below), **Read** (p. 105), **Enrichment** (p. 105), and **Activity** (p. 107).

BAD VIBRATIONS

◄ Tuning fork

Can you see sound?
Have you ever noticed an object shaking back and forth? Maybe you've seen a washing machine struggling through a spin cycle, or a tuning fork after it's been struck against someone's palm. If so, you've seen vibrations. Often, vibrating objects (such as violin strings) create sound waves. But sometimes sound waves cause objects to vibrate.

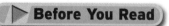
► **Before You Read**

CAN YOU SEE WHAT YOU HEAR? A sound wave traveling through air is a vibration sensed by our ears. When sound travels through a liquid or solid we can sometimes see or feel the vibrations. Walls and windows don't have ears, but loud sounds can make them tremble. Try to remember a time you heard a sound so loud that you saw or felt something in your house vibrate.

► *Describe the sound and the objects you felt or saw vibrating.*

Answers will vary. Examples: When jet planes fly low I hear the glasses

on the shelf rattle; if the thunder is really loud I see the hanging lights

swing; if the music is really loud I hear the windows rattle.

_____

_____

_____

_____

_____

_____

_____

104

UNIT 3: SOUND, LIGHT, AND HEAT

TEACHING PLAN pp. 104–105

INTRODUCING THE LESSON
This lesson encourages students to think about how sound waves can affect matter. Ask students if they have ever seen anything physically changed by sound. Some students may not be aware that sound is something that can sometimes be felt or that could affect objects. Ask them if they have ever heard a car alarm being set off by a loud noise. The sound waves exert pressure on the car just as a person would when trying to open the car door. The car alarm has been fooled— there is no person there, just sound waves hitting the car.

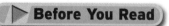
► **Before You Read**

Time: 10 minutes
Materials: (for each student) rubber band

CAN YOU SEE WHAT YOU HEAR? Have students explore sound and vibration by first placing their hand on their throat and humming at different volumes. Ask students to describe what they feel. (Students may note that they feel a vibration and that the vibration gets stronger when the volume increases.) Then have students explore sound and vibration using a variety of other

objects, such as a rubber band. When they pull the rubber band taut and pluck it, they will see that it vibrates while making a sound.

▶ **Read**

Physics professor Walter Lewin showed a group of science teachers a way to see sounds.

A Shattering Sound

[Professor Lewin's presentation made] good use of both sight and sound, and touched a good many eardrums. Professor Lewin used...visual demonstrations...to explain sound waves. [T]hen...[he shattered] a wine glass with a loud, even tone....

...Sound is a pressure wave that compresses and decompresses the air to make a vibration.... [A vibration is] a disturbance that [spreads, like movement] through a [crowd] of people when one begins...shoving the next. When that pressure wave reaches your ear, the eardrum begins to vibrate at the same frequency, and your brain tells you something.

...[Sound can also be destructive when it makes an object] vibrate at a ... special frequency to which it is extremely sensitive.... [To demonstrate this,] Professor Lewin... rubbed a moistened finger around the rim of a wine glass to find the [special] tone, or frequency, ...of that glass. Then [he used] an electronic device to reproduce the tone at high volume. [This]...shattered the [glass] with sound waves.

compress: press together
decompress: push apart
frequency: the number of sound waves produced per second
moistened: wet

From: Brehm, Denise. "Lewin Shows Properties of Sound." Massachusetts Institute of Technology News Office. (web.mit.edu/newsoffice/tt/1998/jul15/conflewin.html)

NoteZone

Underline ways that sound moved or changed matter in the reading.

FIND OUT MORE

SCIENCESAURUS

Forms of Energy	300
Waves	305
Sound	312
Properties of Sound	313

SCILINKS.
THE WORLD'S A CLICK AWAY

www.scilinks.org
Keyword: Sound
Code: GSPD12

105

Enrichment

Time: 20 minutes
Materials: tuning fork, plastic cup, water

Let students do the following activity in small groups. Give each group a tuning fork and a plastic cup filled with water. Instruct students to strike the tuning fork on their palm and then slowly lower its prongs into the plastic cup without touching the water. Ask students to record their observations. (Students should observe that as the tuning fork nears the water, the water begins to move.) Ask students what was causing the water to move. (Students should realize that the sound waves produced by the tuning fork reached the water and caused it to vibrate.)

Have students repeat the exercise a few more times, varying how hard they strike the tuning fork. Have students discuss their observations with the rest of the class. Ask students how sound waves can cause objects to vibrate. Lead students to recognize that the energy in sound waves is transferred to the object, causing it to vibrate.

▶ **Read**

Time: 15 minutes
Materials: water glasses or wine glasses of different shapes and sizes (optional)

Encourage students to make diagrams, models, or other visual aids that illustrate the meaning of *compress, decompress,* and *frequency.* For example, students might draw somebody pushing a group of small objects close together to show the meaning of compress, somebody pulling objects apart to show the meaning of decompress, and objects placed at regular intervals to show frequency. Have students display their visual aids to the rest of the class.

After students have finished reading the passage, you may want to have each student run a moist finger around the rim of a glass to hear the tone that the glass produces. This tone is the one that would shatter the glass if it were loud enough. Provide an assortment of glasses so students can hear that each one produces a different tone.

CHECK UNDERSTANDING
Skill: Recognizing cause and effect
Ask students: *What happens to air when a sound wave moves through it?* (The air is compressed and decompressed over and over again.) *Under what circumstances will an object break when exposed to very loud sound?* (when the frequency of the sound is the one to which the object is particularly sensitive)

More Resources

The following resources are also available from Great Source and NSTA.

ScienceSaurus

Reader's Handbook

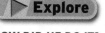

www.scilinks.org
Keyword: Sound
Code: GSPD12

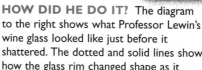

HOW DID HE DO IT? The diagram to the right shows what Professor Lewin's wine glass looked like just before it shattered. The dotted and solid lines show how the glass rim changed shape as it vibrated. The rim was pushed out of shape more and more as each second passed. After several seconds of the sound playing, the glass shattered.

▶ *Describe how sound was able to change the shape of the wine glass. Use information from the diagram in your answer.*

The energy of the sound waves made

the glass vibrate. As it vibrated, the rim moved back and forth.

_____

▶ *How was sound able to shatter the glass?*

As the rim moved back and forth over and over again, the force was

eventually great enough to break the glass.

_____

MAKE INFERENCES

▶ *Energy is the ability to move or change matter. How did Professor Lewin demonstrate that sound is energy?*

He used sound to break a glass.

_____

_____

▶ *The reading states that Professor Lewin used sound at a high volume. What can you infer about the connection between the energy of the sound wave and the volume of the sound?*

The higher the volume the more energy the sound wave has.

_____

_____

_____

Teaching Plan pp. 106–107

▶ Explore

HOW DID HE DO IT? Students may have difficulty understanding that the wine glass actually changes shape a little without breaking. In our everyday experiences, glass is not at all flexible. Explain that the diagram shows exaggerated movement, but the glass can in fact flex a little before shattering. However, because glass is so breakable (brittle), very small vibrations are all that is needed to shatter the glass, which is why sound can carry enough energy to do the job.

MAKE INFERENCES Ask students: *How do you know sound is a form of energy?* (Sound can move or change matter.) After students infer that a louder sound carries more energy, ask them to think about where that energy comes from. Lead students to realize that hitting a gong hard to make a louder sound, for example, takes more energy than tapping it gently to make a soft sound. Similarly, pulling a banjo string farther before letting it go makes a louder sound and requires more energy input.

▶ Activity

CREATE A MODEL

The sound in Professor Lewin's demonstration shattered the wine glass by causing the rim of the glass to quickly flex back and forth between a circular shape and an oval shape. Use the following model to see this effect in slow motion.

What You Need:
• 2 plastic foam coffee cups

What to Do:
1. Hold one cup upright between the palms of your hands. As slowly as you can, press your palms together, gently squishing the rim of the cup until opposite sides touch. Then slowly release the cup.
2. Turn the cup one-quarter turn and hold it between your palms again. Press your hands together very slowly until the rim is flattened.
▶ *What happened to the cup?*

  Either the cup was squished but did not crack, or it cracked only a little.

3. Hold the second cup upright between the palms of your hands. Quickly clap your hands together, flattening the rim of the cup. Release the cup.
4. Turn the cup one-quarter turn and hold it between your palms again. Clap your hands together again quickly.
5. Repeat steps 3 and 4 five more times with the same cup.
▶ *What happened to the second cup?*

  The cup cracked in four places.

▶ Propose Explanations

▶ *In your model, what did your hands represent?*

  the pressure of the sound waves

▶ *Describe the pressure that caused the plastic foam cup to crack.*

  hard , fast, and repeated pressure

107

Connections

MUSIC If any students play a string instrument, ask them if they are aware of the role of a violin's body in creating sound. Let them explain, or ask students to research the answer. (A vibrating string alone does not make a very loud sound. Rather, the vibrations travel though the bridge to the body of the instrument, and the vibrations of the body and of the air in the hollow space inside the body create most of the sound.)

Assessment
Skill: Concept mapping

Use the following task to assess each student's progress:

Tell students to draw a concept map that includes the following key words: *closer together, compress, decompress, farther apart, sound, vibrations, waves.* A sample is shown below.

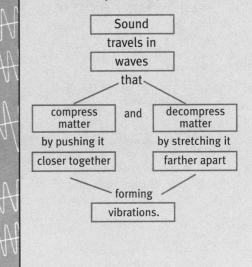

▶ Activity

Time: 10–15 minutes
Materials: 2 plastic foam coffee cups

As students complete the activity, tell them that the wine glass described in the reading cracked after being distorted (pushed out of shape) just a small amount. Remind them that the foam cup required a much larger distortion in order to break. What caused this difference? Most students will realize that it had something to do with the materials that make up the glass and the foam cup.

Extend the concept by explaining that all forms of matter have a set of physical properties that distinguish them from other matter. A material's physical properties determine how it will react to disturbances such as sound waves. Brittleness, the tendency of a material to break when bent, is a physical property that varies between materials. Glass is very brittle, but plastic foam is not.

▶ Propose Explanations

Help students elaborate on the analogy between the foam cup and the wine glass. Ask: *What kind of sound were you modeling when you pressed the sides of the cup together slowly?* (a quiet sound) *What kind of sound were you modeling with the sudden clapping motion you used on the foam cup?* (a loud, high-volume sound) *How do the results of quick clapping model Professor Lewin's results?* (Like the loud sound waves, the hard clapping had enough energy to crack the cup.)

Point of Lesson

Music is a pattern of sounds that are mathematically related.

Focus

- ▶ Motion and forces
- ▶ Transfer of energy
- ▶ Change, constancy, and measurement
- ▶ Form and function

Skills and Strategies

- ▶ Concept mapping
- ▶ Classifying
- ▶ Using numbers
- ▶ Making inferences
- ▶ Comparing and contrasting
- ▶ Analyzing data
- ▶ Forming operational definitions

Advance Preparation

Vocabulary

Make sure students understand this term. The definition can be found in the glossary at the end of the student book.

- ▶ vibration

Materials

Gather the materials needed for *Science Scope Activity* (p. 104B and p. 109), *Explore* (p. 110), and *Take Action* (p. 111).

GOOD VIBRATIONS

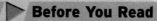

How do you tell the difference between music and noise?

You and your parents may disagree about what's music and what's noise. But the difference between music and noise is more than just a matter of opinion. It's a matter of mathematics and the shape of the sound waves. Long, stretched-out waves produce deep, low tones. Short, close-together waves produce higher pitched tones. How the different-shaped sound waves are combined determines whether a sound is musical or not.

▶ **Before You Read**

THINK ABOUT IT There are many different kinds of sounds. Some are pleasant to listen to, and some are not. Think about different kinds of sounds that are familiar to you. Decide if they are unpleasant or pleasant. List a few of the sounds in the circles below. Around the circles, list words or phrases that describe what makes these sounds pleasant or unpleasant.

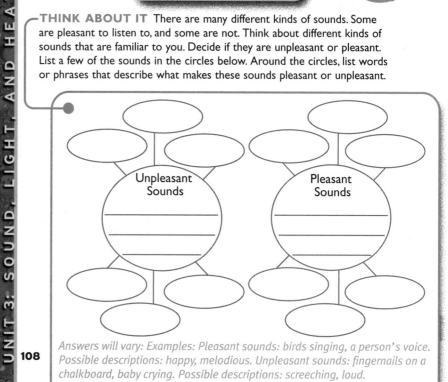

Answers will vary: Examples: Pleasant sounds: birds singing, a person's voice. Possible descriptions: happy, melodious. Unpleasant sounds: fingernails on a chalkboard, baby crying. Possible descriptions: screeching, loud.

108

© GREAT SOURCE. COPYING IS PROHIBITED.

TEACHING PLAN pp. 108–109

INTRODUCING THE LESSON

This lesson introduces the idea that patterns in frequencies determine whether sounds are considered music or noise. Find out what students know about music. Ask them to describe what characteristics all music shares. Many students will say that all music has some degree of rhythm, melody, and harmony.

Have students share with each other some examples of noise and some examples of music. Does the whole class agree on the same items? They probably will not. Tell students that people rarely agree on what exactly distinguishes music from noise.

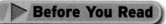

▶ **Before You Read**

THINK ABOUT IT After students fill in the circles in the diagram, poll the class on what sounds they listed as pleasant and unpleasant. List their answers on the board. Then encourage the class to suggest two or three adjectives that characterize all the unpleasant sounds and two or three others that characterize all the pleasant sounds.

NOTEZONE

Underline the three traits of every musical note.

What's the difference between drumming on a Caribbean steel pan and banging on kitchen pots? One is music and the other isn't. That's because master craftsmen carefully heat and pound the surface of a steel pan to form dimples that produce 28 distinct notes.

The Physics of Music

Engineers are still studying the intricacies of steel-pan music, but the basics are simple. Every musical tone has three traits: pitch—how high or low the note is; volume—how loud it is; and timbre—the "color" of the sound, which makes a note played on a steel pan different from the same note played on a trumpet. The sound is created when a source object (a note on the steel pan) is excited (hit) and made to vibrate. The pitch of the sound depends on its frequency—the numbers of times it vibrates per second—which is determined by the size, mass and other physical properties of the source. The bigger the source of the sound, the more room there is for the wave to form and the longer the wavelength will be. Longer wavelengths have lower frequencies, and when the sound waves reach us we hear a lower pitched note.

Lowest notes from largest dimples

Highest notes from smallest dimples

frequency: the number of waves produced per second

wavelength: the distance between one point of a wave and the same point on the next wave

▲ **Steel pan**

From: Miller, Jake. "The Physics of Music." *Scientific American Explorations.*

FIND OUT MORE

SCIENCE SAURUS

Waves	305
Characteristics of a Wave	306
Sound	312
Properties of Sound	313

SCI LINKS.
THE WORLD'S A CLICK AWAY

www.scilinks.org
Keyword: Sound
Code: GSPD12

109

Science Scope Activity
(continued from page 104B)

Procedure
Display the supplies you have provided, and give students the following instructions:

1. Choose supplies to make a musical instrument. Be creative. Your instrument can be simple or complex. It can resemble a real instrument, or it can be a new invention.

2. When you have built your instrument, make adjustments to see if you can alter the pitch, the tone, or the volume.

3. After everyone has created their instruments, you will have a chance to present yours to the class. Demonstrate how to play your instrument, and explain how it creates sound.

Have students reread the last paragraph of the passage and create a concept map of the information presented. Suggest that they start the map with the word *Pitch*. A sample is shown at right.

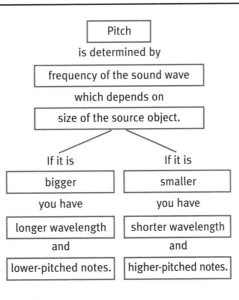

Pitch

is determined by

frequency of the sound wave

which depends on

size of the source object.

If it is **bigger** you have **longer wavelength** and **lower-pitched notes.**

If it is **smaller** you have **shorter wavelength** and **higher-pitched notes.**

CHECK UNDERSTANDING
Skill: Making inferences
Ask students to consider an empty plastic milk jug as a drum. *What would be different about the tuning processes for the jug and a steel drum?* (The jug might be cut instead of pounded.) *How do you think the sound of the jug drum would differ from the sound of a steel drum?* (The jug wouldn't ring like steel, so the timbre would be different. Plastic is softer than steel, so the volume would be lower. The jug is smaller, so the pitch would be higher.)

More Resources

The following resources are also available from Great Source and NSTA.

SCIENCESAURUS

READER'S HANDBOOK

www.scilinks.org
Keyword: Sound
Code: GSPD12

 **Explore**

ANALYZE DATA When an object vibrates, it can create sound waves, which we hear as sounds. A sound's pitch (how high or low it is) depends on the frequency of the sound waves, or how many waves are produced per second. High-pitched sounds have high frequencies (many waves per second). Low-pitched sounds have low frequencies (fewer waves per second).

Some vibrating objects produce sound waves of different frequencies at the same time. Whether a sound is considered music or noise depends on whether there is a pattern among the frequencies. Hertz (Hz) is a unit of measure for frequency, just as meter is a unit of measure for distance. This table shows frequencies of sound waves made by two familiar objects. One of the objects is a musical instrument. The other is not.

Frequency of Sound Waves Produced	
Object 1	Object 2
200 Hz	197 Hz
400 Hz	211 Hz
600 Hz	217 Hz
800 Hz	219 Hz
1000 Hz	287 Hz
	311 Hz
	329 Hz
	399 Hz
	407 Hz

▶ **How are the two sets of frequencies different?**

Object 1's frequencies all end in two zeroes. The frequencies of Object 2

end in different numbers.

▶ **Describe any pattern you see in the frequencies produced by the objects.**

The frequencies of Object 1 are all 200 Hz apart. The frequencies for

Object 2 do not make a pattern.

MAKE INFERENCES

▶ **What can you infer about the sound made by the combinations of frequencies that each object produces? Which object probably makes the more musical sound?**

The frequencies with a pattern are probably more musical. Object 1

probably makes the more pleasing sound.

▶ **Which object do you think is a musical instrument? Explain your answer.**

Object 1 is probably a musical instrument. Frequencies in a pattern are

probably more like music. Frequencies that are not in a pattern are

probably more like noise.

110

TEACHING PLAN pp. 110–111

▶ **Explore**

Time: 15–20 minutes
Materials: (for each pair) 3-m length of rope

ANALYZE DATA Help students visualize sound wave frequency by pairing them and giving each pair a rope. The two students should stand about 3 meters apart, each holding one end of the rope. To create a wave, one student should move his or her end of the rope up and down. Have each pair make a wave with a slow frequency first. Then tell the pairs to slowly increase the frequency by speeding up their up-and-

down movement. Ask students: *If this rope were a sound wave, how would the pitch change as you speeded up your movements?* (The pitch of the sound would become higher, since higher frequency means higher pitch.)

Time: will vary
Materials: recording of sounds at different pitches (optional)

You may want to bring in a recording of sounds at different pitches so students can hear what pitch is. You could also ask a musician or the school's music teacher to demonstrate pitch to the class. If time allows, have the music

teacher or musician tell students how to change the pitch of their voice. Then have the class do some vocal exercises that involve raising and lowering their pitch.

MAKE INFERENCES Have students review the set of frequencies made by each object again. The one that showed the pattern probably made the more musical sound. The more musical sound probably came from a musical instrument. Tell students that Object 1 is actually a flute and Object 2 is a dropped pencil.

▶ Propose Explanations

COMPARE AND CONTRAST

▶ *How are noise and music alike? Explain your answer.*

Noise and music are both sounds. Both result from an object being

made to vibrate and produce sound waves. Both contain energy.

▶ *To one person, a set of sounds may seem like music. To another person, the same sounds seem like noise. What is one way to tell if a set of sounds is more like noise or music?*

Look at the frequencies of the sound waves that produce it. If there is a

regular pattern, it may seem like music to most people. If there is no

clear pattern to the frequencies, most people may think of it as noise.

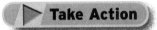

▶ Take Action

WRITE A PARAGRAPH Think about the sounds made by your favorite musical instrument. Describe the instrument and the sounds it produces. Then describe the sounds in terms of their pitch, volume, and timbre. What do they make you think of? How do they make you feel?

Answers will vary but should include the concept that distinct notes

can be played in a pattern of sequences, or melodies, and are pleasing

to hear.

Connections

SOCIAL STUDIES Drums have existed for more than 6,000 years and were probably first invented to transmit messages over long distances. For example, people in West Africa have long used drums to send out announcements to the entire village population. Have the class create a simple code that can be drummed (for example, three quick taps means move to the front of the room, two quick taps means go to the back of the room, and three slow taps means return to your seat). Then allow students to take turns sending messages to their classmates.

Assessment

Skill: Communicating

Use the following task to assess each student's progress:

Tell students to imagine that they are listening to a favorite song when an adult comes by and complains, "Turn that noise off!" Ask students to write down an argument that they could use to explain that the song is music and not noise. (Students might explain that because the song was full of sound waves with patterned frequencies rather than unpatterned frequencies, the song was actually music rather than noise.)

111

▶ Propose Explanations

COMPARE AND CONTRAST After students answer the Propose Explanations questions on their own, write the words *alike* and *different* on the board. Then ask half the class to identify different ways that noise and sound are alike and different. List their answers below the headings on the board. When the lists are complete, ask the other half of the class whether they agree with every item on the list. If not, have them explain. Allow the first half of the class to defend their answers.

▶ Take Action

Time: 20 minutes
Materials: recordings of musical instruments (optional)

WRITE A PARAGRAPH Many students may not have a favorite musical instrument. If necessary, bring in recordings of several different musical instruments for students to listen to before they make their choices. To give students practice describing music, encourage them to use adjectives to describe the sounds of each instrument. For example, if you have a recording of a flute, they might describe the sound as light and airy.

Point of Lesson
Ultrasound is a form of sound energy used in medicine.

Focus
▶ Properties and changes of properties in matter
▶ Motion and forces
▶ Transfer of energy
▶ Evidence, models, and explanation
▶ Change, constancy, and measurement

Skills and Strategies
▶ Making inferences
▶ Communicating
▶ Generating ideas
▶ Problem solving

Advance Preparation

Vocabulary
Make sure students understand these terms. Definitions can be found in the glossary at the end of the student book.
▶ frequency
▶ vibration
▶ wave

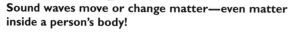

Healing Vibrations

Sound waves move or change matter—even matter inside a person's body!

Doctors often use high-frequency sound waves to make pictures of structures inside the human body. These waves are known as ultrasound. Like other sound waves, ultrasound waves contain energy. Recently, doctors have found a new way to make use of the energy contained in ultrasound waves.

▶ **Read**

NOTEZONE

Underline the three ways of treating internal wounds mentioned in the reading.

Doctors at the University of Washington are using sound waves to stop bleeding deep inside a patient's body.

STOP THE BLEEDING

There is no [easy way to] stop internal bleeding without surgery, which is...risky. As an alternative, some researchers are hoping to use ultrasound to [find], heat and cauterize internal wounds. But cooking tissue in that way is too dangerous if bleeding occurs in areas [like] the brain, or if the problem is hard to [find] and doctors need to treat a large area of the body.

Now a team from the University of Washington in Seattle has discovered that high-intensity focused ultrasound beams can [speed up] natural [blood] clotting, and stop bleeding without heating up tissue.

Sound waves make blood move around more than usual. This activates platelets by tricking them into thinking they are flowing through an open wound. [The platelets then] stick to membranes and each other. [This helps blood] clots to form.

[This] technique could be a...life-saving option when cauterizing is too dangerous. "We are really excited about [it]," says team member Lawrence Crum.

ultrasound: high-frequency sound waves beyond the range of human hearing
cauterize: stop bleeding by burning
high-intensity: high-energy

clotting: forming clots in blood to stop bleeding
platelets: small particles in the blood involved in clotting
membranes: thin layers of tissue that act as a lining

From: "Stop the Bleeding." newscientist.com
(www.newscientist.com/conferences/confarticle.jsp?conf=acsam200006&id=22411500)

FIND OUT MORE

SCIENCESAURUS
Circulatory
System   093
Waves   305
Characteristics
of a Wave   306

SCLINKS.
THE WORLD'S A CLICK AWAY
www.scilinks.org
Keyword: Sound
Code: GSPD12

112

TEACHING PLAN pp. 112–113

INTRODUCING THE LESSON
This lesson introduces some uses of high-frequency ultrasound waves. Remind students that frequency is the number of wave vibrations produced within a certain period of time. Ask a volunteer to draw a low-frequency sound wave on the board. Then ask a second volunteer to draw a high-frequency sound wave. (The high-frequency sound wave should have more waves per meter than the low-frequency sound wave.) Explain that the prefix *ultra-* means "beyond," so *ultrasound* refers to sound waves that are beyond human hearing.

▶ **Read**

After students complete the NoteZone activity, discuss the differences between the three procedures. (Surgery involves cutting; cauterizing uses heat from ultrasound but no cutting; fooling blood cells into clotting uses ultrasound with no heat and no cutting.) Ask students to organize this information into a concept map. Have pairs of students compare and discuss their concept maps.

▶ **Propose Explanations**

MAKE INFERENCES To help students understand the difference between audible sound waves and ultrasound, have them use the information presented in the text to work with you to make a simple diagram. Begin by drawing the longest horizontal line possible across the board. Label the left end point *o*, (zero). Label a point far to the right *10 million*. Have students help you find and label the section of the line that represents the range of frequencies audible to humans. (If you draw to scale, this section may be only a couple

▶ Propose Explanations

MAKE INFERENCES

▶ *The passage describes two ways that ultrasound can be used to heal wounds. Explain how each method uses sound to move or change matter.*

One way is to use ultrasound to cauterize wounds. The sound waves

generate heat, which cooks tissue inside the body and closes up the

wound. A second method uses ultrasound to speed up natural clotting.

The sound waves make the blood move around more than usual.

Remember that sound is vibration, and frequency is a measure of how many vibrations occur per second. The human ear can only hear sounds within a certain range of frequencies, generally between 20 and 20,000 vibrations per second. The frequency of medical ultrasound can reach 10 million vibrations per second. The higher the rate of vibration, the more energy the sound wave carries.

▶ *Explain how ultrasound can burn tissue while the sound of a hair dryer cannot.*

The sound of a hair dryer has many fewer vibrations per second than the

ultrasound. Lower vibration means less energy. The hair dryer sound

wave does not have enough energy to burn tissue. The ultrasound wave

has a very high frequency and therefore lots of energy, enough energy to

burn tissue.

▶ Take Action

WRITE A JOURNAL ENTRY Imagine that you are a scientist trying to come up with a new way to use sound energy. Think about how sound energy affects matter. In your journal, record your latest design idea. Explain what problem you are trying to solve and how your idea would use sound waves to solve it.

Possible answer: Problem: to develop a new way to cook food;

Idea: to use sound waves to heat food by having high-frequency sound

waves penetrate the food and cause the particles in it to start moving

and become heated.

113

More Resources

The following resources are also available from Great Source and NSTA.

SCIENCESAURUS

Circulatory System	93
Waves	305
Characteristics of a Wave	306

SCI LINKS.
THE WORLD'S A CLICK AWAY

www.scilinks.org
Keyword: Sound
Code: GSPD12

Assessment

Skill: Drawing conclusions

Use the following question to assess each student's progress:

Remind students that all sound waves carry energy. Then ask, *How do you know that the sound you make by blowing a high-pitched whistle or beating a drum won't have enough energy to make a wound stop bleeding?* (Sound we can hear has frequencies between 20 and 20,000 vibrations per second. The frequency of waves needed to cauterize a wound is about 10 million vibrations per second. If you can hear a sound, its frequency isn't high enough to cauterize a wound.)

centimeters wide.) Have a volunteer add a label for medical ultrasound frequencies from 500,000 to 10 million. It will be clear that the frequencies of medical ultrasound are significantly beyond the human range.

▶ Take Action

WRITE A JOURNAL ENTRY Before students write their journal entries, lead them in a brief discussion about all the different ways sound waves can affect matter. Students should realize that when sound waves make particles in matter move faster, the material heats

up and sometimes breaks apart. Then have students discuss how this property of sound can be useful to humans. Be sure students mention some medical uses of ultrasound, but encourage them to offer their own ideas for possible new applications as well.

CHECK UNDERSTANDING
Skill: Making inferences
Ask students to explain why doctors who use ultrasound to help a patient with internal bleeding would need to use a very narrow beam and aim accurately. (Ultrasound has a great amount of energy, so it could damage parts it hit by accident. A doctor would not want blood flow to stop anywhere except at the source of the bleeding.)

Light It Up!

LESSON 31

Seeing Near and Far
Point of Lesson: *When Ben Franklin needed to see better, he invented a way to do so.*

Benjamin Franklin's description of how and why he invented bifocal eyeglasses reinforces students' understanding of the steps in technological design, while at the same time introducing students to light and lenses. Students read Franklin's letter, then identify which parts of Franklin's lenses were used for near and distance vision.

Materials
none

LESSON 32

Seeing Colors
Point of Lesson: *The eyes and the brain work together to perceive color.*

Students explore the perception of color in this lesson. After considering their own experiences with how colors appear under different lighting conditions, they read a scientist's explanation of the role of the human brain in interpreting color. Students then reconsider their experiences with color taking into account this new information and describe how an object's background can affect their perception of its color. The lesson ends with an activity in which students explore the role of color receptor cells in the eye and how fatigue of those cells can lead to afterimages.

Materials
Science Scope Activity (p. 114B and p. 117)
for each pair:
► black film canister with lid
► glue
► plastic diffraction grating
for the class:
► 1 or 2 table lamps
for the teacher:
► hobby knife
Explore (p. 118), for each student:
► colored markers or pencils
Activity (p. 119), for each student:
► set of colored markers
Connections (p. 119), for the class:
► books that contain examples of op art

Laboratory Safety
Review the following safety guideline with students before they do the *Science Scope* Activity in this lesson.
► When using the spectroscope to look at different light sources, do not look at the sun.

LESSON 33

Magic Mirrors
Point of Lesson: *Mirrors can be used to create optical illusions.*

A convincing trick performed by two stage magicians leads students to explore the science of mirrors. Students see and read a description of the "floating head" illusion. They then interpret a diagram to understand the role of mirrors in making the illusion seem so real. Students trace lines of sight on the diagram to compare what the viewer thinks he or she is seeing with what is actually seen.

Materials
Enrichment (p. 121), for the class:
► full-length mirror
► masking tape
► tape measure or meterstick
Connections (p. 123), for the class:
► collections of fantasy and science fiction stories

Science Scope Activity

Dissecting Light

NSTA has chosen a Science Scope *activity related to the content in this chapter. The activity begins here and continues in Lesson 32, page 117.*

Time: 25 minutes

Materials: see page 114A (Sheets of plastic diffraction grating are available from scientific supply houses.)

Advance Preparation: Prior to the activity, use a hobby knife to cut a slit that measures 1 cm by 1 mm in the bottom of each film canister. Cut a square that measures 1 cm by 1 cm in each lid.

Cut the sheets of diffraction grating into squares that measure 1.5 cm by 1.5 cm. Prepare one canister and one square of diffraction grating for each pair of students.

Remind students that white light contains all the colors of the rainbow. Rainbows appear when light passes through water droplets or a prism and different colors are bent different amounts. Explain that light also bends when it passes through a narrow opening. This bending is called diffraction.

(continued on page 117)

Background Information

Lesson 32

White light is composed of all the different colors of visible light: red, orange, yellow, green, blue, indigo, and violet. A spectroscope makes use of a plastic diffraction grating, a sheet with parallel grooves that work together to bend, or diffract, light that passes through them. Because each color is a different wavelength of light, each bends at a different angle as it passes through the grating. The bending causes the colors to spread out and produces the visible spectrum.

Point of Lesson

When Ben Franklin needed to see better, he invented a way to do so.

Focus

▶ Form and function
▶ Transfer of energy
▶ Science as a human endeavor
▶ History of science
▶ Abilities of technological design

Skills and Strategies

▶ Interpreting scientific illustrations
▶ Making inferences

Advance Preparation

Vocabulary

Make sure students understand this term. The definition can be found in the glossary at the end of the student book.

▶ lens

SEEING NEAR AND FAR

What image comes to mind when you see the name Benjamin Franklin?

You might imagine a man in knee pants flying a kite in a lightning storm. But Ben Franklin is famous for more than investigating electricity. He was also a printer, inventor, city planner, and diplomat. As an elderly man, Franklin traveled back and forth between the American colonies and France seeking money and support for the American Revolution. During his time in France, he was inspired to improve his eyeglasses.

▲ Ben Franklin

NOTEZONE

Underline the problem Franklin had which led to his invention.

FIND OUT MORE

SCIENCESAURUS

| Light | 308 |
| Steps in Technology Design | 357 |

SCLINKS
THE WORLD'S A CLICK AWAY

www.scilinks.org
Keyword: Lenses
Code: GSPD13

114

UNIT 3: SOUND, LIGHT, AND HEAT

> **Read**

Always an inventor, here's what Franklin wrote to the man who made his eyeglasses back in Philadelphia.

Ben Franklin's Spectacles

I imagine it will be found pretty generally true, that the same convexity of glass, through which a man sees clearest and best at the distance proper for reading, is not the best for greater distances. I therefore had formerly two pair of spectacles, which I shifted occasionally, as in traveling I sometimes read, and often wanted to regard the prospects. Finding this change troublesome, and not always sufficiently ready, I had the glasses cut, and half of each kind [placed] in the same circle....

By this means, as I wear my spectacles constantly, I have only to move my eyes up or down, as I want to see distinctly far or near, the proper glasses being always ready. This I find more particularly convenient since my being in France, the glasses that serve me best at table to see what I eat, not being the best to see the faces of those on the other side of the

© GREAT SOURCE. COPYING IS PROHIBITED.

TEACHING PLAN pp. 114–115

INTRODUCING THE LESSON

This lesson introduces the idea that lenses bend light and can be used to help people see more clearly.

To find out what students know about vision problems, ask, *What does it mean to be nearsighted? Farsighted?* Some students may confuse the terms *nearsighted* and *farsighted*. Explain that *nearsighted* refers to people who cannot see distant objects clearly and that *farsighted* refers to people who cannot see close objects clearly.

> **Read**

Ask students to underline the description of the glasses that Franklin invented. ("I had the glasses cut, and half of each kind [placed] in the same circle.") Then ask students if they know the name of the kind of eyeglasses Franklin was describing. (bifocals) Discuss the meaning of the term *bifocal*. Tell students that the prefix *bi-* means "two" and *focal* refers to focusing, or making the image sharp. Thus, bifocals have lenses that help the wearer see clearly at both distances, near and far.

Ask students if they can think of every-day situations in which bifocals would be helpful to a person who is both near- and farsighted. (Examples: watching TV and seeing the buttons on the remote control; watching a basket-ball game and taking notes for a news-paper article)

> **Explore**

BENDING LIGHT Explain that as light passes through the eye's own lens, it is focused on the area at the back of the eye called the retina. When people are

table who speak to me; and when one's ears are not well accustomed to the sounds of a language, a sight of the movements in the features of him that speaks helps to explain; so that I understand French better by the help of my spectacles.

— Ben Franklin

convexity: curvature, or roundness
formerly: before

spectacles: eyeglasses
prospects: the view or scene
accustomed to: used to

From: a letter to George Whatley by Benjamin Franklin on May 23, 1785.

BENDING LIGHT A lens is a curved piece of glass that bends light moving through it, helping to focus the light for people who don't see clearly. A convex (curved out) lens helps people to read up close. A concave (curved in) lens helps people see far.

Based on the reading, label the photograph of Ben's bifocal spectacles. Show which parts are used to see distant objects, and which are used to see nearby objects. Then label each lens "convex" or "concave."

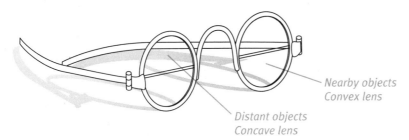

Nearby objects
Convex lens

Distant objects
Concave lens

THE MOTHER OF INVENTION As the old saying goes, "Necessity is the mother of invention."

▶ *How does the saying fit the case of Ben Franklin's spectacles?*

Ben Franklin needed to see better when he read or looked down at his food and when he looked at scenery and the people who sat across the dinner table from him. He was tired of switching his two pairs of glasses, so he invented eyeglasses that could help him focus both near and far.

115

More Resources
The following resources are also available from Great Source and NSTA.

ScienceSaurus
Light	308
Steps in Technology Design	357

SCI LINKS.
THE WORLD'S A CLICK AWAY

www.scilinks.org
Keyword: Lenses
Code: GSPD13

Enrichment
If any students in the class wear eyeglasses, ask them to describe their vision both with and without their glasses. Encourage them to show other students, in small groups, how the lenses function by holding the eyeglasses above the print in a book. Ask students to note which lenses make the print appear larger (the ones for farsightedness) and which make the print appear smaller (the ones for nearsightedness).

Assessment
Skill: Organizing information

Use the following task to assess each student's progress:

Have students make a Venn diagram to compare the shapes and functions of convex and concave lenses.

---

nearsighted or farsighted, the light is focused at a point either in front of (nearsighted) or behind (farsighted) the retina, and the person sees a blurred image. Lenses bend the light before it even enters the eye so that it is focused precisely on the retina.

Write the term *refraction* on the board, and have students find its meaning in a dictionary. (the bending of a light wave) Point out that when light rays enter a new medium (such as a lens) at an angle, their speed changes. The change in speed causes the rays to bend. An example of this can be seen when you place a pencil in a clear glass half-filled with water. The pencil appears to bend where it enters the water.

THE MOTHER OF INVENTION Have students read the quoted saying and discuss its meaning. Ask students to identify a situation in which they used a tool that did not seem to be as helpful as it could be. Then have them imagine a specific alteration to that tool that might make it more useful. Ask students to either write about or make a sketch of such an invention. Have them tell how the invention could improve their lives. Encourage students to share their inventions with the class.

CHECK UNDERSTANDING
Skill: Forming operational definitions
Ask students, *Was Ben Franklin nearsighted or farsighted? Explain your answer.* (He was both. He couldn't see far, which means he was nearsighted. He couldn't see near, which means he was farsighted.)

Point of Lesson
The eyes and the brain work together to perceive color.

Focus
► **Form and function**
► **Transfer of energy**
► **Structure and function in living systems**
► **Nature of science**

Skills and Strategies
► **Observing**
► **Making inferences**
► **Recognizing cause and effect**
► **Drawing conclusions**

Advance Preparation

Materials
Gather the materials needed for *Science Scope Activity* (p. 114B and p. 117), *Explore* (p. 118), *Activity* (p. 119), and *Connections* (p. 119).

SEEING COLORS

Your brain is pretty smart when it comes to seeing colors, but it can be fooled.

If you've seen a rainbow or shined a light through a glass prism, you know that white light is made up of all the colors of visible light. When white light, such as sunlight at midday, strikes an object, some of the colors of light are absorbed by the object. The remaining colors are reflected by the object. The colors of reflected light that enter your eyes are what gives an object its color.

Seems simple, doesn't it? Well, it's not. Scientists who study color and vision have to think about the brain as well as the eyes. Your brain acts like a powerful computer—analyzing color information sent from your eyes and, sometimes, getting fooled.

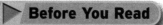
▶ Before You Read

LIGHT EFFECTS Imagine you are served a slice of pizza with red tomatoes and green peppers in a brightly lit school cafeteria. Now imagine the same slice of pizza in a candle-lit restaurant. Now imagine it outside on a picnic table. How might the appearance of the pizza change from place to place?

Answers will vary. Example: The tomatoes look red and the peppers

green in the school cafeteria. The colors are dull in the candle-lit

restaurant because there is so little light. Out in the sunlight the

colors look the brightest.

116

TEACHING PLAN pp. 116–117

INTRODUCING THE LESSON
This lesson explains how the human brain perceives color.

Be sure students understand that the first step in seeing color generally occurs when light is reflected by an object, travels to the eye, and strikes the retina at the back of the eye. As the brain receives signals from the retina, it analyzes the information and interprets the signals as color.

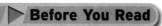
▶ Before You Read

LIGHT EFFECTS To demonstrate the pizza example, have students look at a brightly colored object in the classroom. Ask them to predict how the color of the object would appear to change in a darkened room. Then turn off the lights and close the window shades enough to leave only a little light in the room. Students should note that the object's color is basically the same but appears dimmer in the darkened room.

UNIT 3: SOUND, LIGHT, AND HEAT

▶ Read

Tony Vladusich is a visual scientist from Australia. He is investigating how the brain knows what colors should look like under different lighting conditions.

COLOR IT IN

In the natural world, we see different [colors] depending on the wavelengths of light that are absorbed by and reflected from a surface. As illumination changes in the environment, for example from a midday sun to a reddish sunset, an object's [color], in theory, should also change. But it doesn't; things may seem a slightly different shade, but that's...[all]. ...[T]he fact that a blue book does not [change color] under different light indicates that the brain must have some mechanism to keep [colors] stable during changing environmental conditions....

It performs this feat by consulting its own... "[color] chart." This [system] works by looking at how two blobs of [color] contrast with each other, a factor that is constant whatever the lighting conditions.

"Essentially the brain takes notice of edges and boundaries between objects in the real world," Vladusich says. "It extracts that edge information, which is free from the effects of illumination, and fills the rest in.... It knows that light changes but contrast doesn't."

---

wavelength: the distance from the crest of one wave to the crest of the next wave; the colors of visible light vary in their wavelengths
absorbed: taken in
reflected: bounced off
illumination: lighting

mechanism: process
stable: unchanged
feat: act of skill
consulting: getting the advice of
extracts: pulls out
contrast: the difference between lighter and darker

From: "Colour Scheme." *Beyond 2000.* (www.beyond2000.com/news/Aug_00/story_721.html)

FIND OUT MORE

SCIENCESAURUS

Light	308
Electromagnetic Spectrum	309
Light at a Surface	311

SCiLINKS.
THE WORLD'S A CLICK AWAY
www.scilinks.org
Keyword: Light and Color
Code: GSPD14

117

Science Scope Activity

(continued from page 114B)

Tell students they will create a color spectrum by bending, or diffracting, white light with a spectroscope. Explain that a spectroscope directs a narrow beam of light through a grating of very narrow slits or grooves, bending each color a different amount. Give students the following instructions.

Procedure

1. Position the diffraction grating over the hole in the canister lid, and glue the edges to keep the grating in place. Rotate the lid so the grooves in the grating are parallel to the slit in the bottom of the canister. This is your spectroscope.
2. With the room darkened, hold the grating end of the canister up to your eye. Look through the spectroscope at a light.
3. Draw what you observe. (Students should see one or two full spectrums.)

Have a volunteer explain how this activity shows that white light contains all the colors of light. Encourage students to look at different types of light sources to see if they can find lights that produce only part of the spectrum. (Neon lights, for example, produce a very narrow spectrum of reds and oranges.)

▶ Read

Ask students to underline phrases in the reading that describe how the brain knows what colors should look like. ("by consulting its own [color] chart," "by looking at how two blobs of [color] contrast with each other") Explain that the brain does this kind of interpreting in other situations as well. For example, when you look at a person standing in the distance, you know that the person is not as small as he or she appears to be. Ask students to suggest what the brain might be doing to understand that the person in the distance is actually not very small. (The brain considers the whole scene, and by comparing the size of the person to the size of the surrounding objects, it understands that he or she is far away rather than small.)

CHECK UNDERSTANDING
Skill: Organizing information
Ask students to list as many factors as they can that affect how the brain perceives the color of an object. (the wavelengths of light the object absorbs and reflects, the color of surrounding objects, lighting conditions, and whether some of the eye's color receptors are tired)

More Resources

The following resources are also available from Great Source and NSTA.

ScienceSaurus

SC/LINKS.
THE WORLD'S A CLICK AWAY

www.scilinks.org
Keyword: Light and Color
Code: GSPD14

COLOR CONSTANCY Picture a bowl of lemons and limes outside on a picnic table at sundown. During a reddish sunset, the red light from the sun makes the lemons look orange. But the red light also makes the green limes next to the lemons look different. The brain notices how the lemons and limes contrast, and "sees" them as the same colors they would appear in the midday sunlight. So the brain holds these colors "constant," or the same, even when the light reflected from them has changed.

▶ *Imagine looking at a piece of white chalk on a colored background on a very bright sunny day. Now imagine how the chalk might look as a dark cloud moved overhead. Would the chalk still reflect the same colors of light? Would it still look the same color to your brain? Explain.*

The chalk would reflect more of a gray light, but the brain would still

think of the chalk as white, since it would still appear white compared

to any other colors around it.

FOOLING THE BRAIN As the brain tries to determine what color an object is, it takes in color information about more than just the single object. Background colors are also part of the picture the brain sees.

▶ *Compare the two pictures below. How is the color of the bricks different?*

Answers will vary, but many students will have the impression that

the bricks on the left are darker than the bricks on the right.

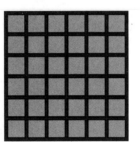 

If you said the bricks on the left are darker, you are not alone. But the color of the bricks is exactly the same in both pictures.

▶ *Explain why you think the bricks on the left look darker.*

The bricks on the left look darker because of the dark background

behind them. The bricks on the right look lighter because their

background is lighter.

118

TEACHING PLAN pp. 118–119

▶ **Explore**

COLOR CONSTANCY Ask students why they think the brain sees the colors of the lemons and limes as yellow and green. (The brain sees but ignores the slightly reddish light. It pays attention to the whole scene, including the contrast between the lemons and limes.)

If your classroom has a chalkboard, demonstrate the white chalk example. Write several sentences on the board, and have students observe the brightness of the color. Turn off the lights and have students observe the color again.

Then pull down the shades to see if the chalk still appears white.

Time: 20 minutes
Materials: colored markers or pencils

FOOLING THE BRAIN When blocks of the same color are arranged on backgrounds of different colors, the brain pays attention to the contrast between the two colors, and this affects how the color is perceived. Artists, designers, and architects use many tricks of color and contrast in their work to get the effect they want. Challenge students to design their own color pictures similar to the one on this page. Have them use

colors other than black or white for the background, and encourage them to predict what the result will be before actually creating the picture. Have students share their color pictures with the class to test the effect.

▶ Activity

BEFORE AND AFTER

Try this to get your brain to "see" what isn't there!

What You Need: set of colored markers

What to Do:
1. Color the stop sign on the left, making the space around the letters red.
2. Hold this book at arm's length. Stare at the stop sign for 30 seconds.
3. Then stare at the blank stop sign on the right.
4. Color the stop sign on the right the way it appeared to you.

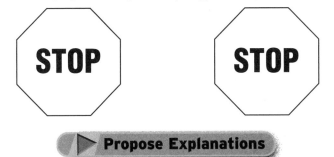

▶ Propose Explanations

WHICH RECEPTORS? There are three kinds of color receptor cells in your eye. Each kind is sensitive to a different range of wavelengths of light. One kind can sense mostly red light, one mostly blue light, and the third mostly green light. If the light reflected from an object is mostly in the red wavelengths, the red color cells will send a stronger signal to the brain than the other receptor cells. The brain compares the strengths of all three signals and "sees" a color.

When color receptors get a strong signal for a long time, they become tired. Then they stop sending messages about that color to the brain.

▶ *In the activity, which color receptor cells do you think got tired?*

the red color receptor cells

An afterimage is the image you see after you stop looking at a real object. When you look at a white page, all colors of light are reflected into your eyes. If your red-sensitive cells are still tired, no red signal is sent to the brain. However, the other two signals are still strong.

▶ *Use this information to explain what you saw when you looked at the blank stop sign.*

When I looked at the blank stop sign, I just saw the colors from cells that

weren't tired—blue and green.

119

Connections

Time: will vary
Materials: books that contain examples of op art

ART During the early 1960s, an art movement known as op art developed in the United States and Europe. Op art was based on optical illusion. Both color and black-and-white images were arranged to take advantage of the effect of color contrast and produce a particular visual experience. Ask students to look through art books to find examples of op art by noted artists such as Victor de Vasarely and Josef Albers. Invite interested students to create their own op art pictures.

Assessment

Skill: Predicting

Use the following question to assess each student's progress:

What would you expect to happen if the green color receptors in the eye got tired by staring at a green object for too long? Explain. (Students should predict that the eye will be fooled into seeing red-blue, or purple, because the receptors stopped sending green color messages to the brain and left only red and blue receptors sending messages.)

▶ Activity

Time: 10 minutes
Materials: set of colored markers

After students stare at the red stop sign on the left, they should see a blue-green color in the stop sign on the right. Ask students to hypothesize why they saw the blue-green color. Record their hypotheses on the board.

▶ Propose Explanations

WHICH RECEPTORS? Have students review the hypotheses they made in the Activity. Do their hypotheses support the information in this section? Ask: *What color do you think you would see if you repeated the activity using blue instead of red?* (Students may guess that they would see red-green. Red light and green light, however, combine to produce yellow light. The afterimage will in fact look yellow if they try it.) Then invite students to experiment with creating their own before-and-after images similar to the

stop sign activity. Have them note which colors produce which colors in the afterimages.

Point of Lesson
Mirrors can be used to create optical illusions.

Focus
► Evidence, models, and explanation
► Transfer of energy
► Nature of science

Skills and Strategies
► Interpreting scientific diagrams
► Making inferences
► Recognizing cause and effect
► Generating ideas
► Abilities necessary to do scientific inquiry

Advance Preparation

Vocabulary
Make sure students understand this term. The definition can be found in the glossary at the end of the student book.

► reflection

Materials
Gather the materials needed for *Enrichment* (p. 121) and *Connections* (p. 123).

MAGIC MIRRORS

Can you believe it? It's a living human head without a body!

Penn and Teller, a team of humorous magicians, can fool almost anyone with their illusions and sleight of hand. In one famous magic trick, Penn explains that Teller lost his head in a car accident. Penn tells the audience that through the wonders of modern medicine, doctors have been able to keep Teller's head alive. Finishing his story, Penn pulls away a cloth. The audience suddenly sees Teller's head—living, breathing, talking, and not attached to a body!

▲ A student demonstrates Penn and Teller's "floating head" trick.

► **Before You Read**

THINK ABOUT IT If you stand in a totally dark room, you can't see a thing. You need light to see your book, your dog, and your best friend. None of these things gives off their own light. So, how can you see them? They reflect light from the sun or some other light source. Some objects reflect light in a more ordered way than others. When you look into these objects—such as calm water or a mirror—you see a reflection.

► *Think about reflections you have seen. Describe one below.*

Answers will vary. Example: I saw the trees and clouds reflected in a puddle on the sidewalk.

► *How far away was the object from the surface that reflected it? How far away did the object's reflection seem to be from the surface?*

Answers will vary. Some students may explain that the object's reflection seemed to be about the same distance behind the surface as the object was in front of the surface. Others might be more literal and say the reflected image was right on top of, or in, the reflecting surface.

120

TEACHING PLAN pp. 120–121

INTRODUCING THE LESSON

This lesson explores how mirrors redirect light rays to create an illusion. Find out what students know about optical illusions by asking them to describe any they may have seen. Ask students to try to explain why the illusions occurred.

Many students will know what optical illusions are but will not know what causes them. Point out that sometimes the brain is fooled by what it expects to see based on its previous experience. Tell students who are interested in stage magic that there are some books,

videos, and Internet sites that explain the illusions that are used.

► **Before You Read**

THINK ABOUT IT Remind students that light is reflected by objects it strikes. That is, when light rays strike an object like a chair or a mirror, they bounce off the object. Light rays always bounce off an object at the same angle they strike it. Because a mirror is perfectly smooth, light rays reflect off all points of the surface at the same angle and so produce a clear image of whatever

object is in front of the mirror. Since light travels in a straight line, objects appear to be behind the mirror, at the same distance as they actually are in front of it.

When the surface of a mirror is badly scratched and no longer perfectly smooth, the incoming rays strike at different angles and so bounce off at different angles. As a result, the incoming light is scattered and no image is produced. Only perfectly smooth surfaces such as glass and polished metal reflect images.

Backstage, the magicians explain the science behind their magic.

MAGIC:
THE SCIENCE OF ILLUSION

Backstage at this illusion...Penn admits that medical science isn't keeping Teller's head alive. Optics, the science of mirrors, drives this illusion.

A large mirror propped in front of Teller's body leaves his head visible. The predictable properties of mirrors—light bounces off it at the same angle it arrives, and a mirror image appears as far behind the mirror as the real thing is in front—let us set up the mirror to control what you see.

The mirror is exactly between the front and the back walls, which are painted the same. So while you think you're looking under Teller's head to the back wall, you're really seeing a reflection of the front wall. And the checkered floor helps the illusion too, with the lines coming closer together in the "distance" just as you'd expect. The story of Teller's accident and the art of Penn & Teller's performance make the illusion complete.

predictable: expected

From: "Living Head Backstage." *Magic, the Science of Illusion.* California ScienCenter. (www.magicexhibit.org/illusions/illusions_LH_backstage.html)

NOTEZONE

Underline two facts about reflecting light that make Penn and Teller's trick possible.

FIND OUT MORE

SCIENCESAURUS

Properties of Light 310
Light at a Surface 311

121

Enrichment

Time: 15 minutes
Materials: full-length mirror, masking tape, tape measure or meterstick

Ask a volunteer to stand in front of a full-length mirror. Place short strips of masking tape on the mirror where the student sees the top of his or her head and the bottom of the feet (not the tip of the toes but below the arch). Measure the distance between the two strips of tape and compare it with the student's actual height. (The distance between the tape strips will be half the height of the student.) Then have the student move farther away from the mirror, and repeat the procedure. (The height in the mirror will not change with distance.)

Have students sketch the mirror and draw lines of sight to show why the mirror height will always be half the volunteer's height. (Light rays from the feet will hit the mirror at a height halfway between the feet and the eyes, hitting and bouncing off the mirror at equal angles. This can be proved with simple geometry, but it is also intuitive. The same is true for light rays from the top of the head. Thus, the distance between the two strips of tape is always half the person's actual height.)

▶ Read

Tell students that a diagram of the trick is shown on page 122. Have them look at the diagram as they read to help them understand the setup.

To help students visualize Penn and Teller's exhibit, kneel on the floor and hold a large sheet of posterboard in front of your upper body so only your head shows above it. Ask students to explain why this does not make your head appear as though it is floating. (It is obvious that your body is behind the posterboard.) Then ask them to imagine that the posterboard is a mirror.

Can they explain why that arrangement would not be any more convincing? (They would see their own reflections, which would make it obvious that a mirror is used.)

After students complete the NoteZone activity, have them look for descriptions in the reading that explain how Penn and Teller use the mirror to create the illusion. (The mirror extends all the way to the floor, and there is a wall in front of you, so you see only a reflection of the front wall; the checkered floor helps the illusion with its lines converging in the distance.)

CHECK UNDERSTANDING
Skill: Drawing conclusions
Ask students, *Why were the front and back walls painted exactly the same on the Penn and Teller set?* (to give the impression that what the audience sees is really the back wall)

More Resources

The following resources are also available from Great Source.

SCIENCESAURUS

MATH ON CALL

Connections

MATH Tell students that distances in space are measured in what are known as "light-years." Light travels at a speed of about 300,000 kilometers per second. A light-year is the distance that light travels in one year—about 9.5 trillion kilometers. The nearest star to Earth after the sun, Proxima Centauri, is about 4.2 light-years from Earth. Ask students to estimate the distance from Earth to Proxima Centauri in kilometers. (about 40 trillion kilometers)

TEACHING PLAN pp. 122–123

▶ **Explore**

TAKE ANOTHER LOOK To the audience, it looks like Teller's head was cut off and placed on a table. But you know it can't be true. Taking a look from another angle helps us understand how the illusion is done. The diagram shows a view of the exhibit from the side.

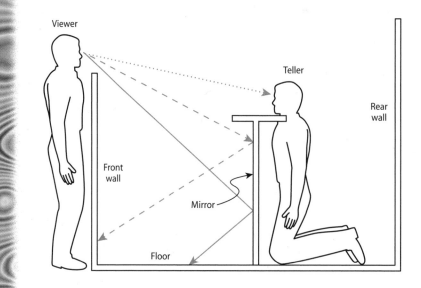

Penn and Teller know that in order to see a real object you must have a line of sight reaching it. (A line of sight is the straight line between the viewer's eyes and the object.) In this illusion, Teller's head is the real object.

▶ *On the diagram, draw a dotted line of sight from the viewer's eye to Teller's head.*

CHECK THE ANGLE The viewer can't see Teller's body because it is behind a large flat mirror. When the viewer looks at the mirror, he or she sees a reflected image of what's in front of the mirror.

▶ *On the diagram, draw a dashed line of sight from the viewer's eye to the top part of the mirror—about level with Teller's chest.*
▶ *Use a protractor to measure the angle made by your dashed line and the top half of the mirror.*
▶ *Then draw another dashed line from the top part of the mirror to make an equal angle with the bottom half of the mirror. The place where the second dashed line ends is the end of the line of sight.*

122

▶ **Explore**

TAKE ANOTHER LOOK Call attention to the diagram, and have students note the position of the front wall and the mirror. Emphasize the importance of having the front wall between the viewer and the exhibit. Ask students: *What would the viewer see when he looked in the mirror if the front wall were not there?* (He would see himself and the other things around him.)

CHECK THE ANGLE You may want to have students work in pairs when they draw the lines. Students can check each other's angles to make sure they are equal.

Ask students: *Why does the line you draw from the viewer's eye to the top part of the mirror have to be at the same angle with the mirror as the line you draw from the mirror to the front wall?* (Light rays bounce off objects at the same angle they strike them.)

▶ **Where does the line of sight end? What will the viewer see?**

The line of sight ends on the front wall of the exhibit. The viewer will

see an image of the front wall.

▶ **Draw a solid *line of sight* to a point in the lower part of the mirror— about level with Teller's hand. Measure the angle and draw where the line of sight ends up.**

▶ **Where does the line of sight end? What will the viewer see?**

The line of sight ends on the floor in front of Teller. The viewer will see

an image of the floor in front of Teller.

▶ **No matter where the viewer looks in the mirror what will he or she see?**

the front wall or the floor

Penn and Teller also know that, to the viewer, each object seen in a mirror appears to be the same distance behind the mirror as it really is in front of the mirror.

▶ **So, what does the viewer think he is seeing when he actually sees the front wall in the mirror?**

the rear wall of the exhibit

▶ **What does the viewer think he is seeing when he actually sees the floor in front of Teller in the mirror?**

the floor in back of Teller

▶ Propose Explanations

COMPLETING THE ILLUSION Penn tells the audience a long story about how Teller lost his head in a car accident.

▶ **How does the story help create the illusion for the viewer?**

Answers will vary. Example: by getting the viewers to want to believe

that Teller's head is not connected to his body

123

LITERATURE Discuss the elements of persuasive storytelling. Explain that the storyteller may use a friendly and familiar manner to connect with readers. He or she may begin the story with vivid and realistic details to "hook" readers and gain their trust. When fantasy elements are introduced into the story, the readers are already willing to "suspend disbelief." Invite students to examine collections of fantasy and science fiction stories to illustrate how readers can be drawn into an imaginary world. Suggest that they try to identify elements that make impossible stories seem believable by reviewing familiar books such as *Chronicles of Narnia*.

Assessment

Skill: Interpreting scientific illustrations

Use the following task to assess each student's progress:

Ask students to use the diagram on page 122 to explain why the viewer cannot see a reflection of his own face in the mirror when looking at the exhibit. (Any line of sight drawn from the viewer's eyes to the mirror hits at an angle and bounces off at an equal angle, so all he can is the floor or the front wall.)

▶ Propose Explanations

COMPLETING THE ILLUSION Remind students that Penn and Teller do not simply present a disconnected head; they first stir the audience's imagination by giving "background information." They also encourage the audience to accept something that might seem unbelievable by referring to "the wonders of modern medicine." They fool the audience by taking advantage of how uncertain the audience members are about what is really possible.

Ask students to recall Lesson 32, in which they viewed pictures that tricked the brain into seeing different colors. Ask volunteers to describe other situations in which they were fooled into seeing or hearing something based on their expectations. (Students may relate a wide variety of examples. A student might mention having "seen" a monster's shadow after hearing a scary story. Another student might recall believing that a plastic apple in a bowl of fruit was real. In this case, the expectation was prompted by the apple's surroundings rather than by a story.)

Heating Things Up

LESSON 34

Head in the Clouds

Point of Lesson: *Heating the gases in a hot-air balloon lifts it into the sky.*

An article describing a modern version of a balloon designed in the late 1700s introduces the idea that gases expand and become less dense when they are heated. After reading the article, students interpret a diagram showing the balloon's construction, then suggest ways in which balloonists could take advantage of the design to change the direction in which a balloon is flying. Finally, students demonstrate their understanding of the balloon design by writing a mock patent application for it.

Materials

Introducing the Lesson (p. 124), for the class:
► 2 balloons—1 filled with air, 1 filled with helium

Science Scope Activity (p. 124B and p. 125), for each group:
► copy of Garbage-Bag Balloon Instructions (copymaster page 229)
► 8 large, lightweight plastic garbage bags (about 1.4 m × 1.8 m when cut open and laid flat)
► scissors
► lightweight tape
► heavyweight tape
► metric ruler
► marker
► hair dryer
► lightweight fishing line
► extension cords
► protective gloves

Propose Explanations (p. 127), for the class:
► world map or globe

Laboratory Safety

Review the following safety guidelines with students before they do the *Science Scope* Activity in this lesson.
► Handle the hair dryers carefully to reduce the risk of electrical shock and burns.
► Wear protective gloves when handling the fishing line to avoid cuts.

LESSON 35

Can You Feel the Heat?

Point of Lesson: *Some materials store more heat energy than others do.*

The concepts of heat energy and temperature are introduced through the example of a hot apple pie. Students read a scientist's explanation of why the filling of an apple pie will burn your tongue but the crust will not, even though both are at the same temperature. After learning about specific heat capacity, students apply the concept to predict which of two different metals would heat and cool more quickly.

Materials

Read (p. 128), for teacher demonstration:
► 2 balloons—1 filled with air, 1 filled with air and about 50 mL of water
► candle
► matches

LESSON 36

Some Like It Hot

Point of Lesson: *Insulators slow the exchange of heat energy.*

Students explore the properties that make synthetic pile fabric such a good insulator. After reading an article describing the invention of Polartec®, students interpret a diagram showing the structure of the fabric on a microscopic scale. They then conduct an experiment to compare how well wool and synthetic pile insulate against heat loss.

Materials

Read (p. 131), for the class:
► Polartec® or polyester fleece gloves and wool gloves
► magnifiers

Enrichment (p. 131), for the class:
► research sources about different types of synthetic fabrics

Activity (p. 133), for each group:
► pitcher of warm water
► thermometer
► measuring cup
► 3 resealable plastic bags
► 1 wool glove
► 1 Polartec® or other synthetic pile fabric glove
► access to a freezer

Laboratory Safety

Review the following safety guideline with students before they do the Activity in this lesson.
► Clean up spills promptly to avoid slips and falls.

Science Scope Activity

Launching Garbage-Bag Balloons

NSTA has chosen a Science Scope *activity related to the content in this chapter. The activity begins here and continues in Lesson 34, page 125.*

Time: 1 hour
Materials: see page 124A

Teacher Safety Notes:

▶ Select a launch area that is free of power lines and other obstructions.

▶ If your launch area is outdoors, use extension cords that are labeled for outdoor use.

▶ Do not use hair dryers and extension cords outdoors if the ground is wet. Wait for a dry day or launch the balloons indoors.

Have students work in groups of four to create their own hot-air balloons using garbage bags. Tell students to follow the directions on the copymaster to make the balloon.

(continued on page 125)

Background Information

Lesson 34

Students may be interested to know that the youngest person ever to apply for and receive a patent was a four-year-old girl from Houston, Texas. Invite interested students to learn more from the United States Patent and Trademark Office Web site at www.uspto.gov. Pages designed specifically for students in grades 6 through 12 describe the patent process and lead readers through creativity exercises.

Lesson 35

What we commonly call "heat" is just another form of energy. All matter is made up of atoms and molecules, and these particles vibrate back and forth. *Thermal energy* is the term used to describe the energy a substance has due to the motion of its molecules. But since students have a more intuitive sense of the word *heat*, we use the term *heat energy* in this chapter rather than *thermal energy*.

Point of Lesson

Heating the gases in a hot-air balloon lifts it into the sky.

Focus

▶ Systems, order, and organization
▶ Abilities of technological design
▶ Science as a human endeavor
▶ Transfer of energy

Skills and Strategies

▶ Communicating
▶ Interpreting scientific illustrations
▶ Making inferences
▶ Comparing and contrasting

Advance Preparation

Vocabulary

Make sure students understand these terms. Definitions can be found in the glossary at the end of the student book.

▶ gas
▶ heat

Materials

Gather the materials needed for *Introducing the Lesson* (below), *Science Scope Activity* (p. 124B and p. 125), and *Propose Explanations* (p. 127).

Head in the Clouds

Floating in a balloon, the sky's the limit.

Balloons were the first aircraft. In the 1700s, hot air lifted explorers skyward—but the balloons couldn't stay up long. In the 1800s, scientists experimented with lighter hydrogen gas to lift balloons. But hydrogen was dangerously explosive! Still, courageous balloonists never quit trying to improve their flights. In the year 2002, adventurer Steve Fossett used the newest balloon technology to become the first person ever to fly solo around the world in a hot-air balloon.

▶ Before You Read

RECALL EXPERIENCES Balloons filled with hot air rise because hot air is lighter than cool air. Can you think of different places where you have seen hot air rising or knew that hot air was rising?

Possible answers: steam from a pot on the stove, smoke from a

chimney, flame above a match, wavy lines above the hood of a car,

hawks coasting on warm air currents, upstairs is hotter than

downstairs

124

TEACHING PLAN pp. 124–125

INTRODUCING THE LESSON

Time: 20 minutes
Materials: 2 balloons—1 filled with air, 1 filled with helium

This lesson focuses on how hot air is used with lighter-tohan-air gases such as hydrogen and helium to control altitude in balloon flights.

Ask students to share what they know about hot-air balloons. Perhaps some students have ridden in a balloon or watched one being launched. Ask volunteers to share their ideas about how a hot-air balloon is able to rise into the air. Point out that hot air is only one part of what makes the balloon rise.

To demonstrate the concept of how lighter-than-air gases are used in ballooning, show a balloon that has been filled with air and one that has been filled with helium. Ask: *Why do you suppose one balloon rises in the air while the other balloon does not?* Record students' ideas on the board. Then explain that the balloon that rises in the air is filled with a gas that is lighter than air.

▶ Before You Read

RECALL EXPERIENCES Ask students to hypothesize why hot air is lighter than cool air. (Hot air is less dense than cold air—that is, its molecules are spaced farther apart.) Remind students that air is a gas. Like all gases, air expands as it is heated and becomes less dense. This means that any given volume of heated air will have less mass than the same volume of cool air. Because heated air is lighter than cool air, it rises above the cool air.

▶ **Read**

The first hot-air balloon flight occurred in 1783, and lasted only a few minutes. But in 1874, French physicist Pilatre de Rozier had a better idea—a balloon that could keep its gases hot longer, and fly farther. Don Cameron, a modern balloon manufacturer, adopted Rozier's design—and the rest was history.

Steady as She Goes

Unlike air, a light gas such as hydrogen (or...helium) remains light without the constant [use] of fuel. Yet it, too, rises when heated and sinks when cooled. That's where burners and hot air can come in handy.

"The secret of making a gas balloon fly [for] long periods is to keep the helium the same temperature day and night," says Alan Noble, director of special projects for Cameron Balloons. "The problem is that during the day the sun is trying to warm it and at night it wants to radiate heat into the blackness of space. Our job is to keep the temperature as stable as possible." Cameron's so-called Rozier design places [two helium-filled balloons] above...air heated by propane. To [rise up], the aeronauts heat the air..., which in turn heats and expands the helium. The balloon's outer envelope consists of two layers, and the dead air space between the layers cuts heat loss at night by 50 percent. During the day the sun takes over to warm the helium, but should the balloon want to rise..., solar-powered fans can draw in cool air so that the temperature inside remains stable. "It's what we call air conditioning...," Noble says. It's also what you would call a success: the majority of distance and duration flights have been flown in Cameron-built Roziers....

radiate: send out
propane: a type of fuel

aeronaut: someone who travels in a balloon

From: "The Balloon that Flew Around the World." *Scientific American.com* (www.sciam.com/article.cfm?co1ID=1&article1D=000CF318-089B-1C74-9B81809EC588EF21)

The author writes as if the sun and the balloon were living things.
Circle the two verbs that describe the balloon's or sun's actions in terms of human feelings.

FIND OUT MORE

SCIENCESAURUS

Properties of Matter	251
States of Matter	253
Temperature versus Heat	302
Methods of Heat Transfer	304

125

Science Scope Activity
(continued from p. 124B)

Procedure

Give students the following instructions:

1. Tie one end of a 4-m piece of fishing line to the balloon to use as a tether. **Caution:** Wear protective gloves when handling the tether to avoid cuts.
2. Choose a cool, breezeless day for your launch. Select a clear area. If an outdoor area is not available, conduct the launch in the school gym.
3. Fill the balloon with hot air from the hair dryer. (Use extension cords as needed for the hair dryers.) Check for leaks at the seams, and tape the seams together if necessary.

Once the balloon is filled with heated air, it should rise. Ask: *Why does the balloon rise?* (The heated air inside is less dense than the cool air outside. Less dense materials float in more dense materials.) Point out that the weight of the garbage bags, tape, and fishing line are factors, too. The combined weight of these materials increases the overall density of the balloon. As long as its overall density is less than the density of the surrounding air, the balloon will rise.

▶ **Read**

Ask students to recall the examples of hot air rising they gave in the Before You Read activity. Ask: *Why do you think a hot-air balloon cannot stay in the air for very long?* (The hot air eventually cools, and the balloon sinks to the ground.) Help students see that by using a lighter-than-air gas such as helium, balloons can be made to float without carrying as much fuel as is needed for heating air.

Students may be interested to know that the early balloons launched by Rozier used another lighter-than-air

gas, hydrogen, since helium was not discovered until 1895. Helium has since mostly replaced hydrogen, which is highly flammable and potentially explosive. Students are probably familiar with the disaster of the Hindenburg, a dirigible filled with hydrogen that ignited and burned as it attempted to land at Lakehurst, New Jersey, in 1937.

Help students understand how dead air space helps keep the temperature of the air in the balloon stable. Explain that "dead air space" refers to air that is not moving. Any pocket of enclosed air is a very poor conductor of heat, meaning heat moves through it very slowly.

CHECK UNDERSTANDING
Skill: Communicating
Ask: *What two factors allow a Rozier balloon to rise?* (It uses a lighter-than-air gas, and it heats the gas to make it even lighter.)

More Resources

The following resources are also available from Great Source.

INTERPRET AN ENGINEERING DIAGRAM When engineering teams create new products, they first make plans of their design. They must think of all the details and requirements that will make their product work, and include these in their plans. These are called specifications. Making diagrams helps engineers communicate their ideas clearly. The diagrams must show how a design meets the specifications to build the product.

▶ *Below is a diagram of the Rozier balloon. For each labeled part of the diagram, add a note that tells what its purpose is. Remember that a Rozier balloon needs:*

1. A source of heat
2. A system for cooling
3. A warm air pocket
4. A layer of dead air to insulate
5. Lighter-than-air gas

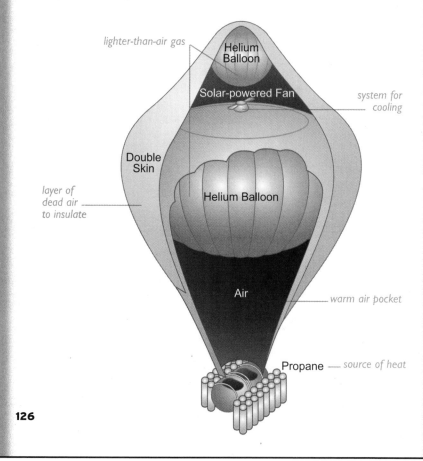

126

Teaching Plan pp. 126–127

INTERPRET AN ENGINEERING DIAGRAM Have students first identify all the labeled parts of the diagram. Then, to help them add notes to the diagram, prompt them to recall the reading. Ask: *What is used to heat the air pocket inside the balloon?* (propane) *How are the balloonists able to keep the temperature inside the balloon stable?* (Air is cooled by solar-powered fans and heated by burners.) *How does the double skin prevent excessive heat loss?* (The dead air space cuts heat loss.)

What special gas enables the balloon to rise? (helium in the helium-filled balloons)

Explain that propane is a colorless, odorless gas that can be burned as fuel. It is held in pressurized tanks that are attached to the gondola (passenger area) of the balloon. Like all gases, propane is not very dense. But when contained under pressure, its density increases and more can fit into a tank.

▶ Propose Explanations

THINK ABOUT IT Balloonists cannot steer a balloon. The only way their direction changes is when air currents push the balloon. Air currents move in different directions at different elevations.

▶ *Explain how balloonists might use their fans or heaters to change direction.*

If the air above them is going the direction they want to go, they would

heat the air more in order to rise. If the air below them is going the

direction they want to go, they would use their fans to cool the balloon

and move lower.

▶ Take Action

BRIGHT IDEAS When inventors get good ideas, they describe them very carefully in a request for a "patent." A patent is a formal record kept on file by the government that proves an idea is yours. If someone else were to later come up with the same idea, they would search the files at the United States Patent Office and find that you thought of it first.

▶ *Imagine you are working for Pilatre de Rozier. Your scientific team is filling out an application for a patent on the design for the Rozier balloon. In order to be given a patent on your invention, you need to show that it is a significant improvement over what already exists. Describe how the Rozier design is better than a simple, single balloon filled with hot air or helium. Remember to use scientific terms found in the passage.*

PATENT APPLICATION

1) Propane heats air below the helium-filled balloons so you can control

the temperature of the air pockets. 2) The skin has two layers with dead

air space between, which insulates the balloon. 3) Solar-powered fans

can cool the air, to control the temperature inside the balloon.

127

Connections

LANGUAGE ARTS Tell students that the first successful balloon flight took place in 1783 in a balloon made by the Montgolfier brothers of France. The first passengers on the balloon were not humans but a duck, a sheep, and a rooster. Tell students to imagine they are reporters covering the Montgolfier balloon flight. Ask them to generate a list of questions they would like to ask the brothers. Then have them write a newspaper article describing the launch.

Assessment

Skill: Using space/time relationships

Use the following task to assess each student's progress.

Have each student draw a diagram to show the flow of heat as it is produced, moves around the balloon, and eventually escapes. (Student diagrams should show arrows indicating the movement of heat from the burners to the air below the helium balloons and then to the helium balloons themselves. Arrows should also indicate the flow of heat from the sun to the balloon. To show cooling, arrows should indicate the flow of heat from the helium balloons into the air pocket as fans bring in cool air. Arrows should also indicate the movement of heat from the outer envelope into the surrounding air.)

▶ Propose Explanations

Time: will vary
Materials: world map or globe

THINK ABOUT IT Explain that *elevation* and *altitude* are terms that refer to an object's height above Earth.

Tell students that many balloon flights today cross over the Atlantic Ocean. Explain that the jet stream is a high-altitude wind that travels in a band from west to east. The jet stream may reach speeds of 300 km/hr and may suddenly swoop northward or southward. Show students a globe or world map. Ask: *How do you suppose the bal-loonists are able to use the jet stream to sail their balloons from the United States to Europe?* (By controlling the altitude of the balloon through heating and cooling, balloonists are able to move in and out of the jet stream.)

▶ Take Action

BRIGHT IDEAS Explain that an application is a form that a person fills out when applying for a job, a scholarship, membership to a club, and so on.

You may want to tell students more about the patent system. The U.S. Patent and Trademark Office gives inventors the exclusive right to make, use, and sell their inventions—for a limited amount of time. In the United States, a patent is good for 20 years. Under the patent system, inventors have been able to develop new technologies knowing that they will someday be able to make money from them. In this way, the patent system is a useful tool for encouraging inventors to come up with new products. Invite interested students to check out the Web site for the United States Patent and Trademark Office at www.uspto.gov.

Point of Lesson
Some materials store more heat energy than others do.

Focus
▶ Change, constancy, and measurement
▶ Transfer of energy
▶ Nature of science

Skills and Strategies
▶ Forming operational definitions
▶ Making inferences
▶ Comparing and contrasting
▶ Drawing conclusions

Advance Preparation

Vocabulary
Make sure students understand these terms. Definitions can be found in the glossary at the end of the student book.

▶ heat
▶ temperature

Materials
Gather the materials needed for *Read* (below).

Can You Feel the HEAT?

How did that pie filling get so hot?

Have you ever put a little frozen pie in the toaster oven for a couple of minutes, and then taken a quick bite? The crust may not have felt too hot on the tongue, but when you bite into the filling—ouch! Some foods feel hotter than others. What do you need to know to keep from getting burned?

NOTEZONE

Circle the two different principles involved in the process of burning your tongue.

Underline what each principle measures.

FIND OUT MORE

SCIENCESAURUS

States of Matter	253
Thermal Energy	301
Temperature versus Heat	302
Methods of Heat Transfer	304

SCILINKS
THE WORLD'S A CLICK AWAY
www.scilinks.org
Keyword: Heat Transfer
Code: GSPD15

▶ Read

Here's a tasty science lesson with a moral for anyone who has ever burned their tongue.

HOT STUFF

Question: Why is an apple pie's sauce always hotter than the pastry even though they have been cooked on the same heat?

Answer: The paradox you describe arises from the [use] of the word "hotter." As you point out, the pastry and filling have been resting in the same oven for long enough to come to the same temperature — and therefore one is not hotter than the other in this sense....

Despite the temperatures being equal, your tongue is still more likely to get burned by the filling than the crust, though. There are 2 principles behind this: thermal conductivity and specific heat capacity.

Thermal conductivity is just the measure of how quickly heat energy travels through a substance. The pastry contains many pockets of air and cannot [conduct] energy...to...your tongue [easily]....

Specific heat capacity...measures how much [heat] energy must be contained in a substance for it to have a certain temperature... For example, 100 grams of aluminum at 100 degrees C has more heat [energy] than 100 grams of copper at the same temperature.... Since the [pie] filling is mostly made of water, and water has a very high specific heat, the filling has

TEACHING PLAN pp. 128–129

INTRODUCING THE LESSON

This lesson introduces the concepts of specific heat capacity and thermal conductivity.

To prepare students for the lesson, ask them what kinds of foods they have burned their tongue on. (Students might mention hot toaster pastries, hot cookies from the oven, hot soup, and so on.)

Remind students that all matter is made up of tiny particles called atoms and molecules. These particles vibrate back and forth. The faster the particles in a substance vibrate, the hotter the substance is.

▶ Read

Time: 5 minutes
Materials: 2 balloons—1 filled with air, 1 filled with air and about 50 ml of water; candle; matches

Once students have completed the reading, demonstrate the capacity of water to absorb heat with the following demonstration. Hold a lit candle against the bottom of the balloon filled only with air. It will pop almost immediately. Then hold the candle against the bottom of the second balloon that also contains water. Students will be anticipating another loud pop, but there will

not be one. Explain that because the specific heat of water is so high, it can absorb a lot of the heat from the flame without increasing significantly in temperature. The water also draws the heat away from the balloon latex, preventing it from rising in temperature and rupturing.

Have students create a graphic organizer that shows the relationship between the following concepts: *specific heat capacity, temperature,* and *heat energy.* (Organizers should show an understanding that heat energy and temperature are two different things and that two objects at the same temperature can contain different amounts of heat energy.)

a lot of heat to give off [before its temperature drops. So] when the pie comes out of the oven, the filling cools down much more slowly....

The long and short of it is—stick to ice cream—it's safer!

paradox: something that doesn't seem to make sense
principles: reasons
thermal conductivity: the ability of a substance to let heat energy pass through it

specific heat capacity: the amount of heat energy a substance needs to change temperature

From: Landolfi, Rob. *PhysLink.com.*
(www.physlink.com/Education/AskExperts/ae463.cfm)

 **Explore**

TAKE THE HEAT Different materials need different amounts of heat energy to warm up. The amount of heat energy needed to warm a substance by 1°C is the property called specific heat.

The excerpt tells you that 100 grams of aluminum at 100°C has more heat energy than the same amount of copper at the same temperature.

▶ *Which material has a higher specific heat, copper or aluminum? How do you know?*

Aluminum, because it has more heat energy at 100°C than copper does

at the same temperature. That means it took more heat energy to raise

its temperature and so it has a higher specific heat.

Think about two different saucepans. Both are the same shape and have the same mass. One saucepan is made of copper and the other is made of aluminum. Say that you put both saucepans into the oven and heated them to 200°C.

▶ *Which of the two saucepans would get hot faster? Explain your reasoning in terms of specific heat.*

The copper pan would get hot faster because it has a lower specific heat

and so it takes less heat energy to raise its temperature.

▶ *When you removed the two saucepans from the oven, which would take longer to cool down? Explain your reasoning in terms of specific heat.*

The aluminum pan would take longer to cool down because it has a

higher specific heat and contains more heat energy at 200°C than the

copper pan does.

129

More Resources

The following resources are also available from Great Source and NSTA.

SCIENCESAURUS

States of Matter	253
Thermal Energy	301
Temperature versus Heat	302
Methods of Heat Transfer	304

SCILINKS
THE WORLD'S A CLICK AWAY

www.scilinks.org
Keyword: Heat Transfer
Code: GSPD15

Assessment

Skill: Making inferences

Use the following task to assess each student's progress:

Have students compare the advantage of cooking with copper saucepans over cooking with aluminum saucepans. Ask: *Which requires more fuel to reach a certain temperature? Explain.* (the aluminum pans because they require more heat energy to reach a certain temperature)

▶ **Explore**

TAKE THE HEAT Encourage students to refer to the graphic organizers they made earlier when they answer the questions in this section.

Help students with the first question by reminding them that when comparing equal amounts of two substances at the same temperature, the one that has more heat energy is the one with the higher specific heat.

Help students as needed with the next two questions. Then, to emphasize the importance of comparing equal quantities of the substances, ask: *If*

the copper saucepan were twice as big as the aluminum saucepan, could you be sure that it would still get hot faster and cool down faster? Explain. (No, a bigger pan may take longer to heat up and cool down. It would not be a fair comparison.) Point out the importance of keeping variables constant in any experiment.

CHECK UNDERSTANDING
Skill: Making inferences
Tell students that in the nineteenth century, people used a warm brick to heat their beds at night or to keep their feet warm during a carriage ride on a cold winter day. Ask: *Which would be better to use as a heating element, a brick of aluminum or a brick of copper? Explain.* (the aluminum brick, because it has a higher specific heat and would take longer to cool down than a copper brick)

Point of Lesson

Insulators slow the exchange of heat energy.

Focus

► Change, constancy, and measurement
► Systems, order, and organization
► Abilities of technological design
► Transfer of energy

Skills and Strategies

► Identifying and controlling variables
► Observing
► Collecting data
► Drawing conclusions

Advance Preparation

Vocabulary

Make sure students understand this term. The definition can be found in the glossary at the end of the student book.

► insulator

Materials

Gather the materials needed for *Read* (p. 131), *Enrichment* (p. 131), and *Activity* (p. 133).

SOME LIKE IT HOT

Brrr! Do you like to stay warm in cold weather? You don't have to shear a sheep to do it.

Humans have used wool, leather, cotton, and linen to make their clothing for thousands of years. Natural materials work fine for some activities. But get a wool sweater wet and it could shrink. It might even smell sheepish. Today's designers often use new kinds of materials. Synthetic, or man-made, fabrics are common choices for making clothing. Some synthetics you might have seen before include acrylic, polyester, and rayon.

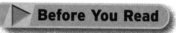
Before You Read

WHAT'S IN A LABEL? Believe it or not, many of the clothes we wear are made from materials that start out as oil. Chemical engineers make plastics from oil-related materials. Liquid plastic gets drawn out into thin threads or fibers. Then machines weave or knit the fibers into fabrics. These fabrics can keep us warmer, cooler, drier, and more comfy than natural materials.

► *Look at the labels from the clothes you are wearing today. Write down all the materials listed. Circle any that are synthetic.*

Clothing materials could include: wool or cotton (natural), rayon,

polyester, acrylic, or nylon (synthetic). Some clothing may include a

combination, or blend, of materials.

UNIT 3: SOUND, LIGHT, AND HEAT

130

TEACHING PLAN pp. 130–131

INTRODUCING THE LESSON

This lesson describes how both natural and synthetic materials keep the body warm by trapping heat.

Make a list of the following natural materials on the board: cotton, wool, linen, leather, fur, silk. Ask: *Where does each of these materials come from?* (cotton—cotton plant; wool—sheep; linen—flax plant; leather and fur—animals; silk—cocoons of silk worms)

To prompt students to think about different types of clothing and their insulating properties, ask: *What are some of the materials that people wear*

in cold climates? (wool, fur, leather) *What types of materials do people wear in warm climates?* (cotton, linen, silk, any lightweight fabric)

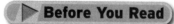
Before You Read

WHAT'S IN A LABEL? Have volunteers list the synthetic fibers that they found in their clothing in one column on the board. Do the same for natural fibers in a second column. Have students compare the number of different synthetic materials listed to the number of different natural fibers. Then tell students

that many types of clothing are made from synthetic fibers because the fabrics can be designed for very specific purposes. Ask students: *What are the properties of different fabrics that you find either comfortable or useful?* (Students may mention fabrics that keep them warm, cool, or dry. Some may prefer fabrics that are stretchy, soft, smooth, or simply attractive. Some may appreciate the durability of a fabric.)

What's cozier than a heavy wool coat? Just ask the folks at the Malden Mills fabric company.

It's Fuzzy Wuzzy Time

Forget Dolly, the infamous test-tube lamb cloned by Scottish scientists. Aaron Feuerstein and the folks at Malden Mills began building a better sheep way back in the 1970s. And what a sheep they built. Their invention, a fuzzy polyester fabric first called Polarfleece®, changed the way backcountry enthusiasts dress for the outdoors.

It all started when ...[Feuerstein] encouraged his research and development team to experiment with synthetic alternatives to wool. Pile fabrics made from [man-made materials] had just hit the scene, and their future looked promising...Malden's team set out to develop a durable but lightweight fabric that would dry quickly, stretch slightly for a more forgiving fit than wool, and accept a variety of dyes. Like good Argonauts, they returned with a fleece [that had] magical properties. Their brainchild was a single-sided polyester material with a fleecy finish that trapped heat as efficiently as wool and fibers that didn't absorb water, shrink, or stink after intense use.... Malden's Polartec® line...now boasts 150 fabrics, including a variety of fleeces designed to handle all sorts of outdoor activities and weather conditions.

So three cheers for the fuzzy stuff. Thanks to an enterprising fabric company, we stay warm and the sheep stay happy.

---

infamous: famous but unpopular
enthusiasts: people who spend a lot of time at an activity
pile: soft and velvety
durable: tough
Argonauts: characters in a Greek story who sailed the world looking for a magical ram with a golden wooly coat

fleece: a sheep's coat of wool, or a fabric that looks like that
efficiently: well
boasts: includes
enterprising: hard-working

From: Dorn, Jonathan. "Polartec: Building a Better Sheep." *Backpacker*.

© GREAT SOURCE. COPYING IS PROHIBITED.

131

NOTEZONE

Imagine you are writing an ad to sell Polartec.® Circle four words or phrases you might use in your ad.

FIND OUT MORE

SCIENCESAURUS

Temperature versus Heat	302
Methods of Heat Transfer	304

SCILINKS.
THE WORLD'S A CLICK AWAY

www.scilinks.org
Keyword: Insulation
Code: GSPD16

Enrichment

Time: will vary
Materials: research sources about different types of synthetic fabrics

Write the following names of synthetic fabrics on the board: nylon, polyester, rayon, acrylic, *Gortex, CoolMax, Thinsulate,* and *Illuminite* (all trademarked names). Have each student or small group research and write a short report on one of the fabrics. Suggest that students try to answer the following questions:

► What are the characteristics of the fabric?
► What purpose was it designed to serve?
► How has it been improved since it was first invented?
► How is it used today?
► What are the scientific principles behind what makes the fabric effective?

▶ **Read**

Time: 15 minutes
Materials: Polartec® or polyester fleece gloves and wool gloves (also used in Activity, p. 133), magnifiers

Ask if any students have clothing made of polyester fleece. Ask: *When do you most commonly wear the article of clothing?* (when it is cool or cold)

Pass around the Polartec® and wool gloves, and have students feel the materials. Ask them to describe the fabrics using descriptive adjectives. Then have students describe the major differences between the two fabrics.

(Polartec® is softer and lighter-weight than wool, which may feel scratchy.)

Next have students examine the gloves with a magnifier. Ask them to sketch the fibers they see. (*Note:* Details will be much easier to see if they hold the fabric close to a bright light.) Ask students: *Which fabric would be easier to poke a pen through? Why do you think so?* (wool, because there are bigger holes and it is stretchier) *How might this make a difference in keeping your hands warm?* (Cold air could go right through the holes.)

CHECK UNDERSTANDING
Skill: Comparing and contrasting
Ask students to make a list of the advantages of Polartec® over wool clothing. (Polartec® is more durable, lightweight, and flexible; dries quickly; and does not absorb water, shrink, or smell bad after use.)

More Resources

The following resources are also available from Great Source and NSTA.

SCIENCESAURUS

WRITE SOURCE 2000

SCiLINKS.
THE WORLD'S A CLICK AWAY

www.scilinks.org
Keyword: Insulation
Code: GSPD16

▶ **Explore**

THAT FLEECE IS GOLDEN Your body generates heat energy, but it has trouble staying warm in very cold weather. That's because heat energy is transferred from warmer objects to cooler objects. If you put your hand on a cold windowpane, the glass draws heat energy away from your hand and cools your hand down. In the same way, cold air takes heat energy from your body.

Clothing helps to stop your body's heat energy from escaping to the cold air. There is a thin but important layer of air between your skin and your clothing. Air is a very good insulator (a material that does not transfer heat energy easily). So, this layer of air helps trap your body's warmth.

▶ *Why would it be smart to wear several layers of clothes in very cold weather?*

Each layer provides another air space that prevents the exchange of heat

energy between my body and the air.

Polartec® is specially designed to trap body warmth. The picture shows a close-up of how the fibers of Polartec® fabric are arranged.

▶ *What do you see that makes Polartec® a good insulator?*

lots of air spaces between the little

fibers

In Lesson 34 you read about a balloon designed to keep helium pockets warm for a long time.

▶ *Look carefully at the picture of the Rozier balloon on page 126. Which part of the balloon design helps keep heat energy trapped in the helium balloons?*

dead air spaces

▶ *In this lesson you read about a fabric designed to keep warm bodies warm. How is the Rozier balloon design similar to the Polartec® fabric design?*

They both have dead air spaces to prevent the exchange of heat.

TEACHING PLAN pp. 132–133

▶ **Explore**

THAT FLEECE IS GOLDEN Tell students that the key to staying warm is keeping body heat in your body. Unfortunately, heat energy always travels from a warmer area to a cooler area. Since normal body temperature is about 36–37°C (97–99°F), body temperature is almost always higher than air temperature. As a result, heat energy is almost always leaving your body. The best you can do is slow down the loss of heat energy so your body has a chance to replace it.

Ask: *What does Polartec® fabric have in common with layered clothing that slows the escape of heat energy from your body?* (It has lots of air pockets, and air does not transfer heat energy easily.)

You may want to mention that many mammals and birds have body coverings that provide insulation by trapping air close to their bodies. Ask: *Why do you think dogs grow thick coats in the winter?* (The thicker coat provides more insulation.) *Why do you think birds fluff up their feathers on cold mornings?* (Fluffing the feathers traps more air, which provides more insulation.)

To answer the last two questions, students can turn back to page 126 and examine the diagram of the balloon. Point out the similarities between the balloon having two layers of fabric and people wearing several layers of clothing. Then ask: *What other objects can you think of that use dead air space to trap heat and provide insulation?* (Examples: thermos containers, ice coolers, padded lunch bags, double-pane windows, down jackets) Clarify for students that although we think of ice coolers as keeping the cold in, what they really do is keep heat energy out.

KEEPING WARM

Which glove will keep your hands toastier?

What You Need:

- pitcher of warm water
- thermometer
- measuring cup
- three resealable plastic bags
- one wool glove
- one Polartec® or other synthetic pile fabric glove
- access to a freezer

What to Do:

1. Fill a pitcher with warm water and put a thermometer in the water.
2. Read the thermometer and record the *Beginning Water Temperature*.
3. Measure and pour $\frac{1}{2}$ cup of water into each bag. Close bags tightly.
4. Fit one bag deeply into each glove.
5. Leave the third bag as a control, without a glove.
6. Place the two gloves and the control bag in a freezer for about 30 minutes.
7. Remove the gloves and the control bag from the freezer.
8. Open each bag one at a time and measure the temperature of the water inside. Record the *Ending Water Temperature* in the chart.

Beginning Water Temperature (°C) _____		
Type of Glove	Ending Water Temperature (°C)	Temperature Change (°C)
Natural material		
Synthetic material		
No glove (control)		

DRAW CONCLUSIONS

▶ *Which of the bags had the coldest water after being in the freezer?*

  the bag with no glove

▶ *Based on your results, what difference does wearing gloves in a cold environment make?*

  Gloves help keep my hands warmer than if I didn't wear gloves.

▶ *Which of the two gloves would keep your hands warmer? What evidence do you have for your answer?*

  Answers will depend on materials chosen, but often, synthetic materials

  insulate better than natural materials. The evidence is that the bag of

  water in that glove had warmer water.

133

Assessment

Skill: Organizing information

Use the following task to assess each student's progress:

Ask students to devise a new synthetic fabric that is specifically designed to trap heat. Have them draw a diagram and explain how the fabric acts as an insulator. Encourage them to describe both the advantages and disadvantages of their new fabric. (Students' diagrams should show a material with many air pockets among the fibers. Students should explain that because air does not transfer heat easily, air pockets create insulation. The advantages and disadvantages of the fabric may be related to its weight, bulkiness, durability, or other factors.)

▶ **Activity**

Time: 40–45 minutes
Materials: (for each group) pitcher of warm water, thermometer, measuring cup, 3 resealable plastic bags, 1 wool glove, 1 Polartec® or other synthetic pile fabric glove, access to a freezer

▶ Have paper towels and mops available in case of spills.
▶ Have students work in groups of four.
▶ Ask students to predict which bag of water will have the highest temperature and which will have the lowest temperature after step 6.

Have them record their predictions and reasoning.
▶ At the end of the activity, ask students to compare their predictions with their results. If the results are different from the prediction, ask them to try to explain why.
▶ Have groups compare their results. Were they all the same? If not, why not?
▶ Encourage students to look at other variables in addition to the type of material. One likely variable is the thickness of the material. Another possible variable is how long the

group waited before reading the thermometer.

UNIT 4 Matter

About the Photo

In icy climates, the same water molecules that all life depends on lock together into sharp crystals of ice that can rupture an organism's cells and kill it. The gray treefrog shown in the smaller photo has a special adaptation to help it cope with water within its body changing from liquid to solid. This frog protects its cells by flooding them with glucose, a sugar that acts as a natural antifreeze and prevents the formation of life-threatening ice crystals.

About the Charts

A major goal of the *Science Daybooks* is to promote reading, writing, and critical thinking skills in the context of science. The charts below describe the types of reading selections included in this unit and identify the skills and strategies used in each lesson.

Matter is all the physical "stuff" around you.

Your shoes, the walls of your classroom, the teeth in the mouth of your pet hamster, even the tiny invisible molecules of air you breathe in and out are all made up of bits of matter. For thousands of years, philosophers and scientists around the world have been trying to describe what matter is and how it combines with other matter.

In this unit you'll take a look at some of the ways matter is described and classified. You'll find out how the model of the atom has changed over the centuries. You'll learn what the melting point of sand is, and what makes a perfect snow globe. You'll even determine whether or not a fictional *Star Trek* creature could actually exist.

134

SELECTION	READING	WRITING	APPLICATION
CHAPTER 13 • BUILDING BLOCKS			
37.	• Read and follow directions	• Evaluate the model	• Hands-on activity • Create a model
38. "An Early Model" (nonfiction science book)	• Brainstorming • Read for details	• Compare and contrast • Use a model to explain	• Analyze an experiment
39. "Countless Particles Make a Flake" (newspaper science Q & A column)	• Problem solving • Read for details	• Use scientific notation • Complete a table	• Make comparisons • Draw conclusions
CHAPTER 14 • IT'S A MATTER OF STATE			
40. "Frog-cicles" (Canadian newspaper article)	• Use prior knowledge • Take notes	• Analyze data • Apply knowledge to propose explanations	• Hands-on activity • Record observations
41.	• Read and follow directions	• Record data in charts	• Conduct an experiment • Analyze data
42. "Underground Lightning" (university Web site)	• Directed reading • Read a data table	• Sort and classify	• Conduct research • Create a display

THE CHAPTERS IN THIS UNIT ARE . . .

135

Answers to *Find Out* Questions

CHAPTER 13
100,000,000,000,000,000,000 (100 quintillion) (p. 143)

CHAPTER 14
Both use an antifreeze to prevent the formation of ice crystals. (pp. 146–147)

CHAPTER 15
Carbon dioxide is forced into the liquid at high pressure. (p. 163)

CHAPTER 16
Both the cave and a rotten egg smell of sulfur, an element whose odor is a distinguishing characteristic. (pp. 169–171)

SCiLINKS
THE WORLD'S A CLICK AWAY

www.scilinks.org
Keyword: Mentoring
Code: GSSD06

SELECTION	READING	WRITING	APPLICATION
CHAPTER 15 • MIXTURES, SOLUTIONS, AND SUSPENSIONS			
43.	• Read and follow directions	• Draw conclusions • Explain your answer	• Hands-on activity • Record observations
44. "The Tale of Henri Nestlé and Daniel Peter" (chocolatier's Web site)	• Brainstorming • Use prior knowledge • Read for details	• Complete a chart • Explain your answer	• Hands-on activity • Record observations • Compare outcomes
45. "The Fizz Factor" (nonfiction science book)	• Brainstorming • Use prior knowledge	• Label diagrams • Make comparisons	• Invent a new product
CHAPTER 16 • PROPERTIES OF ELEMENTS			
46. "The Nifty 92" (newspaper science Q & A column)	• Read for details	• Draw conclusions	• Conduct research • Write expressively
47. "Deadly Haven" (National Geographic article)	• Use prior knowledge • Directed reading	• Create a graphic organizer • Make inferences	• Think about safety issues
48. "Carbon and Silicon" (science museum Web site)	• Read the periodic table of elements	• Make inferences • Make comparisons	• Write a review of science fiction

CHAPTER 13

Overview

Building Blocks

LESSON 37

What's an Atom?

Point of Lesson: *An atom is the smallest part of an element that still has the properties of that element.*

In this lesson, students use a model to explore the definition of an atom. They then evaluate the model by drawing analogies between their model and the nature of real elements and atoms.

Materials

Activity (p. 136), for each pair or small group:

► assorted rubber bands (different sizes and colors)
► scissors

Laboratory Safety

Review the following safety guidelines with students before doing the Activity in this lesson.

► Handle rubber bands responsibly to avoid hurting yourself or others. Return all rubber bands and cut pieces to your teacher after the activity.
► Handle scissors with care. Do not point scissors at anyone's face. Avoid touching the sharp blades.

LESSON 38

Democritus's Tiny Particles

Point of Lesson: *Models of the atom have changed over time.*

In this lesson, students explore an early model of the atom and learn about the process of developing scientific models. Students read about how Greek scholar Democritus imagined atoms, then compare his model with a modern model of the atom. They then identify differences in the methods used to develop the ancient and modern models and consider the role of observation and evidence in modern scientific investigation.

Materials

Science Scope Activity (p. 136B and p. 139), for each student or pair:

► 50 blue beads
► 50 white beads
► 50 red beads
► string
► scissors
► Periodic Table of Elements (copymaster page 230)

Connections (p. 140), for the class:

► dictionary that includes word origins

for each student:

► Periodic Table of Elements (copymaster page 230)

LESSON 39

Molecule Madness

Point of Lesson: *Atoms and molecules are the building blocks of matter.*

An article about the number of molecules in a single snowflake introduces students to the idea that even tiny objects are composed of very large numbers of molecules. After reading the article, students use scientific notation to compare the number of molecules in various objects. They then explore how even a small difference in the combination of atoms that make up molecules can cause big differences in the properties of two similar substances.

Materials

Before You Read (p. 142), for the class:

► large bag of paper clips or other small objects

Read (p. 143), for the class:

► science books or other research sources about snowflakes

Enrichment (p. 143), for the class:

► photographs of snowflakes
► research sources about snow crystals

Explore (p. 145), for each student:

► Periodic Table of Elements (copymaster page 230)
► red and blue highlighters

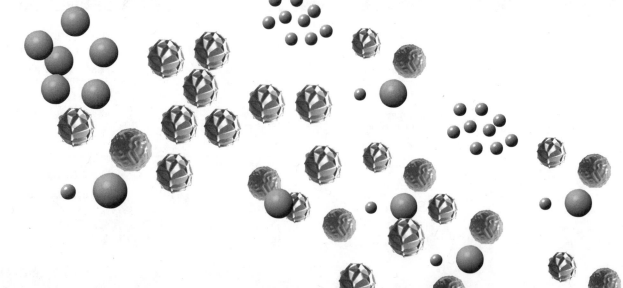

Science Scope Activity

Beads + String = Atoms You Can See

NSTA has chosen a Science Scope *activity related to the content in this chapter. The activity begins here and continues in Lesson 38, page 139.*

Time: 40–45 minutes

Materials: see page 136A

Explain to students that they will be using colored beads to make models of different atoms. First, review the atomic model on page 140 with the class and answer any questions. Then give a copy of the Periodic Table of Elements to each student or group. Point out that the atomic number of an element on the Periodic Table tells how many protons are in the nucleus of one atom of that element. Tell students that in their models the number of neutrons and electrons will be the same as the number of protons. (You may want to point out that although the number of neutrons in an atom often equals the number of protons, this is not true for every atom.)

Write the following color key on the board:

Blue beads: protons
White beads: neutrons
Red beads: electrons

(continued on page 139)

Background Information

Lesson 38

The ideas of the Greek philosopher Aristotle were the reason for the long gap between Democritus's ideas about the atom in 440 B.C. and the next major advance in atomic theory in 1803. About 100 years after Democritus, Aristotle championed a competing theory that matter was composed of four elements: earth, air, fire, and water. Aristotle argued vehemently against the idea that matter was made up of indivisible particles. His theory was that matter is continuous — that is, it can be continually divided into smaller pieces. Aristotle's influence extended for more than a thousand years beyond his death.

Point of Lesson

An atom is the smallest part of an element that still has the properties of that element.

Focus

► Evidence, models, and explanation
► Properties and changes of properties in matter
► Systems, order, and organization

Skills and Strategies

► Observing
► Classifying
► Making and using models

Advance Preparation

Vocabulary

Make sure students understand these terms. Definitions can be found in the glossary at the end of the student book.

► compound
► elements
► matter
► model
► property

Materials

Gather the materials needed for *Activity* (below).

WHAT'S AN ATOM?

What happens when you divide the indivisible?

Just as letters are the units that make up words, sentences, and paragraphs, atoms are the units that make up elements, compounds, and all other kinds of matter. You can break a paragraph down into the single letters that make it up. But you can't break down a letter into anything smaller, or else it isn't a letter anymore! Likewise, you can break matter down into smaller and smaller pieces right down to a single atom. But atoms cannot be broken down into anything smaller without losing the special properties that give them their identity.

 **Activity**

DIVIDING ATOMS

See what happens when you try to divide an atom.

What You Need:
• assorted rubber bands (different sizes and colors)
• scissors

What to Do:
1. Begin with a handful of assorted rubber bands. This will represent a collection of different atoms.
2. Sort the rubber bands into piles so that all rubber bands in each pile are the same size and color.
3. Choose the largest pile. Divide it into two smaller piles.
4. Separate one of these two small piles into two smaller piles.
5. Continue dividing until your pile can't be divided any more.

What Do You See?

► *What do you have in your last pile?*

   one rubber band

► *What would you need to do in order to divide this last pile?*

   cut the rubber band in half with scissors

Go ahead and divide your last pile using the method you just described.

136

TEACHING PLAN pp. 136–137

INTRODUCING THE LESSON

This lesson introduces students to the concept of atoms as indivisible parts of matter. It also provides an opportunity for students to model the relationship between elements and atoms.

Ask students if they can explain the phrase "atoms are the building blocks of matter." If they have difficulty, suggest that they picture a collection of children's wooden blocks. Lead them to see that the individual blocks can be combined in different ways to make a variety of structures, such as houses or skyscrapers. Atoms are like building blocks in that they are the basic unit that is combined in different ways to make up all matter around us.

► **Activity**

Time: 30 minutes
Materials: assorted rubber bands (different sizes and colors), scissors

► Have students work in pairs or small groups.
► To avoid accidents, you may want to distribute the scissors only after students have divided all the rubber band piles.

► Count the rubber bands you give to each group so you can verify that all of them have been turned in after the activity.
► Make sure students understand that they do not need to divide every pile of rubber bands. Point out that in step 3, they are to divide only the largest pile. The other pile is not needed any longer.

▶ Propose Explanations

CHANGING IDENTITIES Review the results of the activity on page 136.

▶ *How was the method you used to divide the last pile different from the method you used to divide the other piles?*

> *I used scissors to cut the rubber band into two pieces, rather than just separating groups of rubber bands into smaller and smaller piles.*

▶ *What property of rubber bands was lost when you divided your last pile?*

> *The cut rubber band cannot hold things together like an uncut rubber band can.*

EVALUATING THE MODEL In the activity, you made a model of the individual atoms that make up elements (pure substances).

▶ *What represented a group of different elements in your model?*

> *the pile of assorted rubber bands*

▶ *What represented a single element in your model?*

> *all the rubber bands of one size and color*

▶ *What represented a single atom in your model?*

> *a single rubber band*

An atom is the smallest part of an element that still has the properties of that element.

▶ *How does your model demonstrate this fact?*

> *The single rubber band represented the atom. It was the smallest pile that still had the properties of a rubber band. When I cut the rubber band in half, it no longer had the properties of the rubber band.*

FIND OUT MORE

SCIENCESAURUS

Atoms	255
Atomic Structure	256
Atomic Size	257
Elements, Molecules, and Compounds	259
Elements	260

SCILINKS
THE WORLD'S A CLICK AWAY

www.scilinks.org
Keyword: Molecules and Atoms
Code: GSPD17

137

More Resources

The following resources are also available from Great Source and NSTA.

SCIENCESAURUS

SCILINKS
THE WORLD'S A CLICK AWAY

www.scilinks.org
Keyword: Molecules and Atoms
Code: GSPD17

Assessment

Skill: Making and using models

Use the following questions to assess each student's progress:

Besides rubber bands, what other everyday items could be used to model elements and atoms? (Example: assorted paper clips) *With that model, what would happen in the last step?* (If you broke apart a paper clip, it would lose the property of being able to hold pieces of paper together.)

▶ Propose Explanations

CHANGING IDENTITIES Before students answer the second question, have them pick up one of their whole rubber bands and describe what it can do. (It can be used to hold a bunch of pencils together; it can be worn like a bracelet on the wrist; it can be twirled around a finger.) Then have them try to do the same things with the cut rubber band. (The cut rubber band will not be able to do any of these things.)

Point out that although people often say an atom is indivisible, the statement is not correct. In reality, an atom is made up of smaller parts called protons, neutrons, and electrons. However, none of those parts acts like the atom does as a whole. Ask: *What do you suppose people mean when they say an atom is indivisible?* (They mean that if you split apart an atom, the parts that make it up do not act like the whole atom does.) Ask: *How is the rubber band like an atom?* (If you divide a rubber band, it does not act like a rubber band any more.)

EVALUATING THE MODEL Remind students that models are not exactly the same as the real thing, but they can help us think about the real thing. Even though it is impossible to see atoms, it is helpful to imagine "make-believe" atoms." Ask: *How does the rubber band model help us understand atoms?* (It shows that there are different types of atoms and that an atom is changed in an important way if it is taken apart.)

CHECK UNDERSTANDING
Skill: Generating Ideas
Ask: *Why do we need to use models to study atoms?* (Atoms are too small to see.)

Point of Lesson
Models of the atom have changed over time.

Focus
► Properties and changes of properties in matter
► Understanding about scientific inquiry
► Systems, order, and organization
► History of science

Skills and Strategies
► Comparing and contrasting
► Understanding that scientists change their ideas in the face of experimental evidence that does not support existing hypotheses
► Understanding that scientists share their results to form a common core of knowledge

Advance Preparation

Vocabulary
Make sure students understand these terms. Definitions can be found in the glossary at the end of the student book.

► atom
► data
► elements
► experiment
► gas

► liquid
► matter
► model
► property

(continued on page 139)

TEACHING PLAN pp. 138–139

Democritus's Tiny Particles

The idea that matter is made up of tiny particles is far from new.

When you hear someone talk about "atomic science," you may think of cutting-edge research. But the study of atoms goes back a long way. In fact, the word *atom* was first used almost 2,500 years ago. It comes from a Greek word that means "not divisible."

Around 440 B.C., a Greek scholar named Democritus came up with the idea that all matter is made up of tiny particles he called atoms. He imagined atoms as tiny, hard spheres that could not be broken apart. His was the first model of the atom. Our understanding of these small bits of matter has changed since then, but Democritus was right about some things.

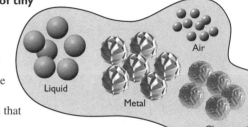

▲ **Democritus's atoms**

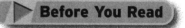
Before You Read

TOO SMALL TO STUDY One way that scientists study things that are too small to be seen or too large to fit into a laboratory is to use models. For example, a map can show the whole world on a tabletop. An architect might make a model of a building she wants to construct. In Lesson 37 you made your own model of atoms and elements.

► *What other models can you think of that might be used to help people study something that cannot be seen easily?*

Students may mention maps and globes, models of the solar system,

and models of complex molecules such as DNA.

138

INTRODUCING THE LESSON
This lesson describes the role of one man—Greek scholar Democritus—in the development of atomic theory.

Ask students to describe how they think scientists "discovered" atoms. Students may think that ancient scholars were completely wrong about the structure of matter and that modern scientists now "know" that matter is made up of atoms. Explain that atomic theory has developed over thousands of years and that it is based on the work and observations of many scientists.

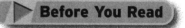
Before You Read

TOO SMALL TO STUDY Ask: *What kinds of models are you familiar with?* (Students may be familiar with model cars and airplanes.) Explain that a model is a representation of something else. A model airplane shows the structure of a real airplane, just on a smaller scale.

Point out that scientists use models to help them think about and discuss things that are too large or too small to examine first-hand. Scientists also use models to discuss and think about things that are far away, such as stars,

and things such as the human heart that are difficult to study for other reasons. Explain that sometimes scientists make models of things they have never seen and can only imagine. Often, as scientists learn more, models turn out to be wrong. Scientists then modify the models to reflect the new information. In this way, models evolve through time, and some are never completely final.

▶ Read

NOTEZONE

Underline words or phrases that tell how Democritus imagined the physical properties of atoms.

Democritus believed that the physical properties of atoms could explain the behavior of different materials.

An Early Model

As we do today, Democritus imagined that there were many different kinds of atoms. Some, he said, are very light and free to dart about this way and that, and they can move far apart from each other. The air and other gases are made of such atoms, Democritus said.

But water had different kinds of atoms, thought Democritus, and they were arranged differently. He pictured the atoms of water and other liquids as larger and heavier than atoms of gases, because the atoms of liquids tend to stick together. And since anyone could see that liquids flow, their atoms must be slick and smooth. If they were not, they would not slip and slide over and around each other.

Atoms that make up copper, iron, rocks, and other heavy solid objects must be even larger and heavier than atoms of liquids, Democritus thought. And since it is hard to break apart such solid objects, their atoms must have very rough and jagged surfaces that cause the atoms to lock together tightly.

dart: move quickly   **slick:** slippery

From: Gallant, Roy. *Explorers of the Atom*. Doubleday.

FIND OUT MORE

SCIENCESAURUS

The Evolution of Atomic Theory   258
Elements, Molecules, and Compounds 259

SCLINKS
THE WORLD'S A CLICK AWAY

www.scilinks.org
Keyword: Molecules and Atoms
Code: GSPD17

139

(continued from page 138)

Materials
Gather the materials needed for *Science Scope Activity* (p. 136B and below) and *Connections* (p. 140).

Science Scope Activity
(continued from page 136B)

Procedure
Make a bead model of a carbon atom as an example. Thread six white beads and six blue beads alternately on a short piece of string and form the string into a ball. Lay the ball on a table. Around it, lay three concentric circles of string to represent orbitals— regions around the nucleus where electrons can be found. Explain that the first orbital can hold two electrons, and the second and third orbitals can each hold eight electrons. Thread two red beads on the first circle of string, and four red beads on the second circle, as shown in the diagram. Tell students that this model represents one atom of the element carbon.

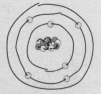

Have students follow your example to create their own models of atoms they choose from the periodic table. Direct them to choose elements with atomic numbers below 18. Encourage them to draw and label each model they create.

▶ Read

Draw students' attention to the introductory sentence. Explain that "physical properties" refers to an object's qualities, such as how it looks or how it feels to the touch. Point out that the first paragraph of the reading describes Democritus's ideas about gases, the second paragraph describes his ideas about liquids, and the third describes his ideas about solids. Encourage students to match the drawings on page 138 to each type of atom that Democritus thought made up the three states of matter. Then ask: *What are the prop-erties of clay?* (It is solid, but its shape can be changed easily.) Ask: *How do you think Democritus would have describe atoms of clay?* (Democritus might have thought the atoms would have some of the properties of a liquid but also some of the properties of a solid. He might have described them as slightly bumpy or uneven.)

When students have finished the NoteZone activity, ask volunteers to read the words and phrases they underlined. Ask: *Do Democritus's descriptions of atoms sound right to you? Why or why not?* (Some students may say that Democritus' way of think-ing makes sense because elements are made of atoms. Others may say that they think atoms have different properties from the elements or substances they make up.)

CHECK UNDERSTANDING
Skill: Communicating
Ask: *How did Democritus explain the differences between various types of materials?* (He thought they were made of atoms with different sizes, weights, and textures.)

More Resources

The following resources are also available from Great Source and NSTA.

SCIENCESAURUS

READER'S HANDBOOK

www.scilinks.org
Keyword: Molecules and Atoms
Code: GSPD17

Connections

Time: 20 minutes
Materials: dictionary that includes word origins, copy of Periodic Table of Elements (copymaster page 230)

LANGUAGE ARTS Remind students that the word *atom* comes from a Greek word. Ask: *Where do you think the elements got their names?* Challenge students to look at the

(continued on page 141)

TEACHING PLAN pp. 140–141

► **Explore**

A MODERN MODEL Democritus's idea that matter is made up of atoms is still accepted. But today, we know atoms are made of even smaller particles. These particles are protons, neutrons, and electrons. What makes one atom different from another isn't the texture of an atom's surface, it's the number of particles in the atom.

If you look at the drawing of an atom shown here, you will see that the particles we call protons and neutrons are in the center of the atom. This is the nucleus of the atom. Almost all of an atom's mass is contained in the nucleus. The number of protons and neutrons is about equal in most atoms. The particles we call electrons zip around through empty space, orbiting the nucleus in electron clouds. Most of the time the number of electrons is also equal to the number of protons.

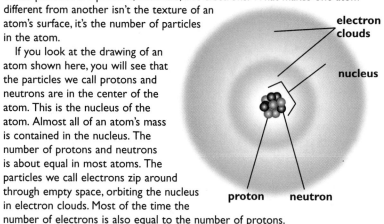

In the modern model, it is the electrons in an atom's outermost electron cloud that interact with other atoms.

► *In what ways does the modern model agree with Democritus's ideas about the surface of the atom? In what ways is it different?*

Since it is the outside layer of electrons that interact, Democritus was

right that it is the surface of the atom that matters. But atoms do not

have smooth or rough surfaces the way he thought.

It wasn't until many centuries after Democritus lived that scientists first started conducting experiments with atoms in the laboratory. In one such experiment, protons were fired at a very, very thin sheet of gold foil. Most of the protons went straight through the foil and out the other side. But a few bounced back.

► *Use the model of the atom above to try to explain the results of this experiment.*

Most of the atom is empty space, so most of the protons went right

through the thin layer of foil. But some must have struck the center of

the atoms—the nucleus—where most of the mass is. These protons

would have bounced off the nucleus, like a ball off a wall.

140

► **Explore**

A MODERN MODEL To help students understand how atomic theory has developed over time, draw a time line on the board, marking off dates when key discoveries were made. You may want to include the following dates and events:

► **around 400 B.C.** Democritus introduces the concept of an atom.

► **1803** John Dalton proposes his theory that all substances are made of small, dense, hard spheres called atoms.

► **1869** Dmitiri Mendeleev arranges the known elements into seven groups with distinct properties—creating the first periodic table.

► **1874** G.J. Stoney describes electrons as negatively charged particles.

► **1909** R.A. Milliken measures the mass and electric charge of an electron.

► **1911** Ernest Rutherford performs the gold foil experiment.

► **1922** Niels Bohr develops a new model of atomic structure that shows electrons orbiting the nucleus.

Explain that Rutherford's gold foil was an extremely thin sheet (about 8.6×10^{-6} cm) of pure, elemental gold. Rutherford made his inferences about atomic structure based on how often and to what degree a proton's path was redirected as it passed through this film of gold atoms. Explain that new discoveries are still being made and the atomic model is still being revised. Although Bohr's model of the atom is still used to teach chemistry, it is a simplified version of the more complex model most scientists use today.

COMPARING METHODS Back in Democritus's time, scientists did not perform experiments and collect data. Instead, they simply thought about questions—debating and arguing their opinions with one another. Today, scientists rely on scientific evidence for answers to their questions.

▶ *Look back at the reading. What did Democritus base his ideas about atoms on?*

He based his ideas on observations of how different materials

in nature behave.

Democritus made an assumption about materials and the atoms that make them up that turned out to be incorrect.

▶ *What was the assumption?*

that the atoms that made up materials have smooth and rough

surfaces just like objects he was familiar with had

Think about the gold foil experiment described on page 140.

▶ *How are the methods used by scientists today better than those used by philosophers in Democritus's time?*

Today's scientists do experiments that produce evidence. People

in Democritus's time could only think about things they couldn't

see, and so had to make assumptions, some of which were wrong.

▶ *What do modern scientists have that might have helped Democritus come up with a more accurate model of the atom?*

modern laboratory equipment that could

study the atom more closely

Democritus ▶

141

periodic table to find names they recognize and then try to determine where the name might have come from. Let students use a dictionary to discover the actual word origins. Then have them think about what the word origin might tell them about the element. (Examples: The name *hydrogen* comes from the Greek words for "water" and "generate"; hydrogen is one part of a water molecule. Tantalum was named after a king in Greek mythology; tantalum is strong. Zinc gets its name from the German word for tin; zinc looks like tin.)

Assessment
Skill: Comparing and contrasting

Use the following question to assess each student's progress:

In some ways Democritus's ideas about atoms were correct. In what ways was he correct? (He was right that matter is made of atoms and that atoms are too small to see. Even though he described atoms inaccurately, he was correct in proposing that different materials were made of different kinds of atoms.)

▶ **Propose Explanations**

COMPARING METHODS Lead a class discussion about the two different methods for investigating questions about the natural world presented in this lesson. Tell students that Democritus's method of trying to understand his world is often called a "thought experiment." If an explanation made sense in his mind, he accepted it as true. Ask: *What would a scientist do before accepting an explanation as true?* (A scientist would do some experiments to test the idea.) *Why isn't it enough to simply think and*

talk about a problem until you come up with an explanation that makes sense? (Sometimes explanations that "make sense" to us are not really true.) Ask students to give you an example from this lesson that illustrates this point. (Democritus reasoned that atoms must have the same physical properties as the materials they made up, when in fact they do not.)

Next, ask: *Do you see any value in a "thought experiment"?* (Example: Yes, because thinking about a question before you do experiments to investigate it in detail makes sense.) Explain

that scientific discoveries depend on both thinking and either laboratory experiments or field studies.

Point of Lesson
Atoms and molecules are the building blocks of matter.

Focus
► Properties and changes of properties in matter
► Science and technology in society
► Systems, order, and organization

Skills and Strategies
► Interpreting scientific illustrations
► Comparing and contrasting
► Using numbers
► Creating and using tables
► Drawing conclusions

Advance Preparation

Vocabulary
Make sure students understand these terms. Definitions can be found in the glossary at the end of the student book.

► atom
► property

Materials
Gather the materials needed for *Before You Read* (below), *Read* (p. 143), *Enrichment* (p. 143), and *Explore* (p. 145).

Molecule Madness

Look out! The molecules are falling!

It's wonderful to stand outside and watch snowflakes collect on your outstretched arm. Snowflakes are delicate, six-sided crystals. Each crystal is made up of smaller ice crystals. And each ice crystal is built from a huge number of water molecules arranged just so. Scientists can actually calculate just how many molecules of water there are in a single snowflake.

Molecules are groups of linked atoms. In living things, most molecules contain atoms of carbon, hydrogen, and oxygen. Many molecules have a few other atoms linked on as well. Exactly how the atoms are arranged makes all the difference between one substance and another.

▲ Microscopic view of a snowflake

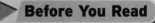 **Before You Read**

A STRATEGY FOR COUNTING It takes a long time to count a large group of objects. Sometimes you lose count in the middle, and have to start all over. What's the best way to count a large number of similar objects?

► *Suppose you have a big bag of paper clips and want to know how many are inside. How would you go about finding the total number?*

Accept all reasonable responses. Some students may choose to count,

possibly by organizing the paper clips into piles of tens or hundreds.

Other students may choose to weigh a few clips to get an average weight

per clip, then weigh the entire package and calculate the number from

that data.

142

TEACHING PLAN pp. 142–143

INTRODUCING THE LESSON
This lesson introduces the idea that atoms combine to form molecules and that very large numbers of molecules combine to form all matter.

Ask: *What is the largest number you can think of?* To whatever numbers students propose, ask: *What happens if you add 1 to that number?* Explain that these silly questions relate to a serious question in science: *How do you deal with incredibly large numbers?*

When confronted with scientific notation or other numbers that use decimals, students may think that the longer number is always greater or that the longer the number after the decimal point, the smaller the number. To address these misconceptions, ask students to compare the following pairs of numbers and to identify which number is greater. Discuss any incorrect answers.

► 4.63 and 4.8 (4.8)
► 0.3 and 0.4 (0.4)
► 5.736 and 5.62 (5.736)

 **Before You Read**

Time: 20 minutes
Materials: large bag of paper clips or other small objects

A STRATEGY FOR COUNTING For an additional challenge, provide a large bag with a known number of paper clips in it. Then have groups of students take turns counting the paper clips. When all groups have reached a final number, have them share their answers. Reveal the actual number of paper clips in the bag, and ask the students who reached the closest count to explain how they arrived at their answer.

▶ **Read**

(Circle) the atoms that make up a water molecule.

Underline the number of water molecules in a single snowflake.

Science writer Kathy Wollard describes the molecules that make up a snowflake.

Countless Particles Make a Flake

How many molecules are in a single snowflake? And what is a molecule, anyway?

A molecule is what you get when atoms link up. There are only slightly more than 100 kinds of atoms in the universe.... A molecule can be made of several atoms (like a molecule of water) or hundreds of billions of atoms (like a molecule of DNA).

Some molecules we know and love: the oxygen we breathe, simply made of two oxygen atoms, linked together. Water, which is made of one oxygen atom linked to two hydrogen atoms. Table sugar, which is made of 12 carbon atoms, 22 hydrogen atoms and 11 oxygen atoms....

Which brings us to snowflakes. A snowflake is made of frozen crystals of water (leaving aside the bits of dirt the crystals may have frozen around). If we know how many water molecules are in an average snow crystal (about 1,000,000,000,000,000,000), and the number of snow crystals in an average snowflake (let's say 100), we can calculate the number of molecules in a flake.

The answer: about 100,000,000,000,000,000,000, or 100 quintillion water molecules. If someone sat you down to count the molecules in a snowflake, you couldn't finish in a million lifetimes.

DNA: the molecule that carries genetic information
crystals: solids whose molecules are arranged in a repeating pattern

From: Wollard, Kathy. "Countless Particles Make a Flake." *Newsday*.

FIND OUT MORE

SCIENCESAURUS

DNA	115
Elements, Molecules, and Compounds	259
Molecules	261
Scientific Notation	377

SCILINKS
THE WORLD'S A CLICK AWAY

www.scilinks.org
Keyword: Molecules and Atoms
Code: GSPD17

143

Enrichment

Time: 30 minutes
Materials: photographs of snowflakes, research sources about snow crystals

Have students research answers to the following questions about snowflakes or questions of their own. (One good source of information is the Caltech Web site, www.its.caltech.edu/~atomic/snowcrystals/.) Allow time for students to share their research results.

▶ *Is it true that no two snowflakes are identical?*
▶ *Why are snowflakes symmetrical? Are they always? What are common snowflake shapes?*
▶ *Water, ice, and snowflakes are all made of water molecules. Why is snow white when ice and water are clear?*

▶ **Read**

Time: will vary
Materials: science books or other research sources about snowflakes

Encourage students to write down any questions they think of while reading the excerpt, then have them share their questions in a class discussion. Provide answers or, if possible, have students answer each other's questions. You may want to provide science books or other research materials for students to use to answer any remaining questions. Provide time for students to share the results of their research.

After students have completed the NoteZone activity, remind them that a water molecule is made of three atoms: one oxygen atom and two hydrogen atoms. Challenge them to determine the number of atoms in one snowflake. (300 quintillion atoms)

To help students visualize the structure of a snowflake, you may want to have them look at photographs of snowflakes. A variety of photographs are available online at www.its.caltech.edu/~atomic/snowcrystals/photos/photos.htm. Point out that each snowflake is made of many snow crystals, each of which is made of many water molecules.

CHECK UNDERSTANDING
Skill: Using space/time relationships
Ask students to describe the relationship between atoms and molecules. (Molecules are made of two or more atoms linked together.)

More Resources

The following resources are also available from Great Source and NSTA.

www.scilinks.org
Keyword: Molecules and Atoms
Code: GSPD17

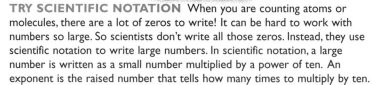

▶ **Explore**

TRY SCIENTIFIC NOTATION When you are counting atoms or molecules, there are a lot of zeros to write! It can be hard to work with numbers so large. So scientists don't write all those zeros. Instead, they use scientific notation to write large numbers. In scientific notation, a large number is written as a small number multiplied by a power of ten. An exponent is the raised number that tells how many times to multiply by ten.

For example, to write 10,000 in scientific notation, you show how many times 1 is multiplied by 10 by writing 1×10^4. It may not be so hard to write the zeros in 10,000. But look again at the reading.

▶ *How many zeros are in the number of molecules in a snow crystal?*

18 zeros

What happens if the number doesn't start with a 1? Put the decimal point after the first number. Then count the places after the decimal. That becomes the exponent you write after the 10. A single drop of water contains 280,000,000,000,000,000,000 molecules of water. In scientific notation, that's 2.8×10^{20} molecules. Now do you see why scientists use this shorter form for writing large numbers?

▶ *Complete the table below. Use information from the reading to fill in the number of molecules. (The last one has been done for you.) Then write each number in scientific notation.*

Object	Number of Molecules	Scientific Notation
Snow crystal	1,000,000,000,000,000,000	1×10^{18}
Snowflake	100,000,000,000,000,000,000	1×10^{20}
Drop of water	280,000,000,000,000,000,000	2.8×10^{20}
A 100-pound person	917,000,000,000,000,000,000,000,000	9.17×10^{26}

▶ *Which contains more molecules, a drop of water or a snow crystal? What's the easiest way to compare the numbers?*

The drop of water has more molecules. You can either count the place values or compare the exponents. It's much easier to compare the exponents. The exponent for the drop of water is 20. For the snow crystal it is only 18.

144

Teaching Plan pp. 144–145

▶ **Explore**

TRY SCIENTIFIC NOTATION To help students learn how to write numbers in scientific notation, work through the example as a class. Ask: *Where do you think the decimal should go when you write the number of molecules in a 100-pound (45-kg) person in scientific notation?* (after the 9) Then ask: *How many places are there after the decimal?* (26) Point out that this is the number used as the exponent. Remind students that the exponent does not necessarily correspond to the number of zeros. Rather, it corresponds to the number of places after the decimal point.

Tell students that about two-thirds of their bodies are water. There are about 20 drops in one gram of water. Challenge them to determine about how many water molecules are in the body of a 45-kg person. ($\frac{2}{3} \times 45 \times 1,000 \times 20 \times 2.8 \times 10^{20} = 1.68 \times 10^{26}$)

GOT A HEADACHE? Scientists sometimes use molecules found in nature as models for new molecules they design in the laboratory. For example, people have known for thousands of years that the bark of the white willow tree could take away headache pain. Chemists studied the molecules in white willow bark to find the one that eased headaches. They then learned to make the molecule, which we now call aspirin, in the laboratory.

Many people find that aspirin upsets their stomachs. Chemists worked to make a similar substance that would not upset the stomach, but would still cure a headache. Acetaminophen is what they came up with.

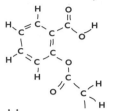
Aspirin

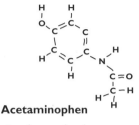
Acetaminophen

Study the diagrams of the aspirin and acetaminophen molecules.

▶ **What do the two molecules have in common?**

Answers will vary. Example: Both molecules have a closed ring of carbon

atoms, and lots of hydrogen atoms hanging off.

Fill in the table to show how many of each type of atom make up one molecule of each pain reliever.

Molecule	Carbon Atoms	Hydrogen Atoms	Oxygen Atoms	Nitrogen Atoms
Aspirin	9	8	4	0
Acetaminophen	8	9	2	1

▶ **Based on the numbers in the table, how do the aspirin and acetaminophen molecules differ?**

The acetaminophen molecule has slightly different numbers of carbon,

hydrogen, and oxygen atoms, and it contains nitrogen.

Aspirin and acetaminophen are very similar molecules. Yet they are different substances with significantly different effects on the human body.

▶ **What can you conclude about the structure of molecules and the properties of the substances they make up?**

Small differences in the atoms that make up molecules can create great

differences in the substances they make up.

145

Connections

MATH Explain that scientific notation can be used to express any number, but it is especially useful for very large and very small numbers. Point out that any number can be written as a base number multiplied by a power of ten. Challenge students to express the number of students in your class in scientific notation. (Example: 26 students = 2.6×10^1) Then have each student write a list of five numbers to convert to scientific notation. For an additional challenge, have students express a number such as 5.7×10^{-4} as a decimal in standard notation. (0.00057)

Assessment
Skill: Solving problems

Use the following task to assess each student's progress:

Have students imagine that they work in a chemistry laboratory. A scientist working next to them announces that she has just created a new kind of water, one with a sulfur atom in place of the oxygen atom that is normally there. She shows them a glass of what looks like normal water. What is their reaction? (Students should say that the scientist is probably joking and just showing them plain water. Changing one of water's three atoms would create a totally different molecule, one with properties different from water.)

Time: 15 minutes
Materials: Periodic Table of Elements (copymaster page 230), red and blue highlighters

GOT A HEADACHE? Point out that each letter in the molecule diagrams represents one atom. A line between two atoms means that the atoms are bonded together; they share one pair of electrons. A double line indicates a double bond; they share two pairs of electrons.

Have students use the periodic table to locate the chemical symbols shown in the diagrams. Ask: *What type of atom*

is represented by the letter C? (carbon) *What type of atom is represented by the letter H?* (hydrogen) *What type of atom is represented by the letter O?* (oxygen) *What type of atom is represented by the letter N?* (nitrogen)

Before asking students to compare the two molecules, have them identify and highlight structures in each molecule as follows:

1. Find the carbon rings (six carbon atoms joined in a ring) in both molecules. Highlight them in red.
2. Find the two "limbs" attached to the carbon ring in the aspirin molecule. Highlight them in blue.

3. Also in blue, trace the "limbs" attached to the carbon ring in the acetaminophen molecule.

Then have students compare the similarities and differences between the molecules.

When students have answered the last question on the page, lead them to conclude that small changes in the atoms that make up a molecule can lead to big changes in the properties of that molecule.

It's a Matter of State

LESSON 40

Frog Antifreeze

Point of Lesson: *Some organisms use natural antifreeze to prevent their cells from being injured by freezing.*

An article describing how certain frog species use glucose to prevent the formation of long, jagged ice crystals in their cells when they freeze begins the lesson. Students conduct an activity to observe that a solution of water and corn syrup has physical properties different from those of pure water. They then relate the results of their activity to frozen frogs and use the results to describe differences in familiar frozen foods.

Materials

Read (p. 147), for teacher demonstration:
► lettuce leaves
► access to a freezer

Enrichment (p. 147), for each pair or group:
► large and small resealable plastic freezer bags
► crushed ice
► 100 g salt
► 100 mL milk
► 15 g sugar
► 1 mL vanilla extract
► towel or newspaper
► spoon

Activity (p. 148), for each pair or group:
► corn syrup
► room-temperature water
► 3 small plastic cups
► masking tape
► permanent marker
► measuring spoons
► freezer

Propose Explanations (p. 149), for each student or pair:
► magnifier

Connections (p. 149), for the class:
► research sources about the harmful effects of and alternatives to salting roads

Laboratory Safety

Caution: Tasting anything in the laboratory is an unsafe practice. Consider conducting the Enrichment in another room, such as the cafeteria.

Review the following safety guidelines with students before doing the Activity or the Enrichment in this lesson.
► Do not taste any substance in the laboratory.
► Promptly wipe up any spilled liquids to avoid accidents.
► Do not sample ice cream with your fingers. Do not share spoons.
► Do not eat ice cream mixtures that have been out of the freezer long enough to reach room temperature, as they may have spoiled.
► Wash your hands thoroughly after each activity.

LESSON 41

Hot Stuff

Point of Lesson: *Adding substances to water can change the boiling point of water.*

Students predict the effect of corn syrup on the boiling point of water, then test their predictions and analyze their results.

Materials

Experiment (p. 150), for each pair or group:
► water
► corn syrup
► 2 beakers (Pyrex® or Kimax®)
► teaspoon
► 100-mL graduated cylinder
► hot plate
► oven mitts
► thermometer
► watch or clock with second hand for each student:
► safety goggles

Propose Explanations (p. 151), for each student:
► graph paper

Laboratory Safety

Caution: The Experiment in this lesson may be too hazardous for some middle school students. If you are unsure of your students' ability to complete it safely, do the experiment as a demonstration.

Review the following safety guidelines with students before they do the Experiment in this lesson.
► Do not taste any substance in the laboratory.
► Wear safety goggles when a hot plate is in use.
► Tie back long hair and fasten any loose clothing such as sweaters.
► Clear away any flammable materials near the hot plate.
► Do not leave the thermometer in the beaker between readings.
► Handle hot containers with oven mitts.
► Wipe up spills promptly.
► Wash your hands thoroughly after the activity.

LESSON 42

What a Change!

Point of Lesson: *Even sand can be melted if heated to a high enough temperature.*

Students read an article about the discovery of the world's longest fulgurite, a glassy tube that forms when lightning strikes the ground and melts sand. Students then compare the melting points of various substances and research how different types of glass are made.

Materials

Enrichment (p. 153), for the class:
► research sources about pottery making and glazing

Take Action (p. 155), for the class:
► research sources about glass-making
► samples of different types of glass (optional)

Background Information

Lesson 40

Cryonics is the practice of freezing the bodies of recently deceased humans in the hope that science will eventually advance enough to revive, repair, and cure them. (This practice is sometimes called cryogenics, but that is a misnomer. Cryogenics is a branch of physics that deals with the behavior of matter at very low temperatures.) The best-known cryonics subject is Ted Williams, the baseball player whose children went to court over whether to cremate or cryogenically preserve his body following his death in 2002. There are a few facilities in North America that offer this service, but no adult has been revived from cryonic preservation, and most scientists do not take the field seriously. In contrast, cryo-preservation of embryos for implantation after in vitro fertilization has been successful.

Point of Lesson

Some organisms use natural anti-freeze to prevent their cells from being injured by freezing.

Focus

- ► Properties and changes of properties in matter
- ► Form and function
- ► Diversity and adaptations of organisms
- ► Abilities necessary to do scientific inquiry

Skills and Strategies

- ► Collecting and recording data
- ► Interpreting data
- ► Drawing conclusions
- ► Making inferences

Advance Preparation

Vocabulary

Make sure students understand these terms. Definitions can be found in the glossary at the end of the student book.

► cell	► mixture
► crystal	► molecule
► freezing point	► states of matter
► liquid	► temperature

(continued on page 147)

FROG ANTIFREEZE

How cold does it get before you reach for a jacket?

Do you live in an area where temperatures fall below freezing in the winter? Does it get cold enough to freeze lakes and ponds? If so, you probably have heard of antifreeze for cars. Antifreeze keeps the water in the radiator from freezing into solid ice. If the water were to freeze, it could no longer be pumped around to cool the engine. Since water expands when it freezes into ice, the radiator could also be cracked open.

Cars in cold climates clearly need antifreeze. But have you ever heard of antifreeze for animals?

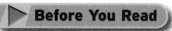 **Before You Read**

IT'S COLD OUTSIDE You can go indoors and stay warm if it is freezing outside. But think about the animals that live where you are. Do you see the same animals all year long? How do you think wild animals in cold climates survive winter's freezing weather?

Students may mention birds that migrate to warmer areas; fish that

go to deeper water; amphibians, reptiles, and mammals that hibernate

or go "dormant." Some animals grow a heavy winter

coat or put on a layer of protective

fat before winter.

► Gray treefrog

146

UNIT 4: MATTER

© GREAT SOURCE. COPYING IS PROHIBITED.

TEACHING PLAN pp. 146–147

INTRODUCING THE LESSON

This lesson describes how some frogs use chemicals to lower the freezing point of water in their cells.

Ask students to identify the temperature at which water freezes. (32°F, 0°C) Then ask: *When the temperature falls below freezing, does everything freeze solid all at once? Explain.* (Students may realize that large bodies of water take longer to freeze or that salt water and moving water often do not freeze.) Students may think that so-called "cold-blooded" animals are not affected by cold weather. Explain that all

organisms have water in their cells and that the cells can be damaged if the water freezes.

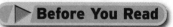 **Before You Read**

IT'S COLD OUTSIDE Encourage students to consider animals that live on land as well as animals that live in or near water, such as fish and frogs. You may also want to ask students to describe how people prepare for cold weather. (People in very cold climates may collect or buy firewood, seal their windows, take their warmer clothes out of storage, and add antifreeze to their car radiators.)

▶ Read

What's a frog-cicle? It's sort of like an icicle, but not quite.

Frog-cicles

[A] bunch of amphibians, all frogs...employ a pretty amazing trick to get through winter. The wood frog, boreal chorus frog, spring peeper, gray treefrog and Cope's gray treefrog don't bother to avoid the cold; they freeze solid and survive! As winter approaches, these frogs find a comfy spot on the forest floor, under some leaves or beneath a log, or under matted grass in a meadow, and just sit there. Next to the ground, with a protective blanket of snow above, the temperatures can often remain above freezing for much of the winter. But eventually they will dip below 0°C.

When temperatures drop below freezing, as much as 65% of the frog's body water is frozen into ice. But the frogs have a special trick to protect their individual cells from the effects of freezing:

[The frogs] arm themselves with antifreeze to protect their [cells]. Cold itself is not what harms living tissues and kills animals; it's the formation of ice crystals that tear up individual cells in tissues, causing death. These frogs flood their cells with glucose, a natural body sugar. This prevents the formation of ice-crystals, similar to what windshield washer antifreeze does in your car....

---

amphibians: animals that live both on land and in water
employ: use
comfy: comfortable

ice crystals: small pieces of ice with sharp edges
tissues: collection of similar cells, such as muscle or skin

From: Collicutt, Doug. "Some frogs hibernate, some become 'frog-cicles'." *Winnipeg Free Press, Sunday Magazine: What's Outdoors.* (www.naturenorth.com)

NOTEZONE

Underline how freezing temperatures can be dangerous to living things.

Jot down something that reading this made you curious about.

FIND OUT MORE

SCIENCESAURUS
States of Matter 253
Mixtures, Solutions, and Suspensions 271

SCILINKS.
THE WORLD'S A CLICK AWAY
www.scilinks.org
Keyword: Compounds
Code: GSPD18

147

(continued from page 146)

Materials

Gather the materials needed for **Read** (below), **Enrichment** (below), **Activity** (p. 148), **Propose Explanations** (p. 149), and **Connections** (p. 149).

Enrichment

Time: 40 minutes
Materials: large and small resealable plastic freezer bags, crushed ice, 100 g salt, 100 mL milk, 15 g sugar, 1 mL vanilla extract, towel or newspaper, spoon

Have students work in pairs or small groups, and give them the following instructions for making ice cream.

1. Combine the milk, sugar, and vanilla in a small freezer bag. Squeeze out all the air and seal the bag.
2. Fill the large freezer bag half full of ice. Add the salt to the ice.
3. Place the small bag into the large bag.
4. Squeeze the air out of the large bag and seal it.
5. Insulate the bags by wrapping them in a towel or several layers of newspaper.
6. Roll the bags back and forth until the mixture thickens and the ice cream is ready to eat.

For an interesting comparison, prepare two additional demonstrations, one without adding salt and the other without using sugar in the small bag. Have students observe the differences in the ice cream and explain them using the ideas presented in this lesson. (Salt

(continued on page 148)

▶ Read

Time: 40–45 minutes
Materials: lettuce leaves, access to a freezer

When students have completed the reading, refer them to the chart on page 154. Explain that the melting point and freezing point of a substance are the same. Then have students compare the melting (freezing) points of water (0°C) and antifreeze (–13°C).

To show students how freezing damages plant and animal cells, place a few leaves of lettuce in a freezer and show students the limp leaves. Ask: *Based on*

the reading, what do you think caused the lettuce to become so limp? (Ice crystals formed in the cells and ruptured them.) Explain that most garden plants cannot survive even a few hours of frost.

Students may think that the frogs described in this lesson and other animals that can survive freezing temperatures could survive being kept in the freezer section of a refrigerator. Explain that a freezer is too cold and that it would be too sudden a temperature change. Also point out that only certain species of frogs that live in very cold climates can survive freezing.

CHECK UNDERSTANDING
Skill: Evaluating source material
Ask: *The reading says that the frogs can "freeze solid and survive." Do the frogs actually freeze solid? Explain your answer.* (No; the reading also says only 65 percent of the water in the frog's body freezes into ice.) *Why do you suppose the author used the expression if it was not really accurate?* (for effect, to grab the reader's attention)

(continued from page 147)

lowers the freezing point of water, making the icewater around the bag of milk and sugar even colder than plain ice. Sugar prevents long ice crystals from forming and makes the mixture smoother.)

More Resources

The following resources are also available from Great Source and NSTA.

www.scilinks.org
Keyword: Compounds
Code: GSPD18

IT'S FREEZING!

Frogs put extra sugar in their cells to keep sharp ice crystals from forming. In this activity, you will see how corn syrup—a mixture of a large amount of sugar in a small amount of water—changes the way water freezes.

What You Need:

- corn syrup
- water, room temperature
- 3 small plastic cups
- masking tape
- permanent marker
- measuring spoons
- freezer

What to Do:

1. Put one teaspoon of water in a small cup. Label the cup "water."
2. Put one teaspoon of corn syrup in another small cup. Label it "corn syrup."
3. Put one-half teaspoon of corn syrup into a third cup. Add one-half teaspoon of water and stir the mixture thoroughly. Label it "water and corn syrup."
4. Observe the liquids in the cups and record your observations in the table.
5. Place the cups in the freezer.
6. After a half hour, remove the cups and observe the contents again. Record your observations in the table. If you see any ice crystals, add drawings of them to your observations.

What Do You See?

Record your observations in the data table.

Liquid	Observations Before Freezer	Observations After Freezer
Water		*The water begins to freeze, and long, somewhat jagged crystals can be seen along the sides of the cup.*
Corn Syrup	*Students will note that the corn syrup is a very thick liquid.*	*The corn syrup does not freeze, although it does become thicker.*
Water–Corn Syrup Mixture	*Mixture is less thick than plain corn syrup.*	*The mixture of corn syrup and water begins to freeze, but it does not form jagged crystals. The ice crystals in this mixture are small and granular. The mixture has a slushy consistency.*

148

TEACHING PLAN pp. 148–149

Time: 40–45 minutes
Materials: corn syrup, room-temperature water, 3 small plastic cups, masking tape, permanent marker, measuring spoons, freezer

- ▶ Have students work in pairs or small groups.
- ▶ Explain that there are different types of sugars. Table sugar is sucrose, corn syrup is fructose, and the sugar in frogs' cells is glucose. All types have a similar effect on the freezing point of water.

- ▶ To prevent spills, have students label the three cups before they add the water and corn syrup.
- ▶ Have students prepare the cups at the beginning of class so they can leave the cups in the freezer for half an hour before observing them.
- ▶ Make sure students fill in the chart on page 148 promptly after removing the cups from the freezer, while the crystals can still be observed.
- ▶ As an extension, students may want to test other mixtures, such as salt water or water mixed with drink mix powder. These mixtures will also

take longer to freeze than plain water, since the dissolved substance will lower the freezing point of the water.

▶ Propose Explanations

ANALYZE THE DATA Review your descriptions of the contents of the three cups that came out of the freezer.

▶ *If any of the cups had ice crystals, describe how the crystals in those cups differed.*

There was a skin of ice forming on the plain water. There was ice in the

water-corn syrup mixture too, but the ice was in little bitty particles. It

did not form long, sharp crystals like the ones in the water.

When sugar-water does begin to freeze, the sugar molecules get in the way of the water molecules as they begin to link up to make long ice crystals.

▶ *What evidence did you find that shows this?*

smaller crystals in the water that had corn syrup in it

When anything is dissolved in a liquid, the mixture will stay completely liquid at lower temperatures than the pure liquid will. We say that the dissolved substance lowers the freezing point of the liquid.

▶ *How might this be helpful to frogs?*

They can use sugar to keep water in their cells from freezing at

temperatures they would normally freeze at.

APPLY KNOWLEDGE Think about some of the foods you might find in your freezer at home. Some items are rock-hard and some are softer.

▶ *Use what you have learned in this activity to explain why ice cubes are hard and brittle while Popsicles are soft enough to bite right through.*

Popsicles have sugar in them, so when they freeze they get little crystals

like slush instead of solid chunks like plain ice.

Sorbet is a soft, frozen, ice cream-like dessert made from frozen fruit juice, sugar, and water. There are lots of recipes for homemade sorbet. Suppose your father tried making sorbet one day. You thought it tasted okay but it was too hard, almost like ice.

▶ *How would you suggest your father change the recipe the next time he made a batch of sorbet? How would you explain your suggestion to him?*

Example: I would tell him to add more sugar, or less water. Water freezes

hard, but when you put enough sugar in water it is more like slush, so if

he added more sugar the sorbet would be slushier.

149

Connections

Time: will vary
Materials: research sources about the harmful effects of and alternatives to salting roads.

SOCIAL STUDIES Tell students that in many parts of the country, trucks spread large amounts of salt on roads to melt any ice that has built up on them and make driving safer. However, there are many drawbacks to salting the roads, the most serious of which is the contamination of groundwater. This can be harmful to humans as well as plant and animal life. Have students research the harmful effects of salting roads, what the alternatives are, and why most communities choose to salt their roads in spite of the drawbacks.

Assessment

Skill: Drawing conclusions

Use the following question to assess each student's progress:

Some ice cream or sorbet makers use a saltwater bath to bring the temperature of the ice cream or sorbet mixture down to below 0°C (32°F). Why is this necessary? (The mixture freezes at a lower temperature than water, so it is important to bring it to an even lower temperature. If they did not, the mixture would get cold but would not freeze.)

▶ Propose Explanations

Time: 10 minutes
Materials: (for each student or pair) magnifier

ANALYZE THE DATA If possible, have students complete the questions on this page while they still have their samples in front of them. Encourage students to use a magnifier to observe the ice crystals closely and compare them.

Explain the crystalline structure of ice. When water begins to freeze, it forms crystals—units with a repeating pattern. These units line up neatly in long rows.

The result is long crystals that can be sharp. The dissolved sugar molecules get between the ice crystals and do not allow them to form long chains. As a result, no long, sharp crystals form. Invite students to make a drawing that shows what you have just explained.

Ask students to explain in their own words what it means to lower the freezing point of a liquid. Offer a series of statements such as the following, and have students fill in the blanks: *If a substance normally freezes at 0°C, it will now need to be ____ °C to freeze.* (some temperature lower than 0°C)

APPLY KNOWLEDGE If practical, provide actual samples of frozen foods for students to observe. Otherwise, have students list foods they have in their freezers at home and then rank them from hardest to softest. Ask: *What trends can you identify from this list?* (Answers should reflect the fact that softer frozen foods contain sugar.)

Point of Lesson
Adding substances to water can change the boiling point of water.

Focus
► Properties and changes of properties in matter
► Abilities necessary to do scientific inquiry
► Change, constancy, and measurement

Skills and Strategies
► Collecting and recording data
► Developing hypotheses
► Interpreting data
► Drawing conclusions

Advance Preparation

Vocabulary
Make sure students understand these terms. Definitions can be found in the glossary at the end of the student book.

► boiling point   ► liquid
► data   ► mixture
► experiment   ► prediction
► freezing point   ► temperature
► hypothesis

Materials
Gather the materials needed for *Experiment* (below) and *Propose Explanations* (p. 151).

Is it possible to change the boiling point of water?
As you learned in Lesson 40, sugar can lower the freezing point of water. Can adding sugar to water change the boiling point, too? Normally, water boils when its temperature reaches 100°C. Would sugar-water boil at the same temperature?

► **Experiment**

IT'S BOILING!
Test the effect of sugar on the boiling point of water.

What You Need:
• water   • teaspoon   • hot plate   • safety goggles
• corn syrup   • 100-mL graduated • oven mitts   • watch or clock
• 2 beakers   cylinder   • thermometer   with seconds

What to Do:
1. Put 100 mL of water into a beaker. Place the beaker on a hot plate.
2. Before you turn on the hot plate, take the temperature of the water, and record it in the data table. Record the time on the same line.
3. Put on the safety goggles. Turn on the hot plate. Take the temperature of the water every two minutes until the water boils. Do not leave the thermometer in the beaker between readings.
4. A liquid has reached its true boiling point when bubbles form within the liquid and break through the surface. Take one more temperature reading two minutes after the water has started to boil. Record your data in the data table. Circle the last temperature. This is the boiling point.
5. Turn off the hot plate. Put on the oven mitts. Carefully move the beaker to a safe place where it can cool.
6. How do you think adding sugar (in the form of corn syrup) to water will affect its boiling point? Write a prediction using an "if/then" statement: IF something happens, THEN something else will happen.

   Accept all hypotheses at this time. Example: If I add sugar to the

   water, then it will boil at a higher temperature.

7. Add 3 teaspoons of corn syrup to 100 mL of water in another beaker. Stir the mixture very well. Place the beaker on the hot plate. Repeat steps 2–5.

TEACHING PLAN pp. 150–151

INTRODUCING THE LESSON
This lesson provides an opportunity for students to measure and compare the boiling points of plain water and a mixture of water and corn syrup.

Ask students what they think is the highest temperature that water can reach. Some students may suggest that water cannot be heated to temperatures higher than 100°C, the boiling point, because it would all boil off. Explain that under ordinary conditions, 100°C is the hottest that pure water can be, but there are some conditions under which water can reach higher temperatures.

► **Experiment**

Time: 40–45 minutes
Materials: water, corn syrup, 2 beakers, teaspoon, 100-mL graduated cylinder, hot plate, oven mitts, thermometer, safety goggles, watch or clock with second hand

Caution: This experiment may be too hazardous for some students. If so, do it as a demonstration.
► Have students work in pairs or small groups.
► Because the beakers will be heated, they must be lab quality, such as Pyrex® or Kimax® beakers.

► To help organize students' work, you may want to announce when it is time to turn on the hot plate and then announce the time every two minutes so all students can take the temperature readings at the same time. However, due to differences in hot plates, some beakers may reach the boiling point before others.
► To save time, have students make their predictions before they start the activity. Then assign half the groups to measure the boiling point of plain water while the other half measures the boiling point of water and corn syrup.

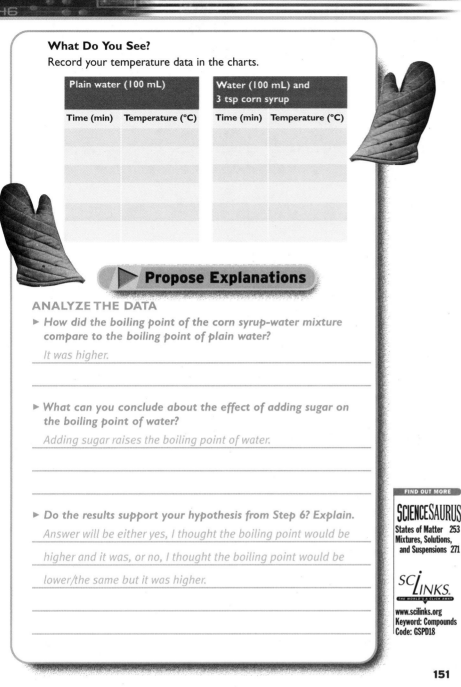

What Do You See?

Record your temperature data in the charts.

Plain water (100 mL)	
Time (min)	Temperature (°C)

Water (100 mL) and 3 tsp corn syrup	
Time (min)	Temperature (°C)

▶ Propose Explanations

ANALYZE THE DATA

▶ *How did the boiling point of the corn syrup-water mixture compare to the boiling point of plain water?*

It was higher.

▶ *What can you conclude about the effect of adding sugar on the boiling point of water?*

Adding sugar raises the boiling point of water.

▶ *Do the results support your hypothesis from Step 6? Explain.*

Answer will be either yes, I thought the boiling point would be higher and it was, or no, I thought the boiling point would be lower/the same but it was higher.

FIND OUT MORE

SCIENCE SAURUS
States of Matter 253
Mixtures, Solutions, and Suspensions 271

SCI**LINKS**
THE WORLD'S A CLICK AWAY

www.scilinks.org
Keyword: Compounds
Code: GSPD18

151

More Resources

The following resources are also available from Great Source and NSTA.

SCIENCE SAURUS

States of Matter	253
Mixtures, Solutions, and Suspensions	271

MATH ON CALL

Graphs and Statistics
Data in Tables	285
Making Graphs	287

SCI**LINKS**
THE WORLD'S A CLICK AWAY

www.scilinks.org
Keyword: Compounds
Code: GSPD18

Assessment

Skill: Predicting

Use the following questions to assess each student's progress:

What do you think would happen to the boiling point if you added 6 teaspoons of corn syrup to 100 mL of water? Would the boiling point be higher than it was for the 3-tsp mixture? Explain how you would test your prediction. (Students should predict either that the boiling point would be higher or that it would be the same. To test the prediction, repeat the procedure with the new mixture. Students would find that the boiling point of the 6-tsp mixture would not be noticeably higher than the 3-tsp mixture.)

▶ Propose Explanations

Time: 20–30 minutes
Materials: graph paper

ANALYZE THE DATA This activity provides a good opportunity to reinforce graphing skills. Have students make a graph for each data table, with time on the horizontal axis and temperature on the vertical axis. Ask: *How do the graphs help you compare the data?* (Examples: You can see that it took more time for the corn syrup mixture to boil; you can see that the boiling point is higher.)

Ask students if they have ever made candy or sugar syrup. Have them describe the process. Tell students that candy makers have to be very careful because hot sugar syrup can cause very serious burns, even worse than those caused by boiling water. Ask students to explain why they think this is so. (Hot sugar syrup can reach higher temperatures than boiling water.) Students who are interested in the science of candy can learn more at www.exploratorium.edu/cooking/candy/sugar-stages.html.

CHECK UNDERSTANDING

Skill: Identifying and controlling variables

Ask: *In this experiment, which variables did you keep the same?* (the amount of water, its temperature at the start, the material that the beakers are made of, the beakers' shape—i.e., the amount of bottom surface exposed to the hot plate) *Which variable did you change?* (the amount of corn syrup added)

Point of Lesson

Even sand can be melted if heated to a high enough temperature.

Focus

► Properties and changes of properties in matter
► Transfer of energy
► Science and technology in society
► Evidence, models, and explanation

Skills and Strategies

► Creating and using tables
► Interpreting data
► Making inferences

Advance Preparation

Vocabulary

Make sure students understand these terms. Definitions can be found in the glossary at the end of the student book.

► boiling point	► mixture
► gas	► prediction
► electrical energy	► property
► energy	► solid
► liquid	► temperature
► melting point	

Materials

Gather the materials needed for *Enrichment* (p. 153) and *Take Action* (p. 155).

TEACHING PLAN pp. 152–153

INTRODUCING THE LESSON

This lesson describes how sand can be melted to produce glass.

Ask students to describe solids they have melted or seen melted. Ask: *What is usually required to melt a solid?* (heat) Students may not realize that many substances that are solid at room temperature also have a liquid state. Use the model of ice, water, and steam to explain that solids also have liquid and gaseous states but that these states sometimes occur at extremely high temperatures.

What a Change!

Flash! Cra-ack! The power of a thunderstorm is amazing!

Have you ever seen a tree that was split in half by a lightning strike? A bolt of lightning carries quite a punch. Scientists at the University of Florida are studying how lightning affects different objects. Martin Uman is part of the research team. He and the team have found fascinating changes in soil that has been struck by lightning.

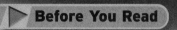 **Before You Read**

THAT'S POWERFUL! You have probably walked across a thick carpet and then felt a shock when you touched a doorknob. That shock is a tiny discharge of electrical energy. A lightning strike is similar, but transfers much more energy. It can also do much more damage than a little shock can.

► *Think about thunderstorms you have experienced or seen reported on news programs. List some effects that lightning can have when it strikes things.*

Lists will vary, but will likely include the possibility of causing power

failures, damage to buildings and trees, starting fires, and so on.

_____

_____

_____

_____

_____

_____

_____

152

UNIT 4: MATTER

▶ **Before You Read**

THAT'S POWERFUL! Students who have seen or heard about the effects of lightning strikes may have dramatic stories to share. Be sensitive to any students who have had frightening experiences with lightning.

Explain that a lightning strike can raise the temperature of an object to about 28,000°C. Point out that heating objects is one way in which lightning transfers energy to them.

Ask: *What do you think would happen if solids such as metal or rock were*

heated to 28,000°C? (Students will probably guess that this temperature is high enough to melt almost anything.) Encourage students to predict what happens when lightning strikes solid objects.

Read

What happens when lightning strikes the ground? It keeps on going!

UNDERGROUND LIGHTNING

When researchers from the University of Florida began digging into the ground where a lightning bolt had hit, they thought it would be just another minor excavation.

But the longer they worked, digging along the glassy path left behind by the dirt-melting lightning, the more apparent it became that this was no ordinary dig. What they finally unearthed was verified recently by the Guinness Book of Records as the world's longest fulgurite ever excavated.... The record-breaking fulgurite includes two branches, one almost 16 feet long and the other reaching 17 feet....

Fulgurites have been described by some as solidified lightning bolts. They are glassy tubes that lightning forms below the ground as it tears through the soil. The lightning melts the sand, which solidifies again when it cools to form the hollow glassy material....

"If a normal citizen tries to dig one of these out of the ground," Uman said, "they would destroy it because fulgurites are so fragile. It takes experts who are skilled in working with special tools and are used to digging up fossil bones. It's definitely an art."

excavation: digging exploration
verified: showed to be true
solidified: made into a solid

From: Meisenheimer, Karen. "Experts From UF Dig Up World's Longest Solidified Lightning Bolt." *University of Florida UF News.* (www.napa.ufl.edu/oldnews/fulgur.htm)

FIND OUT MORE

SCIENCESAURUS
States of Matter 253

SCLINKS.
THE WORLD'S A CLICK AWAY
www.scilinks.org
Keyword: Compounds
Code: GSPD18

153

Enrichment

Time: will vary
Materials: research sources about pottery making and glazing

A material very similar to glass is the glaze used by potters to give clay pieces a glassy finish. The main component of a glaze is silicon dioxide. Since kiln temperatures typically reach only about 1350°C, other materials, known as flux, are added to the silicon dioxide to lower its melting point. Invite a potter to visit the class to describe the glazing process, or invite interested students to research the use of glazes and report back to the class.

Read

Tell students that the word *fulgurite* (FULL-ghur-ite) comes from the Latin word *fulgur*, which means "lightning." Ask students to draw or describe in writing what they think the fulgurite described in the reading looks like. (The reading describes two separate branches, one 16 feet long and the other 17 feet long.)

Draw the following diagram of changes of state on the board:

```
        (melting)        (evaporating)
Solid ──────────▶ Liquid ──────────▶ Gas

        (condensing)     (freezing)
Gas ──────────▶ Liquid ──────────▶ Solid
```

Review the diagram with the class, focusing on what is needed to make each change happen. (addition or subtraction of heat energy) Then ask: *What connection do you see between freezing and melting?* (They are the reverse of each other.) *If water freezes at 0°C, what temperature do you think the melting point of ice is?* (the same temperature, 0°C)

CHECK UNDERSTANDING
Skill: Classifying
Have students identify the state changes mentioned in the reading. (melting—solid sand to melted sand, and freezing—melted sand to glass)

More Resources

The following resources are also available from Great Source and NSTA.

SCILINKS.
THE WORLD'S A CLICK AWAY

www.scilinks.org
Keyword: Compounds
Code: GSPD18

▶ **Explore**

READ A DATA TABLE You are familiar with ice melting into water, and you have certainly seen steam rising from boiling water. We do not often think of rocks melting, though, and it is even harder to imagine a rock boiling.

Melting is the change from a solid to a liquid. The melting point of a substance is a characteristic property of the substance. This means that any solid sample melts at that temperature, no matter how large or small the sample is.

The table below lists the melting points of several substances. As you can see, the melting points cover a wide range of temperatures.

Substance	Melting Point (°C)
Aluminum	660
✓ Baking chocolate	36
Copper	1083
Ethylene glycol (antifreeze)	-13
Iron	1535
Mercury	-39
✓ Paraffin (wax)	51
Sodium chloride (salt)	801
Silicon dioxide (sand)	1610
Titanium	1675
Tungsten	3410
Water	0

Room temperature is usually about 20°C.

▶ Circle the names of substances that are liquid at room temperature.

▶ Place a check mark (✓) next to substances that are solid at room temperature, but could be melted in a kitchen oven set to 200°C.

Lightning itself isn't hot, but everything it passes through is heated to extremely high temperatures.

▶ According to the chart, how high does lightning have to raise the temperature of sand (silicon dioxide) in order to melt it?

1610°C

154

Teaching Plan pp. 154–155

▶ **Explore**

READ A DATA TABLE To help students visualize melted or boiling rock, you may want to discuss volcanic lava, which is molten rock. Explain that rock is not composed of just one substance but is usually a mixture of several different substances, each with a characteristic melting point. Ask: *Do you think rock has a characteristic melting point? Explain why or why not.* (No, each substance in rock would have its own melting point.)

Point out that the melting points listed in the table are for average sea-level

atmospheric pressure. Melting points may be slightly different at different altitudes. This is true of boiling points as well and is particularly true of water. At higher elevations, the boiling point of water is lower. Lead students to infer how a lower boiling point might affect cooking at high altitudes. (Since water cannot reach 100°C before it boils, it cannot cook food at as high a temperature. Therefore, food will need to be boiled longer to cook thoroughly.)

As students review the chart of melting points, ask: *Why could this same table also be called a table of freezing points?*

(The freezing point and the melting point of a substance are the same.)

Caution students against trying any experiments involving melting points. For example, paraffin is easily melted, but it is also flammable and could ignite when heated on a stove.

RESEARCH HOW GLASS IS MADE Every day, you use objects made of glass. You look through glass windows. You might drink out of containers made of glass. Some of the cookware in your kitchen may be made of glass. Perhaps someone in your family collects glass figurines. Even the insulation in the walls of your home could contain glass, in the form of fiberglass.

Glass has many uses, and for each use there is a different kind of glass. All glass starts out as sand—silicon dioxide. The silicon dioxide is melted, and chemicals are added to give the glass the properties that are needed. For example, adding borax to the mixture produces the kind of glass used to make the beakers you use in the laboratory. This kind of glass can stand sudden changes in temperature without breaking.

Choose a kind of glass and find out how it is made. Organize what you learn in a display. You might want to make a flowchart that describes the process. You might make drawings that show the ingredients and the product. Choose any way you like to communicate the information you find.

Answers will vary. Answers might include the following information. The main ingredients of glass are sand, soda ash (to make the sand melt at a lower temperature), and limestone (to help the glass form properly when it cools). The process includes mixing ingredients, melting at high temperature (about 1500°C), shaping (often with a mold), and cooling. You can change the color by adding other ingredients before melting. For red, add gold chloride; for blue, add cobalt oxide; and for green, add iron.

155

Connections

SOCIAL STUDIES Tell students that the first glass windows were made in the 11th century. The windows were used only in churches and palaces because the cost was so high. The glassmaking technique involved creating a cylinder of molten glass, cutting the ends off, and flattening the remaining tube into a sheet. However, this technique did not create glass that was perfectly flat or even. In fact, the glass in many old churches and palaces is thicker at the bottom than at the top. Ask students to find photographs of old glass panes on the Internet.

Assessment

Skill: Interpreting data

Use the following question to assess each student's progress:

Silicon dioxide melts at 1610°C. At what temperature does it freeze? Explain. (It freezes at the same temperature, 1610°C. The freezing point and melting point of a substance are the same.)

▶ **Take Action**

Time: will vary
Materials: research sources about glassmaking, samples of different types of glass (optional)

RESEARCH HOW GLASS IS MADE
Provide time for students to do their research in class, or assign this activity as a long-term project or as homework. Information on making glass can be found at the following Web sites:
Spectrum Glass Company
www.spectrumglass.com/Archives.html
Corning Glass site
www.cmog.org

To help students choose a type of glass to research, you might want to discuss different types of glass, such as lab ware, drinking glasses, light bulbs, optical glass, window glass, safety glass, and lead glass and crystal. If possible, bring in samples of different types of glass for students to compare. (**Caution:** Do *not* include fiberglass, as it is too dangerous to handle without protective gloves, safety goggles, and a face mask.) Encourage each student or pair to choose one type of glass and research its uses and how its unique properties help determine its uses. Provide class time for students to share their findings.

Mixtures, Solutions, and Suspensions

LESSON 43
Suspending Snow
Point of Lesson: *Snow globes provide an opportunity to study suspensions.*

Students explore the properties of suspensions by testing everyday solids and liquids to find a good combination for making a snow globe. After testing the materials and learning how to recognize a suspension, students identify which of the combinations they tested formed a suspension.

Materials
Activity (p. 156), for each pair or group:
► small jar (such as baby food jar, instant coffee jar, or jelly jar)
► test tubes with stoppers
► liquids to test (water, baby oil, corn syrup, vegetable oil)
► solids to test (Epsom salts, baking soda, table salt, borax soap)
► measuring spoons
► hot glue (optional)
► florist clay or aquarium sealant (optional)

Laboratory Safety
Review the following safety guidelines with students before doing the Activity in this lesson.
► Do not taste any substance in the laboratory. Avoid skin contact with substances.
► Keep your hands away from your face during this activity.
► Handle glass jars with care. Alert the teacher immediately if a jar breaks.
► Promptly clean up any spills to avoid accidents.
► Do not mix any substances other than those provided by your teacher.
► Wash your hands thoroughly after the activity.

LESSON 44
Smooth and Creamy
Point of Lesson: *Milk is a mixture that is both a solution and a suspension.*

The history of milk chocolate introduces students to the differences between solutions, suspensions, and colloids. After reading an article about the invention of solid milk chocolate candy, students identify the components of milk, then create their own milk chocolate.

Materials
Enrichment (p. 159), for teacher demonstration or student pairs or groups:
► $\frac{1}{2}$ pint (about 250 mL) heavy cream
► clean plastic 500 mL container with tight seal
► glass marble
Connections (p. 160), for each student:
► Milk Fat Content Sheet (copymaster page 231)
Activity (p. 161), for each pair or group:
► melted dark chocolate (baking chocolate), at least $\frac{1}{4}$ cup
► 2 dishes or bowls
► 2 spoons or stirrers
► whole milk and condensed milk at room temperature
► masking tape
► marking pen

Laboratory Safety
Review these safety guidelines with students before doing the Enrichment and the Activity in this lesson.
► Do not taste any substance in the laboratory.
► If you are allergic to chocolate or milk, do not do this activity.
► Melted chocolate has a high specific heat capacity. Handle it carefully to avoid burning your skin.
► Make sure containers are sealed tightly before shaking.
► Wash your hands thoroughly after the activity.

LESSON 45
Soda Pop Science
Point of Lesson: *Soda pop contains carbon dioxide dissolved into solution.*

An article on why soda pop fizzes introduces the idea that a solution can be made of a gas dissolved in a liquid. After reading the article, students compare the amount of dissolved carbon dioxide in bottles of soda pop before and after opening. They then compare the effect of carbon dioxide dissolved in soda pop with the effect of carbon dioxide trapped in fizzy candy.

Materials
Before You Read (p. 162), for teacher demonstration:
► clear bottle of cold soda pop (optional)
Enrichment (p. 163), for each student or pair:
► drinking straw
► glass of distilled water
► universal pH paper
Explore (p. 164), for teacher demonstration (optional):
► 2 unopened clear bottles of soda pop
► clear bottle of soda pop that has been left open for several hours
Take Action (p. 165), for the class (optional):
► food advertisements from magazines
► poster-making materials

Laboratory Safety
Review the following safety guidelines with students before they do the Enrichment in this lesson:
► Only one student should use the straw.
► Do not drink through the straw. Use it only to blow into the water.

Background Information

Lesson 44

Many people remember a time before homogenization when milk delivered on a doorstep would have a thick layer of cream on top. The layer was formed by fat globules that had separated out and risen to the top. A mixture in which the particles are large enough to separate out is called a *suspension*. Homogenization, as the name suggests, was developed to make the components of milk more homogenous. As part of the homogenization process, milk is forced through small nozzles, breaking the larger fat globules into particles small enough not to separate out. Because the fat particles do not settle out, they no longer form a suspension but rather a colloid. Thus, fat globules in homogenized milk form a colloid, while fat globules in unhomogenized milk form a suspension.

Lesson 45

The lesson material emphasizes that soda pop is a solution of carbon dioxide gas in water. Plain seltzer water usually does not contain anything else. However, most carbonated beverages include other dissolved solutes as well, such as sweeteners and flavorings. When soda pop goes flat, it is still a solution due to these other ingredients.

Point of Lesson

Snow globes provide an opportunity to study suspensions.

Focus

► Properties and changes of properties in matter
► Abilities necessary to do scientific inquiry
► Evidence, models, and explanation

Skills and Strategies

► Collecting and recording data
► Analyzing data
► Drawing conclusions
► Forming operational definitions

Advance Preparation

Vocabulary

Make sure students understand these terms. Definitions can be found in the glossary at the end of the student book.

► liquid
► mixture
► solid

Materials

Gather the materials needed for *Activity* (below).

Suspending Snow

Have you ever bought a snow globe as a souvenir?

A snow globe usually shows a scene of a well-known place. It contains a clear liquid and particles suspended within the liquid. You shake the globe, then watch solid particles of white "snow" drift through a clear liquid and fall over the scene. In order to look like real snow, the white particles can't fall too fast or too slow.

 **Activity**

MAKE A SNOW GLOBE

Figure out what makes the best "snow" by trying different combinations of liquids and solids.

What You Need:
• small jar (such as a baby food jar, instant coffee jar, or jelly jar)
• test tubes with stoppers
• liquids to test (water, baby oil, corn syrup, vegetable oil)
• solids to test (Epsom salts, baking soda, table salt, borax soap)
• measuring spoons

What to Do:
1. Test the first combination in the chart by pouring the liquid into a test tube and adding a small spoonful of the solid. Be sure to stopper the test tube before shaking.
2. Record your observations in the chart.
3. Repeat steps 1 and 2 with other combinations in the chart until you find one that works well. Show your results to your teacher before going on.
4. To make your snow globe, decide how much of each ingredient to use. Add your "winning combination" to the small jar. Make sure the lid is tight before you shake the jar.

UNIT 4: MATTER

156

TEACHING PLAN pp. 156–157

INTRODUCING THE LESSON

This lesson introduces students to suspensions by providing an opportunity for them to determine which materials make the best snow globe.

Ask students if they have ever seen a snow globe and, if so, to describe it in their own words. What "special effect" does it produce? (snow falling on a scene) How do students think the effect is achieved? (Accept all answers for now.) Explain that the liquid and the solid bits inside a snow globe are an example of a type of mixture called a *suspension*. Tell students that they will

learn about other types of mixtures later in this chapter.

▶ **Activity**

Time: 40–45 minutes
Materials: small jar (such as baby food jar, instant coffee jar, or jelly jar); test tubes with stoppers; liquids to test (water, baby oil, corn syrup, vegetable oil); solids to test (Epsom salts, baking soda, table salt, borax soap); measuring spoons; *optional:* hot glue, florist clay or aquarium sealant

Note: You may want to provide different powders or liquids instead of those

listed. If you do, make sure you choose substances that will not react chemically. For example, if baking soda is one of the powders, do not use vinegar as a liquid.

► Have students work in pairs or small groups.
► To save time, you could assign each group a specific combination and have groups pool their results.
► Provide small measuring spoons that can be used with a test tube. If only wide spoons are available, students can roll filter paper into a cone for a funnel and spoon the solid into the cone.

What Do You See?

For each combination you try, write your observations in the appropriate box on the chart.

	Water	Corn Syrup	Baby Oil	Vegetable Oil
Borax Soap	works better than the other solids do in water	forms large clump	works better here than in corn syrup	stays in suspension; doesn't fall
Epsom Salts	sinks too fast	forms large clump	forms large clump	forms large clump
Baking Soda	sinks too fast	forms large clump	works better here than in corn syrup	stays in suspension; doesn't fall
Table Salt	sinks too fast	forms large clump	forms large clump	works best of all combinations

▶ *In your experiment, which mixture of a liquid and a solid looked the most like falling snow? Explain.*

Answers may vary. Possible answer: Table salt in vegetable oil, because the table salt did not dissolve in the vegetable oil and did not form a clump.

DRAWING CONCLUSIONS Snow globes are an example of a special kind of mixture called a *suspension*. In a suspension, tiny particles are suspended—or hung—within the liquid. The tiny particles in a snow globe are suspended in the liquid for a short time after you shake it.

In a snow globe suspension, the particles are large enough to see clearly. In other suspensions, the particles may not be visible but they are large enough to scatter or block light. This makes the mixture appear cloudy. In any suspension, the particles are heavy enough that they slowly fall and collect on the bottom. They will not remain mixed if they are not stirred or shaken.

▶ *Go back to your results chart. Circle any combination that made a suspension.*

FIND OUT MORE

SCIENCESAURUS
Mixtures, Solutions, and Suspensions 271

157

More Resources

The following resources are also available from Great Source.

SCIENCESAURUS

Mixtures, Solutions, and Suspensions   271

READER'S HANDBOOK

Reading Science: Do an Activity 116
How to Read a Chart or Table   600

Assessment

Skill: Drawing conclusions

Use the following questions to assess each student's progress:

Based on your results, what can you conclude about the liquid and solid parts of a suspension? What properties must each have? (The solid must be light enough to drift slowly down through the liquid, but it should not dissolve in the liquid. The liquid must be thick enough to slow the fall of the solid bits.)

▶ Students can personalize their globes with small, insoluble decorations. Supervise students as they attach decorations to the inside of the jar lid with hot glue, florist clay, or aquarium sealant. Students can also apply sealant around the inner rim of the jar lid before screwing it on. Let the sealant dry overnight.

DRAWING CONCLUSIONS Ask: *How can you tell if a mixture is a suspension?* (The particles hang in the liquid after you shake it, but eventually they settle out.) *Did any of the solids form a suspension with water?* (No; they all sank too fast.) *Did any of the solids*

form a suspension with corn syrup? (No; they all formed clumps.) *What do you think is the best kind of liquid to use? What properties does it have that make it work well?* (Oil is the best; it is thick so the solids do not sink very fast, and the solids do not dissolve in it.)

CHECK UNDERSTANDING
Skill: Making inferences
Ask: *How could you tell a suspension from a solution—a mixture in which the solid is dissolved in the liquid?* (In a suspension, the particles eventually settle out.)

Point of Lesson

Milk is a mixture that is both a solution and a suspension.

Focus

► **Properties and changes of properties in matter**
► **Systems, order, and organization**
► **Science and technology in society**
► **Science as a human endeavor**

Skills and Strategies

► **Creating and using tables**
► **Collecting and recording data**
► **Analyzing data**
► **Drawing conclusions**

Advance Preparation

Vocabulary

Make sure students understand these terms. Definitions can be found in the glossary at the end of the student book.

► **mixture**
► **molecule**
► **property**
► **proteins**

Materials

Gather the materials needed for *Enrichment* (p. 159), *Connections* (p. 160), and *Activity* (p. 161).

Smooth and Creamy

Discover the secret of how a very special treat was first created.

From candy bars to chocolate milk to ice cream toppings, milk chocolate is a favorite treat of many. In the 1860s, Daniel Peter, an ambitious young man in Switzerland, was interested in getting into the chocolate business. To create a unique product, he began experimenting with mixing milk and chocolate to make creamy milk chocolate.

Peter started by simply adding plain milk to chocolate, but that didn't work. His neighbor happened to be Henri Nestlé, a baby food manufacturer. Nestlé was working on a new form of milk. You'll see how Daniel Peter was able to use that product to make milk chocolate.

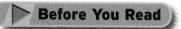 **Before You Read**

ALL THINGS CHOCOLATE Dark chocolate is a mixture made from cacao seeds, sugar, and flavorings. When you add milk to dark chocolate, you get milk chocolate.

► *What foods can you name that contain chocolate?*

Examples: chocolate candy, brownies, chocolate milk, chocolate

covered nuts and fruits like strawberries, and chocolate cereal

► *Describe the flavor of milk chocolate.*

Answers might include adjectives like "sweet" and "creamy."

► *Have you ever had dark chocolate? How does it compare with milk chocolate?*

Students might say that dark chocolate is not as sweet and is harder.

158

TEACHING PLAN pp. 158–159

INTRODUCING THE LESSON

This lesson describes the invention of milk chocolate candy and explains why condensed milk makes a better solution with chocolate than whole milk does.

Ask students if they know where chocolate comes from. Explain that it comes from the beans of the cacao tree, which is native to Central and South America. In ancient cultures, chocolate was consumed as a bitter or spicy beverage; sugar was not added to chocolate until it was introduced to Europe in the 1500s, and chocolate was not mixed with milk to make candy until much later.

► **Before You Read**

ALL THINGS CHOCOLATE Students who are allergic to chocolate may be familiar with other foods or drinks that can be enjoyed either with or without milk, such as tea, coffee, cream of tomato soup, or oatmeal. Ask: *How does the flavor of the food or drink change when you add milk?* (Examples: It is creamy and sweet; it has a richer flavor.) Students who do not eat dairy foods may use soy milk, rice beverages, nut milks, or another milk alternative in the same ways that milk is commonly used.

NOTEZONE

Underline why Daniel Peter's idea of mixing plain milk with dark chocolate did not create creamy chocolate.

Lucky for us, the inventor of milk chocolate candy had a friend, Henri Nestlé, who was an expert on milk.

The Tale of Henri Nestlé and Daniel Peter

...Henri Nestlé...was...an inventive pharmacist and humanitarian. Nestlé wanted to create an alternative to breast milk for mothers who were unable to breast feed their babies.

Infant mortality rates during the 1860s were high due to malnutrition and Henri Nestlé worked hard to battle this widespread problem.... Through his experiments, Henri Nestlé developed a product similar to breast milk that actually saved a child's life. He called this new product Farine Lactée Nestlé.

Around this same time, Daniel Peter, a friend of Henri Nestlé, was trying to successfully mix dark chocolate with milk to create a smooth and creamy chocolate. But his idea was not working because the water present in milk caused the chocolate to separate. He soon combined the dark chocolate with the condensed milk created by Henri Nestlé, and the rest, as they say, is chocolate history. Daniel Peter produced the first milk chocolate bar by adding condensed milk to dark chocolate.

inventive: creative
pharmacist: a person who prepares medicines
humanitarian: a person who tries to help other people

mortality: death
malnutrition: poor diet
condensed milk: milk with some of the water removed and sugar added

From: "The Tale of Henri Nestlé and Daniel Peter." Chocolatevalley.com (www.chocolatevalley.com/history/tale.htm)

FARINE LACTÉE NESTLÉ

FARINE LACTÉE NESTLÉ

ALIMENT COMPLET POUR LES ENFANTS

Mᵒⁿ HENRI NESTLÉ. A.CHRISTEN. 16. Rue du Parc Royal. PARIS.

FIND OUT MORE

SCIENCESAURUS
Mixtures, Solutions, and Suspensions 271

159

Enrichment

Time: 30 minutes
Materials: $\frac{1}{2}$ pint (about 250 mL) heavy cream; clean plastic 500-mL container with tight seal; glass marble

This activity highlights some properties of suspensions by showing what happens to the fat suspended in cream when the mixture is shaken. Perform the activity as a demonstration, or have students work in pairs or small groups.

Pour the cream into the empty container, add the marble, and close the container. Make sure the seal is tight so the container will not leak when shaken. Have students take turns shaking the container. At first, students will be able to hear the marble moving inside the container. When you can no longer hear the marble, open the container. The container should now hold lumps of butter and some liquid. The liquid is buttermilk, a mixture of protein, lactose, and minerals in water. The buttermilk also contains some of the milk fat left over from the butter-making process. Ask: *What happened to the tiny fat globules suspended in the cream?* (The fat globules joined together and settled out of the solution.) *How do you think shaking helped this happen?* (Shaking caused all the particles to move around and collide with each other. When the fat particles collided, they stuck together and eventually became heavy enough to settle out.)

▶ Read

Students may recognize the name Nestlé from the candy bars and chocolate chips sold under that name. Explain that Nestlé is actually the largest food and beverage company in the world; they own many major brands of food, beverages, candy, and pet food. The company was founded in 1866. When Daniel Peter invented milk chocolate in 1875, he started his own company, which later merged with the Nestlé Company.

When students have completed the NoteZone activity, ask volunteers to read the text they underlined. Ask: *Have you ever tried to mix chocolate with water? What happened? What kind of chocolate mixes with water or plain milk?* (Students may have used powdered hot chocolate mix that mixes well with hot water, or they may be familiar with chocolate milk mix in powder or syrup form. These have been specially formulated to dissolve in milk or water.) Explain that Daniel Peter was trying to mix solid dark chocolate—not powder or syrup—with plain milk.

CHECK UNDERSTANDING
Skill: Drawing conclusions
Ask: *Which makes a more creamy solution—chocolate and plain milk or chocolate and condensed milk? Explain why.* (Chocolate and condensed milk make a creamier solution because condensed milk has less water than plain milk, and water does not mix well with chocolate.)

More Resources

The following resources are also available from Great Source.

ScienceSaurus

Reader's Handbook

Connections

Time: 30 minutes
Materials: (for each student) Milk Fat Content Sheet (copymaster page 231)

MATH Have students use the nutritional information on the Milk Fat Content Sheet to answer the following question. *If one cup of 1% milk contains 2.5 grams of fat, how many grams of fat are in one cup of 2% milk?* (5 grams) Have students use the data on the Content Sheet to create a bar graph comparing the fat content of different milk products. Instruct students to use average (mean) values where ranges are given. For example, the fat content of half-and-half is given as 10–18%; students should use 14% on the graph.

▶ **Explore**

MILKY MIXTURES The milk that Daniel Peter first tried to mix with chocolate was plain cow's milk. Cow's milk is about 88 percent water. Fat globules, sugars, and proteins make up the other 12 percent.

The sugar is completely dissolved in the water. You can't see the sugar particles and they will never settle to the bottom.

Tiny fat globules are evenly spread throughout the water. This gives the liquid its creamy white color. But fat molecules always stay separate from water molecules. Since fat is also lighter than water, the fat globules eventually rise. This fat creates a layer of thick cream on the surface of the milk.

Even after the fat has risen to the top, the milk is still whitish in color. This comes from the protein particles that are still spread throughout the water. These protein particles will never settle out, but they are big enough to reflect light. This is why even skim milk, which has no fat globules, is not clear.

The chart below describes three types of mixtures. Complete the chart by writing what components of milk form each type of mixture.

Mixture Type	Properties	Milk Components
Solution	particles are invisible, do not separate	*sugar and water*
Colloid	particles do not separate but are big enough to reflect light	*protein and water*
Suspension	particles separate out	*fat globules and water*

Condensed milk has had about half of the water removed while all the other substances remain. Then extra sugar is added.

▶ *Is condensed milk a colloid, suspension, or solution? Explain your answer.*

  It would be all three since it would still contain water, protein, fat,

  and sugar.

▶ *Why do you think condensed milk mixes better with chocolate than whole milk does? (If you need to, look back at the reading.)*

  It has less water and water does not mix with chocolate.

Teaching Plan pp. 160–161

▶ **Explore**

MILKY MIXTURES Ask students if they know what the term *homogenized* means. Explain that whole milk fresh from a cow separates into layers when it stands; the fat floats to the top and creates a layer of cream. Homogenization is a process that breaks down the fat in milk into very small particles. The small particles remain suspended in the milk and do not settle out for at least as long as the milk remains fresh.

Since the milk available in Daniel Peter's time was unhomogenized (homogenized milk was not available commercially until 1919), the chart on this page shows the mixtures contained in unhomogenized milk.

To help students understand the different types of mixtures listed in the table, you may want to identify examples of each type. Gelatin and tomato paste are examples of colloids; salt water and carbonated water are examples of solutions; oil-and-vinegar salad dressing and orange juice with pulp are examples of suspensions.

To summarize the differences between plain and condensed milk, list the following milk components on the board: *fat, sugar, protein,* and *water.* Then have students write a > or < symbol next to each component to indicate the concentration of each in condensed milk compared with whole milk. (fat >, sugar >, protein >, water <)

A RECIPE FOR DISASTER

Here's a recipe for smooth chocolate milk—or is it?

What You Need:
- melted dark chocolate (baking chocolate)
- 2 dishes or bowls
- 2 spoons or stirrers
- whole milk at room temperature
- condensed milk at room temperature
- masking tape
- marking pen

What to Do:
1. Label one bowl "whole" and the other "condensed."
2. Put some melted dark chocolate in the bowl marked "whole."
3. Add about the same amount of whole milk.
4. Stir to mix well.
5. Record your observations in the table.
6. Pour some melted chocolate into the bowl marked "condensed."
7. Add an equal amount of condensed milk and stir.
8. Record your observations in the table.

Milk Product Added	Observations
Whole milk	*sticky, clumpy like clay*
Condensed milk	*smooth, shiny liquid*

What Do You See?

▶ *What does the mixture in the cup with whole milk look like?*

The chocolate and milk do not mix well. The mixture has a clay-like consistency.

▶ *Describe why Daniel Peter might have found this result unsatisfactory.*

The mixture is not creamy and it does not look very tasty.

▶ *What did Daniel Peter conclude caused the problem when he tried mixing milk and melted chocolate like this?*

The water present in milk caused the problem.

▶ *What did you observe with the condensed milk that supports Daniel Peter's conclusion?*

The condensed milk does not have as much water and it did not make the chocolate lumpy.

161

Assessment

Skill: Designing an experiment to test a hypothesis

Use the following task to assess each student's progress:

Imagine that you have found a container of an unknown mixture. What tests would you perform to determine whether it is a solution, a colloid, or a suspension? (Let the mixture stand to see if any particles settled out. If they do, it's a suspension. If it's cloudy but no particles settle out, it's a colloid. If it's completely clear, it's a solution.)

Time: 40–45 minutes
Materials: (for each pair or group) melted dark chocolate (baking chocolate), 2 dishes or bowls, 2 spoons or stirrers, whole milk at room temperature, condensed milk at room temperature, masking tape, marking pen

Advance Preparation: Before students begin, melt enough dark chocolate to provide each pair or group with at least $\frac{1}{4}$ cup of melted chocolate. The chocolate can be melted in a glass bowl in a microwave oven. (Microwave for 1 minute on high, then stir; continue heating and stirring at 30-second intervals until the chocolate is completely melted.) Finely chopped chocolate will melt more quickly and evenly than larger pieces. Do not use dark chocolate syrup, which is formulated to mix with milk. Make sure students use the recommended proportion of chocolate and milk. If they add too much whole milk, the chocolate and milk will blend.

Caution: Students who are allergic to chocolate or milk should not taste the ingredients or mixtures. As an added precaution, you may want to perform the activity as a demonstration.

▶ As an additional test, students may want to confirm Daniel Peter's conclusion by trying to mix a sample of melted chocolate with an equal amount of plain water. Have students predict what they think will happen before they try this test. Afterward, ask: *Did your results match your prediction?* (Students will probably predict that the chocolate will not mix with water, and their results should confirm their prediction.)

Point of Lesson
Soda pop contains carbon dioxide dissolved into solution.

Focus
► Properties and changes of properties in matter
► Science and technology in society
► Change, constancy, and measurement

Skills and Strategies
► Recognizing cause and effect
► Making inferences
► Comparing and contrasting
► Interpreting scientific illustrations

Advance Preparation

Vocabulary
Make sure students understand these terms. Definitions can be found in the glossary at the end of the student book.

► gas   ► pressure
► liquid   ► solid
► molecule   ► solution

Materials
Gather the materials needed for *Before You Read* (below), *Enrichment* (p. 163), *Explore* (p. 164), and *Take Action* (p. 165).

SODA POP SCIENCE

What puts the *pop* in soda pop?

Old, stale soda pop—blah. It still has the same flavor, but it just doesn't taste as good as a freshly opened bottle. Why? What makes a fresh soda pop different? If you look at the ingredients on a bottle of soda pop, you will notice that one of the many things it contains is "carbonated water." That is just plain water with carbon dioxide gas dissolved in it. But it is this dissolved carbon dioxide that gives fresh soda its sharp, tangy taste. What do you think happens to make a soda pop go flat?

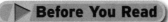 **Before You Read**

GASSY LIQUIDS Imagine you come home from school, open the refrigerator, and take out a can of soda pop.

► *What do you see on the surface of the soda pop right after it is poured into a glass?*

You see the bubbles coming up to the top of the liquid.

► *What happens after the soda has been open for a long time?*

There are no more bubbles.

People who make soda pop want to keep it fizzy until you drink it.

► *Do you know what they do to keep the bubbles dissolved in the liquid? Write any ideas you have.*

Answers will vary. Example: The bottle is tightly closed so that the gas

cannot get out of the liquid.

UNIT 4: MATTER

162

TEACHING PLAN pp. 162–163

INTRODUCING THE LESSON
This lesson describes the use of carbon dioxide to give carbonated beverages and fizzing candies their distinctive "pop."

Ask students to describe the factors they think contribute to how fizzy or bubbly a soda is. (Students may say that the amount of time the soda has been open, its temperature, or how much the can was shaken before opening all affect how fizzy the soda is.) Some students may think that the bubbles rising to the surface of a carbonated drink show that the liquid is changing into a gas, or evaporating.

Explain that the liquid is not evaporating but that gas dissolved in the liquid is being released.

Before You Read

Time: 5 minutes
Materials: clear bottle of cold soda pop (optional)

GASSY LIQUIDS To engage students in answering the questions on this page, you may want to open a clear bottle of cold soda slowly and dramatically. Then encourage students to describe what they hear and what they see when they

open a carbonated beverage. Although students may not answer the last question in this section correctly, encourage them to record their ideas and then compare them later with the information provided in the reading.

▶ Read

Here's how the gas gets into the soda pop and (usually) stays there.

The Fizz Factor

Rarely do you ever drink an entire 2-liter bottle of soda at one sitting. Since leftovers are inevitable, the soda tends to go flat....

Since the fizz in the soda is actually dissolved carbon dioxide gas, the goal is to keep as much of the gas in the bottle as possible. Soda fizzes when dissolved carbon dioxide gas is released in the form of bubbles. At the bottling plant, carbon dioxide molecules are forced into the soda in an amount that is greater than would ordinarily dissolve.... As soon as you open the bottle, ... excess gas escapes into the room...

The higher the gas pressure above the liquid in the bottle, the more gas will be pressed into the liquid. Makes sense. However, here's the kicker. Once you open the bottle, ... carbon dioxide molecules that were forced into the soda at the bottling plant come flying out. It's that unmistakable sound of PSSSSST!

inevitable: unavoidable   excess: extra
dissolved: completely mixed in
and no longer visible

From: Wolke, Robert L. *What Einstein Didn't Know: Scientific Answers to Everyday Questions.* Delacorte Press.

NOTEZONE

Underline the gas that is dissolved in soda pop.

Circle what happens to the gas when you open a bottle of soda pop.

FIND OUT MORE

SCIENCESAURUS

163

Enrichment

Time: 20 minutes
Materials: drinking straw; glass of distilled water; universal pH paper

Note: The pH of pure distilled water should be about 7. However, the pH of the distilled water you are using may be different, depending on its purity. You may want to test the pH yourself before students do the activity. In any case, the important point in the activity is not the specific pH values but the *difference* in values before and after carbon dioxide is added.

Tell students that carbon dioxide forms carbonic acid in solution. This changes the pH of the solution, making it acidic. Students can see this by performing a simple test. Have students work individually or in pairs. Provide each student or pair with a glass of distilled water. Have them use pH paper to test and record the pH of the distilled water. Then have students blow through a straw into the distilled water. Remind students that their breath contains carbon dioxide. Students should then test and record the pH of the water again. Ask: *How did the pH change?* (The water became more acidic; the pH value was lower.) As an extension, you may want to provide samples of different carbonated beverages for students to test with pH paper.

▶ Read

Ask: *How much carbon dioxide gas do you think is dissolved in a bottle of soda pop? Why do you think so?* (Not that much; if you leave the bottle open and the soda pop goes flat, there is not that much less than there was when the bottle was first opened.) Explain that the gas in soda pop is compressed so that more gas fits in a smaller volume. If the compressed carbon dioxide gas in a 454-mL (16-oz) bottle of cola were released at standard temperature and pressure, it would fill a one-liter bottle.

Ask volunteers to share their answers to the NoteZone task. Ask: *Why do you think the gas escapes when the bottle is opened?* Lead students to understand that there is a difference in pressure between the gas inside the closed soda bottle (higher pressure) and the air outside the bottle (lower pressure). When given the chance, gases move from areas of higher pressure to areas of lower pressure. When the bottle is opened, the carbon dioxide gas flows out until the pressure inside the bottle and the pressure outside are the same.

CHECK UNDERSTANDING
Skill: Recognizing cause and effect
Ask: *What makes soda pop hiss, bubble, and fizz when you open it?* (Carbon dioxide gas dissolved in the liquid escapes.)

More Resources

The following resources are also available from Great Source.

SCIENCESAURUS

READER'S HANDBOOK

WRITE SOURCE 2000

Connections

PHYSICAL EDUCATION Ask students if they have ever been scuba diving or if they know anyone who has. Tell students that as a diver goes deeper under water, the water pressure increases. At these high pressures, nitrogen from the air the diver is breathing is forced into solution in his or her blood. If the diver rises to areas of lower pressure too quickly, the dissolved nitrogen forms bubbles in the bloodstream. This condition is known as decompression sickness, commonly called "the bends." Ask:

(continued on page 165)

TEACHING PLAN pp. 164–165

▶ **Explore**

DIAGRAM SOLUTIONS Soda pop is a solution. In a solution, one substance (called the solute) is dissolved in another substance (called the solvent). In many cases, the solute is a powder (a solid) and the solvent is a liquid.

▶ *Can you think of a familiar example of such a solution?*

  Students may think of lemonade or another powdered drink mix.

But not all solutions are made up of solids dissolved in liquids.

▶ *What is the solute in soda pop? What is the solvent?*

  carbon dioxide gas; water

Look at the diagram of three bottles of soda pop. Bottle 1 is unopened, Bottle 2 has just been opened, and Bottle 3 has been open for several hours. Use arrows to show what is happening to the carbon dioxide in each bottle. Beneath each bottle, write a brief description of what is happening in the bottle. Use some of the following terms in your labels or descriptions: *carbon dioxide gas (CO_2), dissolved carbon dioxide gas, in solution, out of solution, pressure.* Use the reading as needed to help you label each diagram.

| Bottle 1 | Bottle 2 | Bottle 3 |

Carbon dioxide gas | *Some of the carbon* | *The pressure inside*
above the level of the | *dioxide gas has escaped* | *and outside the bottle*
liquid is under pressure | *through the neck of the* | *is the same. Most or all*
and keeps dissolved | *bottle. The pressure is* | *of the carbon dioxide*
carbon dioxide gas in | *released.* | *has escaped.*
solution.

164

▶ **Explore**

Time: 20 minutes
Materials: (for teacher demonstration) 2 unopened bottles of soda pop, bottle of soda pop that has been left open for several hours (optional)

DIAGRAM SOLUTIONS To help students visualize the three different soda bottles, you may want to provide examples for them to observe. Students may not realize that there are not many visible bubbles in an unopened bottle of soda. Explain that this is because the carbon dioxide gas is dissolved in the soda, so it is invisible. It is only when

the bottle is opened that the gas forms bubbles. Open one of the unopened bottles so students can observe this.

Remind students to consider the pressure both inside and outside the bottle in each diagram. Encourage them to use analogies that help them understand how the behavior of the carbon dioxide gas is related to pressure. For the first diagram, for example, tell students to imagine that the bottle is a closed room crowded with people. Ask: *What happens when the door is opened?* (People can leave the room. They may rush out as soon as the door is opened.) Then ask: *What happens*

after the door has been opened for a while? (There are not many people left in the room. People can go in and out as they please.) Emphasize that analogies like this one are not scientific explanations, but they are still useful to help us understand scientific ideas.

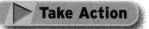

Propose Explanations

CARBONATED CANDY Have you ever tasted the candy that sizzles and fizzles in your mouth? The manufacturer makes it by forcing carbon dioxide gas under high pressure into a hot liquid sugar mixture. When the mixture cools and hardens, tiny pressurized bubbles of carbon dioxide gas are trapped within the hard candy.

▶ *How is making this candy similar to making soda pop?*

To make both, carbon dioxide is forced into a liquid mixture

under high pressure.

What happens when you put the candy on your tongue? First, it begins to dissolve in the water in your saliva—like other candies. Then, your tongue starts to tingle and you hear popping sounds.

▶ *What do you think makes your tongue tingle? What causes the popping sounds? (Think about what you hear when you open a can of soda and what your tongue feels when you drink it.)*

When the candy dissolves, the bubbles burst and the pressurized carbon

dioxide gas escapes. That might tickle your tongue. If the gas is making

the candy break when the walls of the bubble get thin, that might make

the popping sound.

▶ *How is eating a piece of carbonated candy similar to opening a can of soda pop?*

In both cases, carbon dioxide gas that is under pressure is released. You

hear a sound and you feel the effects of the release of carbon dioxide

gas each time.

Take Action

INVENT A NEW TREAT Use your imagination to invent a new food product that uses carbon dioxide to add fizz. On a separate sheet of paper, explain how the food product would be manufactured or packaged to keep the carbon dioxide trapped. Then create an advertisement to describe this new treat.

(continued from page 164)

How is this similar to the carbon dioxide bubbles in soda pop? (The carbon dioxide is forced into solution in the soda. When the bottle is opened, the pressure is lowered, and the dissolved gas forms bubbles.) Invite students to find out more about the bends. (The bends can result in paralysis or even death. The best way for divers to prevent the bends is not to dive too deep and to come to the surface slowly, pausing often at shallower depths.)

Assessment
Skill: Making inferences

Use the following task to assess each student's progress:

Air pressure is lower in the mountains than it is at sea level. Describe how opening a bottle of soda pop on top of a mountain might be different from opening a bottle of soda pop at sea level. (On top of a mountain, the difference between the air pressure and the pressure of the gas in the soda will be greater than at sea level. As a result, the soda will be fizzier as it releases the gas, and all the gas will be released more quickly. At sea level, the soda will bubble less but might stay bubbly longer.)

Propose Explanations

CARBONATED CANDY Ask students if they have ever eaten this type of candy. If so, have them describe the sensations they experienced. Explain that the candy was introduced in 1975 and made by one company until the early 1980s, when a rumor that the candy was dangerous began to spread. The rumor claimed that some children had suffered internal injury when they mixed this candy with carbonated beverages, but the rumor was false. You may want to explain that this type of rumor often spreads quickly and continues to be told for a long time. Although the rumor was not true, the manufacturer eventually stopped trying to sell the candy. However, a few years later, another company began selling the candy again.

Take Action

Time: 40–45 minutes
Materials: food advertisements from magazines, poster-making materials (optional)

INVENT A NEW TREAT Have students work individually or in pairs. In addition to explaining how the carbon dioxide gas would be trapped in the new food, students should include a description of how the carbon dioxide gas would be released. Point out that the method for releasing the gas depends on whether the gas is dissolved in a liquid or trapped in a solid.

You may want to provide samples of magazine advertisements for food, beverages, and candy. Students can choose advertisements they like as models for their own. Some students may want to work in groups to create television commercials for their products. Provide class time for students to share their product ideas and their advertisements.

Properties of Elements

LESSON 46

The Nifty 92

Point of Lesson: *All matter is made up of elements.*

The lesson begins with students reading a popular science article about the 92 naturally occurring chemical elements. Students then examine a periodic table to identify those elements. They compare the atomic masses of natural elements and elements that exist only in laboratories. Finally, students research elements and describe some of their properties.

Materials

Read (p. 166), for each student:
▶ Periodic Table of Elements (copymaster page 230)

Explore (p. 167), for each student:
▶ Periodic Table of Elements (copymaster page 230)

Take Action (p. 167), for the class:
▶ research sources about the properties of elements

Assessment (p. 167), for each student:
▶ Periodic Table of Elements (copymaster page 230)

LESSON 47

Smelly Sulfur

Point of Lesson: *Some elements and compounds have properties that are so distinct, you can recognize them even at a distance.*

Students descend into a cave with a National Geographic explorer to investigate properties of sulfur and the compounds it forms. After reading a description of the smelly, poisonous cave, students examine the chemical reactions involving sulfur that take place in the cave. Students use their new knowledge of sulfur compounds to explain why the explorers must wear protective equipment to safely explore this environment.

Materials

Science Scope Activity, Part 1 (p. 166B and p. 169), for the class:
▶ numbered index cards (see p. 166B)
▶ research sources about elements

LESSON 48

Silicon Creature

Point of Lesson: *The position of an element on the periodic table gives clues to its properties.*

In this lesson, students consider the science behind an episode of the television series *Star Trek*. Students read an explanation of the importance of carbon to life on Earth and a description of the imaginary silicon-based life form introduced in the episode. They examine the periodic table to infer chemical properties that silicon and carbon share, then use that insight to explain why a silicon-based life form might be plausible in the context of science fiction. Finally, students contrast the properties of silicon and carbon to explain why silicon-based life is in reality not very likely.

Materials

Read (p. 173), for the class:
▶ electron-dot diagrams (see *ScienceSaurus*, section 268)

Science Scope Activity, Part 2 (p. 173), for the class:
▶ colored paper squares (about 20 cm × 20 cm): 28 pink, 64 white, and 22 yellow, plus extras of each color in case they are needed
  ▶ pushpins
  ▶ art supplies
  ▶ Periodic Table of Elements (copymaster page 230)
    Explore (p. 174), for each student:
    ▶ Periodic Table of Elements (copymaster page 230)

Science Scope Activity

An Elemental Activity

NSTA has chosen a Science Scope *activity related to the content in this chapter. The activity begins here and continues in Lesson 46, page 169, and Lesson 47, page 173.*

Time: Part 1: will vary

Part 2: 1 class period

Materials: see page 166A

Part 1

Numbering the cards: Prepare a set of index cards numbered from 1 to 92. Alternatively, you may want to skip numbers 43 and 61 and add numbers 93 and 94 to represent elements found on Earth.

A valuable print resource for research is the *Handbook of Chemistry and Physics.* Good Web sites for student research include the following:

www.webelements.com

www.chemicalelements.com

education.jlab.org/itselemental/index.html

(continued on page 169)

Part 2

Prepare squares of colored paper as noted in the materials list on page 166A. In order to complete the giant periodic table in Part 2, you may want to have more than one class collaborate or have each student make more than one square.

(continued on page 173)

Background Information

Lesson 47

The idea that sufuric acid was responsible for the formation of many caves is a relatively new one. Previously, the assumption had been that all caves were formed by slightly acidic river water wearing away limestone. That left some cave formations, such as the Big Room in Carlsbad Caverns, difficult to explain. The Big Room, spacious enough to contain six football fields, has large deposits of gypsum throughout that would have been washed away if the cave had been carved by flowing water. It wasn't until the early 1970s that scientists first proposed that some caves were formed by sulfuric acid. Later, they discovered that in some caves it was bacteria that produced the sulfuric acid.

Point of Lesson
All matter is made up of elements.

Focus
► Properties and changes of properties in matter
► Evidence, models, and explanation
► Systems, order, and organization

Skills and Strategies
► Interpreting scientific illustrations
► Using tables
► Comparing and contrasting

Advance Preparation

Vocabulary
Make sure students understand these terms. Definitions can be found in the glossary at the end of the student book.

► atom	► molecule
► elements	► nucleus
► matter	► proton

Materials
Gather the materials needed for *Read* (below), *Explore* (p. 167), *Take Action* (p. 167), and *Assessment* (p. 167).

The Nifty 92

What are you made of?
How many ingredients do you think it would take to build every different thing in the world?

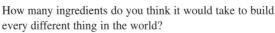
Read

NOTEZONE
Underline the names of elements mentioned in the reading.
Circle the adjectives that describe them.

FIND OUT MORE

SCIENCESAURUS

Properties	
of Matter	251
Atoms	255
Elements	260
Periodic Table	265

SCILINKS.
THE WORLD'S A CLICK AWAY
www.scilinks.org
Keyword: Periodic Table
Code: GSPD20

166

Newspaper writer Kathy Wollard called the 92 naturally occurring elements the "Nifty 92."

The Nifty 92

...The ancient Greeks thought that everything in the world was made of four basic elements: water, fire, earth, and air. You, your dog, and your banana split were simply combinations of the Big Four....

Everything is indeed made of elements....[T]here are 92 natural elements that make everything you see around you. The Nifty 92 are the ingredients in the recipes for cats and clouds, bats and belfries.

(There also are a handful of man-made elements, concocted in laboratories; rather rickety as elements go.)

Many of the Nifty 92 are utterly familiar: good old oxygen. Shiny copper and silver. Slippery mercury. Balloon-lifting helium. Bone-building calcium. Poisonous arsenic. Radiant neon. Others are unfamiliar, tongue-twisting oddballs: Lanthanum. Scandium. Cerium. Praseodymium. Yttrium.

Scientists use a big chart called the Periodic Table that shows all the elements, starting with hydrogen. Why does first place go to hydrogen? Hydrogen is the simplest element....

...[S]tarting with atoms of the Nifty 92, combined in myriad molecules, a whole universe is built, from chocolate-chip cookies to soaring mountains to you and me.

belfries: bell towers	**atoms:** the smallest parts of elements
concocted: made	**myriad:** very, very many
rickety: shaky, unstable	**molecules:** combinations of atoms
utterly: very	

From: Wollard, Kathy. "Atoms Like To Stick Together." *Newsday*.

UNIT 4: MATTER

TEACHING PLAN pp. 166–167

INTRODUCING THE LESSON
This lesson introduces students to the 92 naturally occurring elements and describes how the periodic table organizes the elements by their properties.

Invite students to discuss the questions at the top of the page. Students may think that there must be thousands of "ingredients" needed to build every thing in the world. Explain that all known substances are made up of the elements shown in the periodic table.

Read

Time: 10 minutes
Materials: Periodic Table of Elements (copymaster page 230)

Encourage students to refer to the periodic table as they read the excerpt. Challenge them to locate each element mentioned in the reading.

Point out that of the elements that commonly occur on Earth, element 92, uranium, has the highest atomic number. However, two elements with lower atomic numbers—technetium (43) and promethium (61)—have not been found

to occur naturally on Earth. They have only been created in a laboratory. There are also two elements with higher atomic numbers— neptunium (93) and plutonium (94)—that have been found to occur naturally in very small amounts; these two elements are often created in a lab but are very unstable and do not exist for very long.

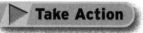

Explore

PERIODIC TABLE OF THE ELEMENTS Look at a copy of the periodic table. You can find one in a reference book such as *ScienceSaurus* or an encyclopedia. You can also find one on the Internet.

▶ *Locate the "Nifty 92" (elements 1–92). What element is number 92?*

Uranium

The number 92 stands for the atomic number, which is the number of protons in the nucleus of a uranium atom. Look at the box for element 92 again.

▶ *What other information about uranium is there?*

Answers may vary. The table should show the atomic mass (for uranium,

atomic mass is about 238 atomic mass units). It will probably also

show the chemical symbol for uranium, U.

▶ *What is the name of the first "rickety" element? (Hint: They start with element 93.)*

Neptunium

▶ *Look at the Nifty 92 as a group. Now look at the "rickety" elements as a group. How do their atomic masses compare?*

The "rickety" elements have more mass.

▶ *What conclusion can you draw about the relationship between atomic mass and stability?*

the more mass, the less stable

Take Action

WRITE EXPRESSIVELY Kathy Wollard uses adjectives to describe how some of the elements look, or what they do.

Do research to find out more about the elements below. Then write your own adjective to describe each one in the blank space beside its name.

Aluminum	*Possible answer: light*	Zinc	*Possible answer: rustproof*
Gold	*Possible answer: valuable*	Iron	*Possible answer: rusts easily*
Lead	*Possible answer: bluish*	Carbon	*Possible answer: black*
Tin	*Possible answer: soft*	Radium	*Possible answer: radioactive*
Iodine	*Possible answer: smelly*	Platinum	*Possible answer: metallic*

167

More Resources
The following resources are also available from Great Source and NSTA.

SCIENCESAURUS
Properties of Matter	251
Atoms	255
Elements	260
Periodic Table	265

READER'S HANDBOOK
Reading a Graphic	537
How to Read a Chart or Table	600

SCILINKS
THE WORLD'S A CLICK AWAY

www.scilinks.org
Keyword: Periodic Table
Code: GSPD20

Assessment
Time: 5 minutes
Materials: Periodic Table of Elements (copymaster page 230)

Skill: Recognizing cause and effect

Use the following question to assess each student's progress:

Have students look at the periodic table. Then ask: *What is the relationship between atomic number and atomic mass?* (As atomic number increases, so does atomic mass.)

Explore

Time: 20 minutes
Materials: Periodic Table of Elements (copymaster page 230)

PERIODIC TABLE OF THE ELEMENTS As students examine the periodic table, explain that an atom's atomic number tells how many protons it has in its nucleus. The atomic mass of an element is approximately equal to the sum of the number of protons and neutrons in the nucleus. (The atomic masses shown on the periodic table include decimal fractions. You may want to explain that these masses reflect an average of all the different isotopes—atoms with variable numbers of neutrons—of the atom.) Also explain that the "rickety" elements are less stable because they are radioactive; in other words, they are in a constant state of decay.

Take Action

Time: will vary
Materials: research sources about the properties of elements

WRITE EXPRESSIVELY Provide reference materials for students to research the elements listed. Provide class time for students to share their adjectives.

CHECK UNDERSTANDING
Skill: Comparing and contrasting
Ask: *What are some facts you can find out about an element from the periodic table?* (its name, atomic number, atomic mass, chemical symbol, and whether it is a metal or nonmetal) *What are some facts about an element that you cannot find out from the periodic table?* (Examples: its color, its melting point, its smell)

Point of Lesson
Some elements and compounds have properties that are so distinct, you can recognize them even at a distance.

Focus
▶ Evidence, models, and explanation
▶ Properties and changes of properties in matter
▶ Natural hazards
▶ Science as a human endeavor

Skills and Strategies
▶ Organizing information
▶ Sequencing
▶ Drawing conclusions

Advance Preparation

Vocabulary
Make sure students understand these terms. Definitions can be found in the glossary at the end of the student book.

- ▶ bacteria
- ▶ compound
- ▶ elements
- ▶ gas
- ▶ molecule
- ▶ periodic table of elements
- ▶ property

Materials
Gather the materials needed for *Science Scope Activity* (p. 166B, p. 169, and p. 173).

Smelly Sulfur

▲ "Snottites"

How can you tell what elements are around you?

Sometimes you can smell the chlorine from a swimming pool before you can even see the pool. The odor of ammonia in window cleaners makes you wrinkle your nose before you notice the bottle. The sulfur smell of one little rotten egg can fill a whole room. Some elements and compounds have properties that are so distinct, your nose can identify them from a distance.

Molecules of chlorine, ammonia, or hydrogen sulfide gases float through the air into your nose. As your nose senses these molecules, it sends a message to your brain, which identifies the smell. With just a sniff and a little knowledge of chemistry, you can actually name many of the elements and compounds in your surroundings. And some day this ability could save your life!

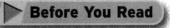 **Before You Read**

CAVE CONDITIONS Have you ever been in a cave? Have you read about caves or seen a movie or television show about caves? What would you expect to see, hear, and smell in a cave?

Answers will vary. Example: It would be dark and damp. There could

be puddles of water or water dripping. Some caves have things that

look like icicles hanging from the top and growing up from the bottom.

I think it would be quiet. There might be bats or other animals living

there. It might smell like mildew in a basement.

UNIT 4: MATTER

168

TEACHING PLAN pp. 168–169

INTRODUCING THE LESSON
This lesson explains the chemical reactions responsible for the distinctive odor associated with sulfur.

To get students thinking about how odors travel, ask: *What happens when you open a bottle of perfume or ammonia and wave it around?* (The smell spreads throughout the room.) Some students may not associate odors with particles of matter. Explain that when you open the bottle, some of the liquid in it evaporates into a gaseous form. Molecules of the gas travel to the nose, where they stimulate the odor receptors.

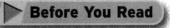 **Before You Read**

CAVE CONDITIONS Encourage students who have visited caves to share their impressions with the class. One exciting highlight of many tours of underground caves occurs when the tour guide turns off all the lights. This allows the visitors to experience total darkness. Ask students who have experienced this to describe what they could hear, smell, or feel in the pitch dark.

Tell students that caves are unique environments for two reasons. First, sunlight cannot penetrate into the

inside of the cave, and second, the cave is insulated by layers of rock, so the climate inside the cave does not change very much with the seasons. Ask: *How do you think these factors would affect the types of organisms that can live in a cave?* (Examples: There would not be any plants. The animals in the cave might not be able to survive in conditions outside the cave.)

▶ Read

Here's how *National Geographic* writer John L. Eliot describes Villa Luz, a cave in Mexico that he and some scientists explored.

DEADLY HAVEN

We could smell the cave long before we saw it. Along the mile-and-a-half (2.4-kilometer) trail from the Almandro River a natural paradise unfolded. Oropendolas, hummingbirds, motmots, and other tropical birds perched in ceiba and quebracho trees. Leafcutter ants paraded across our path in this lush rain forest in southern Mexico's Tabasco state. But as the rotten-egg stench increased, paradise was about to be lost. At the entrance of the cave my scientific companions—all accomplished cavers—and I donned respirators for protection against the vapors within.

Then we descended. Louise Hose, a geologist at California's Chapman University, led me to a rock wall...[covered] with long white mucus-like colonies of sulfur-eating bacteria.

"We joke that this cave has a cold, and we call these 'snottites'," Hose said. The bacteria oxidize sulfur compounds in subterranean springs that feed into the cave. Sulfur is the basis for nearly all [the cave's]...life.

---

paradise: a place of great beauty
stench: a strong, bad odor
donned: put on
respirators: gas masks

vapors: gases
mucus-like: dripping, gooey
oxidize: combine with oxygen
subterranean: below ground

From: Eliot, John L. "Deadly Haven." *National Geographic.* (www.nationalgeographic.com/ngm/0105/feature4)

NOTEZONE

Underline why the explorers had to wear respirators.

Circle the words used to describe the gases in the cave.

FIND OUT MORE

SCIENCESAURUS

Properties
of Matter   251
Elements, Molecules,
and Compounds 259
Chemical
Formulas   267

SCILINKS
THE WORLD'S A CLICK AWAY

www.scilinks.org
Keyword: Elements
Code: GSPD21

169

Science Scope Activity
(continued from page 166B)

Procedure
Part 1

Shuffle the index cards, and have each student select one card. Tell students that the number on the card is the atomic number of the element they are to research. Tell them to find the following information:

► chemical symbol
► atomic number
► atomic mass
► who discovered it
► what year it was discovered
► its physical properties (density, boiling point, freezing point or melting point)
► its state at room temperature (solid, liquid, or gas)
► where it can be found
► at least four ways it is used
► whether it is radioactive
► how much it is worth
► any interesting or unique characteristics

Have each student create a chart or concept map that includes all the information about the element. Then provide class time for students to present their elements to the class.

(continued on page 173)

▶ Read

Point out that this reading provides an opportunity to use context clues to determine the meaning of unknown words. For example, ask students: *What is an oropendola?* (a tropical bird) *What is a ceiba?* (a type of tree)

Students may think that "snottites" is a strange word for scientists to be using. Explain that the formations that hang down from cave roofs are called stalactites, so "snottites" is a play on words. Ask: *What is a snottite composed of?* (a colony of sulfur-eating bacteria) *What can you infer from the statement that*

sulfur is the basis for nearly all life in the cave? (Other organisms in the cave either feed on sulfur or feed on the bacteria that eat sulfur.)

CHECK UNDERSTANDING
Skill: Making inferences
Ask: *What were the cave scientists able to infer about the elements they might find in the cave as they approached it? What evidence did they use?* (The strong smell of rotten eggs alerted them that the cave must contain sulfur or sulfur compounds.)

More Resources

The following resources are also available from Great Source and NSTA.

SCILINKS.
THE WORLD'S A CLICK AWAY

www.scilinks.org
Keyword: Elements
Code: GSPD21

WHAT'S THAT SMELL? When bacteria take sulfur (S) from the rocks and combine it with hydrogen (H), they make hydrogen sulfide (H_2S). Hydrogen sulfide is the stinky gas that John Eliot and the scientists smelled as they approached the cave.

$$S + 2H \rightarrow H_2S$$

Then other bacteria combine some of the H_2S with oxygen (O_2) that enters the cave from outside. H_2S and O_2 make sulfuric acid (H_2SO_4). Sulfuric acid is a powerful acid that can slowly dissolve rock.

$$H_2S + 2O_2 \rightarrow H_2SO_4$$

Use this information to create a graphic organizer. Add action verbs and arrows to the diagram below to show how the bacteria start the process that dissolves rock. Be sure to include the terms *bacteria*, *hydrogen sulfide (H_2S)*, *oxygen (O_2)*, *sulfuric acid (H_2SO_4)*, and *rock* in the diagram.

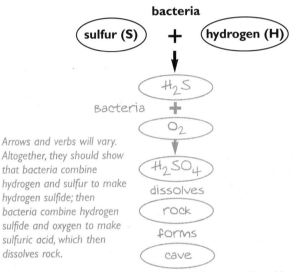

Arrows and verbs will vary. Altogether, they should show that bacteria combine hydrogen and sulfur to make hydrogen sulfide; then bacteria combine hydrogen sulfide and oxygen to make sulfuric acid, which then dissolves rock.

MAKE INFERENCES You know that the acid produced by these sulfur-eating bacteria can slowly dissolve rock.

► *Imagine a small cave that had formed in a giant rock. Describe what could happen if sulfuric acid dripped in that cave for millions of years.*

   The rock would dissolve and the cave would get bigger and bigger.

Go back to your graphic organizer. Add one more step that shows how a cave is formed as rock dissolves.

170

TEACHING PLAN pp. 170–171

► **Explore**

WHAT'S THAT SMELL? To help students interpret the chemical notation, have them read the chemical equations aloud, replacing the symbols with words. For example, the first equation would be read as: One atom of sulfur combines with two atoms of hydrogen to produce one molecule of hydrogen sulfide.

When students have completed their graphic organizers, have them work in pairs to compare their organizers, or ask volunteers to share their organizers with the class. Point out that there may

be more than one way to describe what happens when the bacteria combine sulfur and hydrogen.

Have students refer to their organizers when answering the following question: *What changes to the cave environment might stop the cave from getting larger?* (The water could dry up, the bacteria could be killed, or the oxygen supply could be cut off.)

MAKE INFERENCES Tell students that caves formed by acids that dissolve rock are called "solution caves" (or caverns). Other natural processes result in the formation of other kinds of caves.

For example, waves crashing against sea cliffs can form what are known as sea caves. Similarly, rivers can carve out caves from canyon walls. Lava caves are formed under lava flows. Ice caves are formed within icebergs and glaciers. In desert regions, winds carry sand and other abrasive particles that can carve out caves in rock ledges and cliffs.

SHOULD WE KEEP GOING? The "rotten-egg stench" is caused by the gas hydrogen sulfide (H$_2$S). High concentrations of H$_2$S can damage a person's lungs. Extremely high concentrations can make a person pass out and even die. The gas has a strong odor at first. But after a short while a person gets used to it and can no longer smell it.

▶ *Look at the respirator worn by geologist Louise Hose on the right. Why do you think she is wearing it over her mouth and nose?*

The respirator protects her

from breathing in the

dangerous gas. If she didn't

have it, her lungs could be

damaged.

▶ *The explorers wear gas monitors that tell when hydrogen sulfide is present. Why is it important that the scientists wear gas monitors?*

Since the odor deadens their sense of smell, they need the

monitor to tell them when they need to put the

respirators on.

▶ *Look at the picture of Louise Hose again. What other pieces of safety equipment can you see? Why do you think they are used?*

A helmet protects her head from the rock and

acid, and a light lets her see.

171

Use the following task to assess each student's progress:

Have students identify the two chemical reactions involving sulfur they learned about in this lesson and describe the products of both reactions. (Sulfur combines with hydrogen to form a smelly gas called hydrogen sulfide. Hydrogen sulfide combines with oxygen to form sulfuric acid, which can dissolve rock.)

▶ **Propose Explanations**

SHOULD WE KEEP GOING? Explain that hydrogen sulfide smells like rotten eggs at low levels (up to 30 parts per million) but that the smell changes at high levels to a sickeningly sweet odor. At extremely high levels (above 100 ppm) the gas actually deadens the sense of smell, so it cannot be detected by smell at all. Even low levels of hydrogen sulfide can cause health problems, especially after long exposure.

Tell students that the science of exploring caves is known as speleology, while exploring caves as a hobby is known as

spelunking. Some spelunkers take necessary precautions, but others do not and can find themselves in trouble after entering a cave unprepared. Ask: *Why would it be unsafe to explore a cave you know nothing about with no equipment?* (The levels of hydrogen sulfide gas might be high enough to hurt me. Also, I might get burned by dripping acid.) Have students review the special equipment used by the group exploring Villa Luz. Then ask: *What other equipment would you bring into a cave if you went spelunking?* (Students might mention ropes, ladders, or cables for deep caves. They may also mention

that they should wear heavy shoes and long, heavy pants.)

Point of Lesson
The position of an element on the periodic table gives clues to its properties.

Focus
▶ **Properties and changes of properties in matter**
▶ **Systems, order, and organization**
▶ **Structure and function in living systems**

Skills and Strategies
▶ **Interpreting scientific illustrations**
▶ **Making inferences**
▶ **Comparing and contrasting**

Advance Preparation

Vocabulary
Make sure students understand these terms. Definitions can be found in the glossary at the end of the student book.

▶ **atom**
▶ **elements**
▶ **energy levels**
▶ **nucleus**

▶ **periodic table of elements**
▶ **proton**

Materials
Gather the materials needed for *Read* (p. 173), *Science Scope Activity, Part 2* (p. 173), and *Explore* (p. 174).

TEACHING PLAN pp. 172–173

INTRODUCING THE LESSON
This lesson explains that the properties of an element are determined by its atomic structure and that similar atoms are grouped together on the periodic table. A science fiction example of a silicon-based life form is contrasted with actual carbon-based life to highlight carbon's special properties.

Ask students what forms of pure carbon they have seen. Draw out the fact that diamond, coal, charcoal, and pencil "lead," or graphite, are all forms of the element carbon. Then tell students that all living things contain carbon atoms combined with other types of

---

Properties of Elements

Silicon Creature

The periodic table gives us information about 100+ elements.

Which element in the periodic table is most important to you? Gold? Silver? What about carbon—the element that diamonds are made from? In fact, diamonds are pretty, but plain old carbon is truly precious.

In fact, there is an entire branch of chemistry (called organic chemistry) that involves only molecules that contain carbon atoms with hydrogens hooked on (and a few other atoms here and there). Organic chemistry is important because all living things are made up of these carbon-based molecules.

Before You Read

SCIENCE FICTION Science-fiction writers begin with actual science facts. Then they play with the ideas and write about what they imagine could be different. In the television show *Star Trek,* Captain Kirk and his crew on the starship *Enterprise* explored "strange new worlds" in outer space. Outer space exists, but the fascinating creatures the crew met and the interesting cultures they visited do not.

▶ *What makes science fiction valuable? What value might there be in imagining things beyond those that we know really exist?*

Answers will vary. Example: Science fiction makes you think about what could be possible and sometimes you can get new ideas for things that are possible even if they don't exist yet. Sometimes thinking about something that doesn't seem possible makes you wonder why it isn't possible and then you might understand something new.

UNIT 4: MATTER

172

---

atoms. That is why we say that life on Earth is carbon-based.

Before You Read

SCIENCE FICTION Tell students that science fiction writers usually base their stories on "real" science, but they let their imagination expand on the truth to produce a story that seems as though it might be possible under certain circumstances. When a science fiction work becomes popular, many people may become interested in the related science, which in turn might stimulate research in those areas. Ask:

How do you think science fiction might have contributed to space travel? (Example: Science fiction writers were describing space travel long before it really happened. Some of their ideas may have inspired scientists or given them design ideas.) Encourage students to think of other ideas that were presented first in science fiction but are now used or may soon be available. (Examples: robots, wireless phones, hovercraft)

▶ Read

Neal Meglathery hosts a radio show from a science museum in Vermont. Here he explains why carbon is something we cannot live without.

Carbon and Silicon

Hi this is Neal, and I'm here to talk to you about...you know...the little talk that we need to have at some point in our lives. THE talk. About life. The birds, the bees. So please bear with me. What I'm trying to say is, life as we know it...is based on...carbon. The sixth element in the periodic table. Oh, the other elements are important, all right. Where would we be without hydrogen, or helium, or oxygen? We wouldn't be here having this discussion, I can tell you that! But carbon is special because...[a]bout 24 percent of your body is made up of carbon. So carbon is more than just cheap pencil lead. Carbon makes all life possible.

In an old episode of Star Trek, Captain Kirk and his [brave]...crew stumble across a mining operation where solid, round nodes are being dug up. The miners think these things are inert lumps of silicon but...they turn out to be the eggs of a very displeased creature. ...[T]he Enterprise crew was surprised to find a life form that appeared to be silicon-based. See, we refer to all life forms here on earth as "carbon-based." Carbon is important because it has the ability to form four separate bonds with other atoms. That means a carbon atom can share four of its six electrons with other atoms. Oxygen can make only two bonds and hydrogen only one. So carbon is a bonding champ.

▲ The *Enterprise* crew

nodes: clumps
inert: not moving
bonds: connections

electrons: negatively charged particles that surround the core (or nucleus) of an atom

From: Meglathery, Neal. "Montshire Minute: Carbon." *The Montshire Minute.* Montshire Museum of Science. (www.montshire.net/minute/mm011126.html)

Underline why carbon is special for life.

FIND OUT MORE

SCIENCESAURUS

DNA	115
Properties of Matter	251
Atoms	255
Elements, Molecules, and Compounds	259
Periodic Table	265
Chemical Formulas	267

SCILINKS.
THE WORLD'S A CLICK AWAY
www.scilinks.org
Keyword: Elements
Code: GSPD21

173

Science Scope Activity

(continued from page 169)

Part 2

Give each student a square of paper of the color corresponding to the element they researched in Part 1—students with metals (alkali, alkaline earth, or other metals) receive pink squares, students with transitional metals (including lanthanides and actinides) receive white squares, and students with nonmetals (including noble gases) receive yellow squares. Tell students that they are going to create a square to represent their element on the periodic table. Explain that each square must have the element's atomic mass, atomic number, name, and symbol arranged as they are on the official periodic table, but the lettering and coloring may be unique.

When students have finished their squares, have them use pushpins to place the squares in a giant periodic table on a bulletin board. Encourage students to use what they know about the elements and the periodic table to place each element correctly and then to verify the placement using a copy of the periodic table.

▶ Read

Time: 10 minutes
Materials: electron-dot diagrams (see *ScienceSaurus* section 268)

Draw students' attention to the last four sentences of the excerpt, which describe carbon bonding. To illustrate the text, draw the following electron-dot diagrams for carbon, oxygen, and hydrogen on the board:

·C·   ·O·   H·

Review electron-dot diagrams with students. Explain that the dots around the chemical symbol represent the electrons present in the outermost electron cloud of each atom. The first electron cloud can hold two electrons. The second can hold eight electrons. Use this information to explain the arrangement of electron dots in the diagrams. (Carbon has two of its six electrons in its first electron cloud. That leaves four electrons in its second cloud.) Then relate the diagrams to the last part of the excerpt.

CHECK UNDERSTANDING
Skill: Recognizing cause and effect
Ask: *Why is carbon considered a "bonding champ"?* (It can form four bonds with other atoms.) *Why is the carbon atom's ability form four bonds with other atoms so important?* (It can form big, complex molecules, and that is what makes life possible.)

More Resources

The following resources are also available from Great Source and NSTA.

SCIENCESAURUS

READER'S HANDBOOK

WRITE SOURCE 2000

www.scilinks.org
Keyword: Elements
Code: GSPD21

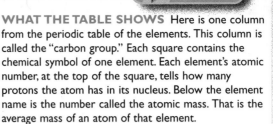

Atomic Number
Chemical Symbol
Name
Atomic Mass

6	
C	
Carbon	
12.011	
14	
Si	
Silicon	
28.086	
32	
Ge	
Germanium	
72.61	
50	
Sn	
Tin	
118.71	
82	
Pb	
Lead	
207.2	

WHAT THE TABLE SHOWS Here is one column from the periodic table of the elements. This column is called the "carbon group." Each square contains the chemical symbol of one element. Each element's atomic number, at the top of the square, tells how many protons the atom has in its nucleus. Below the element name is the number called the atomic mass. That is the average mass of an atom of that element.

Elements are arranged in the table so that all the elements in one column have the same number of electrons in the outermost electron cloud of their atoms. The number of electrons in the outermost electron cloud determines how an atom interacts with other atoms. That means all atoms in one column react to other atoms in similar ways.

You learned in the reading that carbon can share four of its electrons with other atoms. This means it has four electrons in its outermost electron cloud.

▶ *What can you infer about the number of electrons in the outermost electron cloud of a silicon atom based on silicon's position on the periodic table?*

It would also have four electrons in its outermost electron cloud because

it is in the same column as carbon.

▶ *What can you infer about how silicon might bond with other atoms to form molecules?*

Silicon might bond with many of the same atoms as carbon, and form

very similar molecules.

A science-fiction writer combines scientific facts with imagination to create stories that are at least somewhat believable.

▶ *Why do you think the writers of Star Trek chose to base their imaginary life form on the element silicon?*

Because silicon and carbon are in the same column of the periodic table,

they have the same number of electrons in their outermost electron

clouds, and so form similar bonds with other atoms. Since all life on Earth

is carbon-based, you could imagine how carbon might be substituted

with silicon to make another life form.

174

TEACHING PLAN pp. 174–175

▶ **Explore**

Time: 15 minutes
Materials: Periodic Table of Elements (copymaster page 230)

WHAT THE TABLE SHOWS Have students use the periodic table to identify groups of elements with similar properties. For example, ask: *What is another element that has the same number of electrons in its outer shell as hydrogen?* (Students may name any of the elements in the first column of the table, such as lithium, sodium, or potassium.)

Explain that the outermost electron clouds of atoms with atomic numbers under 18 are "complete" when they have eight electrons. Since a single carbon atom by itself has four electrons in the outer level, it needs four more to be full, so carbon can form four bonds. Have students find nitrogen on the periodic table. Tell them that a nitrogen atom, which has five electrons in the outer level, needs only three more to be complete. Ask: *How many bonds can a nitrogen atom form?* (three) Have students find phosphorous on the table. Ask: *Why can you assume that phosphorous will form three bonds?* (It

is in the same column, right below nitrogen, so it has the same number of electrons in the outermost electron cloud.)

Explain that the periodic table gives clues about the behavior of the elements, but there are many exceptions to the "rules" and many different factors that determine how atoms behave.

Propose Explanations

WHY NOT SILICON? Neal Meglathery said that carbon makes all life possible. Silicon is very similar to carbon in some ways, but small differences turn out to matter a lot.

Atoms with higher atomic numbers have more protons, neutrons, and electrons. They are bigger, so they have to "stretch" more to bond with each other. This usually makes the bond weaker.

▶ *How does silicon's atomic number compare to carbon's?*

  It is more than twice as big.

▶ *What can you infer about the strength of a silicon-silicon bond compared to a carbon-carbon bond?*

  It would not be as strong.

Many molecules in the bodies of plants and animals are very long and complex. DNA is one example. This "molecule of life" is built from millions of carbon atoms bonded together.

▶ *Given what you know about silicon-silicon bonds, what can you infer about the likelihood that silicon-based life could exist?*

  Since it cannot form the long molecule chains living things have, it is

  unlikely to be a basis of life.

Take Action

WRITE A REVIEW In the *Star Trek* episode, the crew discovers a life form that is apparently silicon-based and lives in a cave.

▶ *Write a review that discusses the science of this episode. What parts of the episode were based on scientific facts? Which were imagined or made up? Why is it interesting to consider the silicon question?*

  Answers will vary. Example: This might be a fun show but the chances of

  silicon-based life existing is probably pretty small. Although silicon

  bonds with other atoms much like carbon does, it cannot make the very

  long molecules that are necessary for life as we know it. But it's neat to

  look at elements and see which behave similarly, and then to imagine

  how one might be substituted for another.

175

Use the following task to assess each student's progress:

Have students draw a Venn diagram showing the similarities and differences between carbon and silicon. (Venn diagrams should contain the following information: *Silicon*—higher atomic number, has to "stretch" more to make bonds, bonds are weaker; *Carbon*—smaller atomic number, "stretches" less to make bonds, bonds are stronger, makes long chains; *Both*—have four electrons in the outermost electron cloud, bond with many of the same atoms, form similar molecules)

Propose Explanations

WHY NOT SILICON? To help students answer the questions on this page, you might want to explain some differences between the types of bonds formed by carbon and those formed by silicon. For example, the bond that one silicon atom forms with another silicon atom (an Si–Si bond) is only half as strong as the bond that one carbon atom forms with another carbon atom (a C–C bond). Ask: *How do you think the strength of a long chain of silicon atoms would compare with the strength of a long chain of carbon atoms?* (It would be much weaker.)

Explain that a bond between a carbon atom and two oxygen atoms results in carbon dioxide (CO_2), which is gas at room temperature, while a silicon atom bonded with two oxygen atoms forms silicon dioxide, or sand. Remind students that CO_2 is a waste product that we eliminate when we exhale. Ask: *In what way might getting rid of waste products be harder for a silicon-based life form than a carbon-based life form?* (Getting rid of large amounts of solid waste would be harder than getting rid of large amounts of gaseous wastes.)

Take Action

WRITE A REVIEW You may want to suggest that students view the Star Trek episode "The Devil in the Dark," which originally aired on March 9, 1967. Alternatively, students could read a summary of the episode online at www.startrek.com/library/tos_episodes/episodes_tos_detail_68712.asp.

Point out that a good scientific review should include facts to back up the writer's position and should not simply reflect the writer's opinion. Provide class time for students to share their reviews.

UNIT 5 Interactions of Matter

About the Photo

Domesticated horses are shod with metal horseshoes to protect their feet from disease and injury. Horseshoes are made of iron. The blacksmith in this photo heated iron in his forge so he could hammer it into the necessary shape.

Matter is interacting all around you all the time. Can you feel it? When matter interacts with other matter, neat things happen. If the interaction is chemical, new substances are produced. Sometimes heat is given off, or light, or noise. But if you've ever marveled at the wonders of Velcro, you know that physical interactions of matter are just as interesting.

I n this unit you'll take a look at some of the different ways matter interacts with other matter. You'll identify the chemical reactions that make a cake rise. You'll find out what makes Jell-O jiggle and how snakes use venom to disarm their prey. You'll see how chemicals can be mixed to make light, and how scientists experiment to make "super" materials in the laboratory.

About the Charts

A major goal of the *Science Daybooks* is to promote reading, writing, and critical thinking skills in the context of science. The charts below describe the types of reading selections included in this unit and identify the skills and strategies used in each lesson.

176

SELECTION	READING	WRITING	APPLICATION
CHAPTER 17 • CHEMICAL BONDS			
49. "A 'Permanent' Change" (science museum Web site)	• Brainstorming • Read for details	• Draw a concept map • Cite supporting evidence	• Draw a Venn diagram • Compare and contrast
50. "How does [Jell-o] work?" (science Web site)	• Use prior knowledge • Read and follow directions	• Record observations in a table	• Hands-on activity • Create a graphic organizer
51. "I Was Coal, I Was Fire" (children's novel)	• Read for details	• Draw conclusions	
CHAPTER 18 • REACTIONS IN ACTION			
52. "Irving Prager's Chocolate Dump Cake" (recipe)	• Describe an event • Read directions	• Propose explanations	• Hands-on activity • Record observations
53. "SSSSnake Bite" (university science research Web site)	• Assess prior knowledge • Make notes • Read a table	• Critical thinking	• Compare prior and current knowledge
54. "How Mummies Are Made" (science history book)	• Directed reading • Read and follow directions	• Make comparisons • Describe observations	• Compare processes

? Did You Know?

Velcro was invented by a guy who noticed
the burrs that were sticking so well to his
socks after a hike. Examining them under a
microscope, he saw that the hooks of the
burrs fit perfectly into the loops of the
fabric that made up his socks.

177

Answers to *Find Out* Questions

CHAPTER 17
A blacksmith adds heat energy to
steel to make it easier to push the
atoms of metal around. (p. 187)

CHAPTER 18
By removing the moisture with salt
and baking soda and protecting it
from exposure to air, you can "mum-
mify" a potato so it does not decay.
(p. 197)

CHAPTER 19
A chemical reaction inside living
organisms can make ocean water
seem to glow. (p. 203)

CHAPTER 20
A combination of adhesion and cohesion makes tape sticky. (p. 216)

SCI LINKS.
THE WORLD'S A CLICK AWAY

www.scilinks.org
Keyword: Mentoring
Code: GSSD06

SELECTION	READING	WRITING	APPLICATION
CHAPTER 19 • ENERGY FROM CHEMICALS			
55. "Light in the Night Sea" (journal entry)	• Directed reading • Read for details	• Make inferences	• Reflect on historical research
56. "How Light Sticks Work" (science Web site)	• Make an organized list • Read for details	• Create a graphic organizer	• Conduct research • Complete a table
57. "Trying Not to Freeze" (eyewitness account)	• Use prior experience • Read and follow directions	• Record observations	• Hands-on activity • Draw conclusions
CHAPTER 20 • MATERIALS SCIENCE			
58. "Something New Under the Sun" (Smithsonian exhibit)	• Use prior experience • Read for details	• Complete a table	• Interpret a maxim • Explain your reasoning
59. "This Would Be Even Better If..." (university Web site)	• Make notes • Directed reading	• Explain your answer • Use a table	• Draw a Venn diagram
60. "I'm Stuck on You" (science magazine article)	• Read for details • Read and follow directions	• Record observations	• Make a chart • Propose explanations

CHAPTER 17

Overview

Chemical Bonds

LESSON 49

Unnaturally Curly Hair
Point of Lesson: Chemicals can be used to break down and then reconstruct the bonds in hair, changing its natural shape.

Students explore the concept of chemical bonding by looking at the chemistry of hair styling. After reading an article on the difference between curling hair by setting it while wet and curling it with a permanent wave, students compare and contrast the two processes and the types of bonds that are broken and reformed by each.

Materials
Before You Read (p. 178), for the class:
► pages from fashion, entertainment, or hairstyle magazines

Enrichment (p. 179), for each group:
► pH test strips or litmus paper
► samples of 5 different shampoos in test tubes
► test-tube rack

Laboratory Safety
Review the following safety guidelines with students before they do the Enrichment activity in this lesson.
► Do not taste any substance in the laboratory.
► Promptly wipe up any spills to avoid accidents.
► Handle glassware carefully. Immediately report any broken glassware to your teacher.
► Wash your hands thoroughly after the activity.

LESSON 50

Jell-O Jiggle
Point of Lesson: As gelatin dissolves and then resets, bonds are broken and reformed.

In this lesson, students explore the chemistry of a common dessert—flavored gelatin. Students describe the properties of gelatin dessert, then read an article explaining how the process of preparing gelatin involves the breaking and reforming of bonds. Students then prepare gelatin using a variety of water temperature combinations and explain their results in terms of chemical bonding.

Materials
Enrichment (p. 183), for each pair or group:
► modeling supplies, such as pipe cleaners, beads, colored paper, and plastic wrap or cellophane

Activity (p. 184), for each group:
► three 250-mL calibrated beakers
► glass-marking pencil
► package of gelatin dessert
► cold water
► boiling water
► stirring rod or spoon
► oven mitt or pot holders
► measuring spoon (tsp.)
► access to a refrigerator

Laboratory Safety
Review the following safety guidelines with students before they do the Activity in this lesson.
► Do not taste any substance in the laboratory.
► Do not add the boiling water to the beaker yourself. Ask your teacher to do this.
► Use an oven mitt or potholder to handle the beaker that had boiling water added to it.
► Wash your hands thoroughly after the activity.

LESSON 51

Bending Steel
Point of Lesson: Metallic bonds allow metals to bend without breaking.

A passage from a novel introduces students to the process of forging metal. Students examine a diagram to learn about the nature of metallic bonds. They then apply their understanding to explain how the methods used by the novel's characters would help shape steel.

Materials
none

Background Information

Lesson 49

If your students have some knowledge of molecular structure, you may want to illustrate the breaking and reforming of disulfide bonds that occur during a permanent wave. Draw the following simplified diagrams on the board.

1. Before the hair is set on rollers, it is straight and its disulfide bonds are intact.

2. The hair is set on rollers and the waving lotion is applied. The waving lotion (a reducing agent) causes the disulfide bonds to break. The sulfur atoms then form bonds with hydrogen rather than with each other.

3. After the disulfide bonds have been broken, the waving lotion is washed out of the hair with water. Then a neutralizer is applied. Applying the neutralizer (an oxidizing agent) removes the hydrogen and allows disulfide bonds to form again. These bonds hold the hair in its new shape, even off the roller.

1. Before waving lotion

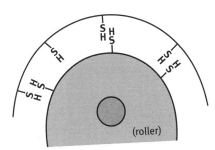

2. After waving lotion

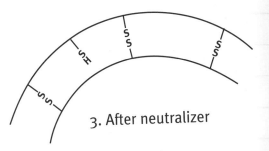

3. After neutralizer

Point of Lesson
Chemicals can be used to break down and then reconstruct the bonds in hair, changing its natural shape.

Focus
► Properties and changes of properties in matter
► Structure and function in living systems
► Systems, order, and organization

Skills and Strategies
► Making inferences
► Concept mapping
► Comparing and contrasting

Advance Preparation

Vocabulary
Make sure students understand these terms. Definitions can be found in the glossary at the end of the student book.
► cell
► chemical
► chemical bond
► molecule

Materials
Gather the materials needed for *Before You Read* (below) and *Enrichment* (p. 179).

Unnaturally Curly Hair

Is your hair curly or straight?

Hair is one of the first things we mention when we are describing a person. There are so many varieties of hair shape—straight, wavy, curly, frizzy, and everything in between. But many people do all kinds of things to change the hair they're born with.

You might be surprised to know that the main substance that makes up hair is the same in everyone. But small differences in the chemical bonds within strands cause big differences in shape and texture.

▲ Curlers give straight hair a different shape

▶ Before You Read

CHANGING HAIR Do you ever do anything to your hair to make it look different? Lots of people do. If you've ever looked at the hair-care aisle of the drug store, you know there are lots of products you can use.

► *Think of the ways you and your friends try to change your hair shape. What products or tools do you use?*

Students will likely list a variety of hair gels, shampoos, and conditioners,

curling irons, hair dryers, hair straighteners, combs, and brushes.

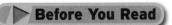

178

TEACHING PLAN pp. 178–179

INTRODUCING THE LESSON
This lesson describes the chemical bonds that cause hair to be curly or straight.

Some students may think of chemical reactions as something that happens only in a laboratory where scientists use test tubes and beakers. Ask: *Where do chemical reactions take place?* Draw out the fact that chemical reactions take place all around us all the time—even at the hair salon.

▶ Before You Read

Time: 15 minutes
Materials: pages from fashion, entertainment, or hairstyle magazines

CHANGING HAIR Discussions about hair care and personal appearance may be difficult or embarrassing for students at this age. Many students may use nothing more than a comb or brush to style their hair. You may want to use images from magazines to represent different hair styles and hair styling products. Try to find images of both men and women and images that show people with different hair types and ethnic

backgrounds. In addition, you may want to challenge students to find advertisements for hair styling products. Ask: *What claims does the ad make about this product? Do you think this is a scientific description of how the product works? Why or why not?* (Answers will vary depending on the advertisement.)

▶ Read

Read about the chemical bonds that make your hair curl.

A "Permanent" Change

When you curl your hair—whether it's with water and styling gel or a permanent-wave kit—you are messing with the chemical bonds that keep the protein fibers of your hair's cortex stuck together. These chemical bonds include hydrogen bonds [and disulfide bonds]..

When you wet your hair, water molecules sneak in between the proteins of the cortex and [break the] hydrogen bonds.... If you set your wet hair in curlers or pull your curly hair straight, then let it dry in this new shape, the hydrogen bonds will reform in a new position. Of course, when your hair gets wet again, those hydrogen bonds will weaken and then reform in their original position, giving you back the hair you didn't want—making curly hair straight, straight hair curly.

If you want a permanent change, you can perm your hair. In a perm, you don't just break hydrogen bonds, you also break the disulfide bonds that hold the proteins together. You add chemicals that break the disulfide bonds (bonds between sulfur atoms). Then you reshape your hair and add chemicals that reconstruct those disulfide bonds, holding your hair in a new shape. Since these disulfide bonds withstand water, your new hairdo will be waterproof.

protein: type of molecule found in the body
cortex: the body of a hair

From: "Better Hair Through Chemistry: It's Enough to Curl Your Hair." *Exploring Online.* The Exploratorium. (www.exploratorium.edu/exploring/hair/hair_4.html)

NOTEZONE

Circle the two kinds of bonds that give hair its shape.

FIND OUT MORE

SCIENCESAURUS
Cell Processes 079
Elements, Molecules, and Compounds 259
Chemical Bonds 263

SCI LINKS.
THE WORLD'S A CLICK AWAY
Keyword: Types of Chemical Bonds
Code: GSPD22

179

Enrichment

Time: 40–45 minutes
Materials: pH test strips or litmus paper, samples of 5 different shampoos in test tubes, test tube rack

Note: Use shampoos intended for different purposes—for example, special shampoos for curly hair, straight hair, and oily hair and products that claim to produce extra body or extra shine.

Tell students that pH is a measure of how acidic or basic a substance is. Acids have more hydrogen ions (H^+) than hydroxide ions (OH^-). Bases have more hydroxide ions (OH^-) than hydrogen ions (H^+). On the pH scale, acids have pH values lower than 7, while bases have values higher than 7. Tell students that pure water has a pH of 7, which means it is neutral.

Have students work in small groups. Provide each group with samples of five different shampoos. Show students how to use the pH test strips. Then have each group test each shampoo sample and record their results. When students have completed the activity, have them share their results. (Students should find that most shampoos are acidic, with pH values slightly lower than 7.) Explain that because extra hydroxide ions (OH^-) can disrupt disulfide bonds while extra hydrogen ions (H^+) are harmless, shampoo manufacturers err on the side of caution and make their products slightly acidic.

▶ Read

Students may think that curling wet hair with curlers is a "physical" process, while using a perm is a "chemical" process. Ask: *According to the reading, what happens to the chemical bonds in your hair if you get it wet and use curlers to curl it?* (When hair is wet, the hydrogen bonds are broken. When the hair dries on curlers, the bonds reform in the new position.) Then ask: *Is this a chemical change in your hair? Is it permanent?* (chemical change—yes; permanent—no) Students with curly hair may be familiar with the

process of using a blow dryer to "blow out" their hair to straighten it. Point out that this is essentially the reverse of the process of letting straight hair dry on curlers.

When students have finished the NoteZone task, ask volunteers to share their answers with the class. Ask: *What is the difference between these two types of bonds?* (Hydrogen bonds are broken by water, but disulfide bonds are not.)

CHECK UNDERSTANDING
Skill: Recognizing cause and effect
Ask: *Why is your hair so messy in the morning when you went to bed with wet hair?* (Example: My pillow pushes my wet hair into weird positions. As it dries, the hydrogen bonds reform between the protein fibers in their weird positions. So whatever messed-up position my hair was in while it dried, that's what it looks like in the morning.)

More Resources

The following resources are also available from Great Source and NSTA.

www.scilinks.org
Keyword: Types of Chemical Bonds
Code: GSPD22

▶ **Explore**

ORGANIZING INFORMATION The reading describes two different processes you can use to curl your hair—setting wet hair in curlers and getting a permanent wave.

▶ *Draw a concept map to show what happens to the different bonds in hair when it gets curled by each of the two different processes. Use terms like hair, water, chemicals, bonds, break, reshape, dry, and reform in your map. Use symbols like arrows and "+" signs to show the relationships between the parts of the map. The map should finish with the term Curly Hair.*

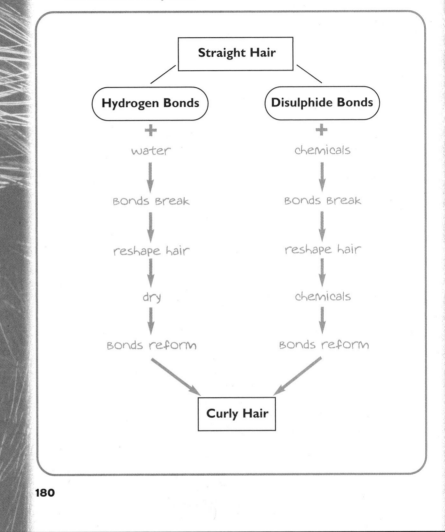

180

Teaching Plan pp. 180–181

▶ **Explore**

ORGANIZING INFORMATION If students are having difficulty getting started on their concept maps, advise them to review the reading and take notes on how the different kinds of bonds are broken and reformed. Then have them construct the maps from their notes.

Next, challenge students to create a concept map that shows the reverse process—curly hair to straight hair. (It will be the same, except that the hair is reshaped in a straight position.) Invite students to consider the significance of

that fact. Lead them to see that bonds are what hold hair in a certain shape.

Students may be interested to know that the technology for perming hair was developed by the textile industry. People working in that industry were trying to straighten curly sheep wool fibers so they would be easier to spin into yarn.

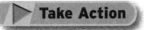

Propose Explanations

HOW PERMANENT? The type of hair you have is determined by your genes. Genes are your body's instructions for how to develop all the parts that make you *you*. Genes control your hair shape by determining how the proteins in your hair will be arranged and which bonds will form between them. Copies of your genes can be found in every cell of your body. In general, things you do to your body do not change your genes.

Let's say that your friend Maya does not like her straight hair. She decides to get a permanent wave. The next day her hair is very curly.

▶ *How will Maya's hair look two years from now if she doesn't have another permanent? Explain in terms of Maya's genes.*

In two years, Maya will have straight hair again. Her curled hair will have

grown out and straight hair coded for by her genes will have replaced it.

WET SET When your hair is wet, it can be molded into practically any shape because the hydrogen bonds between the protein fibers are broken. As hair begins to dry, water molecules between the fibers evaporate away. Hydrogen bonds then reform between the protein fibers. When it's all dry, the hair has a new shape.

▶ *Use this information to explain how hair brushes and blow-dryers can be used to style hair.*

Wet hair can be pulled into the shape you want using a brush. When hot

air blows on the hair, it dries the hair, and the hydrogen bonds reform,

holding the hair in its new shape.

▶ Take Action

COMPARE AND CONTRAST Draw a Venn diagram to compare two methods of hair-styling: permanent wave and blow-drying.

▶ *What do the two methods have in common? How do they differ?*

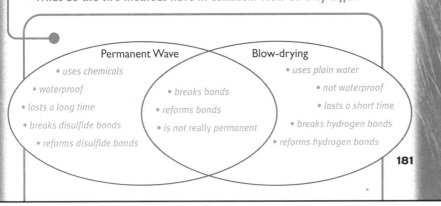

Permanent Wave
- uses chemicals
- waterproof
- lasts a long time
- breaks disulfide bonds
- reforms disulfide bonds

- breaks bonds
- reforms bonds
- is not really permanent

Blow-drying
- uses plain water
- not waterproof
- lasts a short time
- breaks hydrogen bonds
- reforms hydrogen bonds

181

Connections

SOCIAL STUDIES Tell students that hair styles have been important to people throughout history. Have students research popular hair styles and their social implications for the period of history they are currently studying in their social studies classes. For example, during colonial times, it was considered unhealthy to wash hair too frequently, so people wore hats to keep their hair clean. In ancient Egypt, both men and women often shaved their heads and wore wigs. Wearing a wig helped them avoid problems with lice and made elaborate styles possible. You might ask students to explain why "permed" hair on a wig does not lose its curl the way live hair does. (The hair does not grow out.)

Assessment

Skill: Designing an experiment to test a hypothesis

Use the following task to assess each student's progress:

Tell students to imagine that one day their friend with straight hair suddenly has curly hair. They wonder whether their friend's hair has been "permed" or simply curled with rollers. Have students design an experiment to determine which it is. (Students should suggest having the friend wet her hair and then let it dry. If it is still curly, the hair was permed. If it dries straight, it was curled with rollers.)

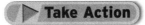

▶ Propose Explanations

HOW PERMANENT? After students answer the question, tell them that the disulfide bonds that link the protein molecules in hair are extremely strong. These bonds contribute to the overall strength of each hair strand. Each time hair is "permed," however, about 10 percent of the disulfide bonds that are broken do not reform again. Ask: *What might happen to a person who gets frequent perms?* (The hair might be weakened.)

WET SET Students may think that wet hair tends to hang straight because the weight of the water is pulling it down. Point out that water weight may contribute to the effect, but the principal cause of wet hair hanging straight is broken hydrogen bonds.

▶ Take Action

COMPARE AND CONTRAST Encourage students to list concepts from the lesson before they draw the Venn diagram. For example, students can write the terms *Blow-drying* and *Permanent Wave* as headings on a sheet of paper. Under each term, students can list the concepts that apply to each. Then they can create the Venn diagram using terms and ideas from their lists. Explain that making lists and creating Venn diagrams are two ways of organizing information and that the two ways can be used together or separately.

Point of Lesson
As gelatin dissolves and then resets, bonds are broken and reformed.

Focus
▶ Properties and changes of properties in matter
▶ Transfer of energy
▶ Abilities necessary to do scientific inquiry
▶ Systems, order, and organization

Skills and Strategies
▶ Collecting and recording data
▶ Interpreting data
▶ Making inferences
▶ Organizing information

Advance Preparation

Vocabulary
Make sure students understand these terms. Definitions can be found in the glossary at the end of the student book.

▶ chemical bond   ▶ mixture
▶ energy   ▶ proteins
▶ liquid   ▶ solid

Materials
Gather the materials needed for *Enrichment* (p. 183) and *Activity* (p. 184).

It wiggles, it jiggles, and it's sweet. What is it?

If you've ever eaten in a cafeteria, you have probably eaten a gelatin dessert. What's in it? The key ingredient is gelatin, a colorless substance made of protein. That's what gives a gelatin dessert its jiggle. What about the rest of the dessert? The sweet taste comes from sugar or artificial sweeteners, and artificial colors are added to make it look appetizing. The fruit flavor comes from natural or artificial flavors.

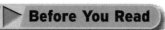

SOLID OR LIQUID?

▶ *Have you ever made a gelatin dessert before? What steps did you follow? Write down what you can remember.*

Answers will vary. Example: I added water and then I put it in the
refrigerator for hours.

▶ *How would you describe gelatin dessert? Would you call it a solid? A liquid? Can you pick it up? Can you drink it through a straw? Write your ideas about what gelatin is below.*

Answers will vary. Example: It's kind of like a solid, but it doesn't really
hold its shape that well. I can't drink it through a straw and it doesn't
pour like a liquid. I would call it a squishy solid.

182

TEACHING PLAN pp. 182–183

INTRODUCING THE LESSON
This lesson describes the chemical bonds that give gelatin desserts their distinctive jiggle.

Ask: *Do you know of any other foods that have characteristics similar to those of gelatin desserts?* (Students may mention cranberry sauce, fruit jelly, or aspic.) Because many of these foods are made from fruit, students may think that gelatin gets its unusual gel characteristics from a substance in fruit. Explain that gelatin is actually derived from a protein found in the bones and hides of certain animals. Gelling agents such as pectin, agar, and

starch, on the other hand, are derived from plants. These vegetable agents are carbohydrates rather than proteins, and the gels they produce are not as springy as gelatin.

Before You Read

SOLID OR LIQUID? If students have not made gelatin dessert or if they cannot remember the steps they followed, encourage them to reason through the steps that must be involved. Ask: *When you buy the box of gelatin at the store, what is in the box?* (powder) Then ask: *How do you think it gets from a pow-*

dered state to its finished state? (add hot water and chill)

Students may have had experience with gelatin desserts of different consistencies, ranging from the traditional types that do not hold their shapes well to a type known as "finger Jell-O" that can be cut into shapes and eaten with the fingers. Explain that "finger Jell-O" is made with a higher ratio of powdered gelatin mix to water, which makes it firmer.

▶ Read

A food scientist describes what makes **Jell-O**, a gelatin dessert, jiggle.

NOTEZONE

Underline the two stages of gelatin preparation.

How does [Jell-O] work?

...When you buy a box of Jell-O (or another brand of gelatin) at the grocery store, you get a small packet of powdered gelatin with artificial flavorings and colors. At room temperature, the gelatin protein is in the form of a triple helix—three separate...polypeptide chains [that] have lined up and twisted around each other.

What happens to gelatin when you add boiling water? The energy of the heated water is enough to break up the weak bonds holding the gelatin strands together. The helical structure falls apart, and you are left with free polypeptide chains floating about in solution.

The next step is to add cold water and stick the dissolved gelatin in the refrigerator to chill for several hours. When you cool down the mixture, the polypeptide chains begin to [bond again] and reform the tight triple helix structure. However, ...the individual strands have been widely dispersed by mixing, so the helices aren't perfectly formed. In some places, there are gaps in the helix, and in others, there is just a tangled web of polypeptide chains. ...[W]ater is trapped inside these gaps and pockets between chains. The protein net that is left after chilling gives the gelatin mold its shape, and the trapped water provides the characteristic Jell-O jiggle....

▲ **Powdered gelatin**

helix: spiral
polypeptide chain: a smaller piece of a protein
helical: shaped like a spiral
dispersed: spread out

From: "What Exactly Is Jell-O Made From? How Does It Work?" *HowStuff Works.* (www.howstuffworks.com/question557.htm)

FIND OUT MORE

SCIENCE SAURUS
Cell Processes   079
Elements, Molecules,
and Compounds   259
Chemical Bonds   263

SCILINKS
THE WORLD'S A CLICK AWAY
www.scilinks.org
Keyword: Types of
Chemical Bonds
Code: GSPD22

Enrichment

Time: 30 minutes
Materials: modeling supplies such as pipe cleaners, beads, colored paper, and plastic wrap or cellophane

Have students work in pairs or small groups to create models showing the structure of the proteins in gelatin. Challenge students to create models that show the structure at three stages: as powder (proteins in triple helix), when hot water is added (triple helix separated), and when the gelatin is chilled (triple helix reformed, tangled, with water in gaps). For example, students may use pipe cleaners to represent the triple helix, beads to represent the chemical bonds, and plastic wrap or cellophane to represent the water.

▶ Read

As students read, encourage them to make sketches of the protein structure described in the reading. Explain that this strategy will help them visualize the helical shape of the polypeptide chains at different stages in the process. Remind students that their drawings do not have to be elaborate or precise; they just want to capture the images described in the text to understand them better. Encourage students to use their sketches to review the information in the reading. (Students' drawings should show three stages: gelatin protein at room temperature—triple helix; gelatin mixed with boiling water—free polypeptide chains in solution; chilled gelatin mixture—triple helices with gaps and tangled web of polypeptide chains.)

CHECK UNDERSTANDING
Skill: Making inferences
Ask: *Where does the energy needed to break the bonds that hold the gelatin strands together come from?* (heated water)

More Resources

The following resources are also available from Great Source and NSTA.

ScienceSaurus

Reader's Handbook

Write Source 2000

www.scilinks.org
Keyword: Types of Chemical Bonds
Code: GSPD22

MAKING A GELATIN DESSERT

What You Need:
- three 250-mL beakers, calibrated
- glass-marking pencil
- package of gelatin dessert
- cold water
- boiling water
- stirring rod or spoon
- oven mitt or pot holders
- measuring spoon (tsp.)

What to Do:
1. Number three 250-mL beakers *1, 2,* and *3.* Mark them with your initials.
2. Put 1 teaspoon of gelatin powder into each of the three beakers.
3. Add 50 mL of cold water to beaker 1 and stir. Ask your teacher to add 50 mL of boiling water to beaker 2 and to beaker 3. Stir.
4. Now add 50 mL of cold water to beaker 1 and to beaker 2 and stir.
5. Ask your teacher to add 50 mL of boiling water to beaker 3. Stir.
6. Put the three beakers into a refrigerator for about 30 minutes.
7. Remove the beakers from the refrigerator and examine the contents. Try shaking the beakers to see if the gelatin jiggles. Try to stir the gelatin or pick up some on a spoon. *Do not taste any of the samples.*

What Did You See?
Record your observations in the table.

Beaker	First Water Added (Hot or Cold?)	Second Water Added (Hot or Cold?)	Appearance of Mixture
1	cold	cold	*grainy powder and water, no thickening*
2	hot	cold	*no powder, mixture began to thicken*
3	hot	hot	*no powder, mixture thickened a little but not as much as in beaker 2*

184

TEACHING PLAN pp. 184–185

▶ Activity

Time: 40–45 minutes
Materials: three 250-mL calibrated beakers, glass-marking pencil, package of gelatin dessert, cold water, boiling water, stirring rod or spoon, oven mitt or pot holders, measuring spoon (tsp.)

▶ Have students work in groups of three or four.
▶ To save time, you may want to have each group work with only one beaker and then have the class pool results.
▶ Have students stand back as you pour boiling water into their beakers. To avoid having to measure the boiling water, use beakers that are marked in 50-mL increments. This is preferable to using a graduated cylinder because the water must be measured when it is hot, and every "pour" increases the risk of accidents.

▶ The amount of time for the gelatin to set may vary depending on the temperature setting of the refrigerator. For best results, test this in advance to get an accurate estimate of how long to leave the gelatin in the refrigerator.

HOLDING IT TOGETHER

Create a graphic organizer to show what happens to the bonds in gelatin during the two stages of preparation described in the reading.

Sample Organizer:

Bonds hold strands of gelatin together.
+
boiling water
↓
Bonds break.
+
cold water/refrigeration
↓
Bonds reform.

Now review your observations from the activity. Use your graphic organizer to explain what was happening to the gelatin bonds in each beaker during the same two stages of preparation.

Beaker	First Water Added	Second Water Added/Refrigeration
1	bonds were not broken by cold water	bonds could not reform because they were never broken
2	bonds were broken by hot water	bonds reformed as the gelatin cooled
3	bonds were broken by hot water	bonds reformed more slowly than in beaker 2

▶ **When making gelatin dessert, what important step must you do when you add the first water?**

You must heat the water, because you need hot water to break the bonds that hold the gelatin strands together.

▶ **Why does the gelatin dessert recipe tell you to add cold water instead of hot water before putting the gelatin in the refrigerator?**

The cold water cools the gelatin down, which makes it cool down faster in the refrigerator. The faster it cools down, the faster the bonds reform and the gelatin gels.

185

Connections

MATH Tell students that according to the company that makes Jell-O brand gelatin, nine boxes of Jell-O are sold every second in the United States. The U.S. population is about 280,000,000 people. Ask: *How many days does it take for enough Jell-O to be sold to give one box to each person in the United States?* (360 days) You can let students use calculators, or you can challenge them to use estimation to find the answer. (Because of rounding, estimates may vary widely but should be between 300 and 400 days.)

Assessment

Skill: Generating questions

Use the following task to assess each student's progress:

Tell students to imagine that a friend has come to them with a bowl of gelatin dessert that did not gel properly. Ask: *What questions would you ask your friend about how the gelatin was prepared?* (Examples: What temperature was the water you added to the powder? Did you stir the powder into the water thoroughly? Did you then add cold water? Did you put it in the refrigerator? For how long?) Challenge students to relate each of their questions to the process of bonds breaking or bonds reforming.

▶ **Propose Explanations**

HOLDING IT TOGETHER To help students organize their thoughts, ask: *Which sample of gelatin was prepared "correctly"?* (beaker 2) Encourage students to describe what happened with that sample first and then compare it with what happened in the other two beakers. Have students answer the following questions and use the answers as they complete the activities on this page: *Which was the second best sample? What did it have in common with the best one, and what was different? What was the worst sample? What was*

different about it? Explain that scientists ask questions like these to help them analyze their results and draw conclusions.

Once students have filled in the table, ask: *What evidence do you have that energy is needed to break the bonds that hold the protein strands together?* (Hot water has more heat energy than cold water, and the bonds broke in hot water but did not in cold water.)

Point of Lesson
Metallic bonds allow metals to bend without breaking.

Focus
► Transfer of energy
► Properties and changes of properties in matter
► Change, constancy, and measurement

Skills and Strategies
► Interpreting scientific illustrations
► Making inferences
► Recognizing cause and effect

Advance Preparation

Vocabulary
Make sure students understand these terms. Definitions can be found in the glossary at the end of the student book.

► atom
► chemical bond
► electron

► energy
► metals
► solid

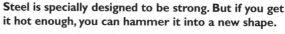

BENDING STEEL

Steel is specially designed to be strong. But if you get it hot enough, you can hammer it into a new shape.

In Gary Paulsen's novel, *Popcorn Days & Buttermilk Nights*, a 14-year old boy from the city is sent to live with his uncle in farm country after getting into some trouble at home. Uncle David has a blacksmith shop. The boy, Carley, becomes his assistant for the summer. He learns how steel is made into horseshoes, farming tools, and other objects.

The atoms that make up metals are held together by metallic bonds—one type of chemical bond. These bonds allow metals to be hammered into different shapes and give them their other characteristic properties.

NoteZone
Underline all the words that give evidence of how hot the forge was.

UNIT 5: INTERACTIONS OF MATTER

FIND OUT MORE
SCIENCESAURUS
Elements, Molecules, and Compounds 259
Chemical Bonds 263

186

 Read

Uncle David gets the idea to create a merry-go-round and Ferris wheel. Carley recalls how he and David became involved in their task.

I Was Coal, I Was Fire

David started as a smithy who was working to build something he needed—a circus for his kids. And I started as a helper. But then everything changed.

I thought we had worked hard before—I didn't know what work was, had no idea. The heat from the forge cooked my face into blisters, peeled the blisters, and then recooked it into more blisters. The process repeated itself until I was leather, until my skin matched my leather sweatband. I was coal, I was fire, I was heat and movement and the *crang CRANG* of hammer to metal and the shower of sparks—I was all of these things just in the first two days and I became a deeper part of them in the following days.

David became steel and smoke and the hammer. When I think of him now, I see him as a flash of white teeth smiling through the burned black of his face and the shower of sparks and the hammer raising and coming down and the steel bending.

forge: fire over which a blacksmith heats metal

From: Paulsen, Gary. *Popcorn Days & Buttermilk Nights*. Puffin Paperback Books.

TEACHING PLAN pp. 186–187

INTRODUCING THE LESSON
This lesson describes how the chemical bonds in metals enable them to be softened with heat and reshaped.

Ask students: *What types of things are made out of metal?* (Examples: some buildings, car parts, machinery) Then ask: *How do you think the metal is shaped?* Students may think that the metal is melted and poured into molds. Explain that some metal objects are formed this way (by a process called casting), but that metals also have properties that allow them to be hammered and bent into shape without breaking.

Read

As students read the passage, encourage them to identify metaphors used by the writer. (Examples: "I was leather," "I was coal, I was fire, I was heat and movement and the *crang CRANG* of hammer to metal and the shower of sparks," "David became steel and smoke and the hammer.") Ask: *Why do you think the writer chose to use these figures of speech?* (Students may say that the metaphors help the writer express how overwhelming the work was.)

When students have completed the NoteZone task, ask volunteers to read the words they underlined. Then ask students to find as many words as they can that give evidence of energy and to identify the type of energy each word represents. (*work:* kinetic energy, or the energy of motion; *heat:* heat energy; *movement:* kinetic energy; *crang:* sound energy; *sparks:* light energy)

▶ **Explore**

WORKING METAL If you were to pound a solid rock with a hammer, little bits of the rock would break off. Unlike most solids, metals bend instead of breaking when hammered. To help us understand why, let's take a look at the atoms that make up metals.

Look at the diagram of a piece of metal. The "plus" signs represent atoms that make up the metal. These atoms have given up one of their electrons, which are negatively charged. This leaves the atoms positively charged. Charged atoms are known as ions. You can see the negatively charged electrons floating around the ions. Bonds between the positively charged ions and the negatively charged electrons are what hold the metal together. These are called metallic bonds.

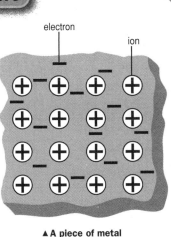

electron

ion

▲ **A piece of metal**

Because the electrons are free to move around the ions, metallic bonds are very flexible. When a piece of metal is hammered, the ions on that side are pushed closer together. In many solids, this would cause the material to break. But because the electrons in metal are free to move around, they can move between the ions in their new positions, and so prevent the material from breaking.

▶ *What did Uncle David and Carley do to the steel before they used hammers to shape it?*

They heated it to a high temperature.

Heat is a form of energy. When you heat metal, you add energy to the atoms that make it up. The added energy causes the atoms to move around more, making the solid less rigid.

▶ *Why do you suppose David and Carley heated the steel before hammering it?*

The heat made it easier to push the metal atoms around, so it was easier to change the shape of the piece of steel.

187

More Resources

The following resources are also available from Great Source.

SCIENCESAURUS
Elements, Molecules, and Compounds   259
Chemical Bonds   263

READER'S HANDBOOK
Elements of Poetry: Metaphor   455

Assessment
Skill: Drawing conclusions

Use the following question to assess each student's progress:

What is it about metallic bonds that makes them so flexible? (The electrons are free to move around the ions.)

▶ **Explore**

WORKING METAL Have students describe the atomic structure of metals under the different conditions described in the text. For example, students should sketch or describe how the ions move when the metal is struck with a hammer and how they move when the metal is heated. Then have students compare how metal and glass react to being struck. Ask: *What happens when a sheet of glass is struck with a hammer?* (It shatters.) *What happens to metal?* (It dents or bends.) *What can you infer about the bonds that hold*

glass together compared with the bonds in metal? (The bonds in glass must be less flexible.)

CHECK UNDERSTANDING
Skill: Organizing information
Ask: *What role did heat play in preparing the metal for shaping?* (Heat made the atoms move around more so the solid became less rigid.)

Reactions in Action

LESSON 52

Batter Up!

Point of Lesson: *Chemical reactions allow a cake to rise when baked.*

Students read a cake recipe and analyze it to identify the chemical reaction that causes this particular cake to rise. Next, they test various liquids used in cooking to determine which could be substituted for vinegar in the recipe. Finally, students identify the substances involved in the reactions and explain why certain steps have to be followed for the recipe to be successful.

Materials

Enrichment (p. 189), for the class:
► research sources about the chemistry of cooking
► food magazines (optional)
for each group:
► markers or paints
Activity (p. 190), for each pair or group:
► clear plastic cups (small)
► marking pen
► baking soda
► water
► white vinegar
► various liquids used in cooking (corn oil, milk, buttermilk, lemon juice, orange juice, etc.)
► teaspoons
for each student:
► safety goggles

Laboratory Safety

Review the following safety guidelines with students before they do the Activity in this lesson.
► Wear safety goggles at all times during this activity.
► Do not taste any substance in the laboratory. Avoid skin contact with laboratory materials.
► Wash your hands thoroughly after the activity.

LESSON 53

Deadly Venom

Point of Lesson: *Snake venom sets off chemical reactions in the snake's prey, causing harm.*

An article on the toxins in snake venom introduces the concept that chemical reactions occur within the bodies of living things. After reading the article, students use the information to predict the kinds of injury that can result from the bite of a venomous snake, based on the chemical reactions the venom causes. They then relate the action of one type of venom to a possible medical use. Finally, students review safety information about snake bites.

Materials

Enrichment (p. 193), for the class:
► research sources about poisonous snakes
for each student:
► drawing paper
► colored markers or pencils

LESSON 54

Mind Your Mummy

Point of Lesson: *Lack of moisture and air slows the chemical reactions of decomposition.*

An account of how Ancient Egyptians prepared a mummy suggests one possible way to slow down chemical reactions. After reading the account, students perform an activity intended to slow the decay of a potato by drying it out.

Materials

Read (p. 196), for the class:
► research sources on the Egyptian mummification process (optional)
Activity (p. 197), for each pair or group:
► 1 small potato
► potato peeler
► knife
► measuring cup
► $\frac{1}{3}$ cup salt
► $\frac{1}{3}$ cup baking soda
► 2 disposable plastic cups
for each student:
► safety goggles

Laboratory Safety

Review the following safety guidelines with students before they do the Activity in this lesson.
► Wear safety goggles at all times during this activity.
► Do not taste any substance in the laboratory.
► Wash your hands thoroughly after preparing the potato, and again after handling it a week later.

Background Information

Lesson 53

Snake venom contains a variety of toxic enzymes, some of which act on the nervous system of the injected prey. Medical researchers are currently investigating snake-venom enzymes and their synthetic equivalents for possible use in treating the neurological symptoms of Parkinson's and Alzheimer's disease. Venom from the black mamba may be useful for Alzheimer's patients, while Asian cobras might provide some relief for those who suffer from Parkinson's disease. Thus far, there have been some encouraging results in small patient trials.

Lesson 54

Human bodies preserved by both human and natural processes have been discovered in different parts of the world. Some examples include frozen sacrifice victims (including children and teenagers) found on the summits of mountains in South America; naturally mummified Native Americans buried in icy graves in near-polar regions; the Urumchi mummies found in China, which were preserved by burial in cold, dry soil; and the leathery bodies found in oxygen-deprived British peat bogs. In each case, conditions were such that the chemical reactions that normally cause tissue to decay were slowed or stopped.

Point of Lesson

Chemical reactions allow a cake to rise when baked.

Focus

▶ Evidence, models, and explanation
▶ Abilities necessary to do scientific inquiry
▶ Properties and changes of properties in matter

Skills and Strategies

▶ Observing
▶ Interpreting data
▶ Classifying
▶ Measuring
▶ Recognizing cause and effect
▶ Making inferences

Advance Preparation

Vocabulary

Make sure students understand these terms. Definitions can be found in the glossary at the end of the student book.

▶ acid   ▶ liquid
▶ chemical reaction   ▶ mixture
▶ gas

Materials

Gather the materials needed for *Enrichment* (p. 189) and *Activity* (p. 190).

TEACHING PLAN pp. 188–189

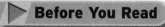

Do you like to cook? If you do, you might be a budding chemist.

It's fun to see how a mixture of ingredients can change as it cooks. The cake that you take out of the oven is very different from the gloppy batter that you started with. Is it just the heat from the oven, or does something else happen to cause the changes?

In many ways, a kitchen is like a chemistry lab. You combine foods to produce a tasty dish, just as a chemist combines chemicals. As your dish cooks, it goes through changes. Some of these changes are chemical reactions.

▶ **Before You Read**

EVERYDAY SCIENCE Even if you haven't done much cooking, you've probably watched someone cook. Think about something you've cooked or watched someone cook. It can be as simple as scrambled eggs, toast, or slice-and-bake cookies.

▶ *Think about the ways in which the food changed as it was cooked. Describe these changes.*

Answers will vary. Example: Scrambled eggs start out as a runny

mixture. As they are cooked, the mixture begins to thicken in places.

Gradually, the whole mixture becomes a moist solid. The longer it is

cooked, the more it dries out. If the eggs are stirred, the solid mass

breaks into pieces. If the eggs aren' t scrambled, the mixture puffs up

as it cooks.

188

INTRODUCING THE LESSON

This lesson introduces a very familiar activity that involves chemical reactions—baking a cake.

Find out what students already know about chemical reactions. Provide examples of changes and ask students to identify which ones are chemical reactions. (Do not use examples from the lesson.) For example, cutting an apple into pieces, crushing a potato chip, and boiling water are physical changes, not chemical reactions. Rusting, food spoiling, and wood burning are chemical reactions. Ask stu-

dents what these chemical reactions have in common. Elicit from them that something new is formed by a chemical reaction.

Students may think that chemistry happens only in a laboratory. Ask them to identify other places where chemistry happens. (Examples: the kitchen, the engine of a car, the human body, a beauty shop, a doctor's office)

▶ **Before You Read**

EVERYDAY SCIENCE As students describe changes in cooked food, encourage them to consider a variety of characteristics, including color, shape, size, texture, state (liquid, solid, or gas), and flavor. Have them also identify the factor that caused the changes. (the addition of heat)

▶ Read

This cake can be prepared in just a few minutes, but the baker still has to follow directions carefully.

IRVING PRAGER'S CHOCOLATE DUMP CAKE

- 1 cup sugar
- $1\frac{1}{2}$ cups flour
- $\frac{1}{3}$ cup cocoa powder
- 1 tsp baking soda
- 2 tbsp vinegar
- $\frac{1}{2}$ tsp salt
- 2 tsp vanilla
- $\frac{1}{2}$ cup corn oil
- 1 cup cold water

Other equipment: 8-inch cake pan [buttered and floured], fork or wire [whisk], mixing bowl

Preheat oven to 375°F. Be sure the oven is at 375°F before you start to mix the ingredients. With a fork or wire [whisk], mix everything together except the vinegar. Blend well. Add the vinegar, stir quickly, [pour into pan,] and put in the oven as fast as you can.

Bake at 375°F for 20 to 25 minutes until slightly puffed in the middle. Dust with confectioner's sugar. Or melt semi-sweet chocolate chips with a pinch of salt, add several tablespoons of sour cream, mix, and spread on the cake.

ingredients: the foods that are mixed together in a cooking recipe

confectioner's sugar: powdered sugar

From: "Irving Prager's Chocolate Dump Cake." Carnegie Mellon University. (www.cs.cmu.edu/People/rapidproto/activities/food/dumpcake.html)

NOTEZONE

In the directions, underline the steps that seem to be the most important to do correctly.

FIND OUT MORE

SCIENCESAURUS

Chemical
Reactions   269

SCILINKS®
THE WORLD'S A CLICK AWAY

www.scilinks.org
Keyword: Chemical Reactions

189

Enrichment

Time: will vary
Materials: research sources about the chemistry of cooking, drawing paper, markers or paints, food magazines (optional)

Note: In addition to using print sources, students could visit Web sites such as *The Exploratorium's* "Science of Cooking" at www.exploratorium.edu/cooking/index.html.

Let students do the following activity in groups of two or three. Tell each group to develop a menu for a breakfast, lunch, or dinner in which every item has undergone a chemical reaction. Have students research the items they want to include in their menus and give a short description of the chemical reactions involved in creating the items. Encourage them to include "before" and "after" pictures or a physical description of each food.

▶ Read

Students can follow the recipe to make the cake either at school or at home. **Caution:** If students do the activity at home, tell them to make sure they have adult supervision. If you choose to bake the cake at school, use the school's kitchen facilities for the entire activity, as students should never taste anything in the laboratory, not even food.

Discuss the importance of measuring the recipe ingredients accurately and following the directions exactly. Also ask students to think about the recipe's "active ingredients" compared with

ingredients that are included for taste. Ask: *Of all the ingredients in the list, which ones seem least likely to be there for taste?* (Students might name flour, water, baking soda, and vinegar.) Give them a few minutes to share ideas. Ask students to suggest possible chemical reactions that might make the cake rise. (Some students may guess that the vinegar and baking soda produce a chemical reaction.)

CHECK UNDERSTANDING
Skill: Sequencing
Have students summarize the observable changes that occur in baking a cake. (You start out with different liquids and powders. When you mix them all together you get a thick liquid. After you bake the cake, you have a soft, puffy solid.)

More Resources

The following resources are also available from Great Source and NSTA.

www.scilinks.org
Keyword: Chemical Reactions
Code: GSPD23

Connections

Time: will vary
Materials: research sources about the history of measurement

MATH Remind students how they measured ingredients for the cake. Ask them if they used a "level" teaspoon or a "heaping" teaspoon. Let this discussion lead to the idea that the lack of a standard system for measurements can create problems.

(continued on page 191)

▶ **Activity**

BUBBLE, BUBBLE

You have probably seen the fizz from the chemical reaction between vinegar and baking soda many times. The "fizz" is what makes the cake rise. Could other liquids be used in place of the vinegar?

What You Need:
- clear plastic cups (small)
- marking pen
- baking soda
- water
- white vinegar
- various liquids used in cooking (corn oil, milk, buttermilk, lemon juice, orange juice, etc.)
- teaspoons
- safety goggles

What to Do:
1. Choose several liquids to test with baking soda. Be sure to include vinegar and water. Show your list to your teacher before you carry out your experiment.
2. After your teacher has approved your list, obtain a cup for each liquid you will test. Label each cup with the name of one of the liquids.
3. Put on your safety goggles. Put about a teaspoon of baking soda into each cup.
4. Add a few teaspoons of water to the cup marked "water" and stir the mixture. Record your observations.
5. Use a clean spoon and repeat step 4 using vinegar and the cup marked "vinegar." Record your observations.
6. Repeat step 5 with the remaining liquids.

Liquid Tested	Observations
Water	*Water, milk and corn oil do not react with baking soda; orange juice,*
Vinegar	*lemon juice, buttermilk, and vinegar do react with baking soda;*
	vinegar produces the fastest reaction, followed by lemon juice,
	orange juice, and buttermilk. Students should note that the bubbles
	rise through the buttermilk slowly, due to the thickness of the liquid.

WHAT DO YOU SEE?
▶ *Which liquids produced a visible reaction with baking soda?*

  vinegar, lemon juice, orange juice, buttermilk

▶ *What evidence of a chemical reaction did you see?*

  The mixture gives off bubbles.

190

TEACHING PLAN pp. 190–191

▶ **Activity**

Time: 25 minutes
Materials: clear plastic cups (small); marking pen; baking soda; water; white vinegar; various liquids used in cooking (corn oil, milk, buttermilk, lemon juice, orange juice, etc.), teaspoons; safety goggles

After students read the instructions, remind them of the need to control variables. Ask: *Which variable will you be changing in this activity?* (the type of liquid) *What variables should be kept the same?* (the amount of baking soda and the amount and temperature of the liquid)

Students can extend the activity by testing the liquids that made baking soda fizz with other powders such as flour, confectioner's sugar, or baking powder. (Since baking powder contains baking soda, it will fizz when mixed with an acid, but neither flour nor confectioner's sugar will.)

WHAT DO YOU SEE? Remind students that chemical reactions produce new products. Ask: *What product was present after the reaction but not before?* (carbon dioxide gas) *What evidence do you have?* (I observed bubbles.)

▶ Propose Explanations

HOW DOES IT WORK? Baking soda is sodium bicarbonate, a chemical that reacts with acids. Vinegar contains acetic acid, so when you mix it with baking soda you get a chemical reaction. Actually, you get two reactions, because the product of the reaction between the sodium bicarbonate and acid breaks down very quickly. Here are the two reactions.

sodium bicarbonate + acetic acid ⟶ carbonic acid

carbonic acid ⟶ carbon dioxide gas + water

▶ *Think about the kinds of liquids that caused a reaction with baking soda. What do these liquids have in common?*

Students might classify them as all having a sour taste, an attribute of

acids. Or, based on the explanation and source, students might infer that

the liquids that reacted must be acids.

The bubbles you saw in the activity were bubbles of carbon dioxide gas escaping from the mixture. Bubbles trapped in the cake batter make the batter rise slightly before the cake is put into the oven. Inside the oven, heat causes the bubbles to expand, making the cake rise even more.

▶ *Notice that the recipe says to put the batter into the pan and get the pan into the oven as quickly as possible. Why do you think it's important to act so quickly when making this cake?*

The chemical reaction takes place very quickly. If you take too long, too

many bubbles will escape, and the cake won't rise.

▶ *Think back to the differences in the liquids you tested in the activity. How is cake batter different from the mixture of vinegar and baking soda you made in the activity? How might this difference help make the cake rise?*

The batter is thicker because it contains flour and sugar and other solid

ingredients. The thickness traps the bubbles, so they don't escape.

191

(continued from page 190)

Then have students use an encyclopedia, other books, and the Internet to find out more about the history of measurement. Students might be interested in how the International System of Units (SI, the metric system) used by most countries and by all scientists throughout the world came into use. Others may be interested in how body parts (feet, distance between knuckles, arm span, and so forth) were used as units of measurement in ancient times.

Assessment
Skill: Making inferences

Use the following questions to assess each student's progress:

▶ *What would happen if you didn't add vinegar to the cake mixture?* (The cake batter would not bubble or fizz, and it would not rise when baked.)
▶ *If you didn't have vinegar, what other liquid might you use to make the cake?* (Answers may include acidic liquids such as lemon juice, orange juice, and buttermilk.)
▶ *Why can't you taste any vinegar or baking soda when you eat the cake?* (The vinegar and baking soda have changed to carbon dioxide and water.)

▶ Propose Explanations

HOW DOES IT WORK? After students have completed the questions, have them draw and label a diagram to show how the cake rose. (Students' diagrams should show baking soda and vinegar reacting to produce carbonic acid and then the acid breaking down into a gas and water. The gas forms tiny bubbles throughout the batter, causing it to expand. As the batter dries and stiffens, most of the bubbles are trapped before they can move to the surface and escape.)

Students might be interested to learn that more is not better. If much larger amounts of vinegar and baking soda were used, more and bigger bubbles would be produced, as expected. But the bubbles would be able to move to the surface much more quickly and would escape before the batter had stiffened.

Point of Lesson

Snake venom sets off chemical reactions in the snake's prey, causing harm.

Focus

► Change, constancy, and measurement
► Properties and changes of properties in matter
► Regulation and behavior
► Personal health
► Science and technology in society

Skills and Strategies

► Generating ideas
► Comparing and contrasting
► Making inferences
► Creating and using tables

Advance Preparation

Vocabulary

Make sure students understand these terms. Definitions can be found in the glossary at the end of the student book.

► cell
► organ
► tissue

Materials

Gather the materials needed for *Enrichment* (p. 193).

TEACHING PLAN pp. 192–193

INTRODUCING THE LESSON

This lesson examines how some predators use venom to set off deadly chemical reactions in their prey.

Ask students to explain the relationship between predators and prey. Help them recall that predators kill other animals—prey—for food. Point out that a predator must have some way to capture and disable its prey.

Tell students that venom is a poison produced by an animal and injected into its victim. Ask students to name any poisonous animals they know of.

(some types of snakes, spiders, insects, and fish; scorpions)

Students may believe that all snakes are poisonous. In fact, most snakes are not (as discussed in the lesson). This may be a good time to discuss poisonous and nonpoisonous snakes that are native to your area. Your local extension service or a nature center should have this information.

DEADLY VENOM

Are you afraid of snakes?

Imagine that you are hiking along a trail with a friend. It's a sunny day, and you and your friend are enjoying the fresh air and exercise. Suddenly, your friend stops walking and points to the path ahead. A snake! It's right there, just a few yards away from you. What do you think the snake will do next? What should you do?

The venom that snakes inject into their prey is a mixture of powerful chemicals. All the workings of an animal's body, including blood cells, muscle cells, and nerve cells, depend on exactly the right chemicals being in the right place at the right moment. The snake's venom changes all that.

Mojave rattlesnake ►

Before You Read

SNAKE CHARMS Many people are afraid of snakes, especially people who know very little about them. How much do you know about snakes? Take this little quiz. Mark the statements that you think are true with a *T*. Mark the statements that you think are false with an *F*.

As you read the rest of this lesson, you'll discover the answers. Remember to go back and check your answers to the quiz. Ready? Then try it!

F	Most species of snakes are venomous (poisonous).
F	A bite from a nonpoisonous snake is harmless.
F	The best first aid for a snakebite is to suck the venom, or poison, from the wound.
T	Snake venom is a kind of saliva.

192

Before You Read

SNAKE CHARMS Ask students what they know about snakes and where they learned it. They may have had first-hand experience, heard stories from others, seen snakes in a movie or television show, or seen live snakes at a zoo. Some students may be familiar with mythological stories about snakes. Have students evaluate the reliability of each of these sources. Which is most reliable? Which is least reliable? Why?

> Read

Allan Bieber is a chemistry professor at Arizona State University. He studies how the toxins, or poisons, in snake venom affect the body's chemical reactions.

SSSSnake Bite

Most toxins in snake venom are proteins.... "Proteins carry out a lot of important functions in cells," says Bieber.

The proteins in snake venom [cause chemical reactions to take place] in the human body, just like our own proteins. For instance, many venoms contain enzymes that set off chemical reactions. But while your body's own enzymes work to help you, the enzymes in snake venom have harmful effects.

Bieber studies the venom of the Mojave rattlesnake.... The Mojave's venom contains a poison called a neurotoxin. Neurotoxins are among the most dangerous kinds of proteins in snake venom. They affect nerve cells, or neurons, and can cause paralysis and eventually, death. Neurotoxins [work by] prevent[ing] neurons from communicating with each other....

Neurotoxins are just one kind of poison found in snake venom. Different snakes carry different kinds of toxins. Some venoms, called myotoxins, damage muscle cells. Others interfere with the blood clotting process. Still others [cause] clotting.

---

proteins: large molecules that carry out chemical reactions in cells

enzymes: proteins that control the rate of chemical reactions in the body

paralysis: being unable to move

clotting: blood cells clumping together into a plug that stops blood flow

From: Boudreau, Diane. "The Virtues of Venom."
(http://chainreaction.asu.edu/desert/digin/venom.htm)

FIND OUT MORE

SCIENCESAURUS

Cell Processes	079
Human Biology	083
Chemical Reactions	269

SCILINKS
THE WORLD'S A CLICK AWAY
www.scilinks.org
Keyword: Chemical Reactions
Code: GSPD23

193

Enrichment

Time: will vary
Materials: research sources about poisonous snakes, drawing paper, colored markers or pencils

Challenge each student to find out more about one type (species) of poisonous snake and prepare a report to share with the class. Explain that the reports should be illustrated with pictures of the snakes. Tell students to include information about the snake's habitat, diet, type of venom, prey, and any unusual adaptations. Some students may be able to link their snake with research being done to discover new medicines. In addition to print sources, students can use the Internet or contact nature centers and museums for information.

Note: In North America, the only poisonous snakes are pit vipers (rattlesnakes, water moccasins, and copperheads) and coral snakes. Pit vipers release hemotoxins; coral snakes release neurotoxins.

> Read

The reading contains a number of terms that may be unfamiliar to students, including *toxins, venom, proteins, enzymes, neurotoxins, neurons, paralysis, myotoxins,* and *muscle cells.* After students have read the passage, have them create a graphic organizer to show the relationships between the terms. A sample is shown at right.

Students may want to know more about enzymes. Explain that an enzyme changes the speed of a chemical reaction. However, each enzyme works for only one reaction (or perhaps a small number of closely related reactions). Because of this, organisms must produce thousands of different enzymes.

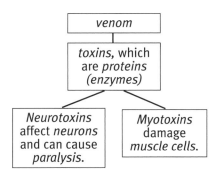

CHECK UNDERSTANDING
Skill: Communicating

Have each student write four true-or-false statements about the proteins found in snake venom, basing the statements on the information in the reading. Then have partners exchange statements and take each other's quiz. Examples are given below.

► Proteins in snake venom cause chemical reactions to take place in our bodies. (T)

► Snake venom is basically the same from snake to snake. (F)

More Resources

The following resources are also available from Great Source and NSTA.

www.scilinks.org
Keyword: Chemical Reactions
Code: GSPD23

Connections

WRITING Ask students if they would like to keep a nonvenomous snake in a glass enclosure in the science classroom. Some classrooms do this, but the practice is controversial. Have each student write a letter to the principal stating his or her position on having snakes in the classroom. Tell students to give at least three reasons for their position. Encourage them to share their letters with the class to see if there is a consensus.

TEACHING PLAN pp. 194–195

▶ **Explore**

WHY POISON? Draw students' attention to the picture of the snake swallowing its rodent prey on this page. Explain that the bones on the left and right sides of a snake's lower jaw are not fused in front, like our lower jaws are, but are connected by cartilage that can stretch so the snake can open its mouth wider. Ask students how this jaw structure might help snakes eat. (It allows snakes to swallow prey much larger than their mouths.)

Write *neurotoxin, hemotoxin,* and *myotoxin* on the board. Explain that the

---

▶ **Explore**

WHY POISON? All snakes swallow their prey whole. To do that, the prey animal can't be moving. Some snakes coil their body around their prey and squeeze until it suffocates. Other snakes puncture the skin of the prey with their fangs and inject venom into the animal. Once the venom does its job, the snake can actually swallow the whole animal.

Snake venom is saliva. That's right, snake spit! The table below lists some of the proteins that may be found in snake venom, their effect on a mouse or other prey animal, and their effect on a human.

Protein	Effect on Prey	Effect on Human
Neurotoxin	paralyzes prey; prey dies because breathing stops	stops nerve cells from communicating with each other and with muscles; makes breathing difficult; can cause death due to paralyzed diaphragm (breathing muscle)
Hemotoxin	destroys blood cells; prey dies because of damage to circulatory system	damages blood cells; can cause bleeding at bite wound, internal organs or brain, leading to death
Digestive enzymes	begins to break down body tissues to help the snake digest the prey	tissue damage in the area around the bite

NEUROTOXINS The human nervous system allows for communication between different parts of the body. All your senses depend on nerve cells being able to send information to the brain. Every movement of your body depends on the brain or spinal cord being able to send messages to muscles.

In the table above, you learned that neurotoxins, which interfere with nerve cell communication, can make it hard to breathe.

▶ *What do you suppose might happen if a snake spit venom with a neurotoxin directly into a person's eye?*

That person might not be able to see.

▶ *What other ways can you think of that neurotoxins might affect the victim of a snakebite?*

Answers will vary. Answers should refer to issues related to a nervous

system problem. Possible answer: They might feel numb, or they might

not be able to walk. They might not even be able to talk.

194

---

prefix *neuro-* refers to the nervous system, *myo-* refers to muscles, and *hemo-* refers to blood (circulatory system). Encourage students to use a dictionary to find other words that begin with these prefixes.

Direct students' attention to the chart. Ask: *Which type of protein in snake venom might you expect to find in human saliva? Why?* (Digestive enzymes; they break down tissues and help digest food.)

NEUROTOXINS Neurotoxins affect the nerve cells of organisms. If necessary, explain that the human nervous system

includes the brain, spinal cord, and all the nerves found throughout the body. It enables the body to detect what is going on in its environment and to react accordingly. The brain, spinal cord, and nerves work together to control all physical activity—both voluntary activities such as muscle movement, and involuntary activities such as the beating of the heart.

▶ Propose Explanations

SNAKES AND PEOPLE When a poisonous snake bites a mouse, it dies. When the same snake bites a human, the human usually doesn't die. Humans have one important factor in their favor—size.

▶ *How might size help a person survive a snakebite?*

A mouse or other prey is small, so a small amount of venom will kill it. A human is many times larger, so that small amount of venom is probably not enough to kill a person quickly.

Although snake venom is scary stuff, it might have uses in medicine. Tiny amounts of snake venom might be used to help a patient with a disease that causes tremors. Tremors are shaking muscles, and are caused by nerve cells telling muscles to contract too frequently.

▶ *Look back at the table on page 194. What protein in snake venom might be useful for such a patient? Why?*

Neurotoxins might be useful. The neurotoxins could stop the nerves from communicating with the muscle and making it shake.

THINK ABOUT IT There are more species of nonpoisonous snakes than poisonous snakes. But it's important to take any snakebite seriously. Even a nonpoisonous snake's bite can cause an infection.

▶ *How do you think a nonpoisonous snakebite could infect you?*

Germs could get in through the open wound.

If someone is bitten by a snake, the person should be taken to a hospital as quickly as possible. It's always good first aid to wash the wound, but don't put ice on it. Don't try to suck out the venom, as you may have seen done in movies. In many cases, this won't remove enough venom to be helpful. And it adds another risk—germs from your mouth may cause an infection.

▶ *Can you think of another safety reason not to try this?*

The venom could get into your body.

Now go back to the quiz you took in *Before You Read* on page 192. How did you do? Make corrections as needed.

195

Assessment
Skill: Concept mapping

Use the following task to assess each student's progress:

Have each student create a concept map to show how snakes use chemical reactions to get food. (Concept maps will vary but should include the following stages: Some snakes produce venom, which contains proteins that cause harmful chemical reactions in their prey. When the snake bites the prey, venom enters the prey's body. Depending on the type of venom, the prey suffers damage to its nervous system, circulatory system, and/or muscles. Once the prey is disabled, the snake can safely swallow it.)

▶ Propose Explanations

SNAKES AND PEOPLE Explain that snake venom may hold the cure for many different types of human diseases. For example, an experimental drug called Ancrod, which is derived from the venom of pit vipers, has been shown to be effective in lowering the level of clotting substances in the blood. The drug could be used to help stroke victims (those who suffer brain damage due to a blockage or rupture of a blood vessel in the brain).

A scientist working at the University of Southern California School of Medicine found that a protein he extracted from the venom of the copperhead snake appeared to prevent breast cancer cells from attaching to and invading nearby healthy cells. In this way, the protein was effective in preventing the spread of the cancer. Point out that snake venom treatments are still controversial, and most have yet to be approved by the U.S. Food and Drug Administration.

THINK ABOUT IT Tell students that the American Red Cross says any snakebite should be considered a medical emer-

gency. Ask students to suggest a reason for this recommendation. (Even if the snake is not poisonous, the wound could still become infected.)

Point of Lesson

Lack of moisture and air slows the chemical reactions of decomposition.

Focus

▶ Change, constancy, and measurement

▶ Properties and changes of properties in matter

▶ History of science

▶ Abilities necessary to do scientific inquiry

Skills and Strategies

▶ Observing

▶ Analyzing data

▶ Making inferences

Advance Preparation

Vocabulary

Make sure students understand these terms. Definitions can be found in the glossary at the end of the student book.

▶ bacteria

▶ chemical reaction

Materials

Gather the materials needed for *Read* (below) and *Activity* (p. 197).

Reactions in Action

Mind Your Mummy

How can you slow down a chemical reaction? Ask your mummy!

About 5,000 years ago, the ancient Egyptians figured out how to preserve bodies. When a living thing dies, a chemical reaction takes place: Bacteria invade and the body begins to decay. Bacteria need moisture to survive. Egyptians mummified a body by removing the moisture from it. This slowed down the chemical reactions of decay.

NOTE ZONE

Circle the stages of mummification that you think slowed down decay of the body.

FIND OUT MORE

SCIENCE SAURUS

Properties of Matter	251
Physical and Chemical Changes	252
Chemical Reactions	269

SCI LINKS
THE WORLD'S A CLICK AWAY

www.scilinks.org
Keyword: Chemical Reactions
Code: GSPD23

Read

Herodotus, a Greek historian, visited Egypt in 450 B.C. and learned how mummies were made. Here's what he wrote:

HOW MUMMIES ARE MADE

"As much of the brain as possible is extracted through the nostrils with an iron hook, and what the hook cannot reach is dissolved with drugs. Next the [body] is slit open with a sharp ...stone and the entire contents of the abdomen are removed.

"The cavity is then thoroughly cleansed and washed out, first with palm wine and again with a solution of pounded spices. Then it is filled with [herbs] .... The opening is sewn up and then the body is placed in natron for 70 days...."

extracted: removed
abdomen: the part of the body between the bottom of the rib cage and the pelvis
cavity: hollowed-out space

solution: mixture of particles dissolved in a liquid
natron: a salt that absorbs moisture

From: Herodotus. *The Histories.* Penguin Group UK.

UNIT 5: INTERACTIONS OF MATTER

196

TEACHING PLAN pp. 196–197

INTRODUCING THE LESSON

This lesson describes how the ancient Egyptians mummified bodies of the dead to prevent decomposition.

Discuss what students know about the ancient Egyptian practice of mummification. If they do not already know, explain that it was a process used to preserve the bodies of pharaohs and other important people before burying them in tombs. Some students might think that mummification simply involved wrapping the corpse in cloth before burial. Tell them the process was much more involved.

Read

Time: will vary
Materials: research sources on the Egyptian mummification process (optional)

Review what the abbreviation B.C. means. (before Christ) Ask: *Which is older, a piece of pottery from 400 B.C. or one from 1400 B.C.?* (the one from 1400 B.C.)

After students have read the excerpt, ask: *What does "contents of the abdomen" refer to?* (organs such as the stomach, intestines, liver, kidneys, pancreas, spleen, gall bladder, and bladder)

Why do you think the Egyptians removed those organs? (Students may realize that these soft, moist internal organs are particularly susceptible to decay after death.) Tell students that the lungs were also removed from the chest cavity. The heart, which was considered to be the center of thought and emotion, was left inside the body.

Students may question whether the wine, spices, and herbs used in the mummification process had an actual preservative effect. Encourage them to do further research on the effectiveness of these materials as preservatives.

MAKE A POTATO MUMMY

The ancient Egyptians preserved bodies by mummifying them. See what happens when you preserve a potato.

What You Need:
- one small potato
- salt
- baking soda
- measuring cup
- two disposable plastic cups
- safety goggles

What to Do:
1. Put on your safety goggles. Peel the potato and cut it in half.
2. Put one potato piece in each plastic cup.
3. Fill the measuring cup with baking soda up to the $\frac{1}{3}$ mark. Then add salt until the cup is filled to the $\frac{2}{3}$ mark.
4. Mix the salt and baking soda together and pour it into one of the cups. Make sure the potato piece is completely covered with the salt mixture.
5. Put both cups in a dark place for a week.
6. After a week, carefully pour out the salt mixture and take a look. Compare the potato piece that was in the salt to the one that wasn't.

WHAT DO YOU SEE?
▶ *Compare the potato pieces. Describe what you see.*

The potato that was left uncovered has a lot of mold on it and is decaying.

The potato that was covered in salt has very little mold and is not decaying.

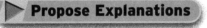

WHAT DO YOU THINK?
▶ *Why didn't the salt-covered potato decay like the other one?*

The salt and baking powder removed the moisture from the potato, which

slowed down decay.

▶ *Look at the phrases you circled in the reading. How is what you did to the covered potato similar to what the Egyptians did to bodies?*

I covered the potato with salt to dry it out, just as the Egyptians covered

bodies with natron to dry them out.

197

More Resources
The following resources are also available from Great Source and NSTA.

SCIENCESAURUS
Properties of Matter	251
Physical and Chemical Changes	252
Chemical Reactions	269

WRITE SOURCE 2000
Researching	55

SCILINKS
THE WORLD'S A CLICK AWAY

www.scilinks.org
Keyword: Chemical Reactions
Code: GSPD23

Assessment
Skill: Generating ideas

Use the following task to assess each student's progress:

Ask students to use what they learned about the ancient Egyptian mummification process to suggest a way to preserve a melon for a long period of time. (Example: Cut the melon open and take out the seeds. Wash the melon and cover it with salt. Stuff paper inside it so it would keep its original shape. Then let it dry out in a cool, dry place.)

Activity

Time: 15–20 minutes for initial setup; 10 minutes for follow-up observations and responses
Materials: one small potato*; potato peeler*; knife*; measuring cup; $\frac{1}{3}$ cup salt, $\frac{1}{3}$ cup baking soda; 2 disposable plastic cups; safety goggles

*Note: To save time and to prevent mishaps, you may want to peel and slice the potatoes yourself beforehand or allow reliable volunteers to do so under your direct supervision.

In step 4, emphasize that the potato should be completely covered with the salt mixture. If a potato piece is too large, have students trim it down.

Propose Explanations

WHAT DO YOU THINK? Point out that the salt and baking soda also kept air from reaching the potato. Air contains oxygen that many types of bacteria need in order to start decomposition.

CHECK UNDERSTANDING
Skill: Making inferences
Tell students that mummified bodies have been discovered in a cold desert in northern China. Although the bodies were not mummified before burial, they have not decayed during hundreds of years. Ask students to explain how this might have happened. (The dry conditions in the desert and burial in the sandy soil kept moisture and air from reaching the bodies, which prevented decay.)

Energy From Chemicals

LESSON 55

Making the Sea Shine
Point of Lesson: *Some organisms use chemicals to produce light.*

An excerpt from the diary Darwin kept while on board the *Beagle* describes the ghostly light that he saw in breaking waves and the ship's wake. Students learn that the light is produced by chemical reactions in microscopic marine organisms. The concept of a catalyst is introduced in the context of this reaction.

Materials
Read (p. 198), for the class:
► globe (optional)

LESSON 56

Lighting Up the Night
Point of Lesson: *Chemicals can be combined to produce light without heat.*

Students explore the chemistry behind the common light stick. An article describes the contents of a light stick and how its construction prevents a chemical reaction from occurring until it is activated. Students sequence the reactions that take place when the chemicals in a light stick mix. Students then compare light produced by heated objects (incandescent) and light that is produced without heat (luminescent).

Materials
Enrichment (p. 201), for teacher demonstration or for each group:
► 3 identical small light sticks
► thermometer
► 3 large beakers
► ice water
► room-temperature water
► hot tap water
► clock
Take Action (p. 203), for the class:
► research sources about different types of light

Laboratory Safety
Review the following safety guidelines with students before they do the Enrichment activity in this lesson.
► Handle glassware carefully. Immediately report any broken glassware to your teacher.
► Do not leave the thermometer in the beaker between readings.

LESSON 57

Keeping Toes Warm
Point of Lesson: *Chemicals can be combined to produce heat.*

In this lesson, a scientist who dives into dangerously cold water beneath the Antarctic ice reveals how he keeps his toes warm: chemical warmers. Students test various combinations of materials to find out which ones release heat energy as the chemicals react with each other. They then improve the design of their chemical toe warmers by testing additives meant to trap the heat energy.

Materials
Read (p. 205), for teacher demonstration:
► chemical toe warmer pack
Enrichment (p. 205), for the class:
► chemical cold pack
Activity, Part 1 (p. 206), for each group:
► 6 small resealable plastic freezer bags
► iron powder
► salt
► antacid tablets
► powdered detergent
► 6 thermometers
► measuring spoons
► water
► safety goggles

Activity, Part 2 (p. 207), for each group:
► 4 small resealable plastic freezer bags
► toe warmer materials from Part 1
► sugar
► marbles
► vermiculite
► small piece of wood
► water
► 4 thermometers
► measuring spoons
► safety goggles

Laboratory Safety
Review the following safety guidelines with students before they do the Activity in this lesson.
► Wear safety goggles at all times during this activity.
► Do not taste any substance in the laboratory. Avoid touching substances directly. Keep your hands away from your face while doing this activity.
► Handle powders carefully to keep them out of the air. Do not inhale any powders.
► Clean up spills promptly.
► Dispose of iron powder and vermiculite in the trash. Do not put these materials in the sink.
► Promptly pick up any marbles that fall on the floor.
► Wash your hands thoroughly after the activity.

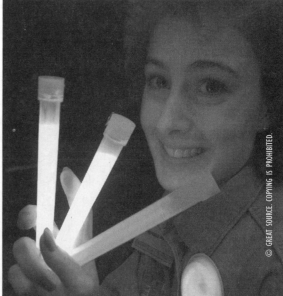

Background Information

Lesson 57

The chemical equation for the reaction that takes place in the toe warmers is as follows:

$$4Fe(s) + 3O_2(g) \longrightarrow 2Fe_2O_3(s) + heat$$

You may recognize this as the reaction for the formation of iron oxide, commonly called rust. The iron powder in the toe warmers is rusting (oxidizing). However, it is doing so much more quickly than it might in nature, for two reasons: the presence of salt, and the small size of the iron grains. Salt, or sodium chloride (NaCl), acts as a catalyst and greatly increases the rate of the reaction. Increasing the surface area of the reactants also increases the rate of a chemical reaction. Iron powder is used rather than iron filings because powder has far more surface area and thus allows the reaction to proceed more quickly. The greater the rate of reaction, the more heat produced in a short amount of time.

Point of Lesson
Some organisms use chemicals to produce light.

Focus
► Properties and changes of properties in matter
► Science as a human endeavor
► Diversity and adaptations of organisms
► Evidence, models, and explanation

Skills and Strategies
► Making inferences
► Recognizing cause and effect
► Generating ideas

Advance Preparation

Vocabulary
Make sure students understand these terms. Definitions can be found in the glossary at the end of the student book.

► cell
► chemical reaction
► light
► organism

Materials
Gather the materials needed for *Read* (below).

Making the Sea Shine

What glows eerily in the dark of night, but isn't a ghost?

Charles Darwin (1809–1892) is best known for his theory explaining the process of evolution. His life in science began at the age of 22. That was when he signed on for a long voyage aboard a ship called the *Beagle*. Darwin was the ship's unpaid naturalist.

The voyage was supposed to last two years but instead lasted five. The trip took Darwin down the Atlantic coast of South America and up the Pacific coast, then through the South Pacific to Australia. Finally, the ship circled around the rest of the world and back to England. In all of these remote places, Darwin had opportunities to observe rocks, plants, and animals that few people had ever studied. Careful observations and brilliant logic helped the young student become an accomplished scientist.

▲ Voyage of the *Beagle*

UNIT 5: INTERACTIONS OF MATTER

NOTEZONE
Circle the words that describe the light Darwin saw.

FIND OUT MORE
SCIENCESAURUS

Relationships Between Populations	132
Chemical Reactions	269
Forms of Energy	300
Light	308

SCILINKS.
THE WORLD'S A CLICK AWAY
www.scilinks.org
Keyword: Chemical Energy
Code: GSPD24

198

▶ Read
Here is a section from the journal Darwin kept during the *Beagle's* voyage. It is from December, 1833. The ship was in the Atlantic Ocean, near the Plata River in South America.

Light in the Night Sea

While sailing a little south of the Plata on one very dark night, the sea presented a wonderful and most beautiful spectacle. There was a fresh breeze, and every part of the surface, which during the day is seen as foam, now glowed with a pale light. The vessel drove before her bows two billows of liquid phosphorus, and in her wake she was followed by a milky train. As far as the eye reached, the crest of every wave was bright, and the sky above the horizon, from the reflected glare of these livid flames, was not so utterly obscure as over the vault of the heavens.

spectacle: an unusual sight
vessel: ship
bow: the front of a ship
billow: wave

phosphorus: substance that glows in the dark
wake: the trail left in the water by a moving boat
crest: upper edge

horizon: imaginary line where the sky meets earth or sea
livid: grayish-blue or pale white
obscure: dark
vault: arched roof

From: Darwin, Charles. *The Voyage of the Beagle.* Doubleday & Co.

TEACHING PLAN pp. 198–199

INTRODUCING THE LESSON
This lesson introduces the idea that chemical reactions enable certain organisms to produce light.

Ask students: *Do you know of any living things that seem to glow in the dark?* (Students may be familiar with foxfire, a type of fungus that grows in the woods, and fireflies. Some students may know about deep-sea animals that produce their own light.) Students may think that bioluminescence is similar to the phosphorescence of glow-in-the-dark toys, which absorb light energy from an external source and then

release it. Explain that some living things actually produce their own light.

▶ Read

Time: 10 minutes
Materials: globe (optional)

Have students locate the Atlantic coast of South America on the map shown on this page. Point out that this map shows a distorted perspective of Earth's land masses and oceans. To orient students to the map, you may want to have them use a globe to find a view that reveals a somewhat similar perspective.

Ask: *Why do you think the map is drawn this way?* (To show Darwin's entire journey on one map.)

Point out that this short excerpt contains several highlighted words, with definitions at the bottom of the page. Encourage students to read the passage replacing the highlighted words with their definitions. For example, students could read "most beautiful spectacle" as "most beautiful and unusual sight."

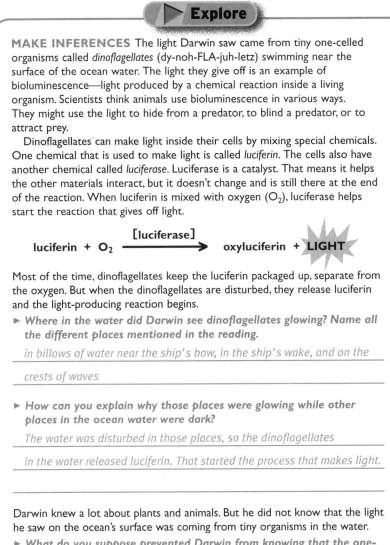

▶ Explore

MAKE INFERENCES The light Darwin saw came from tiny one-celled organisms called *dinoflagellates* (dy-noh-FLA-juh-letz) swimming near the surface of the ocean water. The light they give off is an example of bioluminescence—light produced by a chemical reaction inside a living organism. Scientists think animals use bioluminescence in various ways. They might use the light to hide from a predator, to blind a predator, or to attract prey.

Dinoflagellates can make light inside their cells by mixing special chemicals. One chemical that is used to make light is called *luciferin*. The cells also have another chemical called *luciferase*. Luciferase is a catalyst. That means it helps the other materials interact, but it doesn't change and is still there at the end of the reaction. When luciferin is mixed with oxygen (O_2), luciferase helps start the reaction that gives off light.

$$\text{luciferin} + O_2 \xrightarrow{\text{[luciferase]}} \text{oxyluciferin} + \textbf{LIGHT}$$

Most of the time, dinoflagellates keep the luciferin packaged up, separate from the oxygen. But when the dinoflagellates are disturbed, they release luciferin and the light-producing reaction begins.

▶ *Where in the water did Darwin see dinoflagellates glowing? Name all the different places mentioned in the reading.*

in billows of water near the ship's bow, in the ship's wake, and on the

crests of waves

▶ *How can you explain why those places were glowing while other places in the ocean water were dark?*

The water was disturbed in those places, so the dinoflagellates

in the water released luciferin. That started the process that makes light.

Darwin knew a lot about plants and animals. But he did not know that the light he saw on the ocean's surface was coming from tiny organisms in the water.

▶ *What do you suppose prevented Darwin from knowing that the one-celled dinoflagellates existed? (Hint: Think about what Darwin would need to see the organisms.)*

He probably didn't have a microscope powerful enough to see

one-celled organisms.

199

More Resources

The following resources are also available from Great Source and NSTA.

SCIENCESAURUS

Relationships Between Populations	132
Chemical Reactions	269
Forms of Energy	300
Light	308

READER'S HANDBOOK

Elements of Graphics: Map	555

SCILINKS®
THE WORLD'S A CLICK AWAY

www.scilinks.org
Keyword: Chemical Energy
Code: GSPD24

Assessment
Skill: Making inferences

Use the following question to assess each student's progress:

How might scientists studying dinoflagellate biology have been helped by Darwin's detailed observations about where he saw the light? (His observations might have given scientists the idea that dinoflagellates produce light when they are disturbed.)

▶ Explore

MAKE INFERENCES To help students make sense of the word *bioluminescence*, remind them of other words that include the prefix *bio-* (*biology* and *biography*) and the root word *lumin* (*luminous* and *illuminate*). Lead students to understand that the term *bioluminescence* refers to light from living things.

Have a volunteer read aloud the chemical equation shown on this page and the explanation below it. Ask: *What has to happen first to start this reaction?* (Something disturbs the dinoflagel-

lates, and they release luciferin.) *What happened in the sea that started the reaction?* (The ship passing through made the water move and wind blowing over the surface created waves.)

Help students recognize that bioluminescence involves the conversion of chemical energy to light energy. Students who want to learn more about bioluminescence may be interested in the Harbor Branch Oceanographic Institution's Web site, www.biolum.org/.

CHECK UNDERSTANDING
Skill: Drawing conclusions
Ask: *What is bioluminescence?* (light produced by a chemical reaction inside an organism)

Point of Lesson

Chemicals can be combined to produce light without heat.

Focus

▶ Properties and changes of properties in matter
▶ Transfer of energy
▶ Science and technology in society
▶ Systems, order, and organization

Skills and Strategies

▶ Sequencing
▶ Concept mapping
▶ Generating ideas

Advance Preparation

Vocabulary

Make sure students understand these terms. Definitions can be found in the glossary at the end of the student book.

▶ **chemical reaction**
▶ **energy**
▶ **heat energy**
▶ **temperature**

Materials

Gather the materials needed for *Enrichment* (p. 201) and *Take Action* (p. 203).

Lighting Up the Night

What makes a light stick glow?

Have you ever played with a light stick? You bend or snap the plastic tube and immediately it begins to glow. It might be green or red or purple or yellow. You can wear it around your neck or arm, or put it inside a jack-o-lantern, or just wave it around. You may have also seen light sticks decorating bowling alleys or skating rinks. They're great for outdoor use, too, because they have no electrical parts to keep dry. But, since light sticks don't have batteries or even on–off switches, you may have wondered what makes them work. Where does their energy come from?

▶ **Before You Read**

▲ Light sticks

YOU'RE GETTING COLDER People get light from many different sources. One thing that many (but not all) light sources have in common is that they produce heat as well as light.

▶ *List five things that give off light.*

   Answers will vary. Examples: light sticks; the sun; a light bulb; a candle; a computer monitor

▶ *Now put your list in order, starting with the one that gives off the most heat and ending with the one that gives off the least heat.*

   Answers will vary. Example: the sun; a light bulb; a candle; a computer monitor; light sticks

TEACHING PLAN pp. 200–201

INTRODUCING THE LESSON
This lesson explains how light sticks work: when chemicals inside the sticks mix together, a chain of reactions begin that result in the emission of light.

Ask students if they have ever used light sticks or similar items that produce light. Ask: *What kinds of objects are made from light sticks?* (Students may mention flexible necklaces, bracelets, and hoops.) *What are some popular uses for light sticks?* (Students may list places and events such as carnivals, concerts, circuses, 4th of July picnics, and parties.) Students may believe that the reason light sticks do not feel hot is that they are not very bright. Explain that light bulbs feel hot and light sticks do not because the two objects use different processes to produce light.

▶ **Before You Read**

YOU'RE GETTING COLDER Remind students that light is a form of energy. Ask: *Why do you think light sources are often hot?* (Students may suggest that since both heat and light are forms of energy, one is converted to the other when the light is on.) Ask students: *What are some advantages of having a* *light source that does not produce heat?* (Examples: You do not have to worry about fires or burns; you do not waste as much energy heating things that are not supposed to be heated and then cooling them.)

▶ Read

A series of chemical reactions makes light sticks glow.

How Light Sticks Work

Since their invention 25 years ago, light sticks have become a Halloween staple. They're perfect as safety lights for little trick-or-treaters because they're portable, cheap and they emit a ghostly glow. Light sticks...also...make an ideal lamp for SCUBA divers and campers.

...[L]ight sticks use energy from a chemical reaction to emit light. This chemical reaction is set off by mixing multiple chemical compounds.... The reaction between the different compounds in a light stick causes a substantial release of energy....

The light stick itself is just a housing for the two solutions involved in the reaction—essentially, it is portable chemistry experiment.... Before you activate the light stick, the two solutions are kept in separate chambers. [A chemical solution and a dye fill] most of the plastic stick itself. [Another solution], called the activator, is contained in a small, fragile glass vial in the middle of the stick.

When you bend the plastic stick, the glass vial snaps open, and the two solutions flow together. The chemicals immediately react to one another, and the atoms begin emitting light. The particular dye used in the chemical solution gives the light a distinctive color.

---

staple: a regular part of something
emit: give off
substantial: large
housing: a container that holds something

essentially: basically
activate: make active
chambers: spaces
vial: container
distinctive: special

From: Harris, Tom. "How Light Sticks Work." *HowStuff Works.* (www.howstuffworks.com/light-stick.htm)

201

NOTEZONE
Underline the important ingredients of a light stick.
Circle the sequence of actions that lead to atoms giving off light.

FIND OUT MORE

SCIENCE SAURUS

Compounds	262
Chemical Reactions	269
Forms of Energy	300
Light	308
Electromagnetic Spectrum	309

SCI LINKS.
THE WORLD'S A CLICK AWAY

www.scilinks.org
Keyword: Chemical Energy
Code: GSPD24

Enrichment

Time: 40–45 minutes
Materials: 3 identical small light sticks, thermometer, 3 large beakers, ice water, room-temperature water, hot tap water, clock

Perform this activity as a demonstration, or have students work in groups of three and give them the following directions.

1. Fill one beaker with ice water, the second with room-temperature water, and the third with hot tap water.
2. Place one unactivated light stick into each beaker so as much of the stick is under water as possible.
3. Leave the light sticks in the water for 5 minutes. Measure and record the temperature of the water in the three beakers.
4. Activate all three light sticks at exactly the same time. Return each light stick to its own beaker.
5. Darken the room. Observe the light sticks. Record your observations.
6. Check the light sticks every 15 minutes and record your observations. Note the time at which each light stick stops glowing.

Have students identify which light stick glowed the brightest and which glowed the longest. (The one in warm water glowed brightest; the one in ice water glowed longest.) Ask: *What can you infer about how temperature affected the chemical reaction?* (Higher temperatures made the reaction go more quickly.)

▶ Read

Point out that a diagram of the light stick chambers is provided on page 202. Have students look at the diagram as needed to help them understand the reading.

Ask students to write down any questions they have as they read the passage. Have students share their questions in a class discussion. Interested students may want to visit the Web site from which this reading was taken. Point out the URL address at the bottom of the page, and encourage students to use the Web site to answer any questions they have about light sticks.

When students have finished the reading, help them compare light sticks and electric light bulbs. Write *Similarities* and *Differences* as headings on the board. Then prompt students to identify how the two lights are alike and different by asking questions such as: *Which give off light? Which give off heat? Which require electricity? Which are portable? Which have bulbs? Which can be turned off?* Help students see that each light source uses a very different method to produce light, and each type of light has its own distinct properties.

CHECK UNDERSTANDING
Skill: Organizing information
Ask: *What is the source of energy for a light stick?* (a chemical reaction) *Why doesn't the light stick glow until you bend it?* (The two chemicals that react have not mixed.)

More Resources

The following resources are also available from Great Source and NSTA.

ScienceSaurus

Reader's Handbook

SCILINKS.
THE WORLD'S A CLICK AWAY

www.scilinks.org
Keyword: Chemical Energy
Code: GSPD24

▶ **Explore**

STEP BY STEP Have students read the steps aloud. You may want to remind them that each chemical is made up of one kind of molecule. Molecules are made up of two or more atoms. When two chemicals react, some of the atoms in the molecules of one chemical break off and bond with the atoms in the molecules of the other chemical. The reaction produces two new molecules with properties that are different from the original molecules.

In the light stick, each time one molecule of Chemical A bumps into a molecule of Chemical B, the molecules react. Ask: *What new molecules are formed when Chemicals A and B react?* (molecules of Chemicals C and D) Then ask: *What happens to the molecules of Chemical D?* (Each Chemical D molecule breaks up into two parts—another molecule of Chemical C and a molecule of Chemical E.) *What happens to the molecules of Chemical E?* (The molecules give off energy and turn into carbon dioxide.)

Point out that drawing a picture or using a graphic organizer can help them keep track of complex reactions. When students have completed their graphic organizers, have them work in pairs to compare their organizers, or ask volunteers to share their organizers with the class. Point out that there may be more than one way to represent the chemical processes.

STEP BY STEP This diagram shows the parts of a light stick.

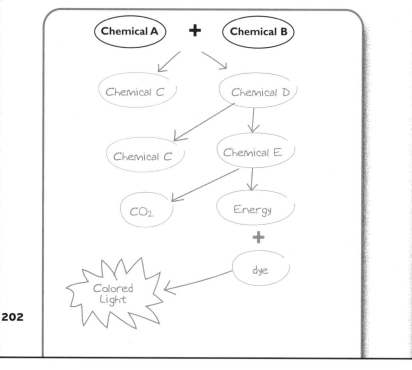

A chemical reaction causes the stick to glow. The reaction starts when you break the glass vial and ends when the light stick no longer glows. The chemical reactions that produce the light occur in four separate steps.

1. Chemical A reacts with Chemical B to form Chemical C and Chemical D.
2. Chemical C does not react with any of the other chemicals. Chemical D breaks down to form Chemical E and more of Chemical C.
3. Chemical E breaks down to form carbon dioxide (CO_2). When it does, it gives off energy.
4. The dye does not react with any of the other chemicals, but it glows when it absorbs energy.

▶ *Use this information to make a graphic organizer that shows the chemical reactions that produce colored light in a light stick.*

202

FIND EXAMPLES Light comes from lots of different sources. The light from common, everyday light bulbs is produced when a wire inside the bulb gets so hot that it glows. Light given off by hot objects is called incandescent light. All other light is called luminescent light.

The table below shows several different kinds of luminescent light. You will probably recognize the type of luminescent light that is often used in classrooms. You learned about another type of luminescent light in lesson 55. Complete the table by adding examples of each type of light. Do research to find examples of types of light you don't know about.

Type of Light		Description	Examples
Incandescent			
light given off by very hot objects		often given off when an object is heated by electricity	*Answers will vary. Examples: regular light bulbs; electric stove burners, toasters*
Luminescent			
light given off by objects that have not been heated	Chemiluminescence	given off by some chemical reactions	*Answers will vary. Examples: glow sticks*
	Bioluminescence	given off by a chemical reaction inside a living organism	*Answers will vary. Examples: glow worms; fireflies; dinoflagellates*
	Fluorescence	given off by some objects when they are hit by ultraviolet waves	*Answers will vary. Examples: fluorescent tubes; glo-paints*
	Phosphorescence	given off by some objects when they are hit by ultraviolet waves even after ultraviolet waves stop	*Answers will vary. Examples: glow-in-the-dark stickers*

203

Connections

WRITING Tell students that a song about a bioluminescent animal was one of the most popular songs of the twentieth century. Ask: *Do you know the song about the glow-worm?* (Some students may be familiar with the song.) If possible, play a recording of the song "The Glow-Worm" with words by Johnny Mercer and music by Paul Lincke. Point out that many songs and poems describe light sources such as candlelight, moonlight, sunlight, and firelight. Have students choose one example of light from the table on page 203 and write a short poem or song about it.

Assessment

Skill: Organizing information

Use the following questions to assess each student's progress:

What two forms of light are produced by chemical reactions? (chemiluminescence and bioluminescence) *What is the relationship between these two forms of light?* (Bioluminescence is simply chemiluminescence that takes place inside a living organism.)

Take Action

Time: will vary
Materials: research sources about different types of light

FIND EXAMPLES Before students begin their research, have them identify in the chart the type of light investigated in this lesson. (chemiluminescent light) Remind students that regardless of the process that produced the light, all visible light has the same basic properties.

Students may not realize that they are probably familiar with at least one example of each type of light. Encourage students to find everyday examples of each type.

Students might simply look back at Lesson 16 in Chapter 6 to review concepts about incandescent light. Point out that bioluminescence refers to chemiluminescence that occurs in living organisms. Remind students that Lesson 55 described an example of bioluminescence. To help students make more sense of the terms in the chart, also point out that fluorescence and phosphorescence refer to light given off by certain materials after being energized by ultraviolet light.

Provide a variety of resources for students to research different types of light. If time is short, you may want to divide the class into five groups, have each group research one type of light, then have groups share their results.

Point of Lesson

Chemicals can be combined to produce heat.

Focus

▶ Properties and changes of properties in matter
▶ Transfer of energy
▶ Science and technology in society
▶ Personal health
▶ Abilities necessary to do scientific inquiry
▶ Change, constancy, and measurement

Skills and Strategies

▶ Collecting and recording data
▶ Analyzing data
▶ Drawing conclusions
▶ Generating ideas

Advance Preparation

Vocabulary

Make sure students understand these terms. Definitions can be found in the glossary at the end of the student book.

▶ heat energy
▶ temperature

(continued on page 205)

Keeping Toes Warm

▲ Suiting up for a dive

When you wish you could take your campfire with you, try this instead.

Throughout human history, people have had to find ways to stay warm in cold places. Of course, some places are colder than others. Dr. Jose Torres teaches classes at the University of South Florida. He also does research that sometimes takes him to unusually cold places.

Dr. Torres studies ecosystems in Antarctica. His work involves being outdoors in extremely low temperatures and extremely high winds. As you can imagine, he wears several layers of clothes designed to trap his body heat. But body heat isn't enough. Fortunately, explorers like Dr. Torres can wear miniature heaters in their clothes.

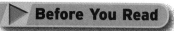 **Before You Read**

YOU'RE GETTING WARMER Few people actually travel to the poles and experience arctic weather, but most of us have been unpleasantly cold at one time or another. Your body needs to stay close to 37°C. When the surrounding air is much colder than that, your body's heat energy is rapidly lost to the cold air. To survive extreme cold, you need to be able to trap your body heat and keep the cold away from your skin.

▶ *Name some cold places you've been and how you stayed warm there.*

Answers will vary. Examples: It was cold when we were at the top of a mountain. We took jackets and hats and gloves, and tried to stay dry and out of the wind. Or: When we went camping in cold weather, we built a fire and kept it going every evening until we got into our sleeping bags.

204

TEACHING PLAN pp. 204–205

INTRODUCING THE LESSON

This lesson describes how Antarctic explorers stay warm using several layers of high-tech clothing and chemical toe warmers.

Students may think that toes are the only body part susceptible to frostbite. Explain that any part of the body can suffer frostbite but that toes are especially vulnerable because they may have poor blood circulation. Circulation to the toes is compromised by the fact that they are so far from the heart and are often restricted by tight boots.

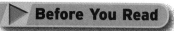 **Before You Read**

YOU'RE GETTING WARMER Provide class time for students to describe their experiences trying to stay warm in cold weather. Encourage students to discuss which types of clothes provide the most warmth. Ask: *What is the best way to trap body heat close to your skin?* (Examples: Down-filled jackets have lots of air between the feathers to trap the heat; wearing multiple layers of clothes helps trap heat close to the skin.) Then ask: *Where does the heat energy in the human body come from?*

(Students will probably know that it comes from metabolizing the food we eat.)

Here, Dr. Torres describes some of the preparations he goes through before diving under the ice in Antarctica.

Trying Not to Freeze

Our last cruise to the Antarctic took place from the 20th of July to the 1st of September, which is in the middle of the Antarctic winter. We routinely experienced temperatures between –25° and –30°C (–13° and –22°F)....

With this report I will give you a little more detail about what it is like to dive underneath Antarctic ice. Let me begin with the type of gear that we use. First, to protect us from the cold, we use a dry suit. A dry suit is basically a heavy rubber suit that has feet integrated into it, much like an old fashioned pair of long johns. It is sealed at the neck and cuffs with tight latex seals to prevent water from entering....

Under the suit we wear expedition-weight long underwear...as our first layer, then a very thick Polartec® fabric suit as our main barrier against the cold. ...On our feet we wear sock liners under a heavy pair of wool or wool/synthetic socks. On top of the socks go a pair of Polartec® booties.... Between the socks and the booties (and this is a trade secret) go a pair of chemical toe warmers that work just great. They are a little bag of what feels like tiny pebbles that heat up when exposed to air. They last for 8 hours or so. I personally think that they are a genius-level invention.

routinely: regularly
integrated: built-in
long johns: long underwear
latex: rubber

expedition-weight: extra heavy
booties: loose-fitting socks

From: Torres, Dr. Jose. "Diving Under Antarctic Ice!" The University of South Florida. (www.marine.usf.edu/bio/physiolab/current_projects/nbp0104-diving-article.html)

NOTEZONE

Underline the phrase that tells how the toe warmers work.

FIND OUT MORE

SCIENCESAURUS
Ecosystems 129
Chemical
 Reactions 269
Thermal Energy 301

SCiLINKS
THE WORLD'S A CLICK AWAY
www.scilinks.org
Keyword: Chemical
Energy
Code: GSPD24

(continued from page 204)

Materials
Gather the materials needed for *Read* (below), *Enrichment* (below), and *Activity, Part 1* (p. 206) and *Part 2* (p. 207).

Enrichment

Time: 10 minutes
Materials: chemical cold pack

Do this activity after students have examined the toe warmer pack in Read below. Pass around an unactivated chemical cold pack, and have students note its temperature. Then activate the pack and pass it around again. Ask students what change they noticed. (The pack is getting colder.) Explain that some chemical reactions absorb heat, leaving the mixture colder than it was before. These types of reactions are known as *endothermic* reactions. Tell students that chemical cold packs like this one are commonly used to treat sports injuries. They work by mixing together two chemicals that absorb heat when they react. Then ask: *How is the cold pack reaction different from the chemical toe warmer reaction?* (The toe warmer produces heat rather than absorbs it.) Tell students that chemical reactions that produce heat are known as *exothermic* reactions.

205

► **Read**

Time: 5 minutes
Materials: chemical toe warmer pack

Point out the chemical warmer in the diver's hand in the photograph on page 204.

You may want to demonstrate how a chemical toe warmer works. First show students the unactivated pack. Then activate it and pass it around for students to feel as it warms up. Ask: *How is this similar to the light stick you studied in the last lesson?* (Both release energy when activated but do not do anything until activated.) *How is it different?* (The light stick produces light with no heat, and the toe warmer produces heat with no light.)

After students complete the NoteZone task, ask them to hypothesize about what happens inside the toe warmer that causes it to heat up. (Students will probably suggest that some sort of chemical reaction is taking place.) Explain that when you take the warmer out of its cellophane packaging, chemicals inside react with oxygen in the air. This reaction produces new chemicals and heat.

CHECK UNDERSTANDING
Skill: Recognizing cause and effect
Tell students that extreme cold usually slows chemical reactions drastically. Ask students to explain how a toe warmer that depends on a chemical reaction could work effectively even in Antarctic temperatures of –25°C. (Some heat from the toes would help get the reaction started. As the reaction began to produce heat, the chemicals would heat up a little, and the reaction would occur more and more quickly.)

More Resources

The following resources are also available from Great Source and NSTA.

SCIENCESAURUS

READER'S HANDBOOK

www.scilinks.org
Keyword: Chemical Energy
Code: GSPD24

 **Activity**

MAKING TOE WARMERS

Can you make a toe warmer like the one Dr. Torres described?

Part 1: Finding the Right Reaction

What You Need:
- 6 small resealable plastic freezer bags
- iron powder
- salt
- antacid tablets
- powdered detergent
- safety goggles
- 6 thermometers
- measuring spoons
- water

What To Do:
1. Label the plastic bags with numbers 1–6. Put on your safety goggles.
2. Put one antacid tablet in bags 1 and 2. Put 2 teaspoons of powdered detergent in bags 3 and 4. Put 2 teaspoons of iron powder in bags 5 and 6.
3. Add $\frac{1}{8}$ teaspoon of salt to one of the antacid-tablet bags (bag 2), one of the detergent bags (bag 4), and one of the iron-powder bags (bag 6). Seal the bags without squeezing the air out, and shake to mix the contents.
4. Place a thermometer in each bag, making sure it reaches into the materials inside. Record the temperatures in the table.
5. Add 1 teaspoon of water to each of the six bags. Seal each bag without squeezing the air out, and shake it to mix the contents. Open a corner of each bag and reinsert the thermometer, making sure it reaches into the material inside.
6. Observe each bag every 5 minutes for 15 minutes. Record the temperatures.

Time (min)	Temperature (°C)					
	Bag 1 antacid tablet water	**Bag 2** antacid tablet salt water	**Bag 3** detergent water	**Bag 4** detergent salt water	**Bag 5** iron powder water	**Bag 6** iron powder salt water
Start						
5						
10						
15						

▶ *Which of the bags, if any, got warmer?*

the bag with iron powder, salt, and water

▶ *What materials would you use to make a chemical toe warmer?*

iron powder, salt, and water

206

TEACHING PLAN pp. 206–207

▶ **Activity**

PART 1: FINDING THE RIGHT REACTION

Time: 50 minutes
Materials: 6 small resealable plastic freezer bags, iron powder, salt, antacid tablets, powdered detergent, safety goggles, 6 thermometers, measuring spoons, water

▶ If you do not have enough thermometers to give each group six, assign only one or two bags to each group and have groups pool their results.
▶ Have students read the entire procedure before they begin measuring materials. Make sure they know to open the bags only slightly in step 5.
▶ Encourage students to predict which mixture(s) will get warmer when water is added. Later, have students compare their results with their predictions.
▶ Be sure all students recognize that the mixture of iron powder, salt, and water became warmer.
▶ Tell students that the iron combined with oxygen in the air to produce iron oxide. The reaction happens more quickly when the reactants are wet and even more quickly when there is salt present. (The salt acts as a catalyst.) Any time iron combines with oxygen to form iron oxide (also known as rust), heat is given off.
▶ Ask students to explain why chemical toe warmers cannot be reused. (Once all the iron has reacted with oxygen, the reaction stops.)

Part 2: Improving the Product

What You Need:
- 4 small resealable plastic freezer bags
- toe warmer materials from Part 1
- safety goggles
- sugar
- marbles
- vermiculite
- small piece of wood
- water
- 4 thermometers
- measuring spoons

What to Do:
1. Label the plastic bags with numbers 1–4. Put on your safety goggles. Then prepare four of your toe warmers from Part 1, but don't add the water yet.
2. Put 2 tablespoons of sugar in bag 1. Put 6 marbles in bag 2. Put 2 tablespoons of vermiculite in bag 3. Put the piece of wood in bag 4.
3. Seal each bag without squeezing the air out, and shake it to mix.
4. Measure the temperature in each bag as you did in Part 1.
5. Add 1 teaspoon of water to each of the four bags. Seal without squeezing the air out, and shake to mix. Open each bag and reinsert the thermometer, as in Part 1.
6. Observe each bag every 10 minutes for 30 minutes. Record the temperatures in the table.

Time (min)	Temperature (°C)			
	Bag 1 toe warmer materials sugar water	**Bag 2** toe warmer materials marbles water	**Bag 3** toe warmer materials vermiculite water	**Bag 4** toe warmer materials wood water
Start				
10				
20				
30				

▶ *Which of the bags stayed warm the longest?*

the bag with the vermiculite

▶ *What materials would you use to make an improved chemical toe warmer?*

iron powder, salt, water, and vermiculite

Use the following question to assess each student's progress:

How else might you improve your chemical toe warmer? (Possible answers: I could add more iron powder or more salt or just use a lot more of everything. I could wrap it in fleece or something to insulate it better. I could try squeezing it to make sure the salt, water, iron powder, and air mix more completely.)

▶ Activity

PART 2: IMPROVING THE PRODUCT

Time: 50 minutes

Materials: 4 small resealable plastic freezer bags, toe warmer materials from Part 1, safety goggles, sugar, marbles, vermiculite, small piece of wood, water, 4 thermometers, measuring spoons

▶ Make sure students understand that the "toe warmer materials from Part 1" are the ones that they used in bag 6. Have them follow the instructions on page 206 to prepare duplicates of bag 6 when they set up the four bags for this part of the activity.

▶ Broken craft sticks can be used as the small pieces of wood.

▶ Ask students to propose some possible reasons that the bag with the vermiculite stayed warm longest. (The vermiculite absorbed heat and held it instead of releasing it into the air. Two of the other materials were in larger chunks, so they could not mix as well to absorb heat before it was lost to the air outside the bag. The sugar simply dissolved.) Then ask students to propose other materials that might work nearly as well as the vermiculite did. (Examples: sawdust, rice)

▶ Students may want to know what vermiculite is. Tell them that vermiculite is a mineral similar to mica that contains water, magnesium, aluminum, and an iron silicate compound. The name vermiculite comes from the Latin word *vermiculare*, which means "to breed worms." When it is exposed to heat, vermiculite expands into worm-like shapes as water inside the vermiculite is converted to water vapor.

Materials Science

LESSON 58

Stronger Than a Speeding Bullet

Point of Lesson: *Creating new materials in the laboratory takes lots of persistence, and a little luck.*

The invention of the material used to make bullet-resistant vests provides a case study of how technological design is advanced by both careful planning and trial-and-error approaches. After reading an account of the invention of Kevlar, students identify which properties of this material make it useful for a variety of applications. They then compare the process used to invent Kevlar with the process Edison used to invent the light bulb.

Materials

Enrichment (p. 209), for the teacher:
► saucepan
► hot plate(s)
► thermometers
► Thermos bottles or similar insulated jugs
► funnel
► enough whole milk to provide 100 mL for each student or pair

for each student or pair:
► 10 mL vinegar
► small calibrated cup
► 250-mL beaker
► spoon
► running water
► paper towel
► safety goggles

Connections (p. 210), for the class:
► research sources about prosthetic devices and implants for the human body

Laboratory Safety

Review the following safety guidelines with students before they do the Enrichment activity in this lesson.
► Wear safety goggles while doing this activity.
► Do not taste any substance in the laboratory.

LESSON 59

Lighter, Stronger, Better

Point of Lesson: *Sometimes an existing material can be improved upon and used for a new purpose.*

A lively description of an inquisitive engineer tinkering with plastic bottles introduces this lesson. Students explore how the arrangement of molecules produces different properties in different kinds of plastic. Students explain what makes the soda pop bottle strong, on a structural level, then compare and contrast the properties of glass and plastic soda pop bottles. Finally, students brainstorm aspects of creativity and identify those that may be common to both artists and inventors.

Materials

Enrichment (p. 213), for the class:
► research sources about recycled plastics

Explore (p. 214), for each student or pair:
► string
► scissors
► masking tape

LESSON 60

Sticky Business

Point of Lesson: *The physical properties of a material determine how it interacts with other materials.*

Students explore the concepts of adhesion and cohesion in this lesson. They read an explanation of why tape is sticky, then test assorted adhesive products and compare the adhesive and cohesive properties of each.

Materials

Activity (p. 217), for each group:
► assorted adhesives (such as clear cellophane tape, masking tape, cloth adhesive tape, self-stick note)
► sheet of paper, cut into small squares
► small squares of cardboard

Background Information

Lesson 58

Kevlar is a type of synthetic polymer called an aramid. Before Stephanie Kwolek worked her magic in the laboratory, aramids were not very useful because unlike other synthetic polymers, they could not be broken down and made manageable by heat or solvents. Kwolek put together the right combination of chemicals that were finally able to break down the aramid so it could be spun into a fiber. This aramid became commerically available as Kevlar and was used to make such items as bullet-resistant vests and helmets. Stephanie Kwolek became known as the guardian angel of those who put themselves in harm's way in the course of their duties.

Lesson 60

The first adhesive tape was invented by an engineer named Richard Drew, who worked for the 3M company. Complaints from auto body painters who were having trouble applying two-tone finishes led Drew to experiment with recipes for sticky tapes. After many false starts and repeated field tests, a two-inch wide masking tape was introduced in 1925. Later, when a colleague was talking about using cellophane to package rolls of masking tape, Drew had the idea of making a see-through cellophane tape. The first roll of cellophane tape was delivered in late 1930. The product quickly became popular as customers found numerous uses for it.

Point of Lesson

Creating new materials in the laboratory takes lots of persistence, and a little luck.

Focus

▶ Properties and changes of properties in matter
▶ Abilities of technological design
▶ Science as a human endeavor
▶ Form and function

Skills and Strategies

▶ Generating ideas
▶ Classifying
▶ Understanding that scientists share their results to form a common core of knowledge

Advance Preparation

Vocabulary

Make sure students understand these terms. Definitions can be found in the glossary at the end of the student book.

▶ force
▶ molecule
▶ laboratory
▶ property

Materials

Gather the materials needed for *Enrichment* (p. 209) and *Connections* (p. 210).

TEACHING PLAN pp. 208–209

INTRODUCING THE LESSON

This lesson discusses the role of trial and error in the invention of the synthetic material called Kevlar.

Students may not realize how important luck and persistence are in scientific research. Ask: *What do you think makes a scientist successful?* Many students will realize that knowledge and intelligence are important factors, and some will realize that having adequate equipment is also key. Tell students that this lesson will describe some other essential qualities of a successful scientist.

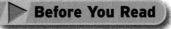

STRONGER THAN A SPEEDING BULLET

Which comes first, the invention or a use for it?

What do silk, wood, and nylon have in common? They are all polymers. A polymer is a substance whose molecules are made up of many smaller units strung together in long chains. Some polymers, like silk and wood, occur in nature. Others, like nylon, were invented in a laboratory.

Scientists and engineers use their understanding of chemistry to invent new materials. Sometimes they want to develop a material to fill a specific need. Other times they stumble upon a material and then find a use for it. Either way, the result is new materials that are useful to people.

▲Stephanie Kwolek in the lab

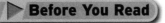

Before You Read

EFFORT OR LUCK? Was there ever a time when you were trying to do something that you found very difficult? Maybe you even wanted to quit. Did you quit? Or did you keep trying and finally succeed? Or, maybe there was a time when you understood something or did something right away because of sheer luck.

▶ *Think about learning to play an instrument, learning a sport, or perhaps looking for a lost object. Describe why the experience was or was not difficult for you, and whether your success was due to hard work or luck.*

Answers will vary. Example: When I first started to learn to play the

flute, I couldn't even make a noise come out of it. I wanted to quit, but

my mom wouldn't let me. Now I can play it. That was hard work.

One time I wanted to get a cat. I thought I would have to work hard to

convince my mom. Then a stray kitten wandered right into our house.

We tried to find his owner, but we couldn't. So my mom said we

should keep him. That was good luck.

208

Before You Read

EFFORT OR LUCK? Ask students to share their experiences. Have them determine whether the outcomes of their experiences were the result of effort or luck. Make a list on the board in two columns labeled *Effort* and *Luck*. Ask students to compare the experiences in the two columns. Then point out that many experiences are a combination of both effort and luck. You may also be able to identify other influences as well, such as help from other people, access to equipment, and creative thinking.

▶ Read

Stephanie Kwolek spent most of her time in the lab combining, heating, stirring, and spinning different substances to see what she could create.

Something New Under the Sun

Imagine this. It is 1964. You are a chemist working in a research laboratory of a major company. Your boss has asked you to find new synthetic polymers.... One day, you combine some substances and heat up your mixture carefully, just as you do every day. But this day, something strange happens. The mixture is cloudy instead of clear. When you stir it, it doesn't look the way you expect. Something clicks in your head, and you rush to find the person in charge of testing new polymers. He isn't at all sure he wants to test this strange glop, but, after talking to him for a long time, you convince him. You're just sure there is something unusual about the substance in your test tube. You are right.... You have just invented a brand new polymer that weighs very little but is strong and stiff beyond anyone's imagination. A few years later, your discovery is used to make bullet-resistant vests and helmets. Your name and picture are in advertisements and billboards as the woman who saved thousands of lives.

synthetic: man-made
polymer: substance whose molecules are made up of many smaller units strung together in long chains
substances: stuff, materials
bullet-resistant: difficult or impossible for bullets to go through

From: Howell, Caitlyn. "Kevlar, The Wonder Fiber." Smithsonian Institution. (www.si.edu/lemelson/centerpieces/ilives/lecture05.html)

Kevlar products ▶

Underline the physical properties of the polymer Stephanie Kwolek invented.

FIND OUT MORE

SCIENCE SAURUS
Properties of Matter   251

www.scilinks.org
Keyword: Physical Properties of Matter
Code: GSPD25

Enrichment

Time: 45 minutes
Materials: *for teacher:* saucepan, hot plate(s), Thermos bottles or similiar insulated jugs, funnel, enough whole milk to provide 100 mL for each student or pair
for each student or pair: 10 mL vinegar, small calibrated cup, 250-mL beaker, spoon, running water, paper towel, safety goggles

Advance Preparation: Before class, warm milk to about 50°C or until it is warm to the touch. Pour the milk into insulated containers to keep it warm.

Tell students that although most of today's plastics are made from petroleum products, the first plastics were made from plant and animal materials. Explain that in this activity, they will make plastic from common substances. Have students work individually or in pairs. Give them the following instructions:

▶ Measure 100 mL of warm milk in the beaker. Add 10 mL of vinegar and stir. With a spoon, remove the clumps that form and rinse them under running water.

▶ This material is plastic. Shape it into discs, rings, balls, cubes, or any shape you like. Place your plastic shapes on the paper towel to dry and harden. If you want, you can color the objects by adding food coloring before the plastic dries or painting them after the plastic hardens.

▶ Read

Ask: *What two things did Stephanie Kwolek do that day in the lab that another person might not have done and that led to her success?* (She recognized that the mixture's being cloudy instead of clear might mean something, and she insisted that the person in charge do tests on it even when he at first didn't want to.)

Explain that most plastics are synthetic polymers made from petroleum. Brainstorm with students to identify other items that are made of synthetic polymers. (Examples: plastics, laminated countertops, vinyl floors, carpets, compact discs, computer parts, foam, food containers, fabrics such as nylon and rayon)

Point out that most synthetic polymers were developed in the past 75 years or so. Challenge students to identify what materials might have been used for items such as toothbrushes, pens, sandwich wrappers, loose-leaf binders, or telephones before plastic was available. Discuss with students how plastics have affected their lives. Then ask them to describe what their lives would be like without plastics.

CHECK UNDERSTANDING
Skill: Communicating
Ask: *What physical properties made Kevlar such a unique and valuable material?* (It was lightweight, stiff, and strong.)

More Resources

The following resources are also available from Great Source and NSTA.

SCIENCESAURUS

Properties of Matter   251

READER'S HANDBOOK

Elements of Textbooks: Charts   157

www.scilinks.org
Keyword: Physical Properties of Matter
Code: GSPD25

Connections

Time: will vary
Materials: research sources about prosthetic devices and implants for the human body

HEALTH Tell students that scientists have learned to create synthetic materials that mimic different tissues in living things. Ask students if any of them have had a tooth crowned. (A crowned tooth may be the most familiar example of a synthetic replacement for human tissue.) Ask students to brainstorm a list of artificial organs or tissues they may have heard of that are used to repair the human body.

(continued on page 211)

TEACHING PLAN pp. 210–211

 **Explore**

FIND THE USE The polymer Stephanie Kwolek discovered was later named Kevlar. Inside the box are a number of products that are made from Kevlar. Below the box is a chart that lists some of the properties of Kevlar.

Think about which properties are important for each product. Write the products in the table next to the appropriate properties. (You may write a product in more than one box.)

Products Made from Kevlar	
• airplane body parts	• protective gloves
• automobile brake pads	• rope
• bicycle helmets	• skis
• bullet-resistant clothing	• tennis rackets
• kayaks	

Property of Kevlar	Products
Lightweight	*Possible answers: airplane body parts, bicycle helmets, bullet-resistant clothing, kayaks, rope, skis, tennis rackets*
Will stretch without breaking	*Possible answers: bicycle helmets, bullet-resistant clothing, rope, tennis rackets*
Resists bending	*Possible answers: kayaks, tennis rackets*
Does not change size or shape with change in temperature	*Possible answers: airplane body parts, automobile brake pads, skis*
Does not cut easily	*Possible answers: protective gloves, rope*
Very hard	*Possible answers: airplane body parts, bicycle helmets, kayaks, skis, tennis rackets*
Flame-resistant	*Possible answers: airplane body parts, automobile brake pads*

THINK ABOUT IT What other use can you imagine for Kevlar in your own life? Think of something you own or use that might work better if it were made of Kevlar. Which properties of Kevlar would be important?

Answers will vary. Example: I think it would be good to have a Kevlar umbrella. Our umbrellas rip but a Kevlar umbrella would not. It would be lightweight so your arm would not get tired. You could stretch it tight and it would not tear. You could make the cloth part and the handle out of Kevlar.

210

 **Explore**

FIND THE USE Before students begin to fill in the chart, briefly discuss the products listed in the box above it. Students will need to know, for example, that brake pads press against the wheels to slow a car and that this friction produces a large amount of heat. If students are unsure about which properties are desirable for each item, allow them to work in small groups. Encourage students to visit the official Web site for Kevlar at www.kevlar.com to learn more about its many practical uses.

THINK ABOUT IT If students need help coming up with ideas, suggest that they begin by listing any 10 or 12 items they use frequently. Then have them consider whether any of those items would be improved if they had Kevlar's properties. Have students share their ideas. You may want the class to vote on the most original or creative idea for the use of Kevlar.

GETTING IT RIGHT Sometimes Stephanie Kwolek experimented with polymers that she or other members of her team had already invented. Other times, she would mix together different substances even though she wasn't entirely sure what the result would be. It was this second, trial-and-error method that produced Kevlar.

► *What are the advantages of each method?*

Answers will vary. Example: The advantage of the first method is that

you are working with something you already know about. Improving

something that already exists is probably easier than inventing

something brand new. The advantage of the second method is that you

might come up with something that you had never even dreamed of —

like Kevlar.

The first light bulb that Thomas Edison invented burned out very quickly. The problem was the filament—the glowing wire inside the bulb. Edison and his team of scientists tested more than 6,000 materials before they found one that made a good filament.

► *How was the method used by Edison's team similar to the one used by Kwolek's team?*

Both involved lots of trial and error before the usable discovery was

made.

Thomas Edison once said, "Genius is one percent inspiration, 99 percent perspiration."

► *Look up any words you do not know the meaning of. Then describe what you think Edison meant by this statement.*

Edison meant that doing something great takes a good idea, but it also

takes lots and lots of hard work.

► *Would you say Kwolek's work was more perspiration or inspiration? Explain your reasoning.*

Answers will vary. Example: I think it was inspiration because she could

have just ignored the cloudy stuff she found. Or: I think it was more

perspiration because it took a long time and lots of experimenting, and

she had to convince the other person to do the testing.

211

(continued from page 210)

List their answers on the board. (The list may include pins or screws, pacemakers, dentures, artificial joints, artificial limbs, and even artificial hearts and lungs.) For each organ or tissue on the list, ask students what properties would be required in a synthetic replacement—hard or soft, stiff or flexible, and so forth. Point out that when scientists try to create replacement materials for the body, they look for properties that closely match those of the tissue they are replacing. Encourage interested students to research the technology currently used in one type of prosthetic device or implant.

Assessment
Skill: Communicating

Use the following task to assess each student's progress.

Have students choose one Kevlar product from the table on page 210 and explain how the material is well-suited to the product. (Answers should reflect an understanding of the relationship between Kevlar's form and the function of the product.)

GETTING IT RIGHT Ask students if they have ever attempted to do something by trial and error. Encourage them to give examples.

Have students try the trial-and-error method in a game of 20 questions. Pick an object that will be relatively difficult for students to guess, and have them ask questions to narrow down the possibilities. Students will find that logical thinking limits the possibilities, but inspired guessing plays an important role as well. If time allows, play more than one round, and analyze the type(s) of questions that were most effective.

Ask students: *Do you think trial and error is a good way of getting something accomplished?* (Examples: No; if you don't succeed, then trial and error can be a waste of time. Yes; trial and error can send you in a direction you had not considered, and this direction might turn out to be the right one.)

Point of Lesson

Sometimes an existing material can be improved upon and used for a new purpose.

Focus

- ▶ **Science as a human endeavor**
- ▶ **Understanding about science and technology**
- ▶ **Properties and changes of properties in matter**
- ▶ **Form and function**

Skills and Strategies

- ▶ **Comparing and contrasting**
- ▶ **Drawing conclusions**
- ▶ **Interpreting scientific illustrations**

Advance Preparation

Vocabulary

Make sure students understand these terms. Definitions can be found in the glossary at the end of the student book.

- ▶ **molecule**
- ▶ **plastics**
- ▶ **property**

Materials

Gather the materials needed for *Enrichment* (p. 213) and *Explore* (p. 214).

Lighter, Stronger, Better

Even the most ordinary objects have to come from somewhere.

In the early 1960s, people paid a deposit (a small amount of money) when they bought a bottle of soda pop. They got the deposit back when they returned the bottle. But the bottle was glass, not plastic. "Recycling" meant washing the bottle thoroughly, filling it with more soda pop, and putting it back in the stores.

The plastic soda pop bottle was developed by a man named Nathaniel Wyeth. Nat's father, brother, and sisters were all famous artists. But Nat followed in his uncle's footsteps and became an engineer. He worked for a chemical company called DuPont. DuPont employs engineers and scientists to invent new materials that might be used in new products.

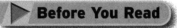

GLASS OR PLASTIC? Think about different drinks and other foods that are sold in glass or plastic jars or bottles. For instance, plastic soda pop bottles are common now, but you can sometimes find glass bottles, too. Apple juice is often sold in plastic bottles but apple sauce is usually sold in glass jars. Which do you prefer? Why? Do you prefer glass for some products and plastic for others? Write some of your thoughts about plastic and glass containers.

Answers will vary.

_____

_____

_____

_____

_____

_____

_____

212

TEACHING PLAN pp. 212–213

INTRODUCING THE LESSON

This lesson relates the story of how one inventor took an existing product— plastic—and improved on it.

Students may not be aware that soda bottles, as well as other everyday objects, were not always made of plastic. Before the 1970s, there was no plastic suitable for soda pop bottles. At that time, all soda pop came in glass bottles or cans. Students also may not know that there are many different kinds of plastics. Some are stiff, some are flexible, some are clear, some are opaque, and so on. Each plastic is suited to a particular task.

▶ Before You Read

GLASS OR PLASTIC? Ask students to think about the kinds of bottles they have in their cupboards at home. Have them describe the materials that are packaged in plastic bottles and those that are packed in glass bottles. Ask: *Can you see any pattern to whether a product comes in a glass bottle or jar or a plastic bottle or jar?* (Students may note that items that are often handled by children or items that are very heavy are more often bottled in plastic.) If students have difficulty remembering, encourage them to look at food containers at home.

▶ Read

In order to make a plastic bottle that could hold soda pop, Wyeth first had to improve plastic.

This Would Be Even Better If...

After wondering out loud at work why plastic was not used for carbonated beverage bottles, Wyeth was told that they would explode. He promptly went to a store, bought a plastic bottle of detergent, returned home, replaced the detergent with ginger ale, sealed the bottle, and put it in the refrigerator. The next morning, the bottle had swollen up so much that it was wedged solidly between the refrigerator shelves.

...Wyeth knew that stretching out nylon thread strengthened it by forcing its molecules to align. The challenge he faced was stretching plastic so that its molecules would align in two dimensions, rather than just one. He managed this by creating a "preform" mold...with screw threads running...in a diamond criss-cross pattern. When the plastic was pressed...through this mold, the molecules aligned in the...fashion Wyeth intended. [Then he replaced] the polypropylene material he had been using with polyethylene-terephthalate ("PET"), which has superior elastic properties. The final product was light, clear, resilient, and safe: a complete success.

carbonated: made fizzy by the addition of carbon dioxide

wedged: jammed; stuck

align: line up

dimensions: directions

polypropylene: a type of plastic

polyethylene-terephthalate: another kind of plastic

elastic: returns to its original shape

resilient: easily returned to its original shape after stretching or bending

From: Dorchak, Joshua. "Inventor of the Week: Nathaniel Wyeth." *Invention Dimension (MIT).* (web.mit.edu/invent/www/inventorsR-Z/wyeth.html)

NOTEZONE

Underline the names of the two types of plastic Wyeth worked with.

Circle the syllables they have in common.

FIND OUT MORE

SCIENCESAURUS

Properties of
Matter   251
Nonrenewable
Material
Resources   331
Conservation of
Material
Resources   336

SCLINKS
THE WORLD'S A CLICK AWAY

www.scilinks.org
Keyword: Physical
Properties of Matter
Code: GSPD25

213

Enrichment

Time: will vary

Materials: research sources about recycled plastics

Review with students what is meant by the slogan "reduce, reuse, recycle." (The slogan encourages people to reduce the amount of packaging they buy, reuse the packaging when they can, and recycle the packaging if they have no other use for it.)

Have students list plastic products that can be recycled. (Examples: plastic bags, milk jugs, foam cups, packing material, soda bottles) Encourage students to find out what products are made from recycled plastics. Finally, have students choose one of the recycled items and name ways the product could be reused before being recycled.

▶ Read

Explain that the detergent bottle expanded when Wyeth put ginger ale in it because the gas that bubbled out of the soda exerted pressure on the plastic. (Since the detergent was not carbonated, it did not put that kind of pressure on the bottle.)

To help students understand the terms *polyethylene-terephthalate* and *polypropylene,* write the terms on the board and underline the prefix *poly-* in each word. Ask students to use a dictionary to find the prefix's meaning. (more than one, many) Tell students

that these two plastic materials are made up of long chains of many molecules. Point out that the word *polymer* itself has the same prefix.

Next, underline the suffix *-ene* in each word. Explain that this suffix indicates that the long chains contain carbon atoms bonded to each other. Tell students that each polymer name describes the arrangement and combinations of atoms in the molecules that make up the polymer. This information tells scientists about the polymer's specific properties. Ask: *What property was Wyeth hoping his new plastic would have?* (resistance to stretching)

CHECK UNDERSTANDING

Skill: Designing an experiment to test a hypothesis

Ask: *How could Wyeth test his new type of plastic to see whether he had succeeded?* (He could make a bottle from it, put soda pop in the bottle, close it up, then wait to see if it stretched out of shape. If it didn't expand like the detergent bottle, it was a success.)

More Resources

The following resources are also available from Great Source.

ScienceSaurus

Properties of Matter   251

Reader's Handbook

Connections

SOCIAL STUDIES Refer students back to Lesson 36, page 131. Point out that Polartec® fabric is made in part from recycled PET plastic. Have students contact their local recycling center and report on the recycling opportunities in the community. Ask students to find out what happens to plastic products after they are picked up from the recycling bin. Have students display their findings in a flow chart. Suggest that the flow chart show the life of a plastic item beginning on a store shelf (or earlier), then going to someone's home, to a recycling center, to a manufacturing plant as raw material, and finally as a new product.

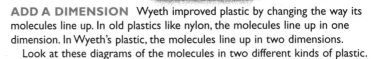

> **Explore**

ADD A DIMENSION Wyeth improved plastic by changing the way its molecules line up. In old plastics like nylon, the molecules line up in one dimension. In Wyeth's plastic, the molecules line up in two dimensions.
    Look at these diagrams of the molecules in two different kinds of plastic.

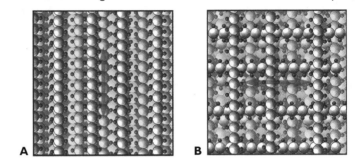

A   B

▶ *Which diagram shows the molecules aligned in two dimensions?*

B (the one on the right)

When long molecules of plastic are lined up side by side, the plastic is strong in the direction of those molecules.

▶ *On diagram A, draw arrows to show which way the material could be pulled without being stretched out of shape. Explain how you know.*

(Vertical arrows) It is strong in the up-and-down direction because the

molecules go up and down.

▶ *On diagram B, draw arrows to show which way the material could be pulled without being stretched out of shape. Explain how you know.*

(Vertical and horizontal arrows) It is strong up and down and sideways

because the molecules are lined up both ways.

Early plastic bottles would burst if they were filled with carbonated liquid. Wyeth's plastic bottles do not.

▶ *Using the diagrams, explain why this might be.*

The molecules in Wyeth's bottles are lined up in both directions, so the

plastic is strong in both directions. The other kind of plastic was only

strong in one direction so it could still be stretched out of shape.

214

Teaching Plan pp. 214–215

 **Explore**

Time: 15 minutes
Materials: string, scissors, masking tape

ADD A DIMENSION Make sure students understand the difference between one dimension (aligned in one direction) and two dimensions (aligned in two directions).

To help students visualize the strength of two dimensions compared with one dimension, have them construct the following two models:

1. Cut several lengths of string, lay them side-by-side on a desk and tape the ends down.
2. Cut several more lengths of string, and tape them side-by-side on the desk as before. Now cut the same number of lengths again and weave them across the other lengths to form a two-dimensional model. Tape these lengths to the desk as well.

Have students poke and pluck the strings to see how they stretch. (Students should find that the strings laid in only one direction are easily stretched, while the strings laid in two

directions do not move much.)

Students who want to find out more about polymer plastics can visit www.psrc.usm.edu/macrog/index.htm. Have students share their findings.

▶ Propose Explanations

The table compares some of the properties of glass and PET soda pop bottles.

Property	Glass Soda Pop Bottles	PET Soda Pop Bottles
Weight	Heavier to transport to store, and from store to home	Only 6% of the weight of a glass bottle
Clarity	Thick glass made it hard to see the contents	Very thin and clear, easy to see contents
Breakability	Could shatter into sharp pieces when dropped, causing cuts	Shatterproof
Scratch	Scratch when bottles rub up against one another	Not easily scratched by other PET plastic

▶ *Which property might be most important to people who buy one bottle at a time from a vending machine? Explain.*

Answers will vary. Example: breakability, because it is easy to drop a bottle that is carried while walking around

▶ *Which property do you think is most important to people who buy soda pop at the grocery store? Explain.*

Answers will vary. Example: weight, because heavy bottles are hard to carry home

▶ Take Action

A CREATIVE FAMILY Nathaniel Wyeth's father, N.C. Wyeth, was a famous painter and illustrator. His brother Andrew was probably the most famous American artist of the 20th century. His sisters Henriette and Caroline were also painters, and Ann was a composer.

Think of the skills and personality traits that would make someone a good inventor. How are they similar to the skills and traits that would make someone a good artist? How are they different? List your ideas in the Venn diagram below.

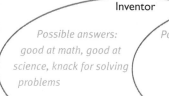

Inventor — Artist

Possible answers: good at math, good at science, knack for solving problems

Possible answers: creative, imaginative, dedicated

Possible answers: good at drawing, expressive, good at coming up with completely new ideas

215

Assessment

Skill: Comparing and contrasting

Use the following question to assess each student's progress.

What made Wyeth's plastic bottles more suitable for carbonated beverages than existing plastics? (They had molecules aligned in two dimensions and so could be pulled in two directions without stretching. This meant they would not be stretched by expanding gas bubbles.)

▶ Propose Explanations

As students examine the table, ask them to describe whether the properties described are advantages or disadvantages. Students should notice that advantages were listed only for PET plastic, while disadvantages were listed only for glass. Ask students whether they can think of any advantages glass has over plastic. (Examples: Glass can be washed and reused. The lids can be sealed tightly. Some people think glass is prettier. Others have health concerns about the possibility of chemicals from plastics contaminating foods and drinks.) Encourage students to see that consumer concerns influence how a food will be packaged.

▶ Take Action

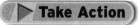

A CREATIVE FAMILY This question does not have absolute answers. Each scientist and each artist has different traits, but creative minds often share some similar traits. Encourage students to share the traits they wrote in their Venn diagrams. Students may disagree about what traits are important for each career. Encourage students to discuss their ideas thoughtfully, to support them with facts or examples, and to listen to each other respectfully.

UNIT 5 Interactions of Matter

Point of Lesson
The physical properties of a material determine how it interacts with other materials.

Focus
► Abilities necessary to do scientific inquiry
► Properties and changes of properties in matter
► Motion and forces
► Form and function

Skills and Strategies
► Collecting and recording data
► Analyzing data
► Drawing conclusions

Advance Preparation

Vocabulary
Make sure students understand these terms. Definitions can be found in the glossary at the end of the student book.

► force
► molecule

Materials
Gather the materials needed for *Activity* (p. 217).

Materials Science

Sticky Business

Why does adhesive tape stick to things?

From the beginning of civilization, people have used adhesives. The ancient Egyptians made paste from flour and water. Other peoples used tree sap or beeswax to stick things together. Most of the products you use today are inventions from the 1900s. That's when scientists began to focus on improving adhesives in the laboratory.

NOTE ZONE

Underline the name of the force that makes things stick to themselves.

Circle the name of the force that makes things stick to something else.

FIND OUT MORE

SCIENCE SAURUS
Properties of Matter 251

SciLINKS
THE WORLD'S A CLICK AWAY
www.scilinks.org
Keyword: Physical Properties of Matter
Code: GSPD25

► **Read**

Benjamin E. Russ from the University of California at San Diego talks about why tape sticks to itself and other things.

I'M STUCK ON YOU

…There are two fundamentally different components of tape's sticky nature; adhesion and cohesion. Adhesion is the binding force between two different materials, whereas cohesion is the binding force between two similar materials. When two materials are brought into contact with each other, the surface molecules interact…. When the molecules are similar, as in the case of two "glue molecules," the cohesive force causes the glue to stick to itself. When the molecules are dissimilar, as in the case of a glue molecule and a molecule of the substrate (the surface the glue is sticking to), the adhesive force holds the glue to the substrate. Hence, the "stickiness" of tape is caused by a combination of the molecular forces of the glue material sticking to itself as well as holding onto the substrate.

fundamentally: basically
components: parts
interact: have an effect on each other
dissimilar: not alike

From: Russ, Benjamin E. "Ask the Experts." *Scientific American.com* (www.sciam.com/askexpert_question.cfm?articleID=000E47BD-6690-1C71-9EB7809EC588F2D7&catID=3)

216

UNIT 5: INTERACTIONS OF MATTER

TEACHING PLAN pp. 216–217

INTRODUCING THE LESSON
This lesson introduces the concepts of adhesion and cohesion.

Ask students to brainstorm all the substances they can think of that could be used to stick things together. Write their suggestions on the board. The list may include materials such as honey, sugar water, frosting, wet snow, pine sap, candle wax, wet clay, and Silly Putty®. Point out that these items have at least one property in common that makes them good adhesives. Challenge student to identify that property. (They are all somewhat gooey.)

► **Read**

Remind students that molecules interact when they are close to each other. Ask: *Why do you think adhesive tape sticks better when you press on it?* (When you press on the tape, you push the molecules of the sticky material closer to the molecules of the other material.) Then ask: *Why do you think sticky materials are a little liquid-like, or gooey?* (The molecules of a liquid can ooze between the fibers of the other material, so the molecules can get closer. When they are closer, the force of attraction is stronger.)

► **Activity**

Time: 30 minutes
Materials: (for each group) assorted adhesives (such as clear cellophane tape, masking tape, cloth adhesive tape, self-stick note); sheet of paper, cut into small squares; small squares of cardboard

► Make sure students understand the difference between the terms *adhesion* and *cohesion* before they begin the activity. Ask: *If I stick a piece of tape on the wall, what property does that demonstrate?* (adhesion) *If I stick two pieces of tape together,*

▶ Activity

LET'S STICK TOGETHER

There's an adhesive for every need.

What You Need:
- assorted adhesives (clear cellophane tape, masking tape, cloth adhesive tape, self-stick note, etc.)
- sheet of paper, cut into small squares
- small squares of cardboard

What to Do:
1. Test the cohesion of each adhesive. Fold the sticky side back on itself, being sure to leave the two ends unstuck. Press the halves together, then try to pull them apart. Decide whether the cohesion is poor, good, very good, or excellent. Record your observations in the chart below.
2. Test the adhesion of each adhesive. Stick it to the paper, the cardboard, and a desktop. Press it down, then try to pull it off. Record your observations in the chart.

Adhesive	Cohesion	Adhesion
cellophane tape	very good	good
masking tape	very good	good
cloth adhesive tape	very good	excellent
self-stick note	poor	poor

WHAT DO YOU SEE?

▶ *Which adhesive(s) showed the greatest cohesion?*

Answers will vary. Example: masking tape

▶ *Which adhesive(s) showed the greatest adhesion to the paper? to the cardboard? to the desk?*

Answers will vary. Example: adhesive tape; adhesive tape; masking tape

▶ Propose Explanations

APPLY KNOWLEDGE

▶ *How do the adhesive properties of self-stick notes make them well-suited to their job?*

They stick to paper, but can be easily removed.

217

More Resources

The following resources are also available from Great Source and NSTA.

ScienceSaurus

Properties of Matter 251

www.scilinks.org
Keyword: Physical Properties of Matter
Code: GSPD25

Assessment

Skill: Classifying

Use the following task to assess each student's progress:

Have students identify each of the situations as an example of cohesion or adhesion:

▶ chocolate fingerprints sticking to the wall (adhesion)
▶ a big ball of clay used to pick up little bits of clay (cohesion)
▶ wet snow used to build a snowman (cohesion)

---

what property does that demonstrate? (cohesion)
▶ Have students work in small groups.
▶ Be careful about which tapes students put onto which surfaces. Tape can peel paint off walls, for example.

▶ Propose Explanations

APPLY KNOWLEDGE Point out that self-stick notes show poor cohesion and adhesion. Ask: *How could you reduce the cohesion and adhesion of a piece of cellophane tape?* (Students might suggest sticking the tape on fuzzy fabric a few times.) *Why would this action reduce the cohesion and adhesion of the tape?* (It would put nonstick materials—clothing fibers—between the tape and the other material.)

CHECK UNDERSTANDING
Skill: Concept mapping
Have students make a concept map showing what makes tape sticky. (A sample concept map is shown below.)

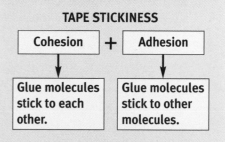

Glossary of Scientific Terms

A

acceleration: change in an object's speed or direction (its velocity) over time

acid: any compound that produces hydrogen ions (H^+) in water, and reduces its pH to below 7

adhesion: the force of attraction between molecules of two different substances

alternating current (AC): flow of electricity through a conductor, in which electric charges change direction many times per second

amplitude: total distance a wave moves (oscillates) from its resting position

atmosphere: layers of air surrounding Earth

atom: smallest particle into which an element can be divided and still have the properties of that element

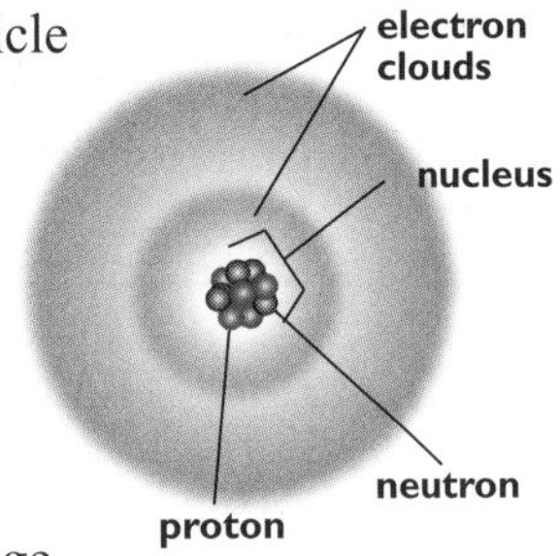

electron clouds
nucleus
neutron
proton

atomic mass: average mass of one atom of an element

atomic number: number of protons in the nucleus of one atom of an element

aurora: display of light in sky, usually at high latitudes; formed where particles from the sun enter Earth's atmosphere and magnetic field

B

bacteria: one-celled organism that lacks a true nucleus; sometimes causes disease

balanced forces: occur when the total of all forces on an object equals zero and the object's motion does not change

base: any compound that produces hydroxide ions (OH^-) in water and raises its pH to above 7

battery: a device that converts chemical energy into electrical energy

binary code: code used by computers that represents all data with strings of 0s and 1s

boiling point: temperature at which a substance changes from a liquid state to a gaseous (vapor) state

bond: a force of attraction that holds atoms, ions, or molecules together; also called **chemical bond**

C

catalyst: substance that helps start or speed up a reaction between two other substances, without being changed by the reaction

cell: basic unit of structure and function in living things

charge: *See electric charge*

chemical: any element or compound

chemical bond: *See bond*

chemical change: occurs when one or more substances are changed into new substances with different properties; cannot be undone by physical means

chemical reaction: change that takes place when two or more substances (reactants) interact to form new substances (products)

chemistry: the study of the structure, properties, and interactions of matter

circuit: path that electric current flows through; a closed circuit has no breaks; an open circuit has a break and current cannot flow through it

cohesion: the force of attraction between molecules of the same substance

colloid: a mixture containing tiny particles of one substance scattered evenly throughout another

color: light of various wavelengths; the eyes see each wavelength of light as a different color

compound: matter made of two or more elements; the elements in a compound are chemically bonded and cannot be separated by physical means; a compound has properties that are different from the elements that make it up

compound machine: a machine made of two or more simple machines that work together

concave: curved in

conductor: substance that conducts heat readily; also a substance that allows an electric current to pass through it

convex: curved out

crystal: a solid made up of molecules arranged in a regular, repeating pattern

current: *See electric current*

D

data: collected information, the results of an experiment or other investigation

direct current (DC): flow of electricity through a conductor, in which electric charges move in only one direction

E

electric charge: a property of the particles in an atom; may be positive (protons), negative (electrons), or neutral (neutrons)

electric current: the amount of electric charge that moves past a certain point each second; measured in amperes (A)

electrical energy: form of energy that consists of the flow of electric charges through a conductor

electricity: general term for interaction of electric charges

electromagnet: magnet made by passing an electric current through a wire wrapped around an iron rod

electromagnetic spectrum: full range of electromagnetic waves

Radio waves	Micro-waves	Infrared waves	Visible light	Ultraviolet light	X rays	Gamma rays

Low Frequency   High Frequency

Long Wavelength   Short Wavelength

Electromagnetic Spectrum

electromagnetic wave: form of energy that can travel through empty space as well as through matter; includes visible light, radio waves, X rays, and many other wavelengths

electron: negatively charged particle found outside the nucleus of an atom

electron cloud: in the electron cloud model of the atom, region around the nucleus where an electron may be found

electronics: relating to devices that work by controlling the movement of electrons

elements: substances that are the building blocks of all matter; an element is made up of one kind of atom

energy: ability to do work

energy levels: in an atom, specific areas at definite distances around the nucleus; each energy level can hold a specific number of electrons

engineer: a person who uses knowledge of science to design machines, systems, or products

environment: surroundings and conditions in which an organism lives

enzyme: a protein in the body that helps control a chemical reaction, such as digestion

experiment: series of steps that, under controlled conditions, produces data that test a hypothesis or prediction

exponent: the number above and to the right of a base number that tells how many times to multiply the base number by itself

F

focus: to adjust lenses so that an image is clear and sharp

force: a push or a pull

freezing point: temperature at which a substance changes from a liquid state to a solid state; same as **melting point** for that substance

frequency: the number of wave vibrations (oscillations) produced in one second; measured in hertz (Hz)

friction: force that resists the motion of two surfaces that are touching each other

G

gamma ray: a type of high-frequency electromagnetic wave

gas: matter that has no definite volume or shape; for example, air

gear: a wheel with teeth, sometimes considered a simple machine

gene: segment of DNA, found on a chromosome, that determines the inheritance of a particular trait

gravitational potential energy: energy stored in an object due to its height above ground

gravity: force of attraction between any two objects

H

habitat: the place in an ecosystem where an organism lives

heat: transfer of thermal energy between substances that are at different temperatures; sometimes used to mean thermal energy

heat energy: total kinetic energy contained in all the particles of a substance; also called thermal energy

hertz (Hz): measurement of wave frequency equal to vibrations per second

humidity: amount of water vapor in the air

hypothesis: an idea that can be tested by experiment or observation

I

incandescent: producing light as a result of being hot

inclined plane: simple machine that consists of a flat, sloping surface (ramp); *See also screw and wedge*

infrared: a type of electromagnetic wave with a frequency just less than the frequency of red light

insulator: a material that does not transfer heat energy easily; also a substance that does not allow electric current to pass through it

ion: atom or molecule that has an overall electric charge due to loss or gain of electrons

K

kinetic energy: the energy an object has because it is moving

L

laboratory: a workroom with equipment for scientific research

lens: curved, transparent piece of glass or plastic that bends light rays to form an image

lever: simple machine made of a long rigid bar that rests on and turns around a support called a fulcrum

light: a type of energy that humans can see; part of the electromagnetic spectrum

liquid: matter that has a definite volume but not a definite shape; for example, water

luminescent: producing light without getting hot

M

magnet: object that attracts iron

magnetic field: region of magnetic force around a magnet

magnetic force: the attractive or repulsive force that acts between magnetic materials; strongest at the poles of magnets

magnetic pole: one of two ends of a magnet, called north and south, that produce opposing forces

mass: amount of matter in something; measured in grams (g)

matter: the material that all objects and substances are made of; anything that has mass and takes up space

mechanical wave: energy that travels through matter; examples include sound, ocean waves, and earthquake waves

melting point: temperature at which a substance changes from a solid state to a liquid state; same as **freezing point** for that substance

metallic bond: bond that holds metal atoms together; positive metal ions are surrounded by a sea of shared electrons

metals: elements, usually solid, with a shiny surface; metals conduct electricity and heat energy well; examples include gold, iron, lead, copper, and silver

mixture: a combination of two or more substances that have not combined chemically and that can be separated by physical means

model: a simplified version of some part of the natural world that helps explain how it functions

molecule: smallest particle of a substance that still has the properties of that substance

motor: a machine that uses electricity to produce movement

N

negative charge: *See electric charge*

neutron: in an atom, particle with a neutral charge; located in the nucleus

Newton's First Law of Motion: An object at rest will stay at rest unless acted on by an unbalanced force. An object in motion will stay in motion at the same speed and in the same direction unless acted on by an unbalanced force.

Newton's Second Law of Motion: The acceleration of an object by a force is inversely proportional to the mass of the object and directly proportional to the force.

Newton's Third Law of Motion: For every action, there is an equal but opposite reaction.

nucleus: the center of an atom, made up of protons and neutrons

O

optics: the study of light and vision

organ: in an organism, structure made of two or more different tissues that has a specialized function; for example, the lungs

organic chemistry: the study of compounds that contain the element carbon

organism: a living thing

P

patent: a government document giving a person the sole right to make, use, and sell their invention for a set period of time

periodic table of elements: a chart where all elements are organized into periods and groups according to their properties

physics: the study of energy, forces, and motion

pitch: how high or low a sound is; determined by the sound's frequency

plastics: chemical compounds that can be easily shaped into many different products; often made from refined petroleum

pole: *See magnetic pole*

pollution: any change in the environment that is harmful to organisms

polymer: a substance whose molecules are made up of many smaller, identical molecules

positive charge: *See electric charge*

potential energy: stored energy an object has because of its position or shape

power: the amount of work done or energy used in a unit of time

prediction: a guess about what will happen under certain conditions, that is based on observation and research

pressure: amount of force exerted on a given area by an object or substance; SI unit is the pascal (Pa)

property: characteristic of a material that helps to identify or classify matter

proteins: organic compounds that make up living things and are essential for life

proton: positively charged particle located in the nucleus of an atom

pulley: simple machine consisting of one or more wheels with a rope wrapped around them

R

reaction: *See chemical reaction*

receiver: a device that converts electro-magnetic or electric signals to sound or light

reflection: bouncing back of a wave from a surface

resistance: measure of how much a material opposes the flow of electric current through it

robot: a machine that can carry out a variety of tasks automatically

S

scientific notation: a way of writing extremely large or extremely small numbers; uses a number between 1–10 multiplied by a power of 10, such as 9.8×10^6

screw: a simple machine consisting of an inclined plane wrapped around a cylinder

simple machine: a device that makes work easier by changing the size or direction of the force applied to it

solar energy: energy from the sun in the form of heat and light

solid: matter that has a definite shape and volume; for example, a rock

solute: *See solution*

solution: mixture in which the molecules of one substance, known as the **solute**, are dissolved in another substance, known as the **solvent**; the solute is present in a smaller quantity than the solvent

solvent: *See solution*

sound: energy that travels through matter as mechanical waves, and can be heard by the ear

specific heat: thermal energy needed to change the temperature of 1 gram of a substance by 1°C

speed: distance traveled by an object in a given amount of time

states of matter: the forms matter can take, as in liquid, solid, or gas; also called phases of matter

static electricity: electricity in which electric charges build up on an object; the movement of the charge off the object is called electric discharge or static discharge

suspension: mixture in which particles of a solid are spread throughout a liquid, and the particles are large enough to settle out

T

technology: the use of scientific knowledge and processes to solve practical problems

temperature: measure of the average kinetic energy of the particles in a substance; measured in degrees Celsius (°C) or degrees Fahrenheit (°F)

theory: an idea that is the best explanation of many observations and helps make new predictions

thermal energy: *See heat energy*

tissue: in plants and animals, a group of cells that work together and do a specific job

transformer: device used to change the voltage of an alternating current

transmitter: a device that sends out signals, usually electrical or radio wave

U

ultrasound: any sound wave whose frequency is too high to be heard by humans

ultraviolet light (UV): a part of the electromagnetic spectrum that is invisible to humans; also called ultraviolet radiation and ultraviolet rays

unbalanced force: occurs when the net force on an object does not equal zero; results in the object changing its motion

V

vacuum: a complete absence of matter

velocity: an object's speed and direction at a given instant

vibration: a rapidly repeated back-and-forth movement over a short distance

voltage: the difference in electrical energy per unit of charge at two different points in a circuit; measured in **volts (V)**

volts: the SI unit of electrical energy per unit of charge

volume: Measurement: amount of space an object or substance takes up; measured in liters (L) or cubic centimeters (cm³); Sound: loudness

W

wave: a back-and-forth motion that travels from one place to another

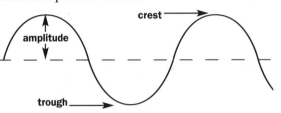

wavelength: distance from any point on one wave to a corresponding point on the next wave, such as crest to crest or compression to compression

wedge: simple machine consisting of an inclined plane that moves

weight: a measure of the force of gravity on an object; directly related to an object's mass

wheel and axle: simple machine made of a shaft (the axle) inserted through the middle of a circle (the wheel)

wind: movement of the air caused by differences in air pressure

work: occurs when a force is used to move an object through a distance; measured in joules (J)

X

X ray: very high frequency electromagnetic radiation; can be used to make images of the human body by passing radiation through the body onto photographic film

Name _____ Assignment _____ Date _____

	Gold 4	Silver 3	Bronze 2	Copper 1
Comprehension ____ %	Specific facts and relationships are identified and well-defined.	Most facts and relationships are defined.	Some facts are identified but relationships are missing.	No facts or relationships are stated.
Application and Analysis ____ %	A strong plan is developed and executed correctly.	A plan is developed and implemented with some scientific errors.	Some organized ideas toward a weak plan.	Random statements with little relation to the question. No plan present.
Science Content ____ %	Appropriate, complete, and correct scientific facts, ideas, and representations.	Appropriate and correct but incomplete scientific facts, ideas, and representations.	Some inappropriate, incomplete, and/or incorrect ideas, leading to further errors.	Lacking understanding of scientific facts or ideas.
Communication ____ %	Strong and succinct communication of results.	Strong communication of results. Justification for outcome may be weak.	Communication of results is present, but lacks any justification.	No results are communicated. No justification is to be found. A correct answer may have appeared.
Aesthetics ____ %	Exceptional. Attractive. Encourages attention. All requirements exceeded.	Neat and orderly. Requirements met.	Messy and disorganized. Some requirements missing.	Illegible and random information. Most or all requirements missing.

Light Bulb Efficiency and Cost Worksheet

Use this table to compare the efficiency of different types of bulbs.

Bulb type	Lumens	Watts	Lumens per watt
Clear incandescent			
Frosted incandescent			
Halogen incandescent			
Mercury vapor incandescent			
High-pressure sodium bulb			
Fluorescent			

Use the following steps to compare the total cost of buying and lighting two different types of bulbs.

	Bulb type	
1. Package cost	$	$
2. Number of bulbs in a package		
3. Cost of one bulb (divide package cost by number of bulbs)	$	$
4. Watts (from package)	W	W
5. Hours of life (from package)	h	h
6. Kilowatt-hours of energy used over life of bulb (multiply Watts by hours of life and divide by 1000)	kWh	kWh
7. Cost of one kWh (from electricity bill)	$	$
8. Electricity cost over life of bulb (multiply cost of one kWh by number of kWhs used)	$	$
9. Total cost of buying and lighting bulb (cost of one bulb + cost of electricity)	$	$

Migratory Routes

Route A

Compass Heading	Direction	Distance
90°	due East	5 m
0°	due North	15 m
45°	Northeast	10 m
180°	due South	15 m

Route B

Compass Heading	Direction	Distance
45°	Northeast	10 m
0°	due North	10 m
90°	due East	5 m
225°	Southwest	15 m

Route C

Compass Heading	Direction	Distance
180°	due South	15 m
270°	due West	5 m
45°	Northeast	10 m
90°	due East	15 m

Route D

Compass Heading	Direction	Distance
270°	due West	10 m
0°	due North	5 m
45°	Northeast	5 m
180°	due South	15 m

International Morse Code

A .—   B —...   C —.—.   D —..

E .   F ..—.   G ——.   H ....

I ..   J .———   K —.—   L .—..

M ——   N —.   O ———   P .——.

Q ——.—   R .—.   S ...   T —

U ..—   V ...—   W .——   X —..—

Y —.——   Z ——..   0 —————   1 .————

2 ..———   3 ...——   4 ....—   5 .....

6 —....   7 ——...   8 ———..   9 ————.

Period .—.—.—   Question Mark ..——..

Garbage-Bag Balloon Instruction Sheet

Follow these instructions to assemble your garbage-bag balloon.

You will need: 8 large lightweight plastic garbage bags (about 1.4 m by 1.8 m when cut open and lying flat), scissors, tape (lightweight and heavy), metric ruler, marker

❶ Cut open each of the eight plastic garbage bags. Tape them together to form a large rectangle about 5.6 m long by 3.6 m wide.

❷ Fold the sheet in half widthwise to create a 2.8 m by 3.6 m rectangle. Tape the two sides together along the edges.

❸ Fold the sheet in half lengthwise to create a 1.4 m by 3.6 m rectangle. Then fold it in half lengthwise again. Your sheet should now be 0.7 m by 3.6 m.

❹ Use the ruler and the marker to mark off a triangle at each end of the rectangle, as shown in Figure 1. Cut along the dotted lines, and remove the triangle.

❺ Unfold the bags to create the double-layer shape shown in Figure 2. Tape along the seams of the bottom and top layers marked **a**. Then, at each end of the balloon, join the edges marked **b** and tape them together. The finished balloon should look like Figure 3.

❻ Cut a hole at one end of the balloon that is large enough to accommodate the nozzles of one or two hair dryers. Attach strips of heavy vinyl tape or other weighted material evenly around the base of the balloon.

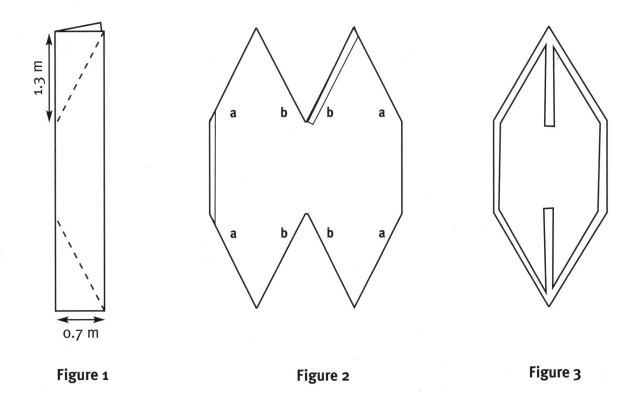

Figure 1 **Figure 2** **Figure 3**

Periodic Table of Elements

Key:
Atomic Number — 6
Chemical Symbol — C
Element Name — Carbon
Atomic Mass — 12.011

1	2	3	4	5	6	7	8	9	10	11	12	13	14	15	16	17	18
H 1 Hydrogen 1.0079																	**He** 2 Helium 4.0026
Li 3 Lithium 6.941	**Be** 4 Beryllium 9.0122											**B** 5 Boron 10.811	**C** 6 Carbon 12.011	**N** 7 Nitrogen 14.007	**O** 8 Oxygen 15.999	**F** 9 Fluorine 18.998	**Ne** 10 Neon 20.180
Na 11 Sodium 22.990	**Mg** 12 Magnesium 24.305											**Al** 13 Aluminum 26.982	**Si** 14 Silicon 28.086	**P** 15 Phosphorus 30.974	**S** 16 Sulfur 32.066	**Cl** 17 Chlorine 35.453	**Ar** 18 Argon 39.948
K 19 Potassium 39.098	**Ca** 20 Calcium 40.078	**Sc** 21 Scandium 44.956	**Ti** 22 Titanium 47.867	**V** 23 Vanadium 50.942	**Cr** 24 Chromium 51.996	**Mn** 25 Manganese 54.938	**Fe** 26 Iron 55.845	**Co** 27 Cobalt 58.93	**Ni** 28 Nickel 58.693	**Cu** 29 Copper 63.546	**Zn** 30 Zinc 65.39	**Ga** 31 Gallium 69.723	**Ge** 32 Germanium 72.61	**As** 33 Arsenic 74.922	**Se** 34 Selenium 78.96	**Br** 35 Bromine 79.904	**Kr** 36 Krypton 83.80
Rb 37 Rubidium 85.468	**Sr** 38 Strontium 87.62	**Y** 39 Yttrium 88.906	**Zr** 40 Zirconium 91.224	**Nb** 41 Niobium 92.906	**Mo** 42 Molybdenum 95.94	**Tc** 43 Technetium (97.907)	**Ru** 44 Ruthenium 101.07	**Rh** 45 Rhodium 102.91	**Pd** 46 Palladium 106.42	**Ag** 47 Silver 107.87	**Cd** 48 Cadmium 112.41	**In** 49 Indium 114.82	**Sn** 50 Tin 118.71	**Sb** 51 Antimony 121.76	**Te** 52 Tellurium 127.60	**I** 53 Iodine 126.90	**Xe** 54 Xenon 131.29
Cs 55 Cesium 132.91	**Ba** 56 Barium 137.33	57-70 *	**Hf** 72 Hafnium 178.49	**Ta** 73 Tantalum 180.95	**W** 74 Tungsten 183.84	**Re** 75 Rhenium 186.21	**Os** 76 Osmium 190.23	**Ir** 77 Iridium 192.22	**Pt** 78 Platinum 195.08	**Au** 79 Gold 196.97	**Hg** 80 Mercury 200.59	**Tl** 81 Thallium 204.38	**Pb** 82 Lead 207.2	**Bi** 83 Bismuth 208.98	**Po** 84 Polonium (208.98)	**At** 85 Astatine (209.99)	**Rn** 86 Radon (222.02)
Fr 87 Francium (223.02)	**Ra** 88 Radium (226.03)	89-102 **	**Rf** 104 Rutherfordium (263.11)	**Db** 105 Dubnium (262.11)	**Sg** 106 Seaborgium (266.12)	**Bh** 107 Bohrium (264.12)	**Hs** 108 Hassium (269.13)	**Mt** 109 Meitnerium (268.14)	**Uun** 110 Ununnilium (272.15)	**Uuu** 111 Unununium (272.15)	**Uub** 112 Ununbium (277)		**Uuq** 114 Ununquadium (289)		**Uuh** 116 Ununhexium (289)		

Lawrencium entry: **Lr** 103 Lawrencium (262.11)

Group labels: alkali metals (1), alkaline earth metals (2), transitional metals (3–12), other metals, nonmetals (13–17), noble gases (18)

*Lanthanides

La 57 Lanthanum 138.91	**Ce** 58 Cerium 140.12	**Pr** 59 Praseodymium 140.91	**Nd** 60 Neodymium 144.24	**Pm** 61 Promethium (144.91)	**Sm** 62 Samarium 150.36	**Eu** 63 Europium 151.96	**Gd** 64 Gadolinium 157.25	**Tb** 65 Terbium 158.93	**Dy** 66 Dysprosium 162.50	**Ho** 67 Holmium 164.93	**Er** 68 Erbium 167.26	**Tm** 69 Thulium 168.93	**Yb** 70 Ytterbium 173.04	**Lu** 71 Lutetium 174.97

**Actinides

Ac 89 Actinium (227.03)	**Th** 90 Thorium 232.04	**Pa** 91 Protactinium 231.04	**U** 92 Uranium 238.03	**Np** 93 Neptunium (237.05)	**Pu** 94 Plutonium (244.06)	**Am** 95 Americium (243.06)	**Cm** 96 Curium (247.07)	**Bk** 97 Berkelium (247.07)	**Cf** 98 Californium (251.08)	**Es** 99 Einsteinium (252.08)	**Fm** 100 Fermium (257.10)	**Md** 101 Mendelevium (258.10)	**No** 102 Nobelium (259.10)	

Milk Fat Content Sheet

Type of milk	Percent fat
Skim or nonfat milk	0.5% or less
1% milk	1%
2% milk	2%
Whole milk	at least 3.25%
Evaporated milk	7.50%
Sweetened condensed milk	8.50%
Half-and-half	10% to 18%
Whipping cream	30% to 36%
Heavy cream	36% to 40%

Use the grid below to create a bar graph showing the average percentage of fat in each milk product.

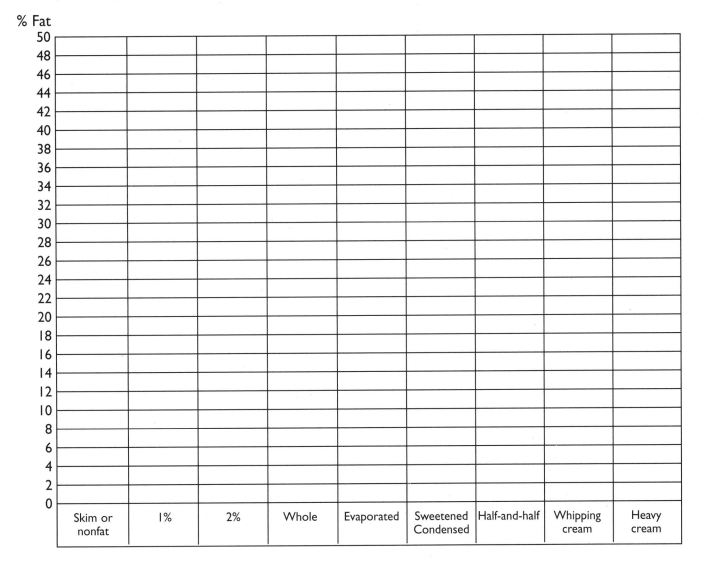

10 From "Thrown for a Loop...Roller Coaster Science," by Samatha Beres. Copyright © 1999 by Scientific American, Inc. All rights reserved.

14 Louis Bloomfield, howthingswork.virginia.edu, 2002.

20 © Exploratorium, www.exploratorium.edu

24 Glubock, Shirley and Alfred Tamarin. *Olympic Games in Ancient Greece.* © HarperCollins, 1976.

28 Hickam, Homer H., Jr. *Rocket Boys.* New York: Delacorte, 1998. (pages 295–296).

30, 36 Boston Museum of Science, Inventor's Workshop. (http://www.mos.org/sln/Leonardo/Inventor'sWorkshop.html)

40 "MIT Senior's Robot Begets 'Ant' Farm." MIT Tech Talk. *MIT News.* Massachusetts Institute of Technology. (http://web.mit.edu/newsoffice/nr/1995/40009.html)

42 From "With the Right Equipment, Cows Can Be Trained to Milk Themselves" by Diane Langipan. Popular Science Newsfiles. (www.popsci.com) Popular Science 2002.

46 Used with permission from *TIME for Kids* magazine, © 2002

52 "Can a Static Charge on Plastic Playground Equipment Harm Someone?" *ScienceNet QuickLinks.* (www.sciencenet.org.uk)

52 Fowler, Steve. "Are Children's Slides at Fast Food Restaurants a Static Hazard?" *ESD Journal.* Fowler Associates, Inc. (www.esdjournal.com)

56 Reprinted with permission of *The Associated Press.*

60 Frostick, Robert. *An Amazon Adventure—Electric Eel.* (http://jajhs.kana.k12.wv.us/amazon/eel.htm)

62, 66, 68 From "AMERICAN EXPERIENCE" at www.pbs.org/wgbh/amex/Copyright © 2002 WGBH/Boston.

72 From *Aurora: The Mysterious Northern Lights.* Copyright © 1994 by Candace Savage. Published by Douglas & McIntyre Ltd. Reprinted by permission of the publisher.

74 Wollard, Kathy. "Sea Turtles' Magnetic Personalities." *Newsday.* 6 August 2002.

78 Adapted from "Fast Track" by Chana Stiefel, published in SCHOLASTIC SCIENCE WORLD, March 23, 1998. Copyright © 1998 by Scholastic Inc. All rights reserved. Used by permission of Scholastic Inc.

82 Excerpt from "Philo T. Farnsworth: Plowboy Inventor" from *Brainstorm! The Stories of Twenty American Kid Inventors* by Tom Tucker. Copyright © 1996 by Tom Tucker. Reprinted by permission of Farrar, Straus and Giroux, LLC.

86 Sandburg, Carl. *Chicago Poems.* 1916.

88 From *Mathematicians Are People, Too. Stories from the Lives of Great Mathematicians,* Vol. 2 by Luetta Reimer and Wilbert Reimer. © 1995 by Pearson Education, Inc., publishing as Dale Seymour Publications. Used by permission.

94 Excerpt from *The Voyage of the Frog* by Gary Paulsen. Published by Orchard Books, an imprint of Scholastic Inc. Copyright © 1989 by Gary Paulsen. Reprinted with permission.

98 Plait, Phil. "What Does Outer Space Feel Like?" Online posting. *Phil Plait's Bad Astronomy: Mad Science.* (http://www.badastronomy.com). © Phil Plait. All Rights Reserved.

102 Special permission granted, *Current Health* magazine, published and copyrighted by Weekly Reader Corporation. All rights reserved.

104 This excerpt from an article by Denise Brehm appeared in *MIT Tech Talk.* It is reprinted with permission of the Massachusetts Institute of Technology, where Professor Walter Lewin teaches physics.

108 From "The Physics of Music," by Jake Miller. Copyright © 1998 by Scientific American, Inc. All rights reserved.

112 Reproduced with permission from www.NewScientist.com

116 Hardy, Mat. "Science: Color Scheme." *Beyond 2000.* (http://www.beyond2000.com)

120 California Science Center Web site: Magic, the Science of Illusion. "Living Head Backstage." (http://www.magicexhibit.org)

124 "The Balloon that Flew around the World." *Scientific American Explorer.* November 1999.

128 "Why is an Apple Pie's Sauce Always Hotter Than the Pastry Even Though They Have Been Cooked on the Same Heat?" Rob Landolfi, *Physlink.com Expert, Physics & Astronomy Online:* (http://www.physlink.com)

130 "Polartec: Building a Better Sheep" by Jonathan Dorn, *Backpacker,* April 1998.

138 Gallant, Roy. *Explorers of the Atom.* Doubleday and Co., 1974.

142 HOW COME?/ DISCOVERIES FOR YOUNG PEOPLE/ Countless Particles Make a Flake, NEWSDAY (Long Island, NY); May 15, 2001, p. C2 (Copyright © 2001 Kathy Wollard.)

146 What's Outdoors, by Doug Collicutt, *Winnipeg Free Press, Sunday Magazine:* Feb. 4, 2001. (http://www.naturenorth.com/column/col18.html).

152 Meisenheimer, Karen. "Experts from UF Dig Up World's Longest Solidified Lightning Bolt." *UF News.* University of Florida. (http://www.napa.ufl.edu)

158 From "The Tale of Henri Nestlé and Daniel Peter." *Chocolate Valley.com.* Indotronix International Corporation (www.chocolatevalley.com)

162 Wolke, Robert. *What Einstein Didn' t Know.*

166 HOW COME?/Atoms Like To Stick Together, Newsday (Long Island, N.Y.) Oct. 21, 1997, p. C2. Copyright © 1997, Kathy Wollard.

168 Eliot, John L. "Deadly Haven." National Geographic Magazine. (http://www.nationalgeographic.com)

172 "Montshire Minute: Carbon." Montshire Museum of Science. (http://www.montshire.net/minute/mm011126.html)

178 "Better Hair Through Chemistry: It's Enough to Curl Your Hair." The Exploratorium. (www.exploratorium.edu)

182 "What Exactly is Jell-O Made from? How Does it Work?" *How Stuff Works.* (http://www.howstuffworks.com)

186 From POPCORN DAYS AND BUTTERMILK NIGHTS by Gary Paulsen, copyright © 1983 by Gary Paulsen. Used by permission of Lodestar Books, an affiliate of Dutton Children's Books, an imprint of Penguin Putnam Books for Young Readers, a division of Penguin Putnam, Inc. All rights reserved.

188 "Irving Prager's Chocolate Dump Cake." *Carnegie Mellon: School of Computer Science.* Carnegie Mellon University. (http://www.cs.cmu.edu)

192 The Virtues of Venom. (http://chainreaction.asu.edu/desert/digin/venom.htm) © Diane Boudreau

196 From THE HISTORIES by Herodotus, translated by Aubrey de Sélincourt, revised by John Marincola (Penguin Classics 1954, Second revised edition 1996) Translation copyright 1954 by Aubrey de Sélincourt. Revised edition copyright © John Marincola, 1996.

198 Darwin, Charles. *The Voyage of the Beagle.*

200 Harris, Tom. "How Light Sticks Work." *How Stuff Works.* (http://www.howstuffworks.com/light-stick.html)

204 Torres, Dr. Jose. "Diving Under Antarctic Ice!" The University of South Florida: College of Marine Sciences. (http://www.marine.usf.edu)

208 "Innovative Lives." Jerome and Dorothy Lemelson Center. National Museum of American History, Behring Center. © 2002 Smithsonian Institution.

212 "MIT Inventor of the Week: Nathaniel Wyeth." Massachusetts Institute of Technology. (http://web.mit.edu/invent/www/inventorsR-Z/wyeth.html)

216 From "What Exactly is the Physical or Chemical Process That Makes Adhesive Tape Sticky?" Copyright © 1997 by Scientific American, Inc. All rights reserved.

The editors have made every effort to trace the ownership of all copyrighted selections found in this book and to make full acknowledgment for their use. Omissions brought to our attention will be corrected in a subsequent edition.